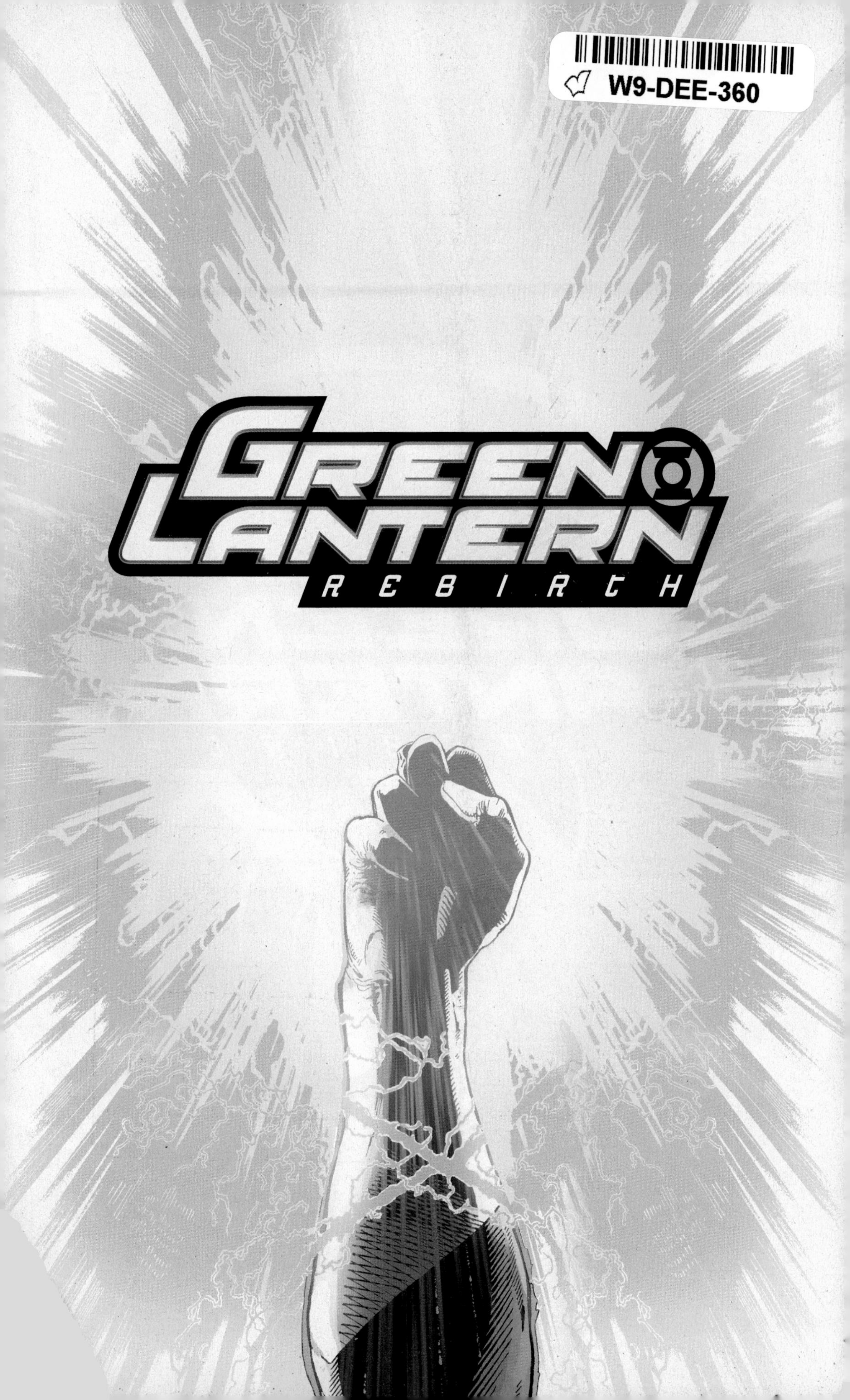
GREEN LANTERN
REBIRTH

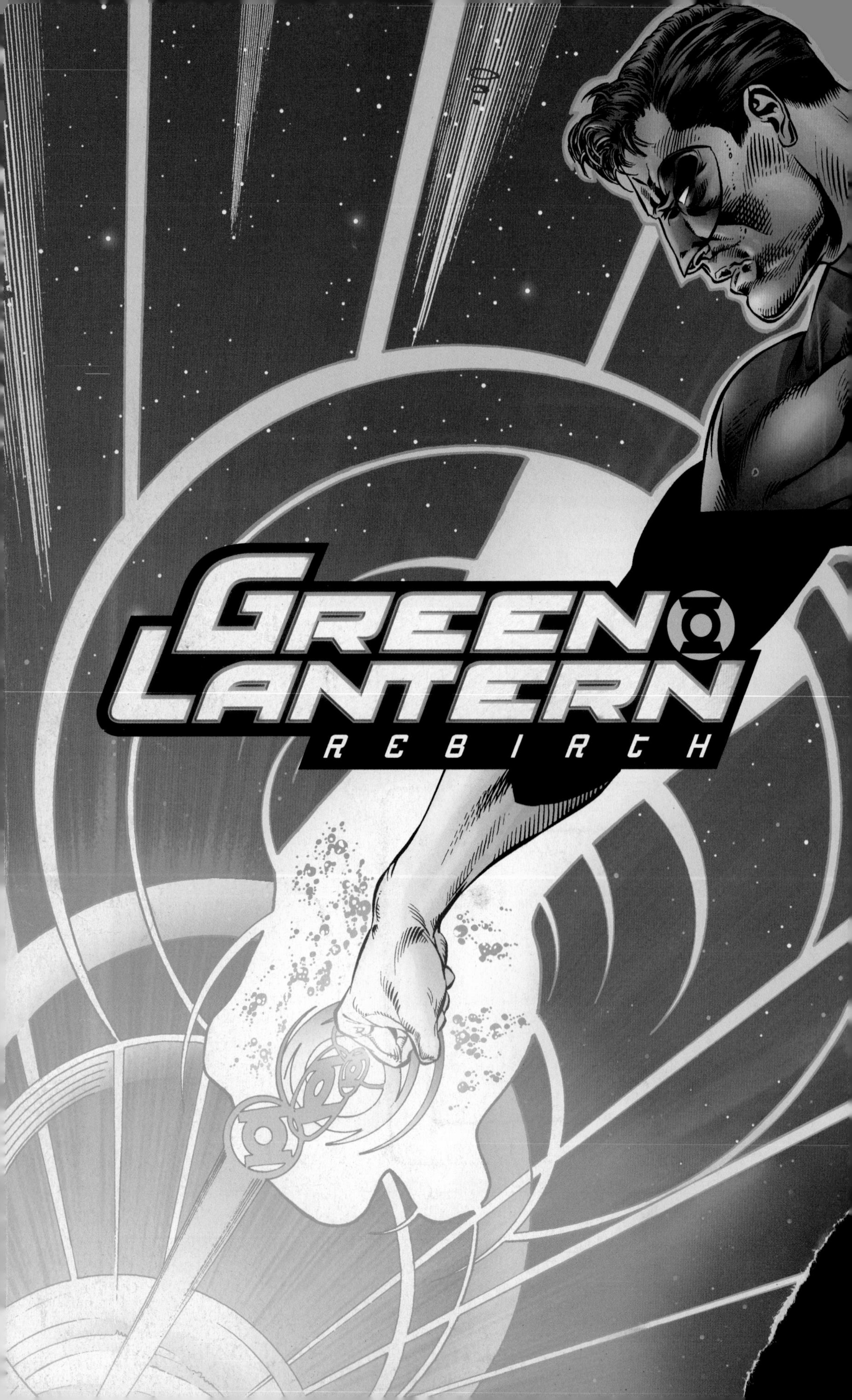
GREEN LANTERN
REBIRTH

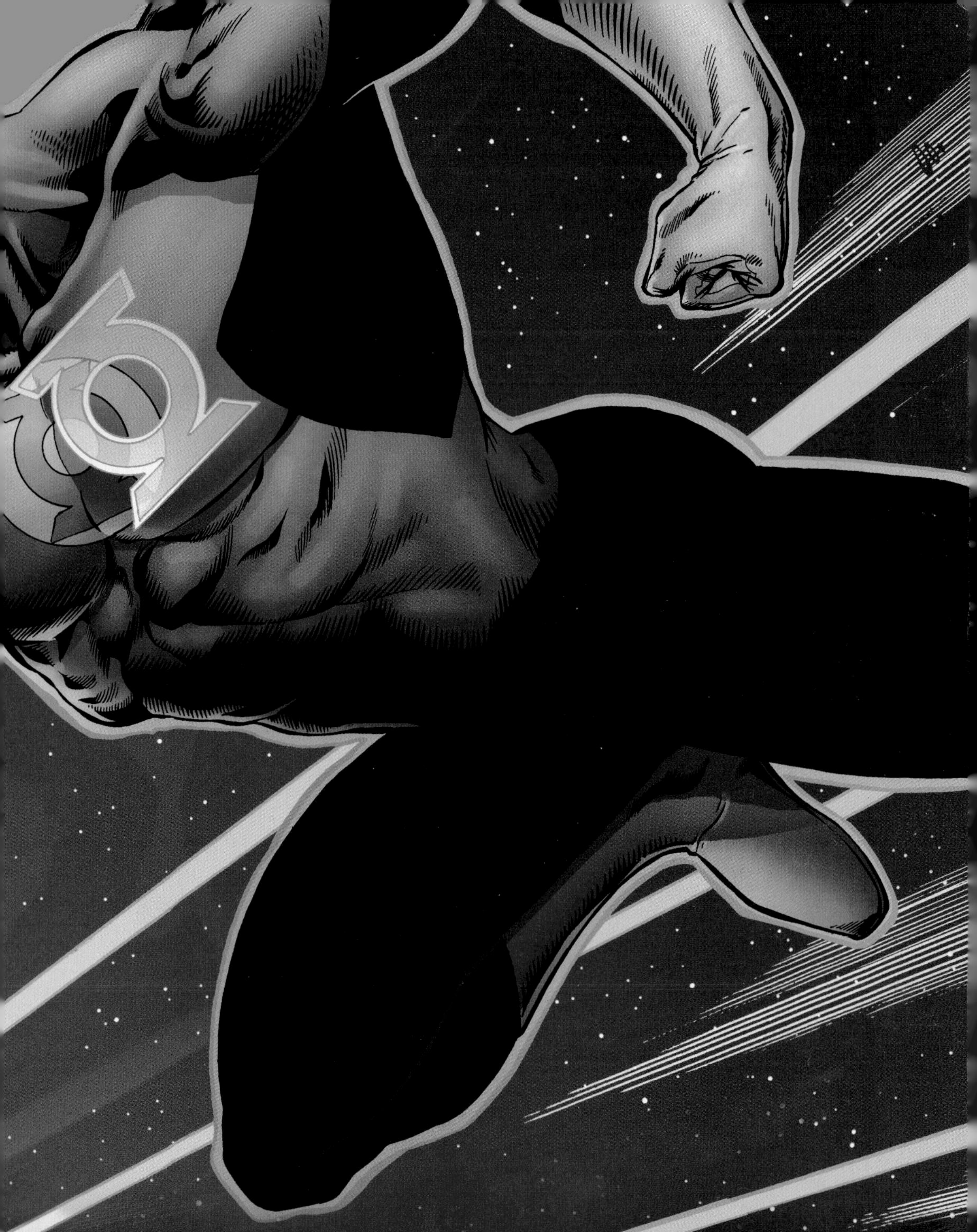

GEOFF JOHNS WRITER

ETHAN VAN SCIVER PENCILLER

PRENTIS ROLLINS/MARLO ALQUIZA

MICK GRAY/ETHAN VAN SCIVER INKERS

ROB LEIGH LETTERER

MOOSE BAUMANN COLORIST

ETHAN VAN SCIVER ORIGINAL SERIES COVERS

DC COMICS

Dan DiDio VP-Executive Editor
Peter Tomasi Senior Editor-original series
Stephen Wacker Associate Editor-original series
Robert Greenberger Senior Editor-collected edition
Robbin Brosterman Senior Art Director
Paul Levitz President & Publisher
Georg Brewer VP-Design & DC Direct Creative
Richard Bruning Senior VP-Creative Director
Patrick Caldon Senior VP-Finance & Operations
Chris Caramalis VP-Finance
Terri Cunningham VP-Managing Editor
Stephanie Fierman Senior VP-Sales & Marketing
Alison Gill VP-Manufacturing
Rich Johnson VP-Book Trade Sales
Hank Kanalz VP-General Manager, WildStorm
Lillian Laserson Senior VP & General Counsel
Jim Lee Editorial Director-WildStorm
Paula Lowitt Senior VP-Business & Legal Affairs
David McKillips VP-Advertising & Custom Publishing
John Nee VP-Business Development
Gregory Noveck Senior VP-Creative Affairs
Cheryl Rubin Senior VP-Brand Management
Jeff Trojan VP-Business Development, DC Direct
Bob Wayne VP-Sales

Cover Illustration by Ethan Van Sciver. Cover color by Moose Baumann. Logo designed by Daniel Gelon.

GREEN LANTERN: REBIRTH

DC Comics
1700 Broadway
New York, NY 10019
A Warner Bros. Entertainment Company
Printed by World Color Press, Inc, St-Romuald, QC, Canada, 9/02/09. Fourth Printing.

ISBN: 978-1-4012-0465-5

SUSTAINABLE FORESTRY INITIATIVE
Certified Fiber Sourcing
www.sfiprogram.org

INTRODUCTION **BRAD MELTZER**

There were infinite ways to bring Hal Jordan back. There were simple ways ("Just give him the ring and move on already"), complex ways ("And then, if you look at *Green Lantern*, volume 2, #188 on the last page, you can see from the trees that Mogo's a healer, which'll be vital for understanding that..."), and the tried and true only-in-comics ways ("I was brainwashed." "Replaced..." "My clone..."). We, however, got the best way of all. The Geoff Johns way.

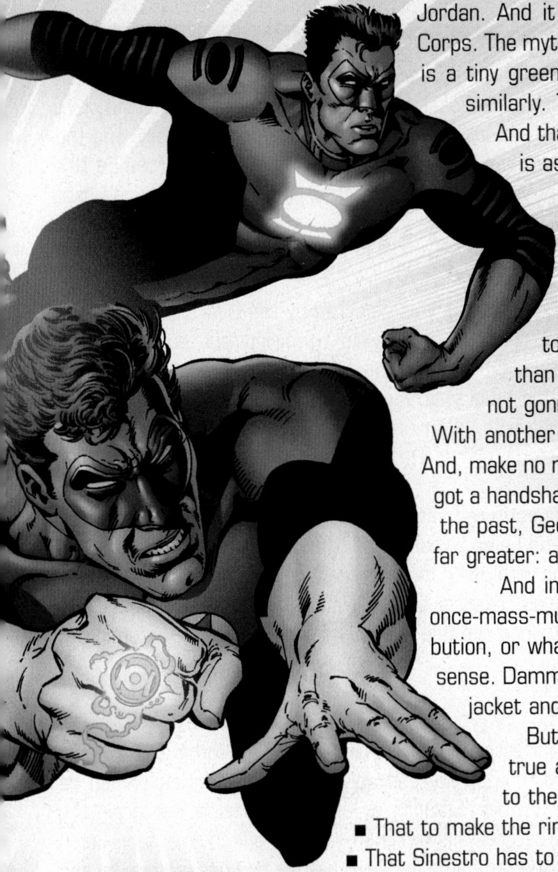

Now let me be clear here. People think *Rebirth* is about the return of Hal Jordan. And it is. But it's also about the return of Green Lantern. The Corps. The mythos. The idea that the most powerful weapon in the universe is a tiny green ring, and that each ring-bearer wields it differently. And similarly. That the ring can empower, corrupt, create, and destroy. And that the history of the spacefaring Knights of the Round Table is as vital as the present.

In lesser hands, *Rebirth* would've given us exactly what we wanted: Hal Jordan back in the costume. In Geoff's able hands, we got the return of the lore that made Hal Jordan great. You can see it on every page. From the irony of Kyle's first words in the series being, "Don't be afraid," to Sinestro's warning, "Never challenge those more powerful than you," to Hal's pitch-perfect response of, "Um...yeah. That's not gonna work for me."

With another writer, the return of Hal could've meant the death of Kyle. And, make no mistake, it would've been so easy to kill Kyle. With Geoff, we got a handshake – and introduction. Instead of plowing over the new with the past, Geoff combined the two and gave these characters something far greater: a future.

And in the center ring of this nostalgia-filled circus, littered with once-mass-murdering heroes merged with spirits of vengeance, or retribution, or whatever they called it that week, Geoff even made it all make sense. Dammit, he even took the time to explain the origin of the bomber jacket and the disappearance of Hal's once-gray hair.

But beyond all the walks down memory lane, what rang most true about *Rebirth* was the brand new nuggets that were added to the gold mine of continuity:

- That to make the ring work, it hurts. Every time.
- That Sinestro has to be close for the ring to translate.
- That John's constructs are built like blueprints, that Guy's ring sprays wild, that Kyle sketches like a never-satisfied artist, that Hal just wants the precision of a good old boxing glove.
- And my personal favorite: that Batman dislikes Hal because Hal has no fear – the one thing Batman relies on for his own "power."

In that single moment, early in issue one, I realized what a fanboy tale this is. Written by a fan. Written for the fans. For us. I love it for that. Like the character it returns, *Rebirth* has no fear embracing its own myths. Instead of trying to be cool or meta or the oh-so-popular self-aware, *Rebirth* succeeds simply because it's what all comics need to be and so often forget to be: a great story with great art.

Which, of course, brings me to the art. Why is the sci-fi craziness within these pages so believable? Because the hyper-detailed beauty of Ethan Van Sciver's art sells us every single moment. From Guy's statue in Warrior's being bigger than the rest, to the true scariness of Hector Hammond, to the fish-inspired look on Kilowog, Ethan brought it all back. This world is real. The Green Lanterns exist, and – with nothing more than sweat beading on their foreheads and skiing down their masks – they will save us. Even the chapter titles tell us so. Unlike nearly every other comic out there, Geoff and Ethan began with blackest night – and left us in brightest day. And that, as you'll see inside, is what heroes are made of.

So buckle up and start memorizing the oath. Hal Jordan hasn't just returned. He's returned to greatness.

BRAD MELTZER Ft. Lauderdale, Florida June 2005

WHO'S WHO

The legacy of the Green Lantern can be traced back almost to the dawn of time. To atone for a great sin, a race of beings who came to call themselves the Guardians of the Universe sought to use great power to tame the spread of evil. After different methods failed, they settled on equipping sentient beings with rings that drew tremendous energy from a central Power Battery located on their adopted world of Oa.

The Green Lantern Corps helped to maintain peace throughout the known universe for eons. Recent events, though, saw all the Guardians but one leave this plane of existence. Soon after, the Central Battery was destroyed and the Corps shattered, all because of one man...

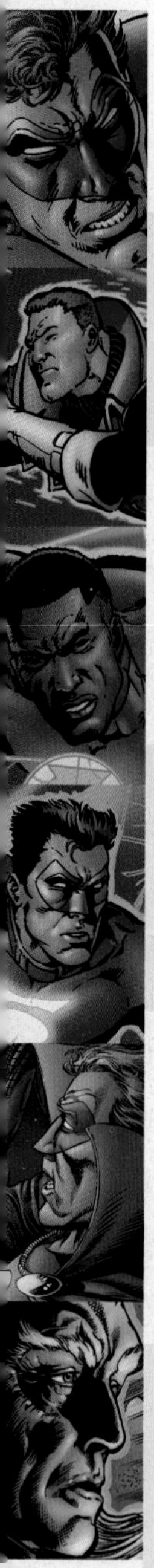

HAL JORDAN

Perhaps the greatest Green Lantern of them all. Test pilot Hal Jordan was bequeathed the ring and served Earth and the Corps well, but not without incident. A series of disastrous events drove Jordan past the point of mental endurance and into a crazed rampage that eventually destroyed the Corps, the Battery, and the Guardians themselves. Jordan regained his sense of purpose in time to sacrifice himself to save the Earth's dying sun. His soul has been merged with God's Spirit of Vengeance, the Spectre, and he has sought redemption before earning his final rest.

GUY GARDNER

A college football star, unable to settle on a career, Guy Gardner was selected by the Guardians to be Hal Jordan's backup. Eventually, during a cosmic crisis, Gardner earned his own ring but suffered brain damage on a mission. He healed, only to lose his ring, but discovered his DNA had been spliced with that of the alien Vuldarians. He became a living weapon and fought as Warrior until settling down, becoming proprietor and host at New York City's premier watering hole, Warriors.

JOHN STEWART

The second man chosen by Hal Jordan to act as his substitute, John Stewart didn't necessarily want to be a hero. As an architect he had a good career going, and he saw the role of Green Lantern as a distraction. In time he knew the tremendous satisfaction that came with using the ring responsibly, but after his actions led to the destruction of the planet Xanshi his spirit was crushed, and he suffered a series of ordeals that left him physically crippled as well. Recently John regained the use of his limbs, and he is now coming to terms with the traumatic incidents of his past.

KYLE RAYNER

Kyle's eagerness and fertile imagination helped him to master the power ring and adapt to his new role as Green Lantern. Eager to live up to Hal Jordan's heroic reputation, he ably handled his duties. When he attained ultimate power, Kyle, calling himself Ion, proved his humanity by using it for good, restoring the Guardians to this plane of existence. In time, though, he grew disillusioned with his effectiveness on Earth and sought to explore space. When Kyle recently returned to Earth, he saw that life had passed him by and now searches for a purpose.

ALAN SCOTT

Years ago, train engineer Alan Scott encountered an old lantern, and his life was never the same. The lantern was forged from a meteor known as the Starheart, a concentrated physical form of magical energy created in a failed attempt by the Guardians of the Universe to rid the universe of magic. Scott forged a ring from a portion of the lantern and became Earth's first Green Lantern, one of the first generation of super-heroes. He fought during World War II, switching from engineering to working at Gotham Broadcasting. Recently Scott internalized the Starheart and is now a living Lantern, imparting his wisdom to younger heroes and fighting the good fight as a member of the legendary Justice Society of America.

GANTHET

Last surviving immortal hailing back billions of years. Originally born on Maltus, he was among those who migrated to Oa and subsequently evolved into the powerful Guardians of the Universe. When the Guardians left this plane of existence, Ganthet was left behind, the final guardian of the remaining emerald energy that powered the few power rings still intact. Hal Jordan's old friend Tom Kalmaku honored his fallen comrade's last request and brought new life to Oa. Later, after being imbued with unimaginable power, Kyle Rayner expended it all to reignite the Central Power Battery. He also brought fresh life to the barren world, a new generation of Guardians. Ganthet is now raising them, teaching them of their powers and their responsibility to the universe.

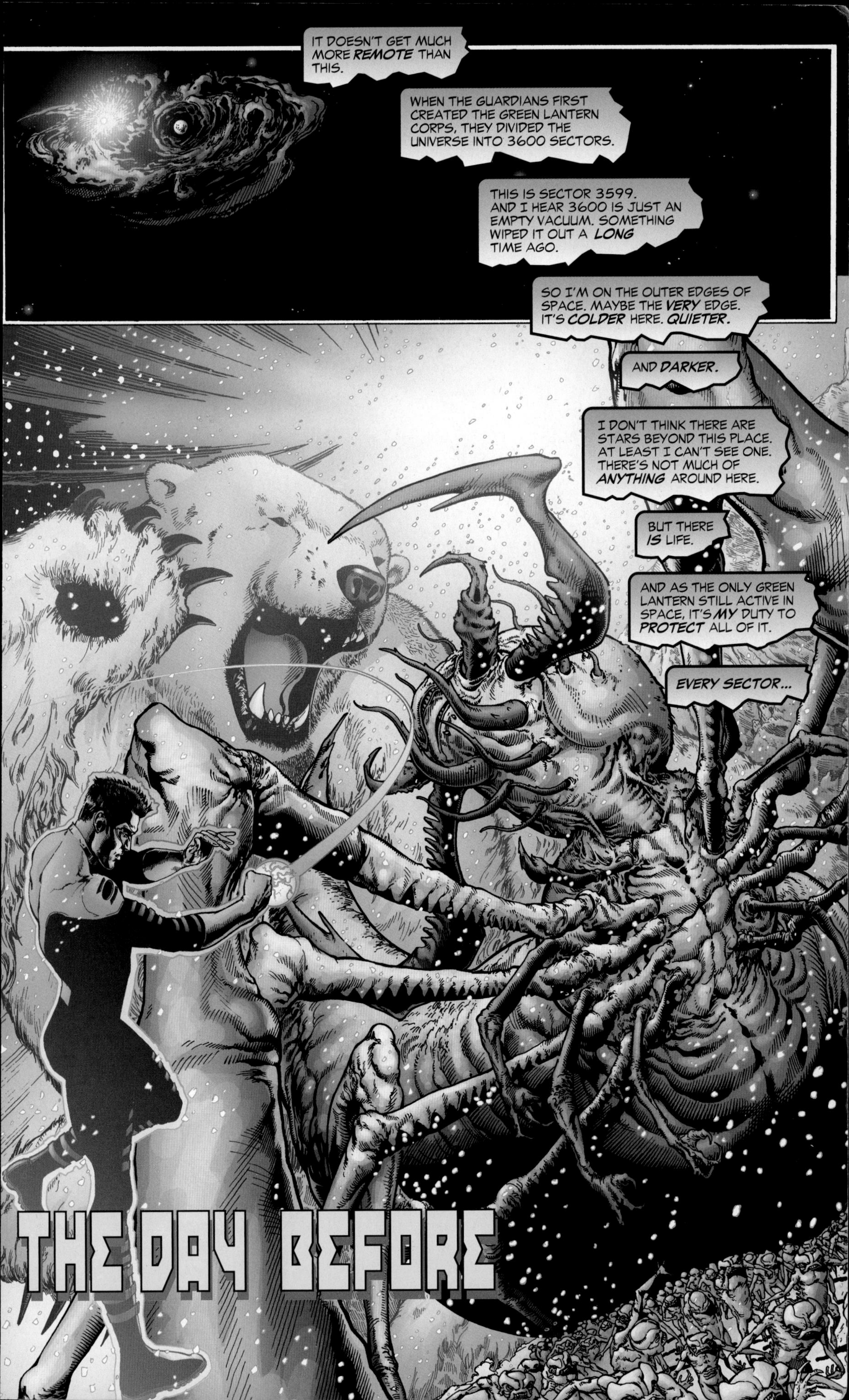
IT DOESN'T GET MUCH MORE *REMOTE* THAN THIS.
WHEN THE GUARDIANS FIRST CREATED THE GREEN LANTERN CORPS, THEY DIVIDED THE UNIVERSE INTO 3600 SECTORS.
THIS IS SECTOR 3599. AND I HEAR 3600 IS JUST AN EMPTY VACUUM. SOMETHING WIPED IT OUT A *LONG* TIME AGO.
SO I'M ON THE OUTER EDGES OF SPACE. MAYBE THE *VERY* EDGE. IT'S *COLDER* HERE. *QUIETER.*
AND *DARKER.*
I DON'T THINK THERE ARE STARS BEYOND THIS PLACE. AT LEAST I CAN'T SEE ONE. THERE'S NOT MUCH OF *ANYTHING* AROUND HERE.
BUT THERE *IS* LIFE.
AND AS THE ONLY GREEN LANTERN STILL ACTIVE IN SPACE, IT'S *MY* DUTY TO *PROTECT* ALL OF IT.
EVERY SECTOR...
THE DAY BEFORE

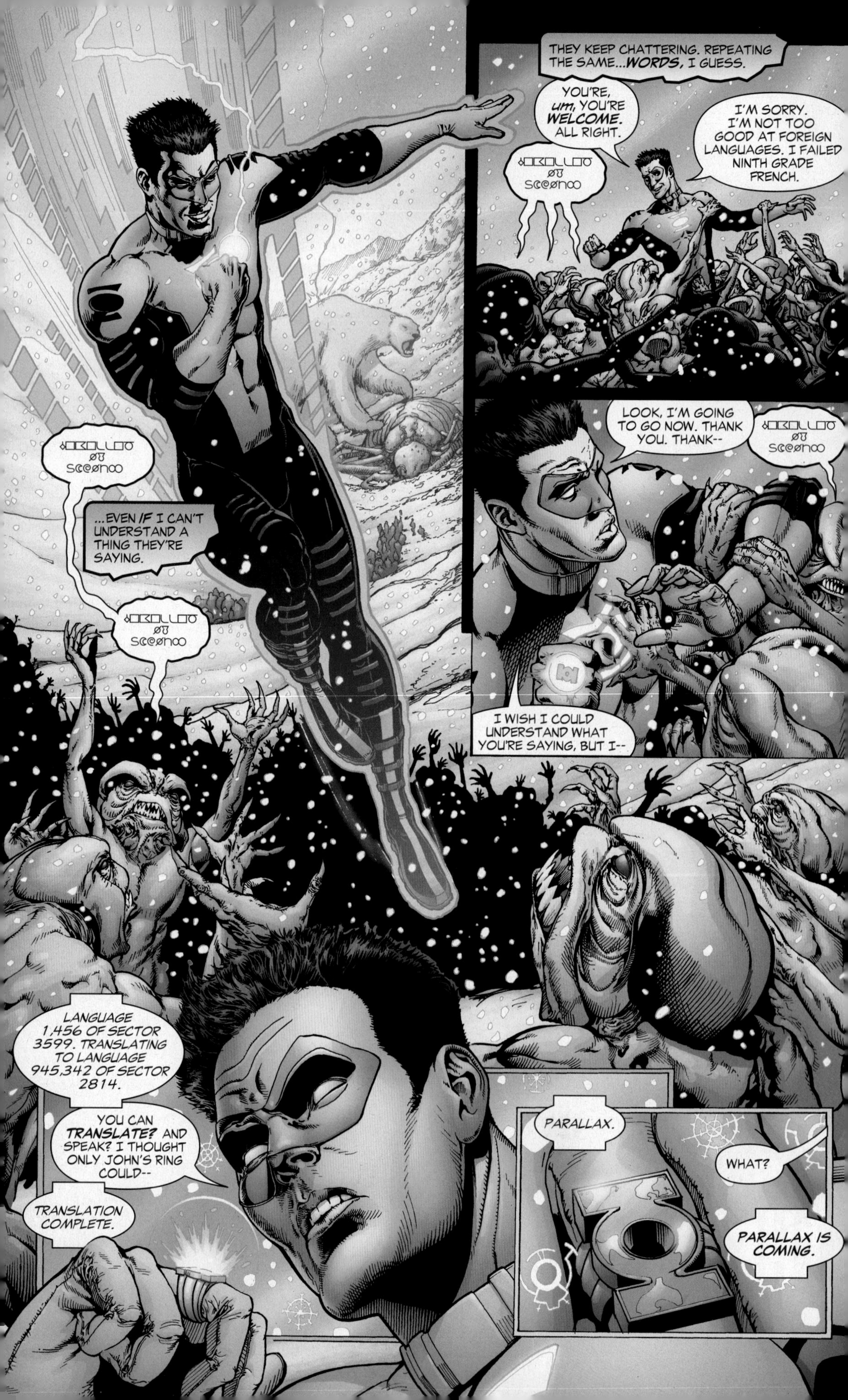
...EVEN IF I CAN'T UNDERSTAND A THING THEY'RE SAYING.
THEY KEEP CHATTERING. REPEATING THE SAME...WORDS, I GUESS.
YOU'RE, UM, YOU'RE WELCOME. ALL RIGHT.
I'M SORRY. I'M NOT TOO GOOD AT FOREIGN LANGUAGES. I FAILED NINTH GRADE FRENCH.
LOOK, I'M GOING TO GO NOW. THANK YOU. THANK--
I WISH I COULD UNDERSTAND WHAT YOU'RE SAYING, BUT I--
LANGUAGE 1,456 OF SECTOR 3599. TRANSLATING TO LANGUAGE 945,342 OF SECTOR 2814.
YOU CAN TRANSLATE? AND SPEAK? I THOUGHT ONLY JOHN'S RING COULD--
TRANSLATION COMPLETE.
PARALLAX.
WHAT?
PARALLAX IS COMING.

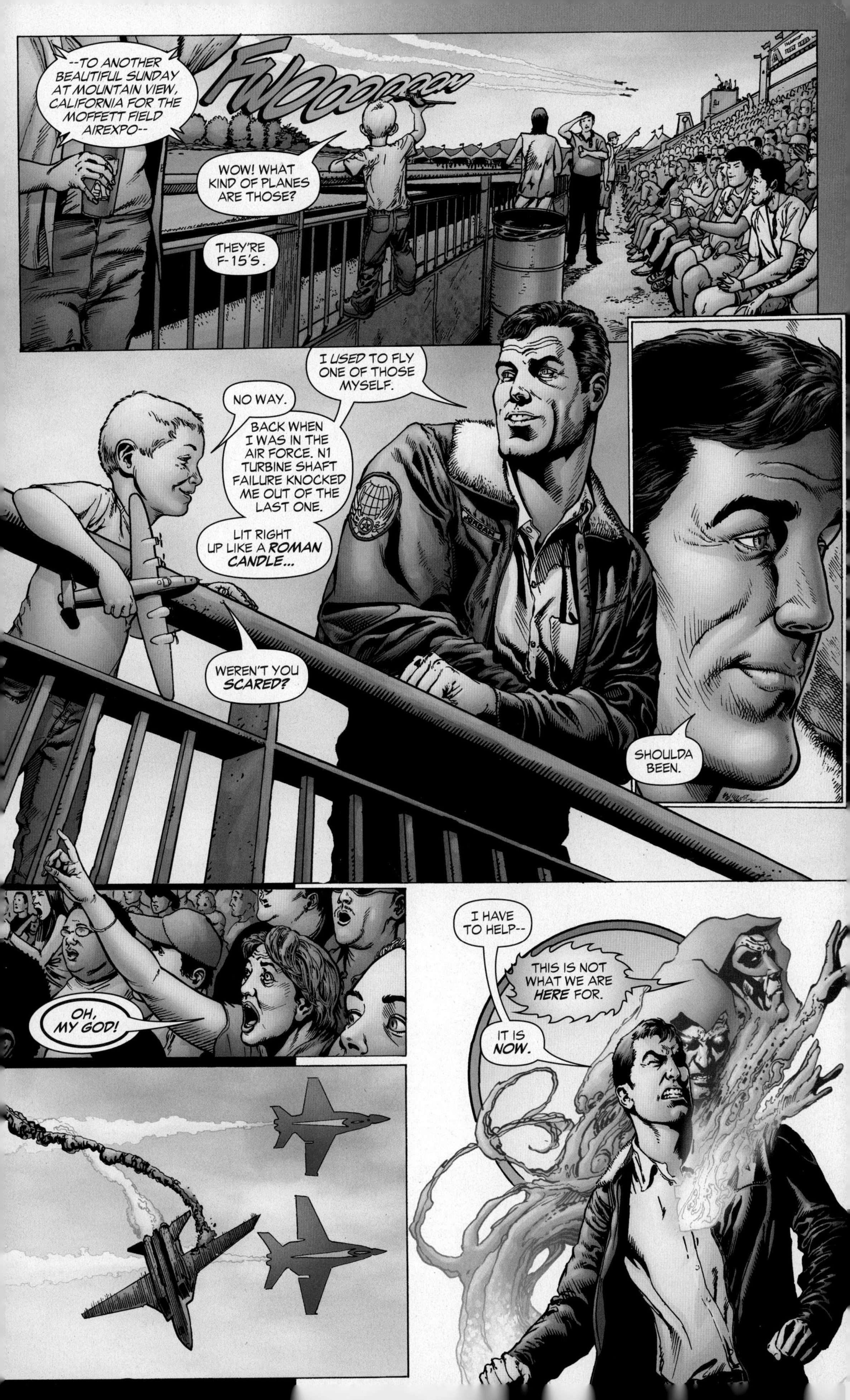

--TO ANOTHER BEAUTIFUL SUNDAY AT MOUNTAIN VIEW, CALIFORNIA FOR THE MOFFETT FIELD AIREXPO--
FWOOOOOOOM
WOW! WHAT KIND OF PLANES ARE THOSE?
THEY'RE F-15'S.
I USED TO FLY ONE OF THOSE MYSELF.
NO WAY.
BACK WHEN I WAS IN THE AIR FORCE. N1 TURBINE SHAFT FAILURE KNOCKED ME OUT OF THE LAST ONE.
LIT RIGHT UP LIKE A ROMAN CANDLE...
WEREN'T YOU SCARED?
SHOULDA BEEN.
OH, MY GOD!
I HAVE TO HELP--
THIS IS NOT WHAT WE ARE HERE FOR.
IT IS NOW.

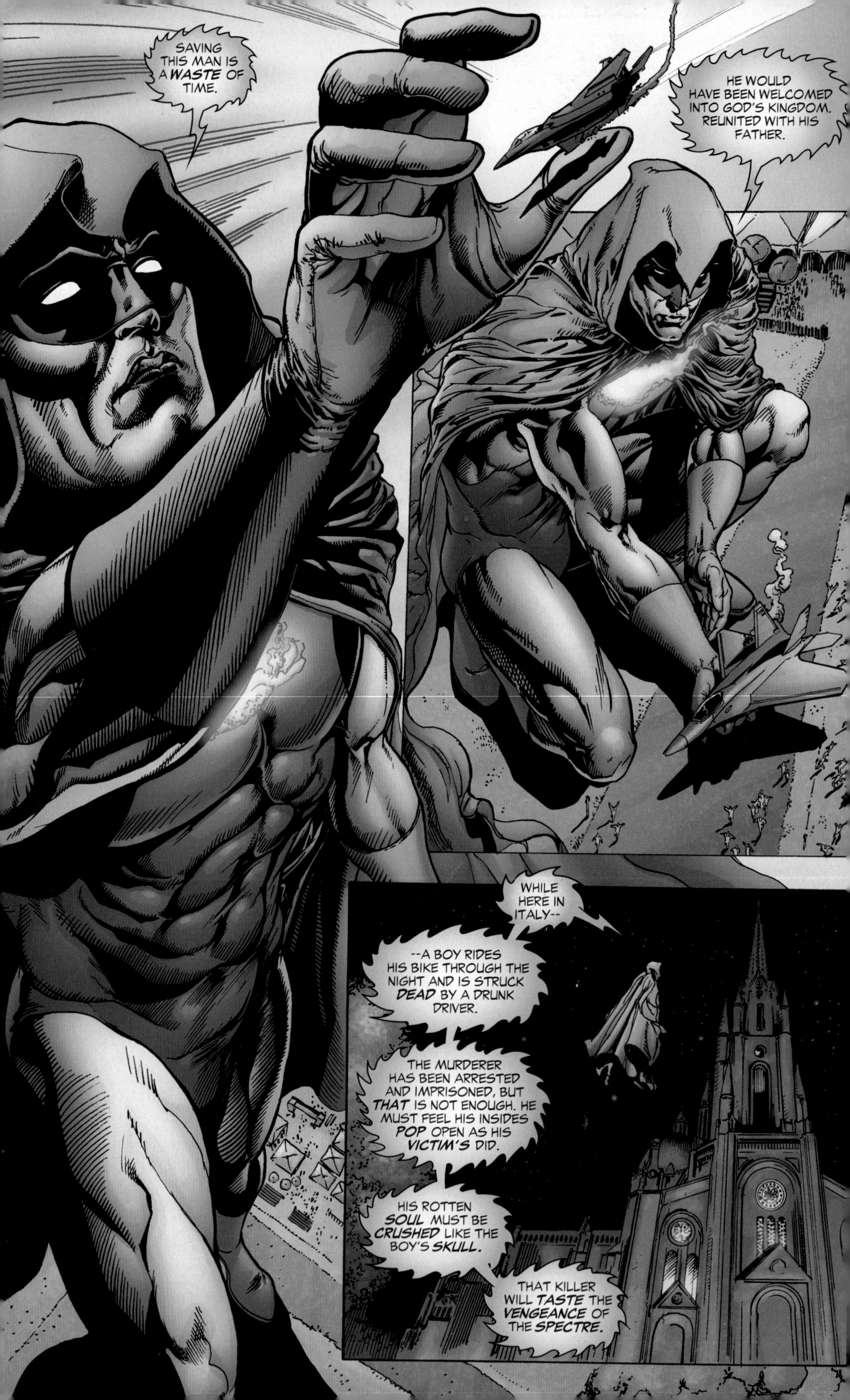
SAVING THIS MAN IS A WASTE OF TIME.
HE WOULD HAVE BEEN WELCOMED INTO GOD'S KINGDOM. REUNITED WITH HIS FATHER.
WHILE HERE IN ITALY--
--A BOY RIDES HIS BIKE THROUGH THE NIGHT AND IS STRUCK DEAD BY A DRUNK DRIVER.
THE MURDERER HAS BEEN ARRESTED AND IMPRISONED, BUT THAT IS NOT ENOUGH. HE MUST FEEL HIS INSIDES POP OPEN AS HIS VICTIM'S DID.
HIS ROTTEN SOUL MUST BE CRUSHED LIKE THE BOY'S SKULL.
THAT KILLER WILL TASTE THE VENGEANCE OF THE SPECTRE.

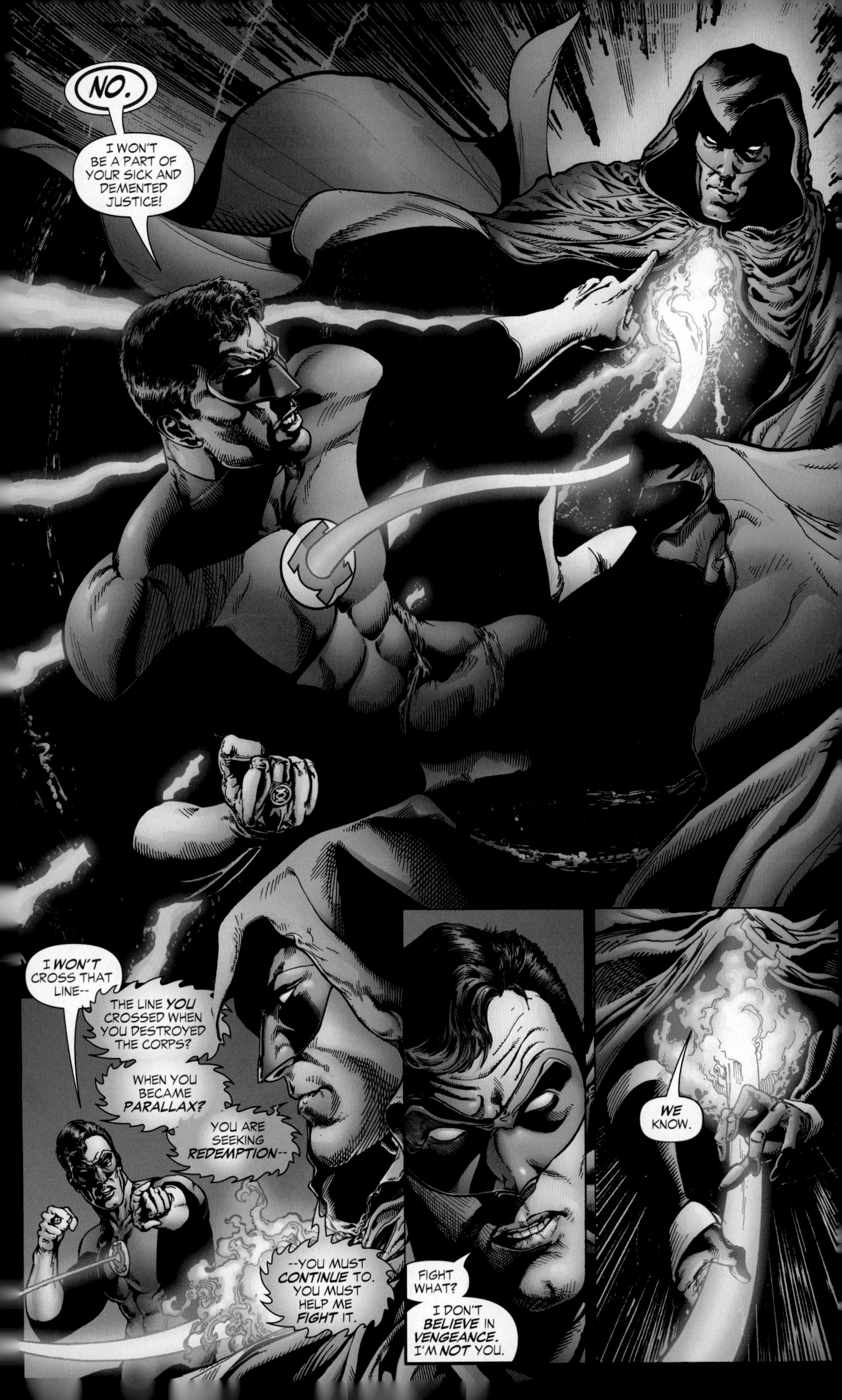
NO.
I WON'T BE A PART OF YOUR SICK AND DEMENTED JUSTICE!
I WON'T CROSS THAT LINE--
THE LINE YOU CROSSED WHEN YOU DESTROYED THE CORPS?
WHEN YOU BECAME PARALLAX?
YOU ARE SEEKING REDEMPTION--
--YOU MUST CONTINUE TO. YOU MUST HELP ME FIGHT IT.
FIGHT WHAT?
I DON'T BELIEVE IN VENGEANCE. I'M NOT YOU.
WE KNOW.

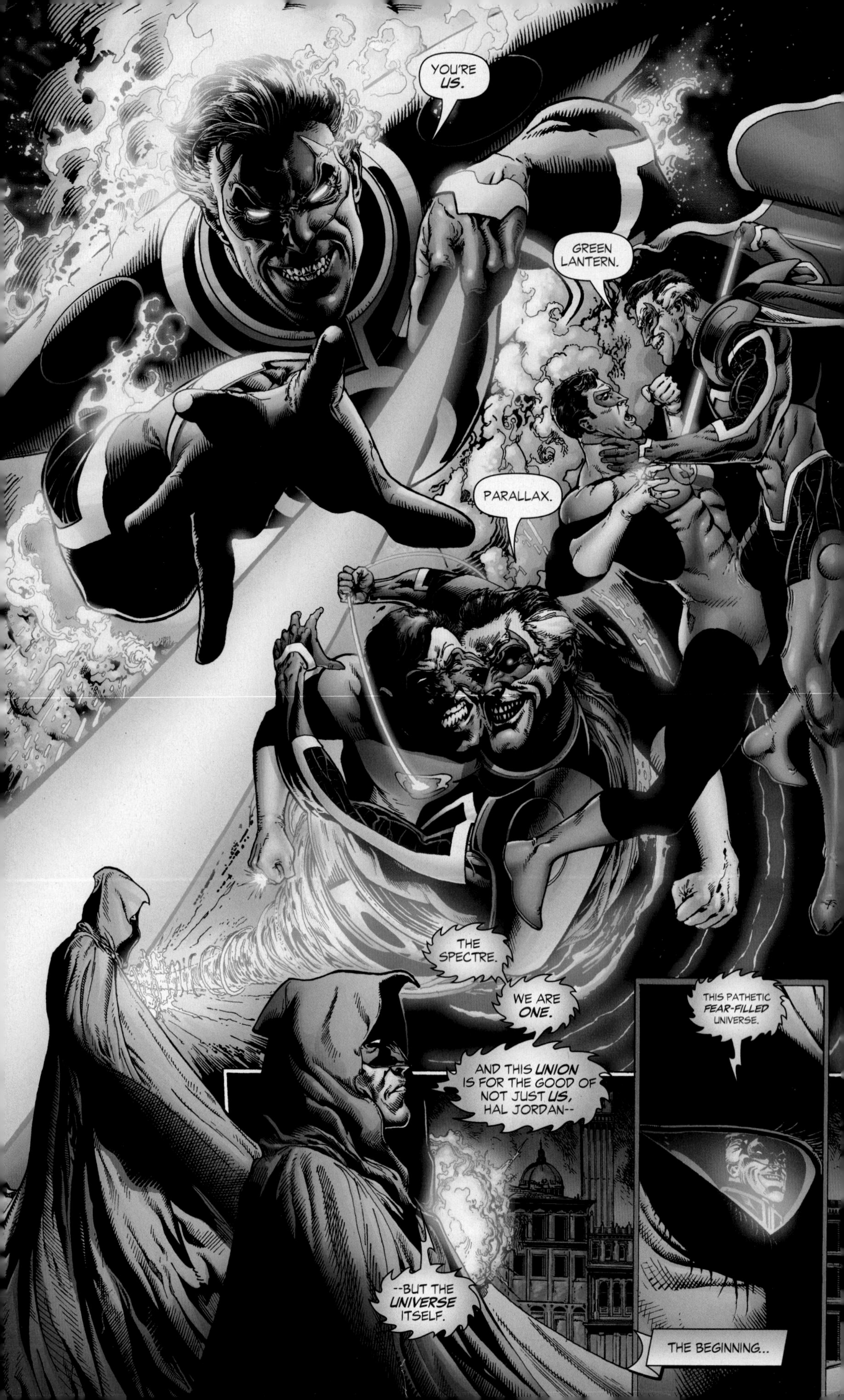
YOU'RE US.
GREEN LANTERN.
PARALLAX.
THE SPECTRE.
WE ARE ONE.
AND THIS UNION IS FOR THE GOOD OF NOT JUST US, HAL JORDAN--
--BUT THE UNIVERSE ITSELF.
THIS PATHETIC FEAR-FILLED UNIVERSE.
THE BEGINNING...

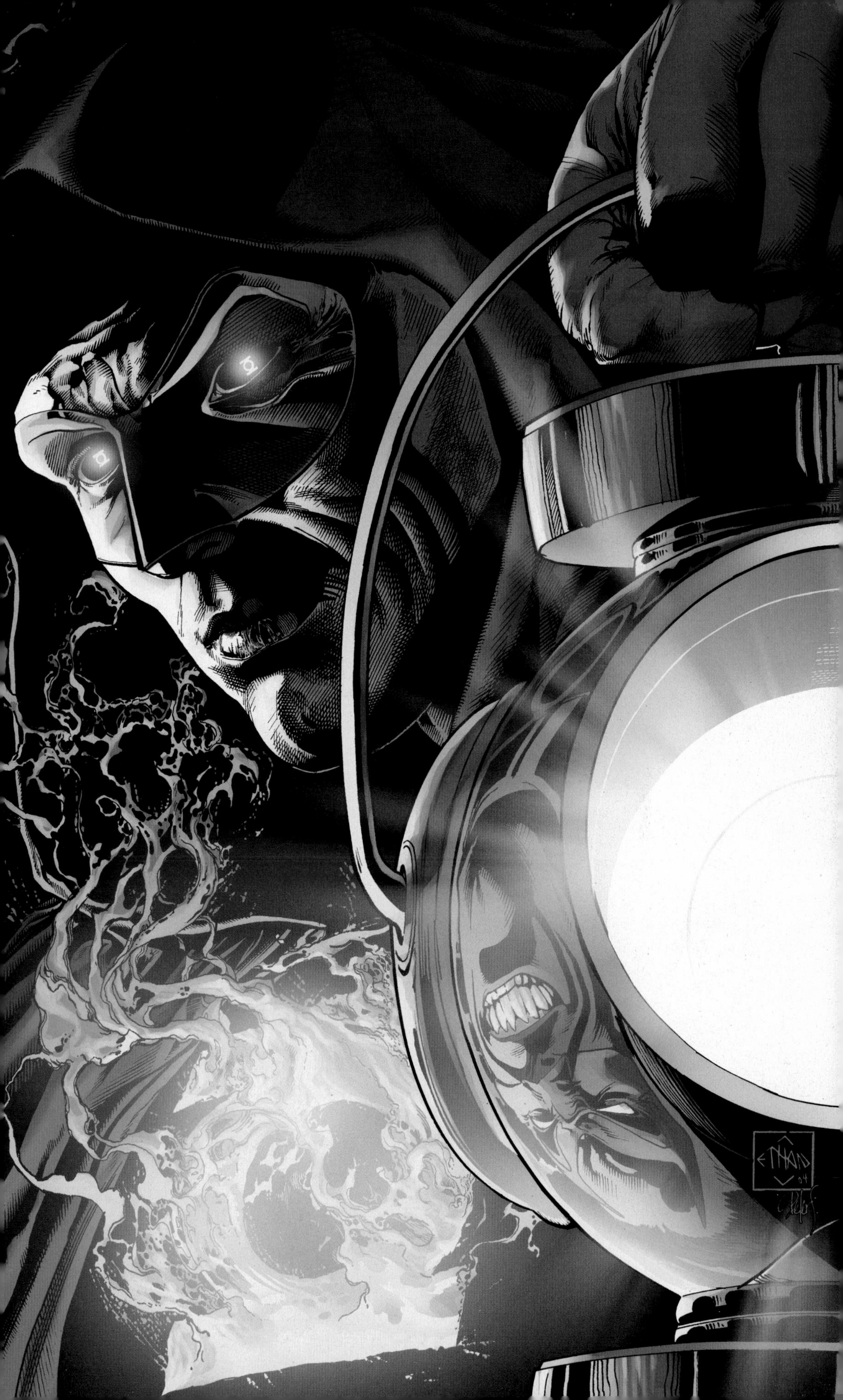

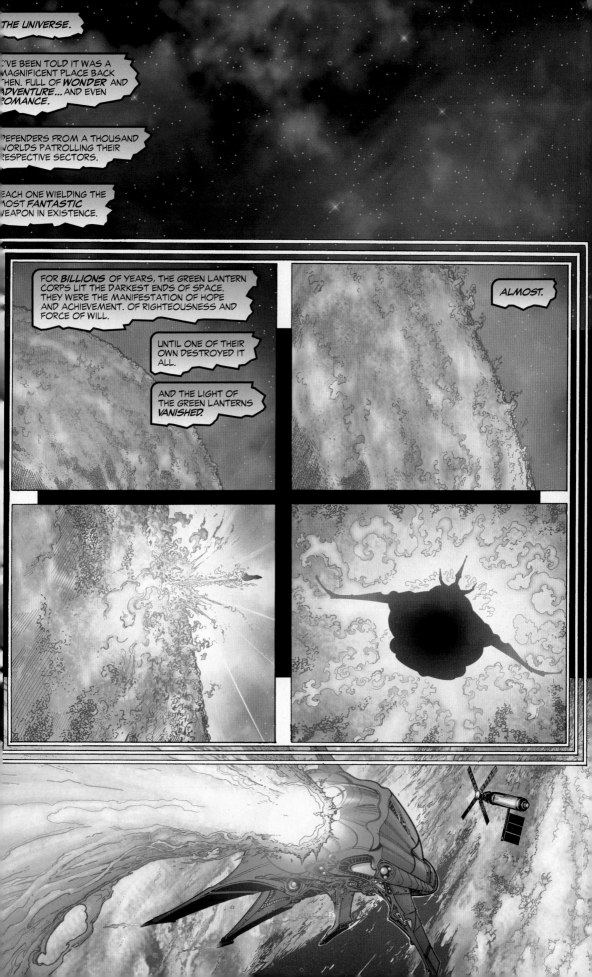

THE UNIVERSE.

I'VE BEEN TOLD IT WAS A MAGNIFICENT PLACE BACK THEN. FULL OF *WONDER* AND *ADVENTURE...* AND EVEN *ROMANCE*.

DEFENDERS FROM A THOUSAND WORLDS PATROLLING THEIR RESPECTIVE SECTORS.

EACH ONE WIELDING THE MOST *FANTASTIC* WEAPON IN EXISTENCE.

FOR *BILLIONS* OF YEARS, THE GREEN LANTERN CORPS LIT THE DARKEST ENDS OF SPACE. THEY WERE THE MANIFESTATION OF HOPE AND ACHIEVEMENT. OF RIGHTEOUSNESS AND FORCE OF WILL.

ALMOST.

UNTIL ONE OF THEIR OWN DESTROYED IT ALL.

AND THE LIGHT OF THE GREEN LANTERNS *VANISHED*.

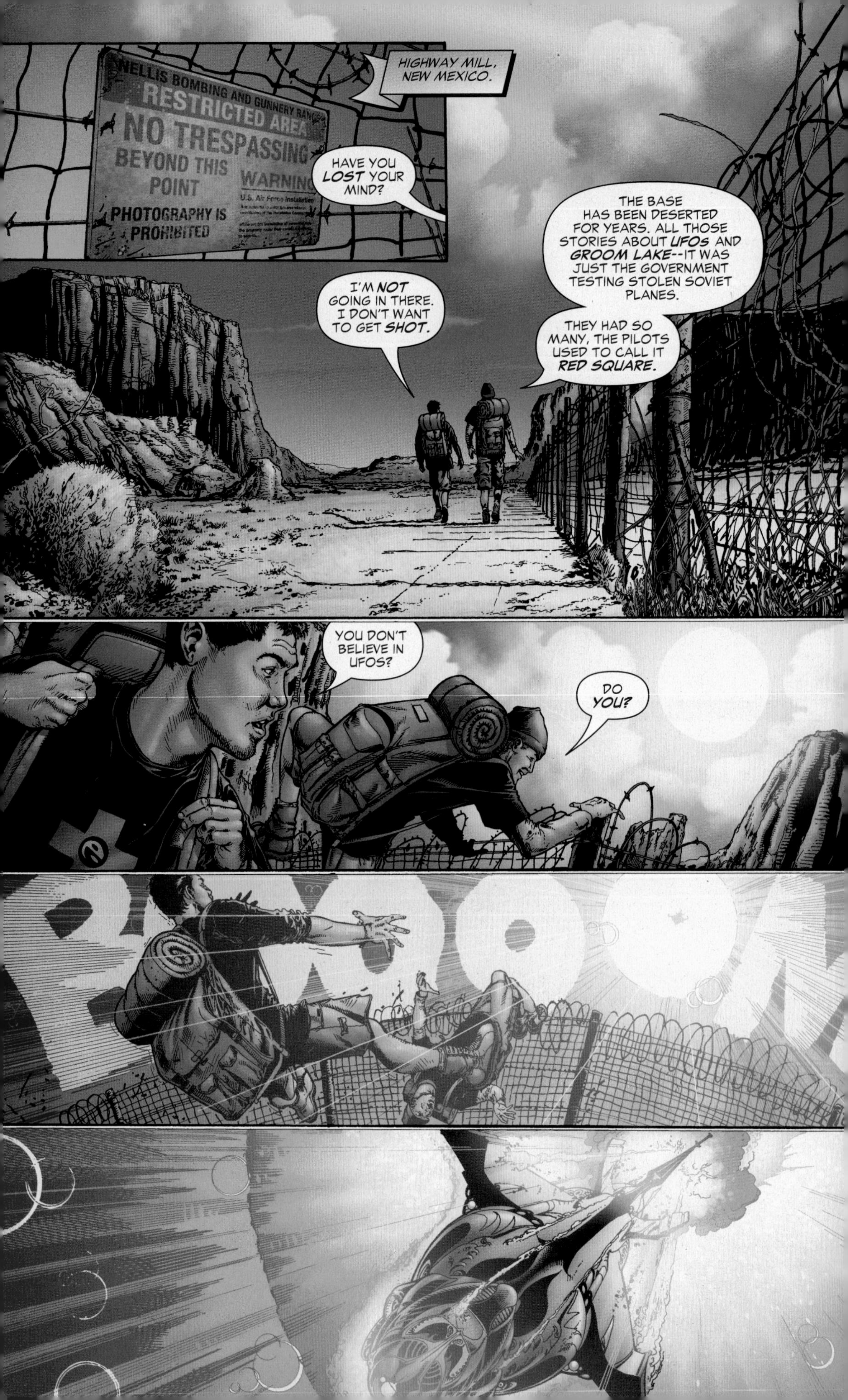
HIGHWAY MILL, NEW MEXICO.
NELLIS BOMBING AND GUNNERY RANGE
RESTRICTED AREA
NO TRESPASSING BEYOND THIS POINT
WARNING
U.S. Air Force Installation
PHOTOGRAPHY IS PROHIBITED
HAVE YOU LOST YOUR MIND?
THE BASE HAS BEEN DESERTED FOR YEARS. ALL THOSE STORIES ABOUT UFOS AND GROOM LAKE--IT WAS JUST THE GOVERNMENT TESTING STOLEN SOVIET PLANES.
I'M NOT GOING IN THERE. I DON'T WANT TO GET SHOT.
THEY HAD SO MANY, THE PILOTS USED TO CALL IT RED SQUARE.
YOU DON'T BELIEVE IN UFOS?
DO YOU?

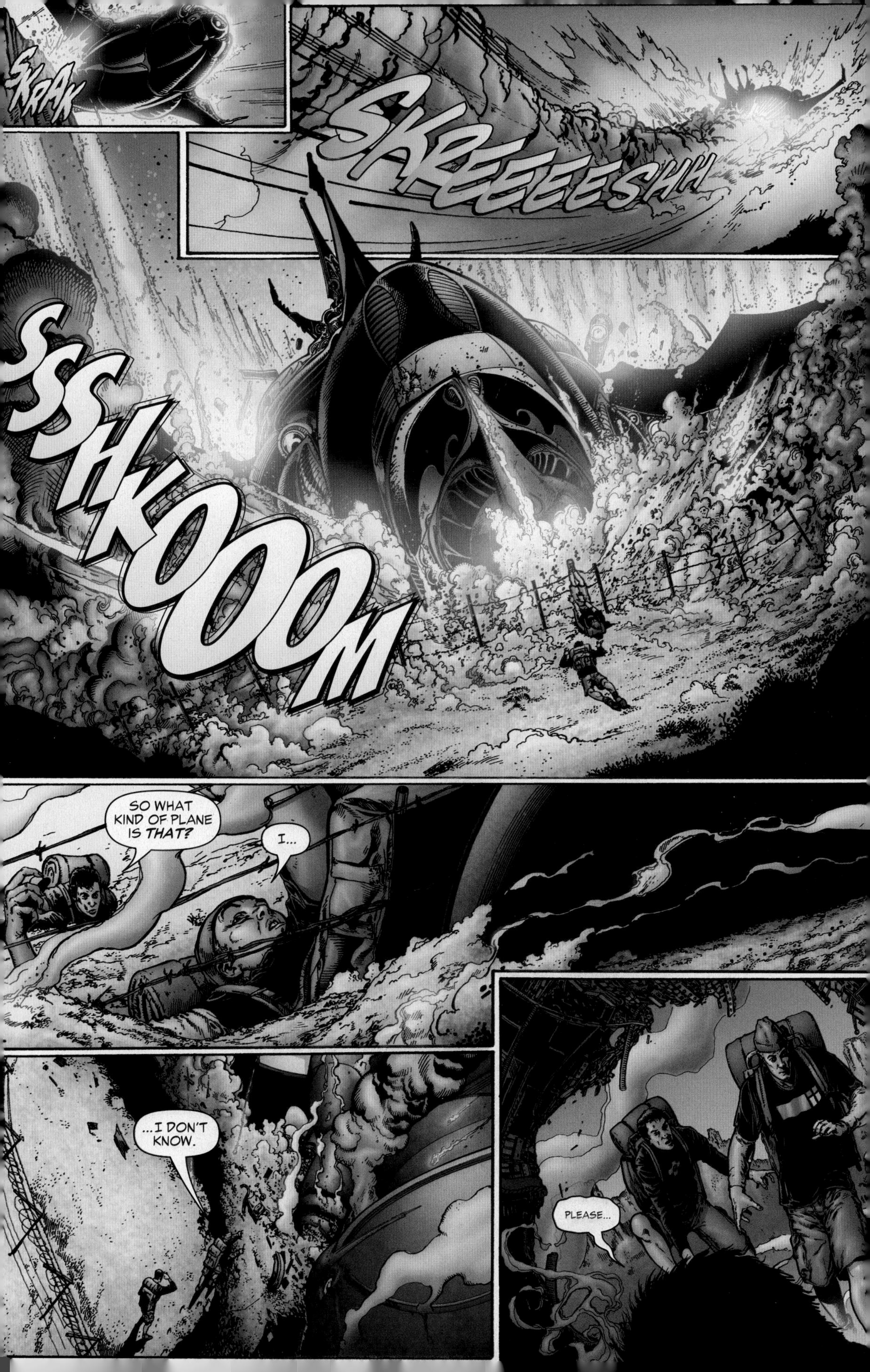
SKRAK
SKREEEEESHH
SSHKOOOM
SO WHAT KIND OF PLANE IS *THAT?*
I...
...I DON'T KNOW.
PLEASE...

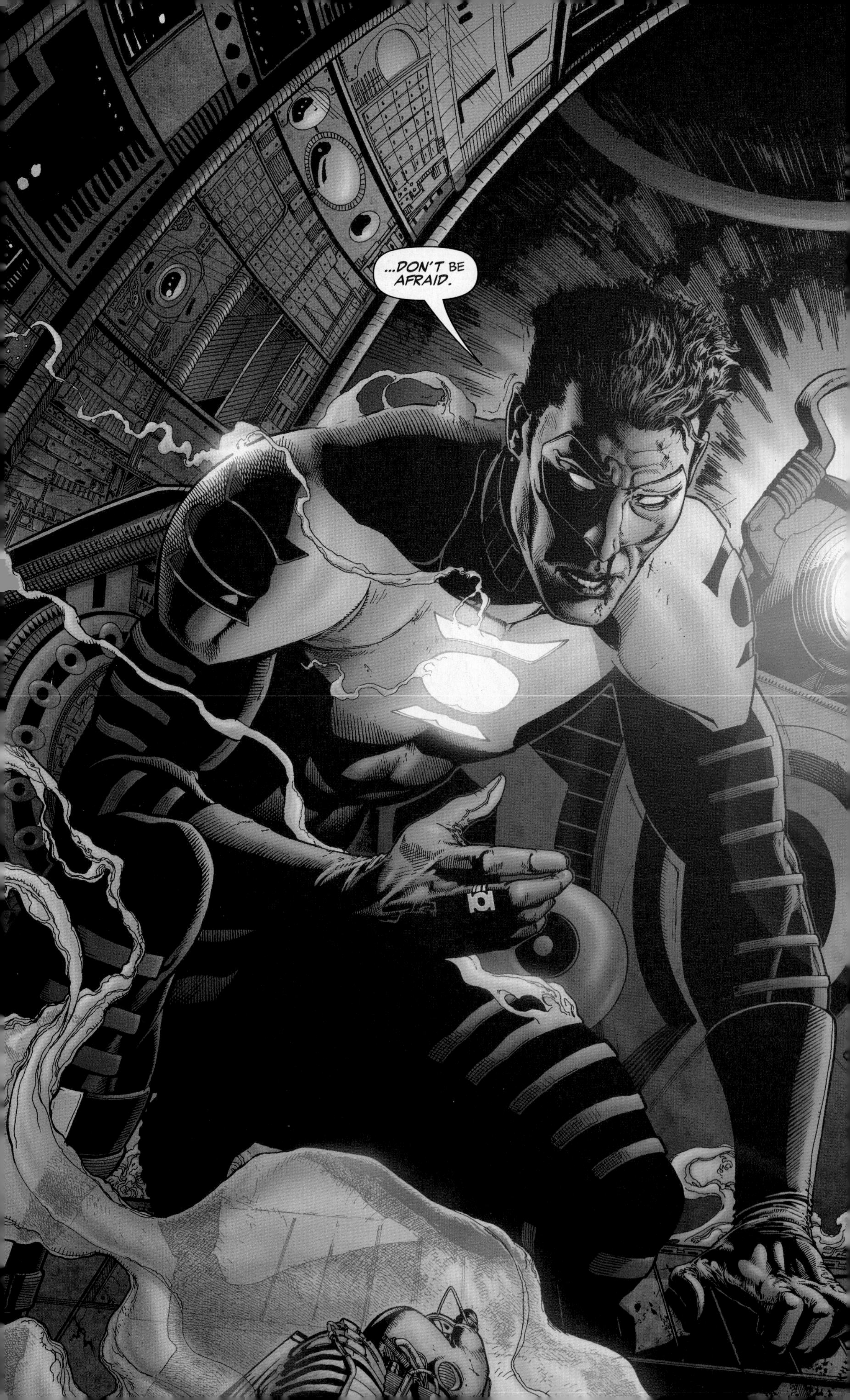
...DON'T BE AFRAID.

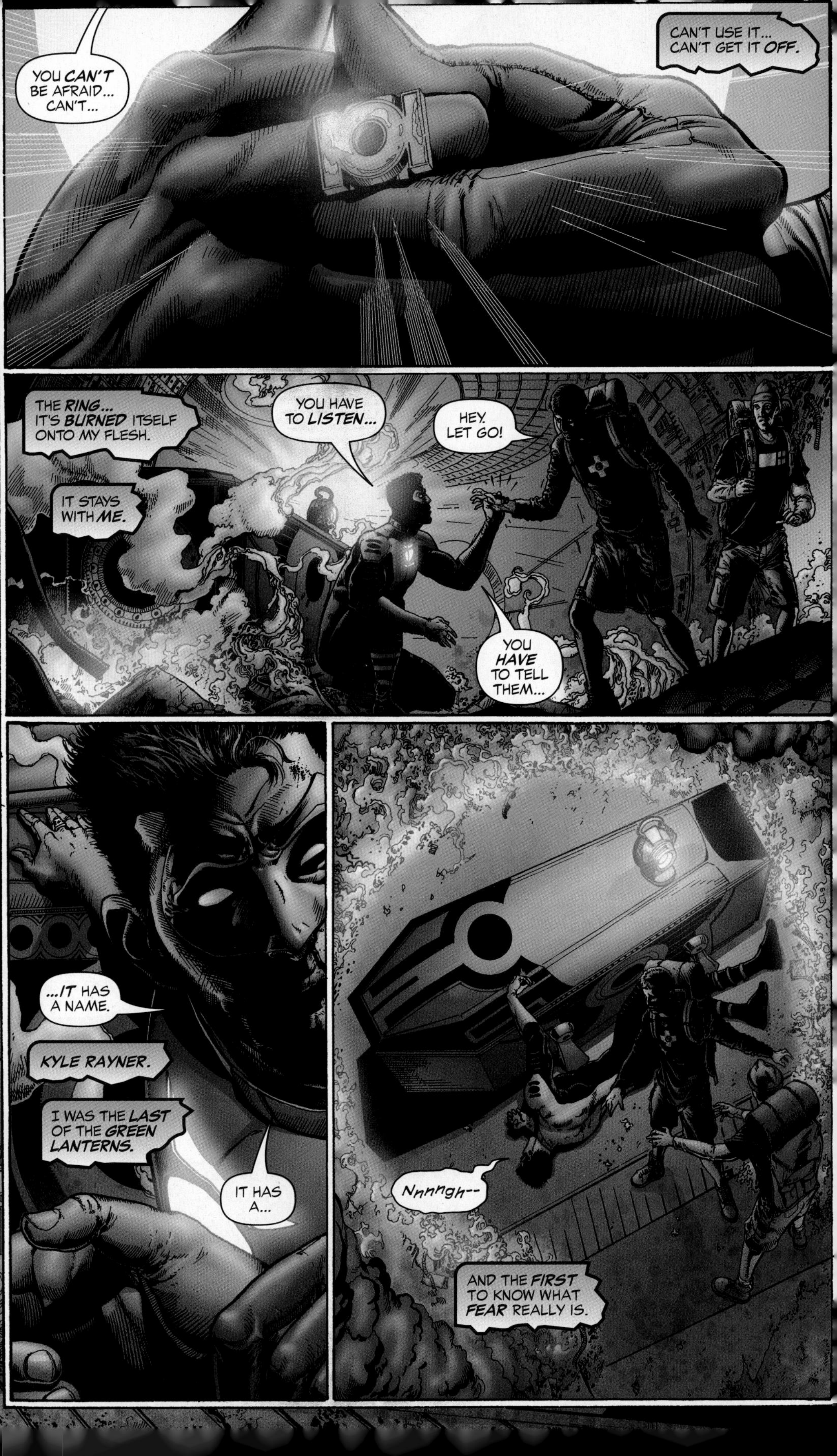
YOU CAN'T BE AFRAID... CAN'T...
CAN'T USE IT... CAN'T GET IT OFF.
THE RING... IT'S BURNED ITSELF ONTO MY FLESH.
IT STAYS WITH ME.
YOU HAVE TO LISTEN...
HEY. LET GO!
YOU HAVE TO TELL THEM...
...IT HAS A NAME.
KYLE RAYNER.
I WAS THE LAST OF THE GREEN LANTERNS.
IT HAS A...
Nnnngh--
AND THE FIRST TO KNOW WHAT FEAR REALLY IS.

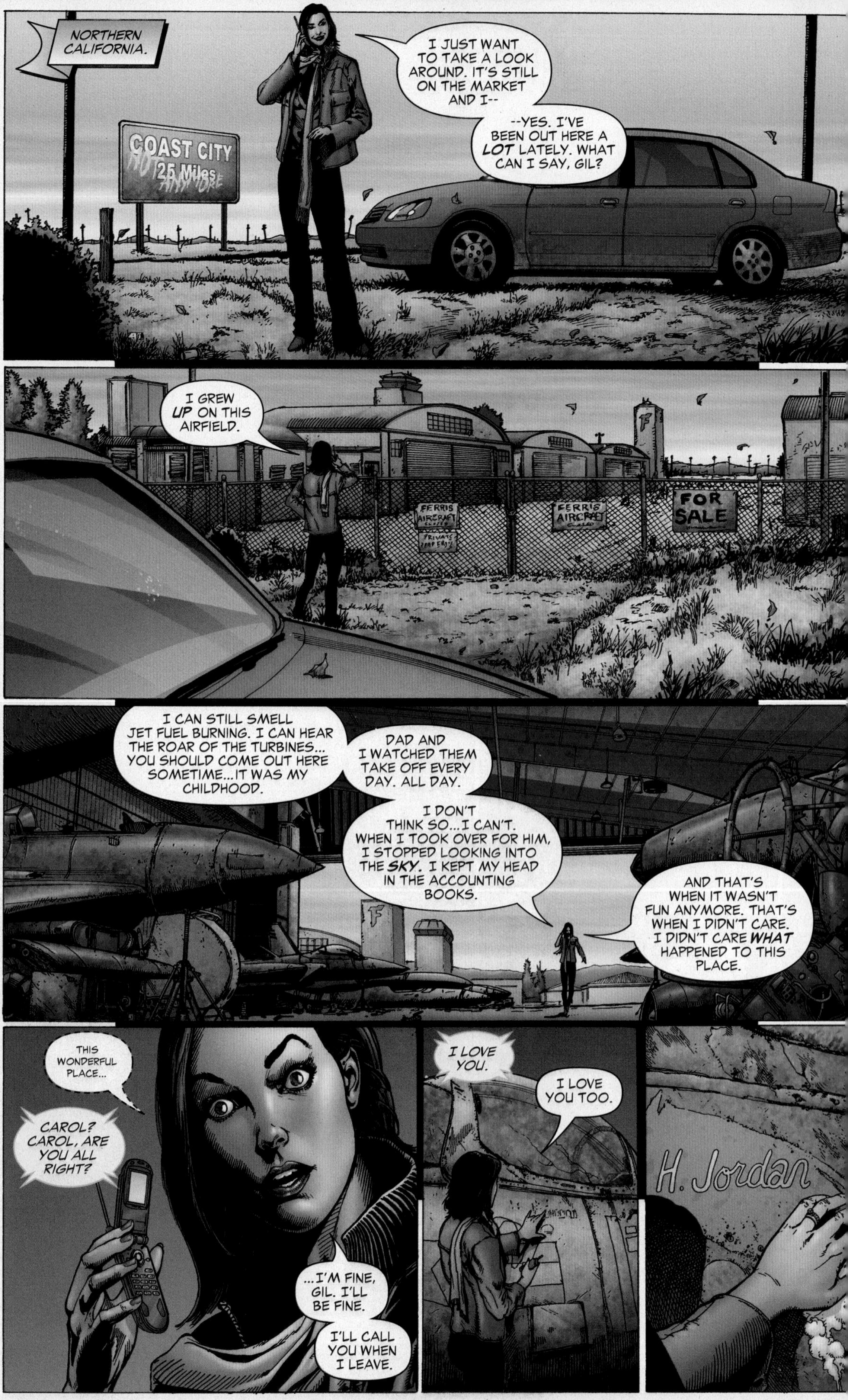
NORTHERN CALIFORNIA.
I JUST WANT TO TAKE A LOOK AROUND. IT'S STILL ON THE MARKET AND I--
--YES. I'VE BEEN OUT HERE A LOT LATELY. WHAT CAN I SAY, GIL?
COAST CITY
25 Miles
I GREW UP ON THIS AIRFIELD.
FERRIS AIRCRAFT
PRIVATE PROPERTY
FERRIS AIRCRAFT
FOR SALE
I CAN STILL SMELL JET FUEL BURNING. I CAN HEAR THE ROAR OF THE TURBINES... YOU SHOULD COME OUT HERE SOMETIME...IT WAS MY CHILDHOOD.
DAD AND I WATCHED THEM TAKE OFF EVERY DAY. ALL DAY.
I DON'T THINK SO...I CAN'T. WHEN I TOOK OVER FOR HIM, I STOPPED LOOKING INTO THE SKY. I KEPT MY HEAD IN THE ACCOUNTING BOOKS.
AND THAT'S WHEN IT WASN'T FUN ANYMORE. THAT'S WHEN I DIDN'T CARE. I DIDN'T CARE WHAT HAPPENED TO THIS PLACE.
THIS WONDERFUL PLACE...
CAROL? CAROL, ARE YOU ALL RIGHT?
...I'M FINE, GIL. I'LL BE FINE.
I'LL CALL YOU WHEN I LEAVE.
I LOVE YOU.
I LOVE YOU TOO.
H. Jordan

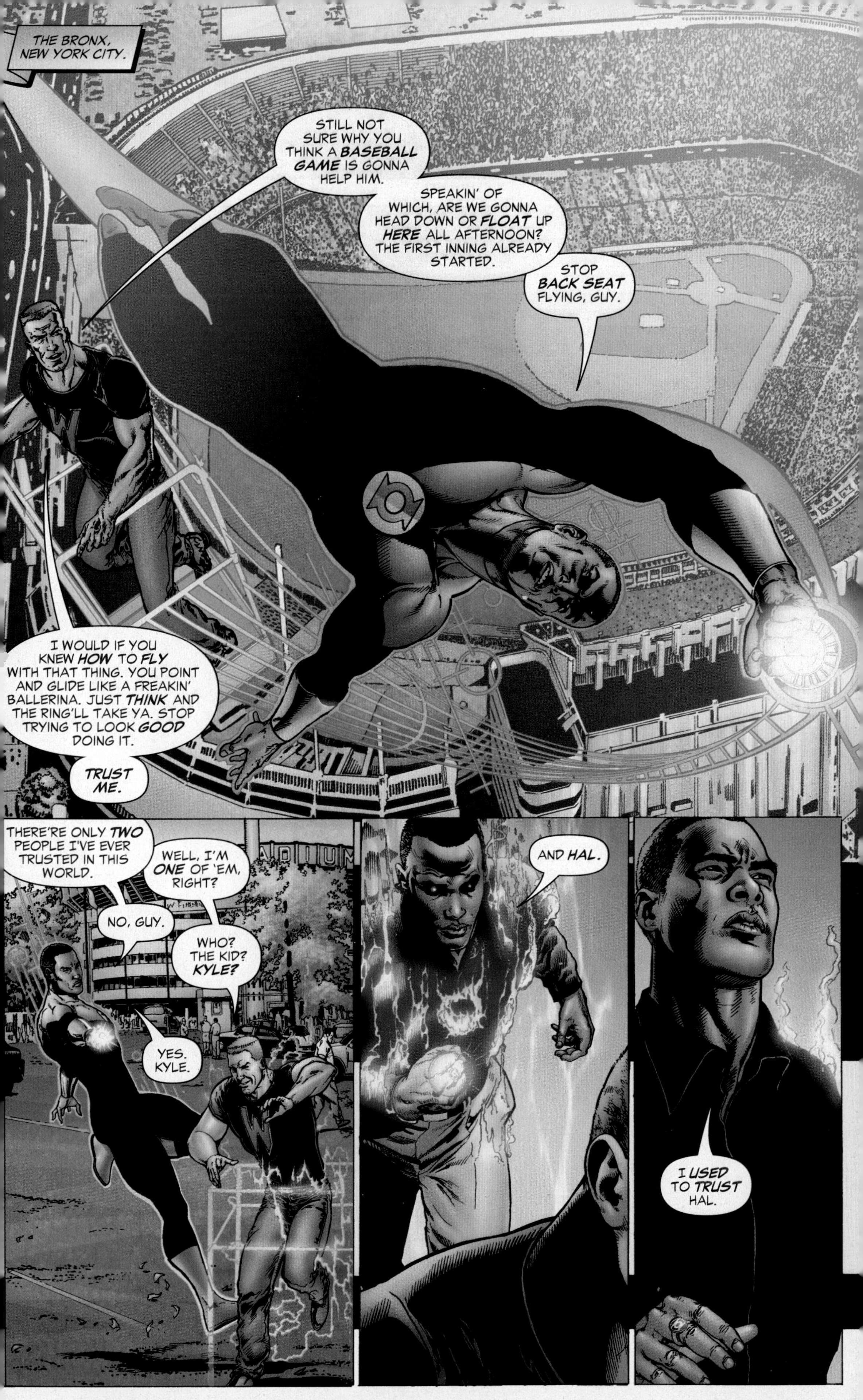
THE BRONX, NEW YORK CITY.
STILL NOT SURE WHY YOU THINK A BASEBALL GAME IS GONNA HELP HIM.
SPEAKIN' OF WHICH, ARE WE GONNA HEAD DOWN OR FLOAT UP HERE ALL AFTERNOON? THE FIRST INNING ALREADY STARTED.
STOP BACK SEAT FLYING, GUY.
I WOULD IF YOU KNEW HOW TO FLY WITH THAT THING. YOU POINT AND GLIDE LIKE A FREAKIN' BALLERINA. JUST THINK AND THE RING'LL TAKE YA. STOP TRYING TO LOOK GOOD DOING IT.
TRUST ME.
THERE'RE ONLY TWO PEOPLE I'VE EVER TRUSTED IN THIS WORLD.
WELL, I'M ONE OF 'EM, RIGHT?
NO, GUY.
WHO? THE KID? KYLE?
YES. KYLE.
AND HAL.
I USED TO TRUST HAL.

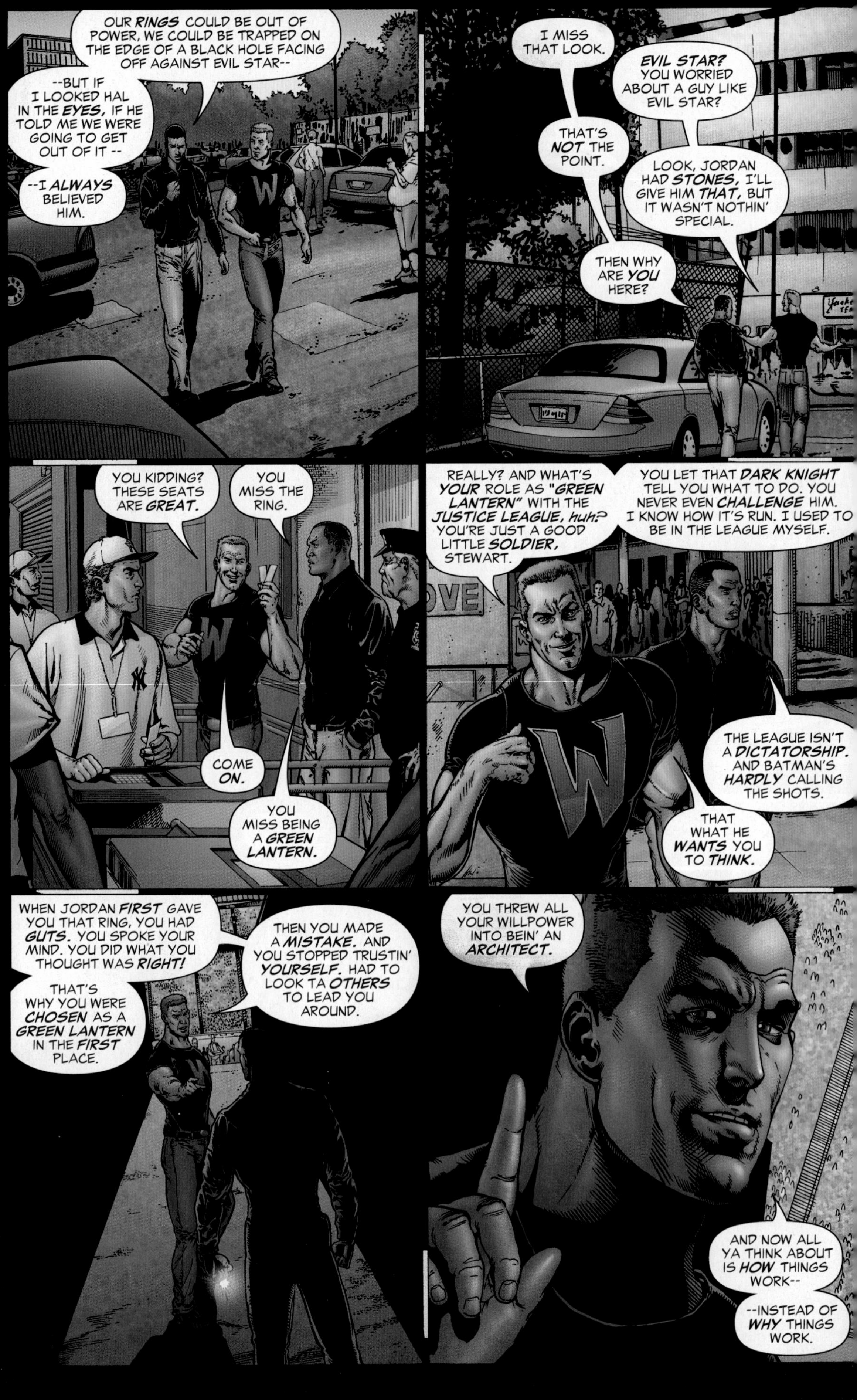
OUR RINGS COULD BE OUT OF POWER, WE COULD BE TRAPPED ON THE EDGE OF A BLACK HOLE FACING OFF AGAINST EVIL STAR--
--BUT IF I LOOKED HAL IN THE EYES, IF HE TOLD ME WE WERE GOING TO GET OUT OF IT --
--I ALWAYS BELIEVED HIM.
I MISS THAT LOOK.
EVIL STAR? YOU WORRIED ABOUT A GUY LIKE EVIL STAR?
THAT'S NOT THE POINT.
LOOK, JORDAN HAD STONES, I'LL GIVE HIM THAT, BUT IT WASN'T NOTHIN' SPECIAL.
THEN WHY ARE YOU HERE?
YOU KIDDING? THESE SEATS ARE GREAT.
YOU MISS THE RING.
COME ON.
YOU MISS BEING A GREEN LANTERN.
REALLY? AND WHAT'S YOUR ROLE AS "GREEN LANTERN" WITH THE JUSTICE LEAGUE, huh? YOU'RE JUST A GOOD LITTLE SOLDIER, STEWART.
YOU LET THAT DARK KNIGHT TELL YOU WHAT TO DO. YOU NEVER EVEN CHALLENGE HIM. I KNOW HOW IT'S RUN. I USED TO BE IN THE LEAGUE MYSELF.
THE LEAGUE ISN'T A DICTATORSHIP. AND BATMAN'S HARDLY CALLING THE SHOTS.
THAT WHAT HE WANTS YOU TO THINK.
WHEN JORDAN FIRST GAVE YOU THAT RING, YOU HAD GUTS. YOU SPOKE YOUR MIND. YOU DID WHAT YOU THOUGHT WAS RIGHT!
THAT'S WHY YOU WERE CHOSEN AS A GREEN LANTERN IN THE FIRST PLACE.
THEN YOU MADE A MISTAKE. AND YOU STOPPED TRUSTIN' YOURSELF. HAD TO LOOK TA OTHERS TO LEAD YOU AROUND.
YOU THREW ALL YOUR WILLPOWER INTO BEIN' AN ARCHITECT.
AND NOW ALL YA THINK ABOUT IS HOW THINGS WORK--
--INSTEAD OF WHY THINGS WORK.

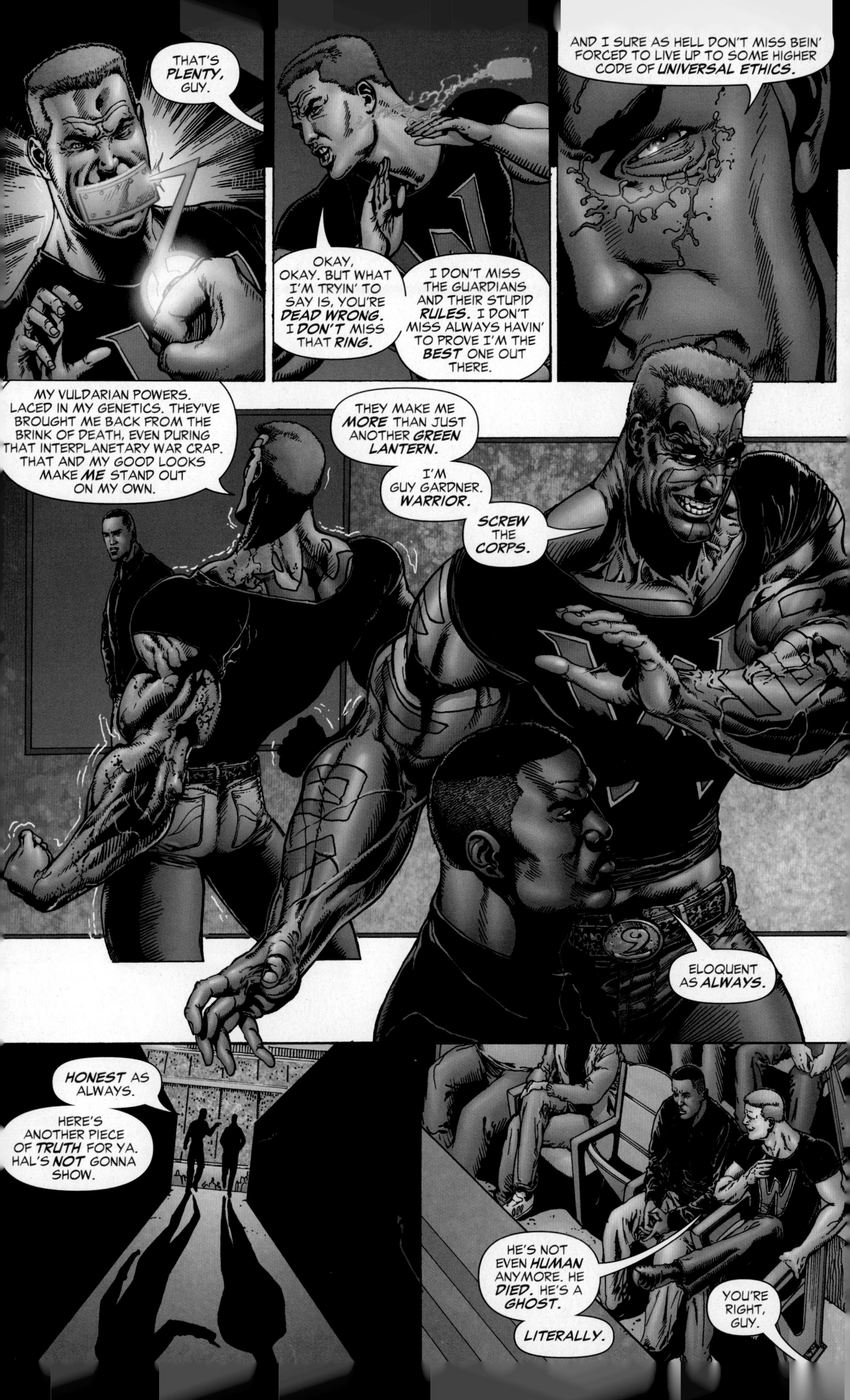
THAT'S PLENTY, GUY.
AND I SURE AS HELL DON'T MISS BEIN' FORCED TO LIVE UP TO SOME HIGHER CODE OF UNIVERSAL ETHICS.
OKAY, OKAY. BUT WHAT I'M TRYIN' TO SAY IS, YOU'RE DEAD WRONG. I DON'T MISS THAT RING.
I DON'T MISS THE GUARDIANS AND THEIR STUPID RULES. I DON'T MISS ALWAYS HAVIN' TO PROVE I'M THE BEST ONE OUT THERE.
MY VULDARIAN POWERS. LACED IN MY GENETICS. THEY'VE BROUGHT ME BACK FROM THE BRINK OF DEATH, EVEN DURING THAT INTERPLANETARY WAR CRAP. THAT AND MY GOOD LOOKS MAKE ME STAND OUT ON MY OWN.
THEY MAKE ME MORE THAN JUST ANOTHER GREEN LANTERN.
I'M GUY GARDNER. WARRIOR.
SCREW THE CORPS.
ELOQUENT AS ALWAYS.
HONEST AS ALWAYS.
HERE'S ANOTHER PIECE OF TRUTH FOR YA. HAL'S NOT GONNA SHOW.
HE'S NOT EVEN HUMAN ANYMORE. HE DIED. HE'S A GHOST.
LITERALLY.
YOU'RE RIGHT, GUY.

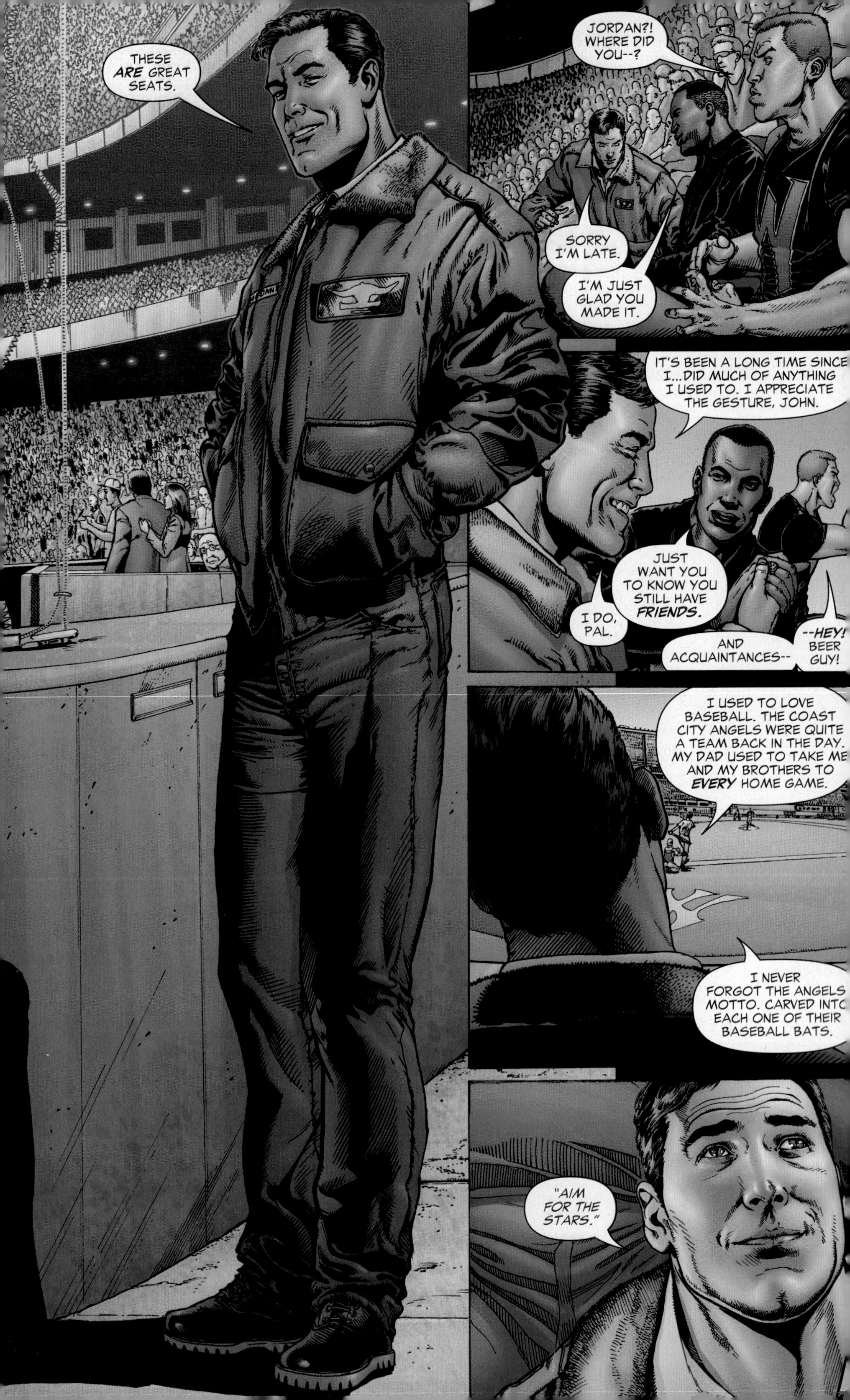
THESE *ARE* GREAT SEATS.
JORDAN?! WHERE DID YOU--?
SORRY I'M LATE.
I'M JUST GLAD YOU MADE IT.
IT'S BEEN A LONG TIME SINCE I...DID MUCH OF ANYTHING I USED TO. I APPRECIATE THE GESTURE, JOHN.
JUST WANT YOU TO KNOW YOU STILL HAVE *FRIENDS*.
I DO, PAL.
AND ACQUAINTANCES--
--*HEY!* BEER GUY!
I USED TO LOVE BASEBALL. THE COAST CITY ANGELS WERE QUITE A TEAM BACK IN THE DAY. MY DAD USED TO TAKE ME AND MY BROTHERS TO *EVERY* HOME GAME.
I NEVER FORGOT THE ANGELS MOTTO. CARVED INTO EACH ONE OF THEIR BASEBALL BATS.
"AIM FOR THE STARS."

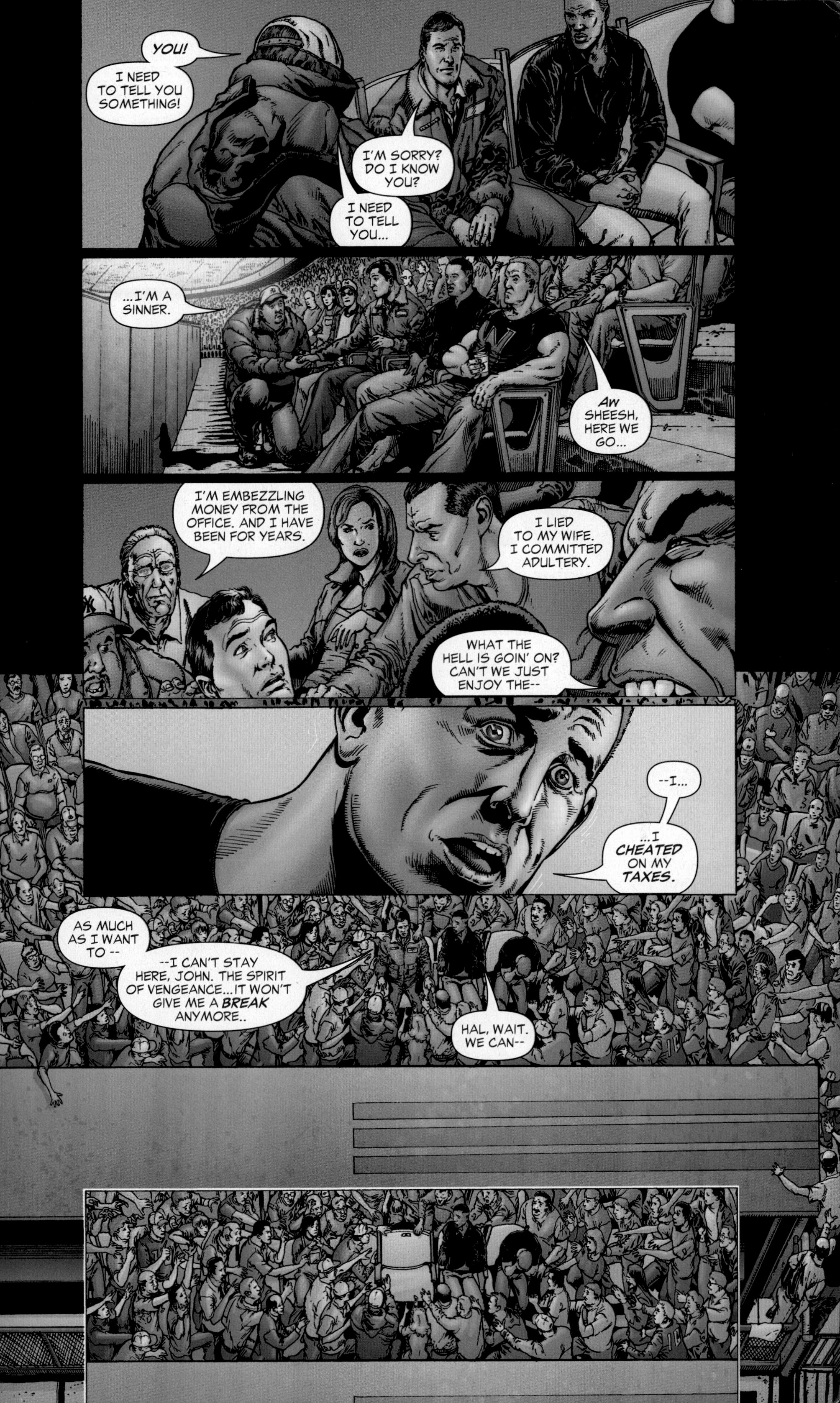
YOU!
I NEED TO TELL YOU SOMETHING!
I'M SORRY? DO I KNOW YOU?
I NEED TO TELL YOU...
...I'M A SINNER.
AW SHEESH, HERE WE GO...
I'M EMBEZZLING MONEY FROM THE OFFICE. AND I HAVE BEEN FOR YEARS.
I LIED TO MY WIFE. I COMMITTED ADULTERY.
WHAT THE HELL IS GOIN' ON? CAN'T WE JUST ENJOY THE--
--I...
...I CHEATED ON MY TAXES.
AS MUCH AS I WANT TO --
--I CAN'T STAY HERE, JOHN. THE SPIRIT OF VENGEANCE...IT WON'T GIVE ME A BREAK ANYMORE..
HAL, WAIT. WE CAN--

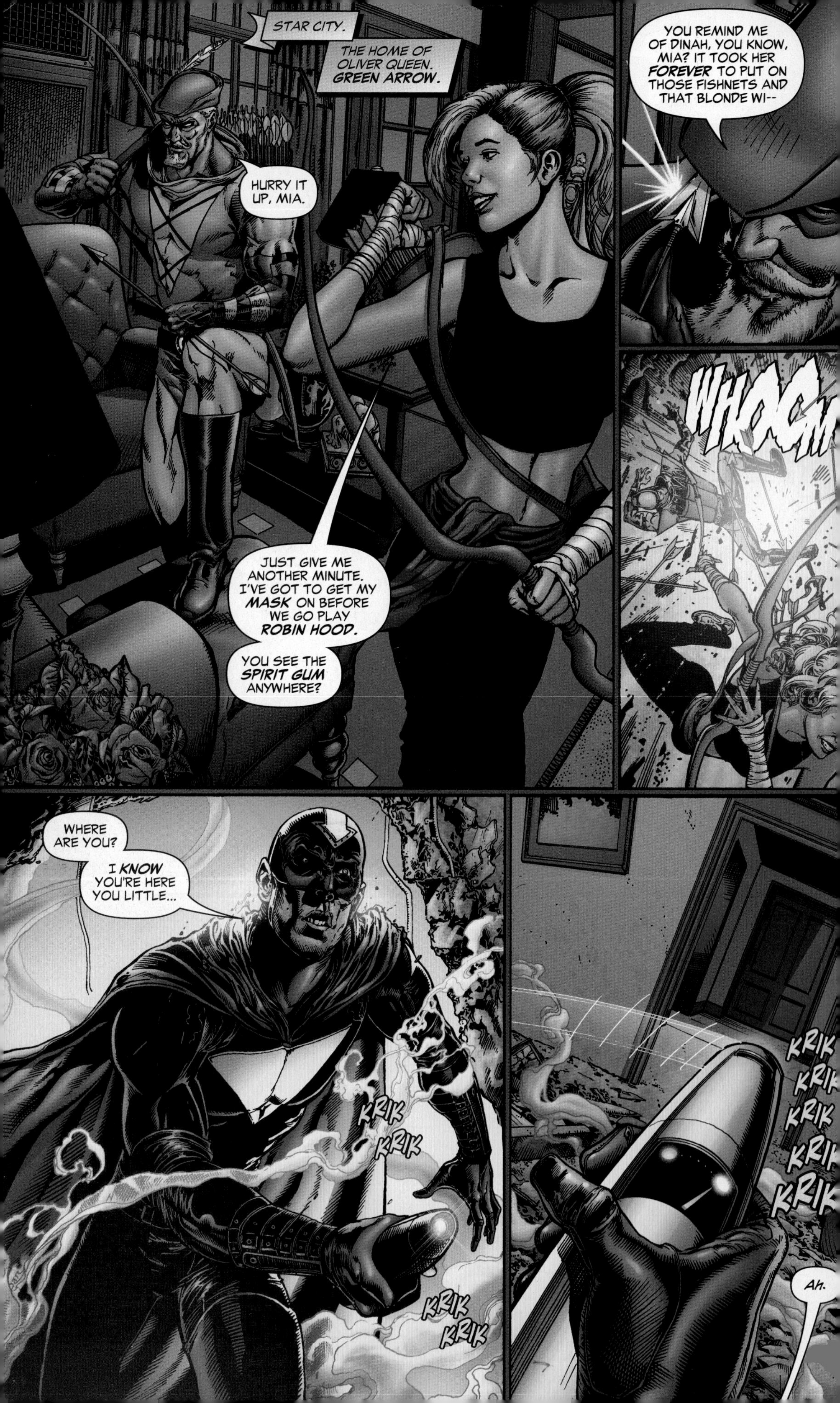
STAR CITY.
THE HOME OF OLIVER QUEEN. GREEN ARROW.
HURRY IT UP, MIA.
JUST GIVE ME ANOTHER MINUTE. I'VE GOT TO GET MY MASK ON BEFORE WE GO PLAY ROBIN HOOD.
YOU SEE THE SPIRIT GUM ANYWHERE?
YOU REMIND ME OF DINAH, YOU KNOW, MIA? IT TOOK HER FOREVER TO PUT ON THOSE FISHNETS AND THAT BLONDE WI--
WHOOM
WHERE ARE YOU?
I KNOW YOU'RE HERE YOU LITTLE...
KRIK
KRIK
KRIK
KRIK
KRIK
KRIK
KRIK
KRIK
KRIK
Ah.

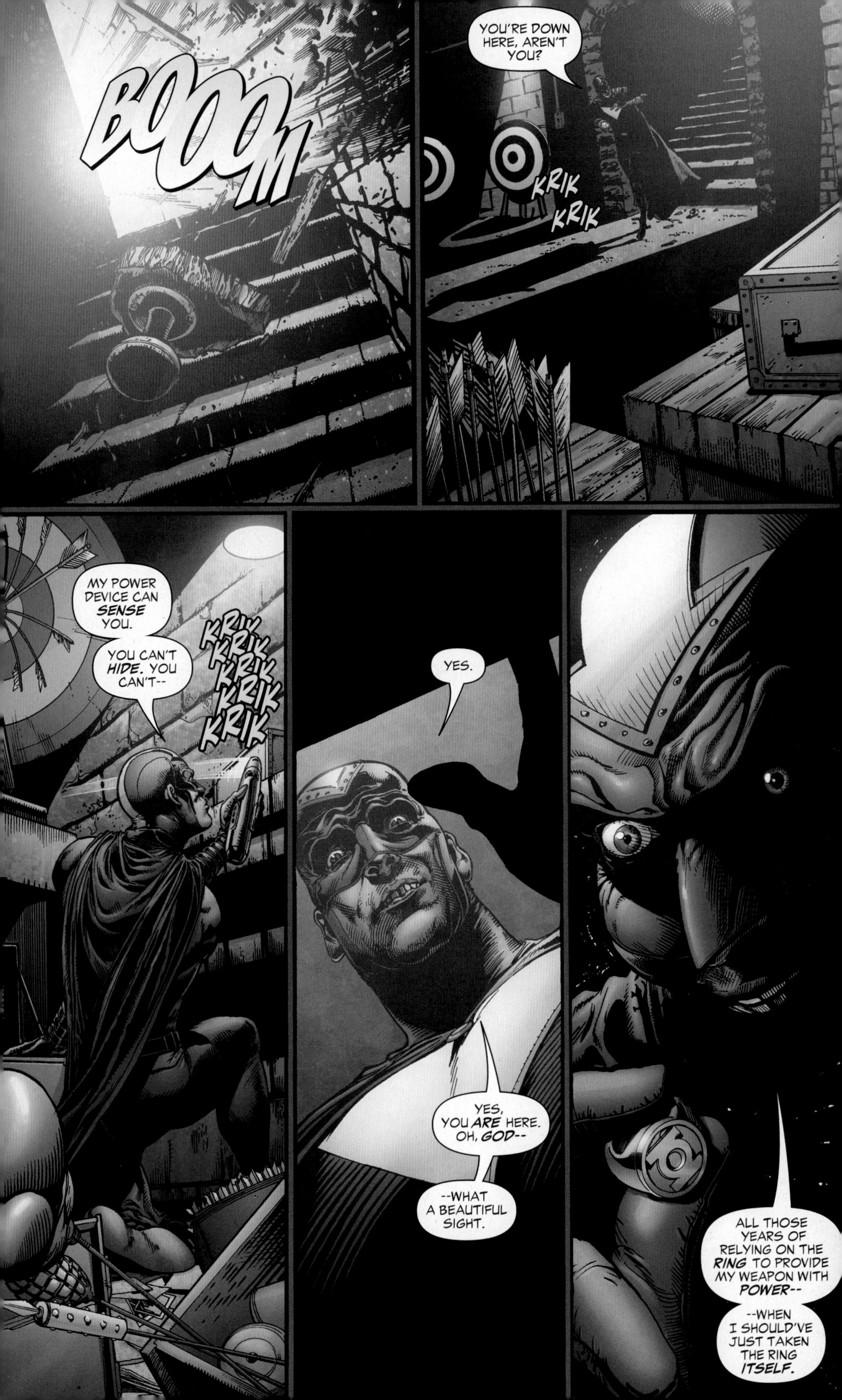
BOOOM
YOU'RE DOWN HERE, AREN'T YOU?
KRIK KRIK
MY POWER DEVICE CAN SENSE YOU.
YOU CAN'T HIDE. YOU CAN'T--
KRIK KRIK KRIK KRIK KRIK
YES.
YES, YOU ARE HERE. OH, GOD--
--WHAT A BEAUTIFUL SIGHT.
ALL THOSE YEARS OF RELYING ON THE RING TO PROVIDE MY WEAPON WITH POWER--
--WHEN I SHOULD'VE JUST TAKEN THE RING ITSELF.

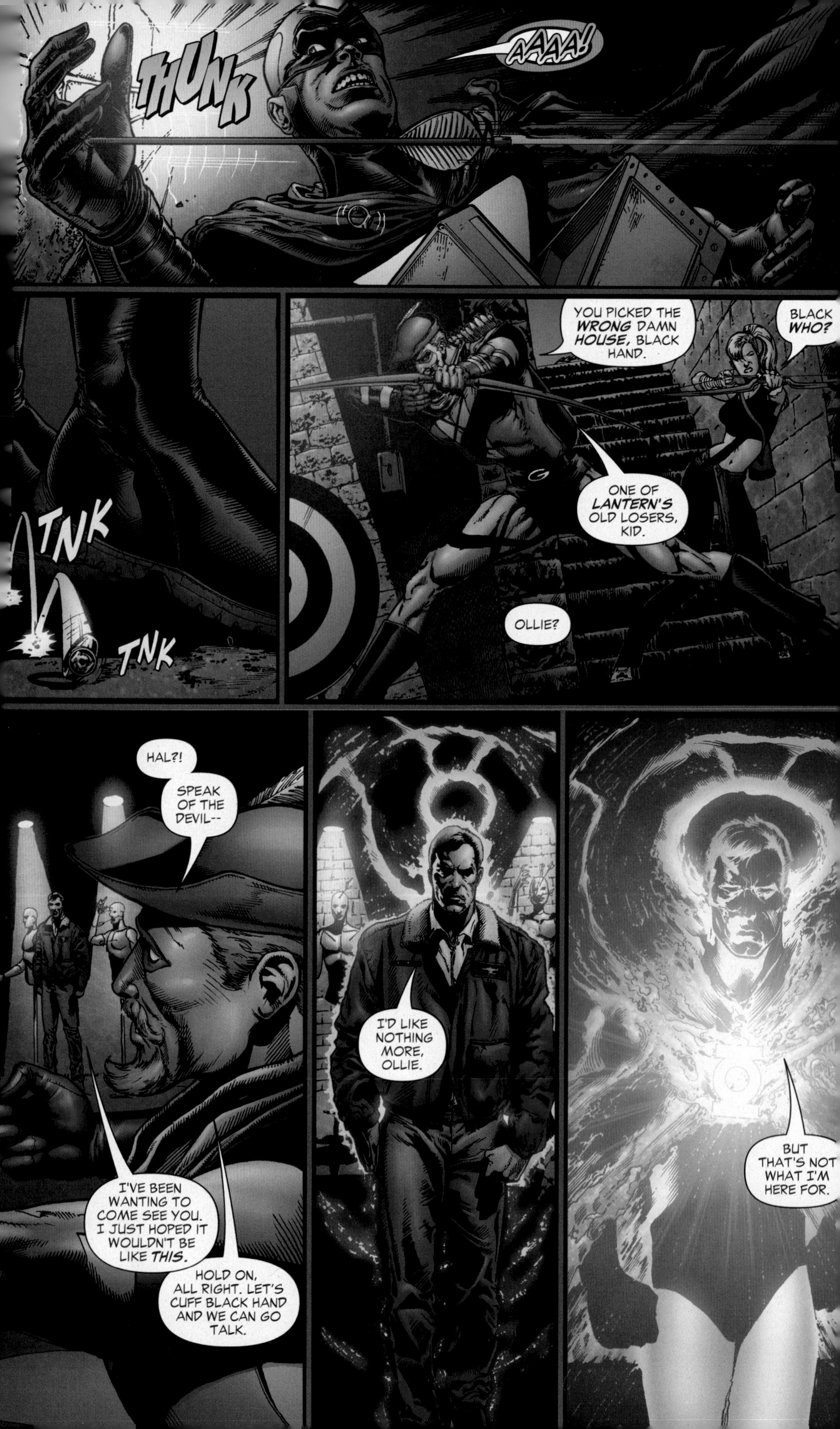
THUNK
AAAA!
TNK
TNK
YOU PICKED THE WRONG DAMN HOUSE, BLACK HAND.
BLACK WHO?
ONE OF LANTERN'S OLD LOSERS, KID.
OLLIE?
HAL?!
SPEAK OF THE DEVIL--
I'D LIKE NOTHING MORE, OLLIE.
BUT THAT'S NOT WHAT I'M HERE FOR.
I'VE BEEN WANTING TO COME SEE YOU. I JUST HOPED IT WOULDN'T BE LIKE THIS.
HOLD ON, ALL RIGHT. LET'S CUFF BLACK HAND AND WE CAN GO TALK.

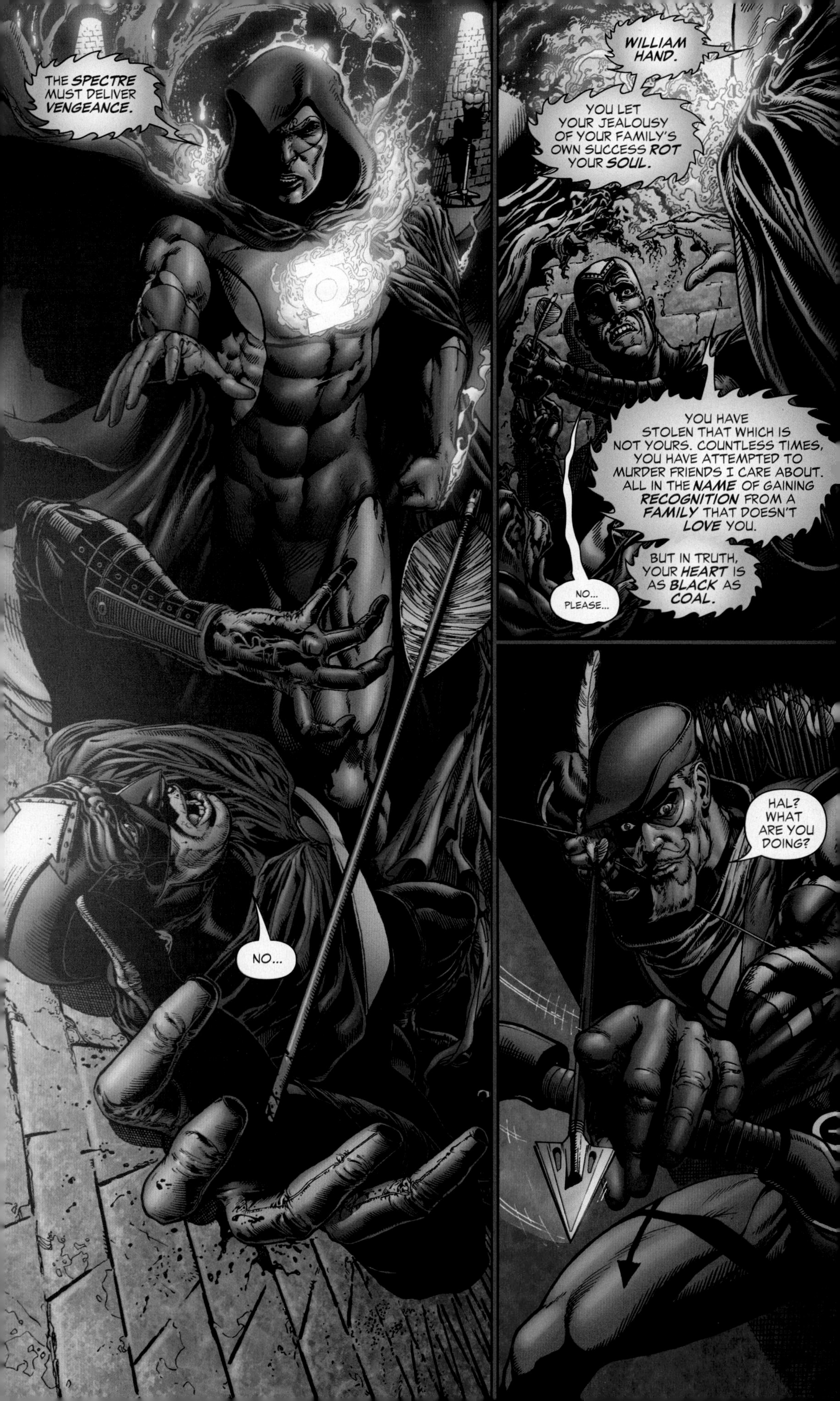

THE SPECTRE MUST DELIVER VENGEANCE.
NO...
WILLIAM HAND.
YOU LET YOUR JEALOUSY OF YOUR FAMILY'S OWN SUCCESS ROT YOUR SOUL.
YOU HAVE STOLEN THAT WHICH IS NOT YOURS. COUNTLESS TIMES, YOU HAVE ATTEMPTED TO MURDER FRIENDS I CARE ABOUT. ALL IN THE NAME OF GAINING RECOGNITION FROM A FAMILY THAT DOESN'T LOVE YOU.
BUT IN TRUTH, YOUR HEART IS AS BLACK AS COAL.
NO... PLEASE...
HAL? WHAT ARE YOU DOING?

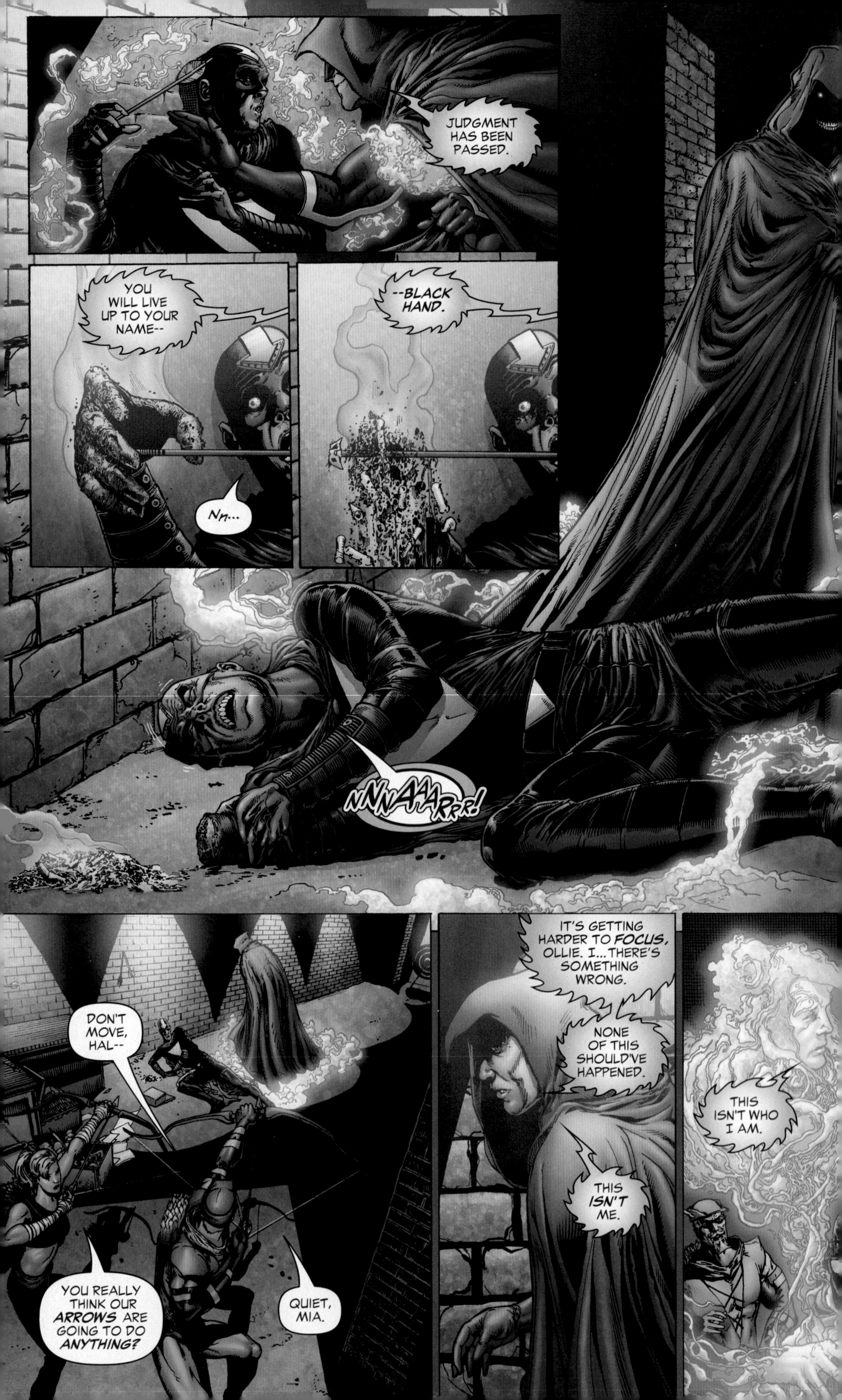
JUDGMENT HAS BEEN PASSED.
YOU WILL LIVE UP TO YOUR NAME--
Nn...
--BLACK HAND.
NNNAAARRR!
DON'T MOVE, HAL--
YOU REALLY THINK OUR ARROWS ARE GOING TO DO ANYTHING?
QUIET, MIA.
IT'S GETTING HARDER TO FOCUS, OLLIE. I...THERE'S SOMETHING WRONG.
NONE OF THIS SHOULD'VE HAPPENED.
THIS ISN'T ME.
THIS ISN'T WHO I AM.

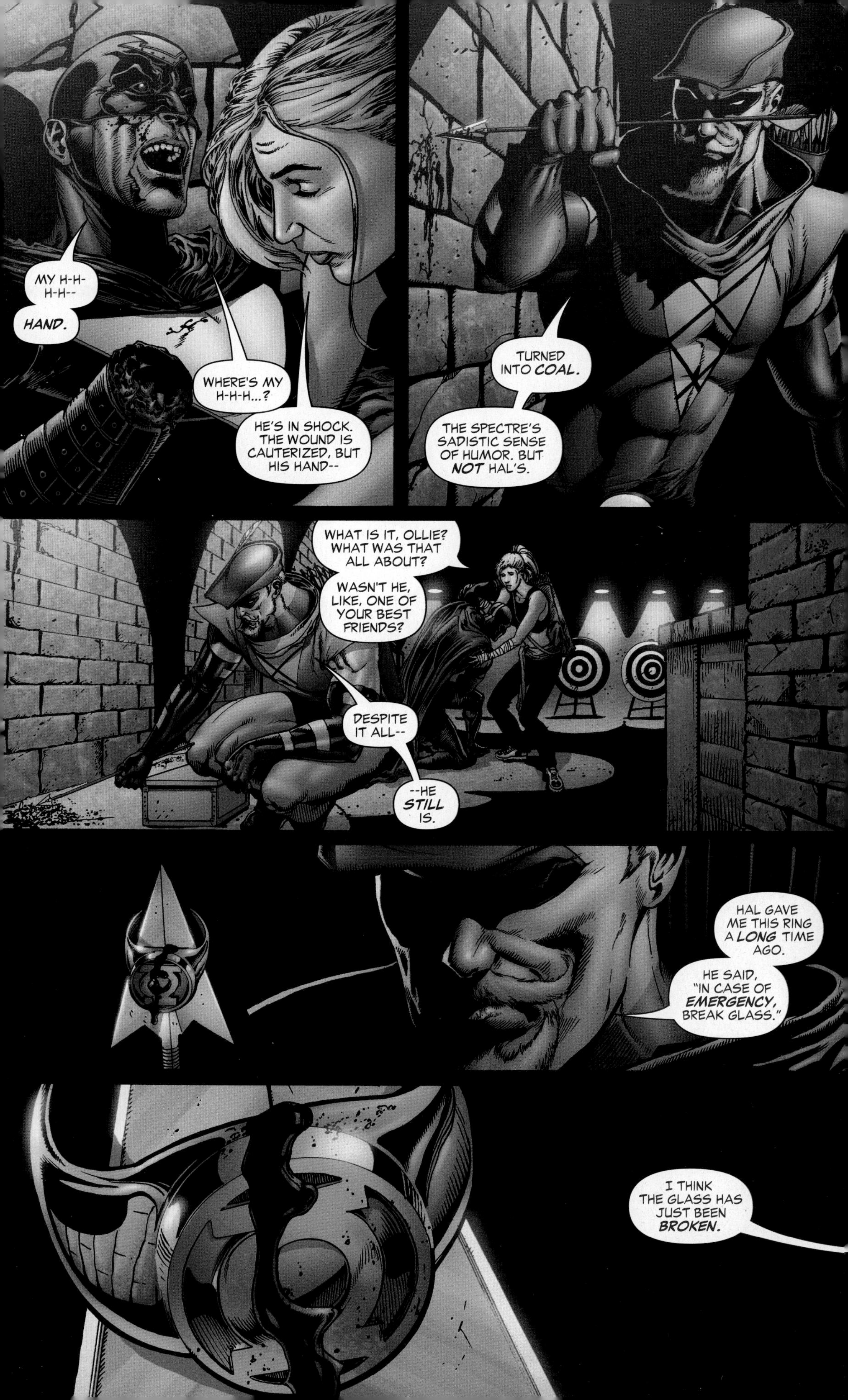

MY H-H-H-H--
HAND.
WHERE'S MY H-H-H...?
HE'S IN SHOCK. THE WOUND IS CAUTERIZED, BUT HIS HAND--
TURNED INTO COAL.
THE SPECTRE'S SADISTIC SENSE OF HUMOR. BUT NOT HAL'S.
WHAT IS IT, OLLIE? WHAT WAS THAT ALL ABOUT?
WASN'T HE, LIKE, ONE OF YOUR BEST FRIENDS?
DESPITE IT ALL--
--HE STILL IS.
HAL GAVE ME THIS RING A LONG TIME AGO.
HE SAID, "IN CASE OF EMERGENCY, BREAK GLASS."
I THINK THE GLASS HAS JUST BEEN BROKEN.

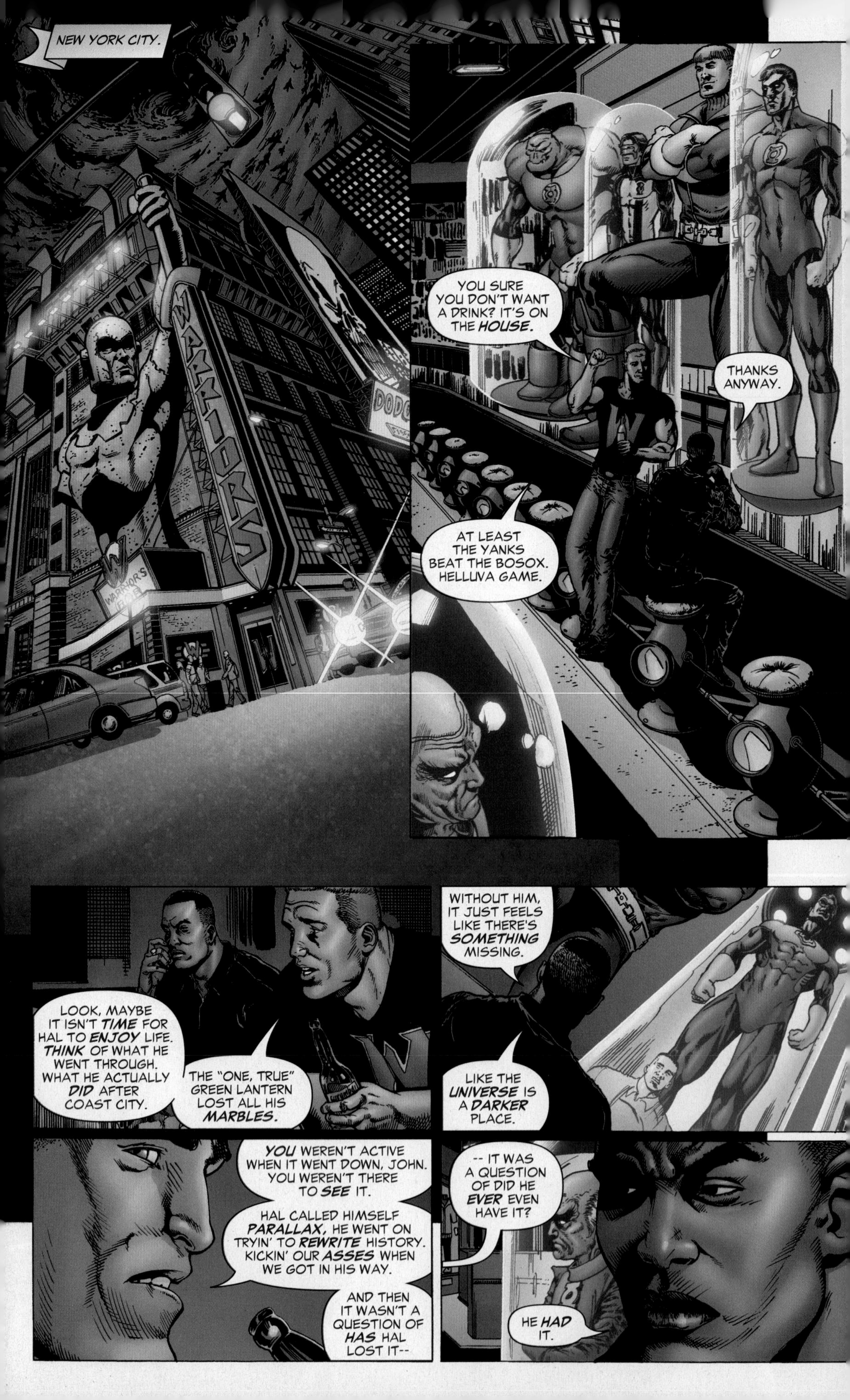
NEW YORK CITY.
WARRIORS
WARRIOR'S
YOU SURE YOU DON'T WANT A DRINK? IT'S ON THE HOUSE.
THANKS ANYWAY.
AT LEAST THE YANKS BEAT THE BOSOX. HELLUVA GAME.
LOOK, MAYBE IT ISN'T TIME FOR HAL TO ENJOY LIFE. THINK OF WHAT HE WENT THROUGH. WHAT HE ACTUALLY DID AFTER COAST CITY.
THE "ONE, TRUE" GREEN LANTERN LOST ALL HIS MARBLES.
WITHOUT HIM, IT JUST FEELS LIKE THERE'S SOMETHING MISSING.
LIKE THE UNIVERSE IS A DARKER PLACE.
YOU WEREN'T ACTIVE WHEN IT WENT DOWN, JOHN. YOU WEREN'T THERE TO SEE IT.
HAL CALLED HIMSELF PARALLAX, HE WENT ON TRYIN' TO REWRITE HISTORY. KICKIN' OUR ASSES WHEN WE GOT IN HIS WAY.
AND THEN IT WASN'T A QUESTION OF HAS HAL LOST IT--
-- IT WAS A QUESTION OF DID HE EVER EVEN HAVE IT?
HE HAD IT.

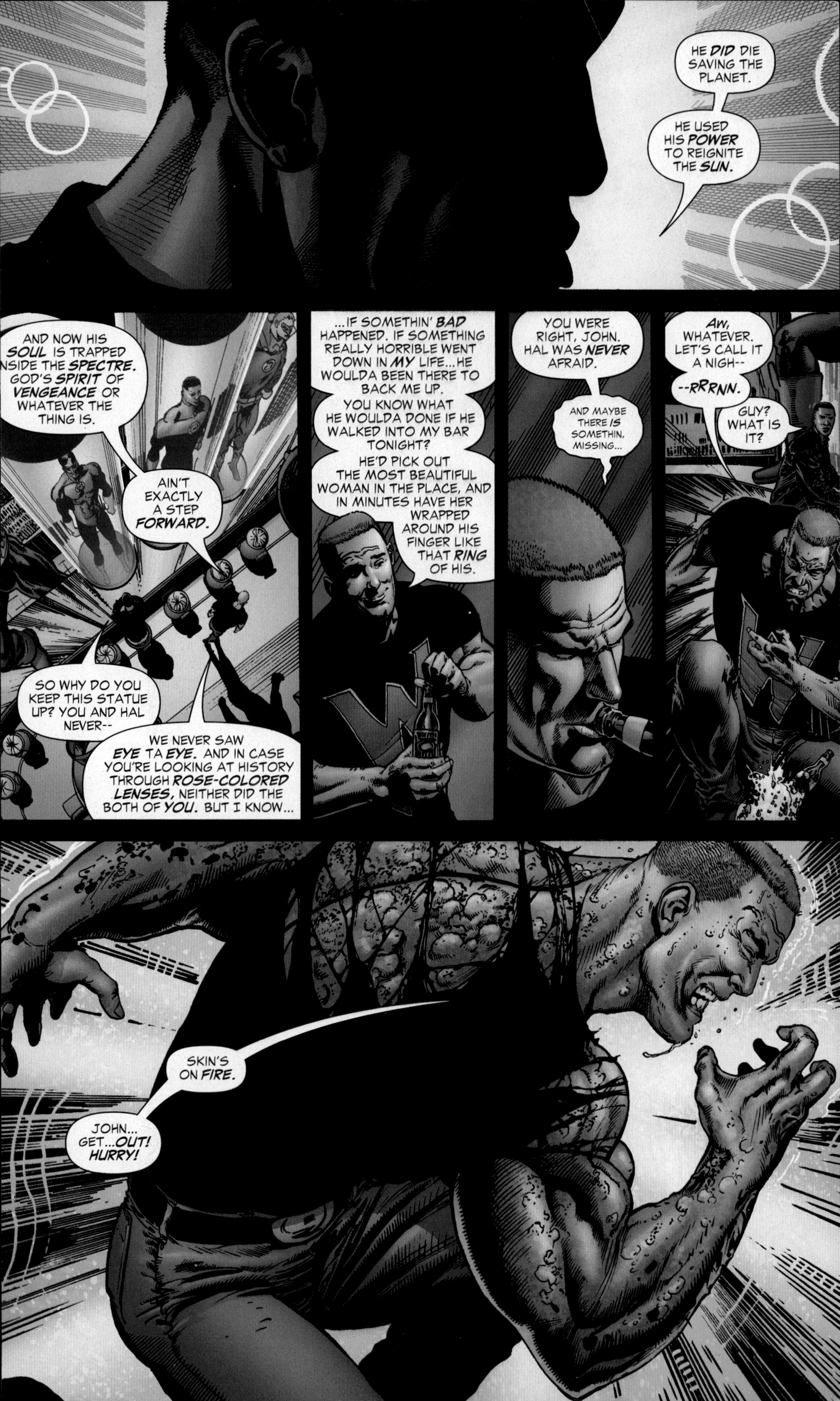

HE DID DIE SAVING THE PLANET.
HE USED HIS POWER TO REIGNITE THE SUN.
AND NOW HIS SOUL IS TRAPPED INSIDE THE SPECTRE. GOD'S SPIRIT OF VENGEANCE OR WHATEVER THE THING IS.
AIN'T EXACTLY A STEP FORWARD.
SO WHY DO YOU KEEP THIS STATUE UP? YOU AND HAL NEVER--
WE NEVER SAW EYE TA EYE. AND IN CASE YOU'RE LOOKING AT HISTORY THROUGH ROSE-COLORED LENSES, NEITHER DID THE BOTH OF YOU. BUT I KNOW...
...IF SOMETHIN' BAD HAPPENED. IF SOMETHING REALLY HORRIBLE WENT DOWN IN MY LIFE...HE WOULDA BEEN THERE TO BACK ME UP.
YOU KNOW WHAT HE WOULDA DONE IF HE WALKED INTO MY BAR TONIGHT?
HE'D PICK OUT THE MOST BEAUTIFUL WOMAN IN THE PLACE, AND IN MINUTES HAVE HER WRAPPED AROUND HIS FINGER LIKE THAT RING OF HIS.
YOU WERE RIGHT, JOHN. HAL WAS NEVER AFRAID.
AND MAYBE THERE IS SOMETHIN, MISSING...
AW, WHATEVER. LET'S CALL IT A NIGH--
--RRRNN.
GUY? WHAT IS IT?
SKIN'S ON FIRE.
JOHN... GET...OUT! HURRY!

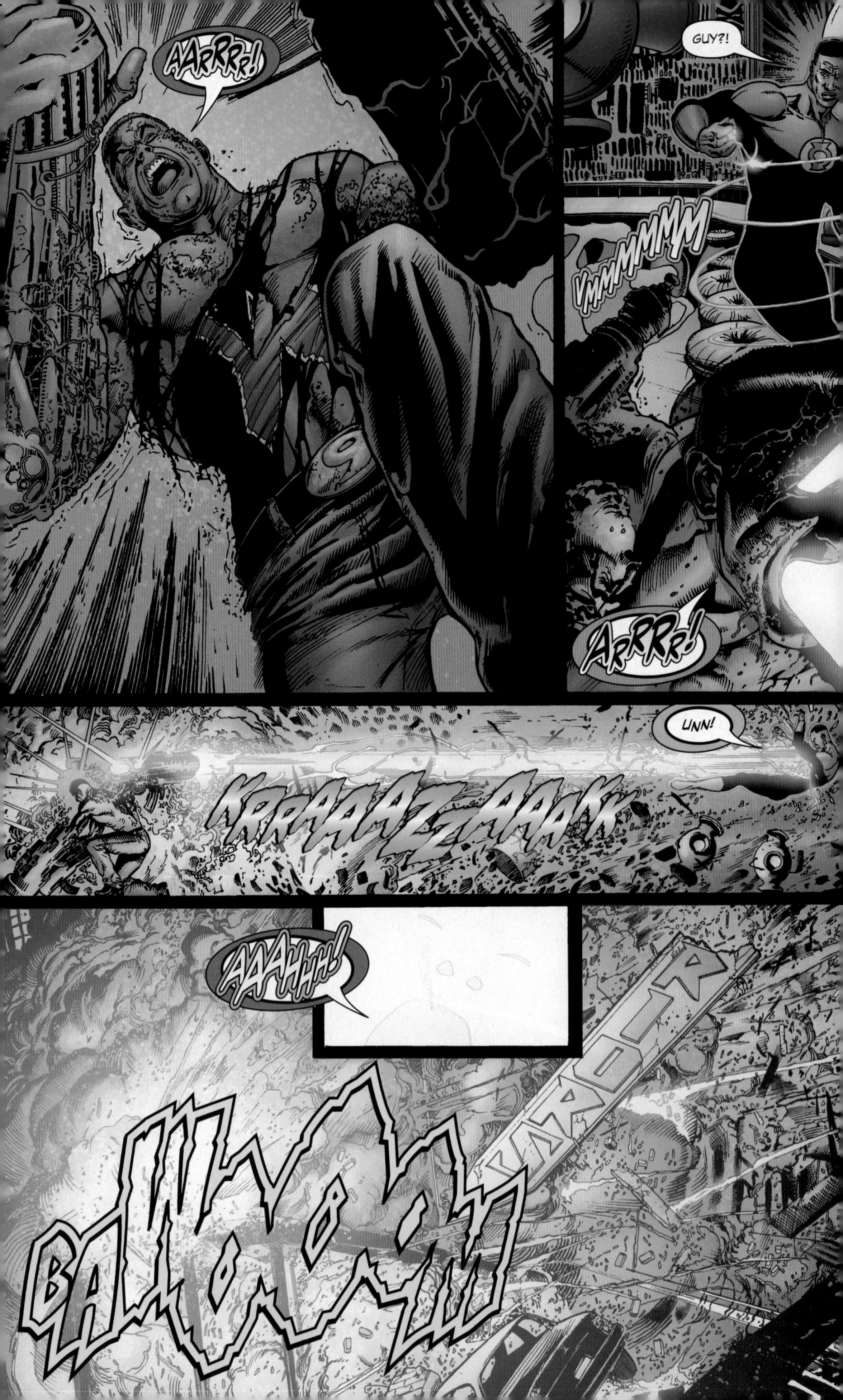
AARRRR!
GUY?!
VMMMMMMM
ARRRR!
UNN!
KRRAAAAZZAAAKK
AAAHHH!

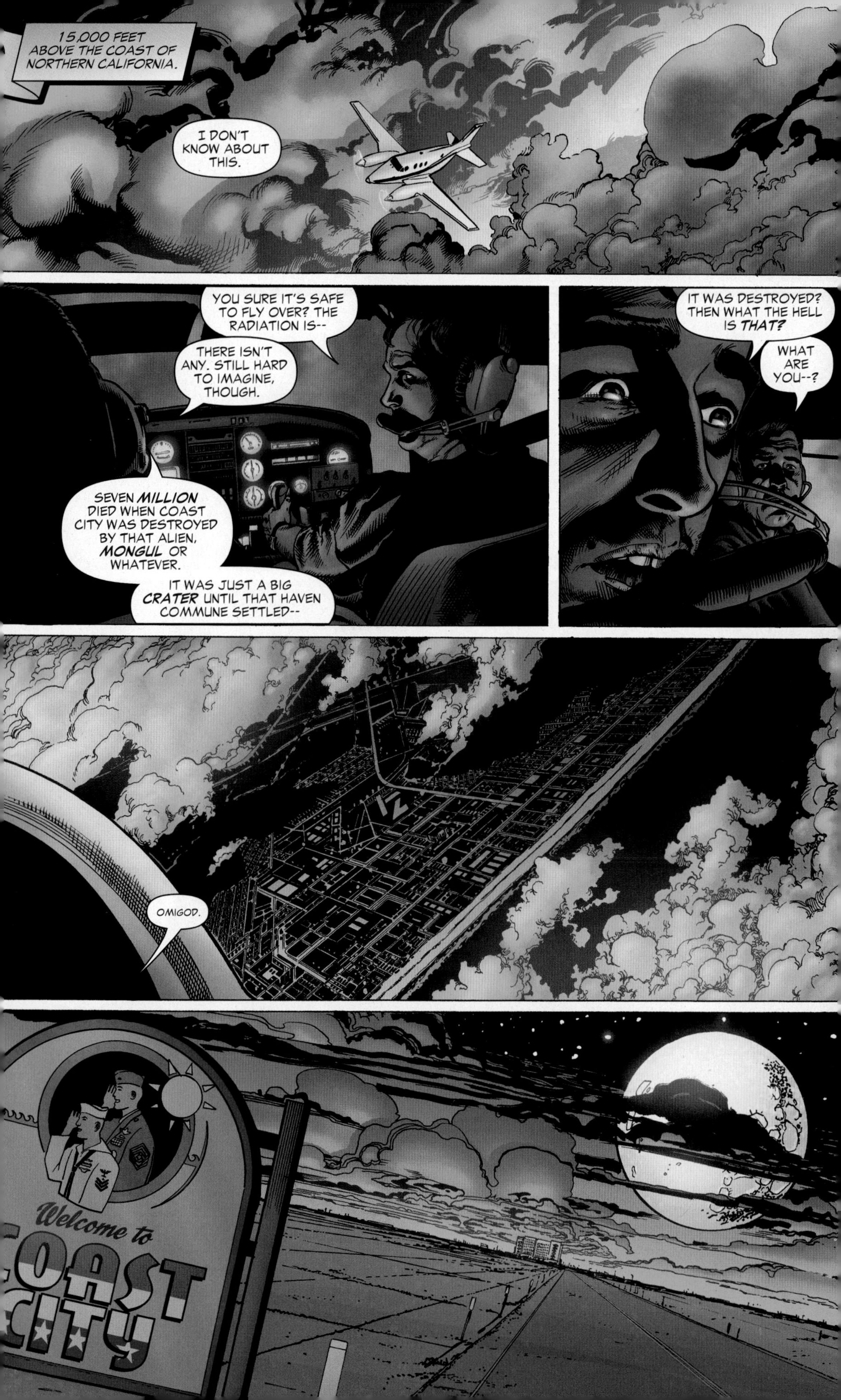
15,000 FEET ABOVE THE COAST OF NORTHERN CALIFORNIA.
I DON'T KNOW ABOUT THIS.
YOU SURE IT'S SAFE TO FLY OVER? THE RADIATION IS--
THERE ISN'T ANY. STILL HARD TO IMAGINE, THOUGH.
SEVEN MILLION DIED WHEN COAST CITY WAS DESTROYED BY THAT ALIEN, MONGUL OR WHATEVER.
IT WAS JUST A BIG CRATER UNTIL THAT HAVEN COMMUNE SETTLED--
IT WAS DESTROYED? THEN WHAT THE HELL IS THAT?
WHAT ARE YOU--?
OMIGOD.
Welcome to
COAST CITY

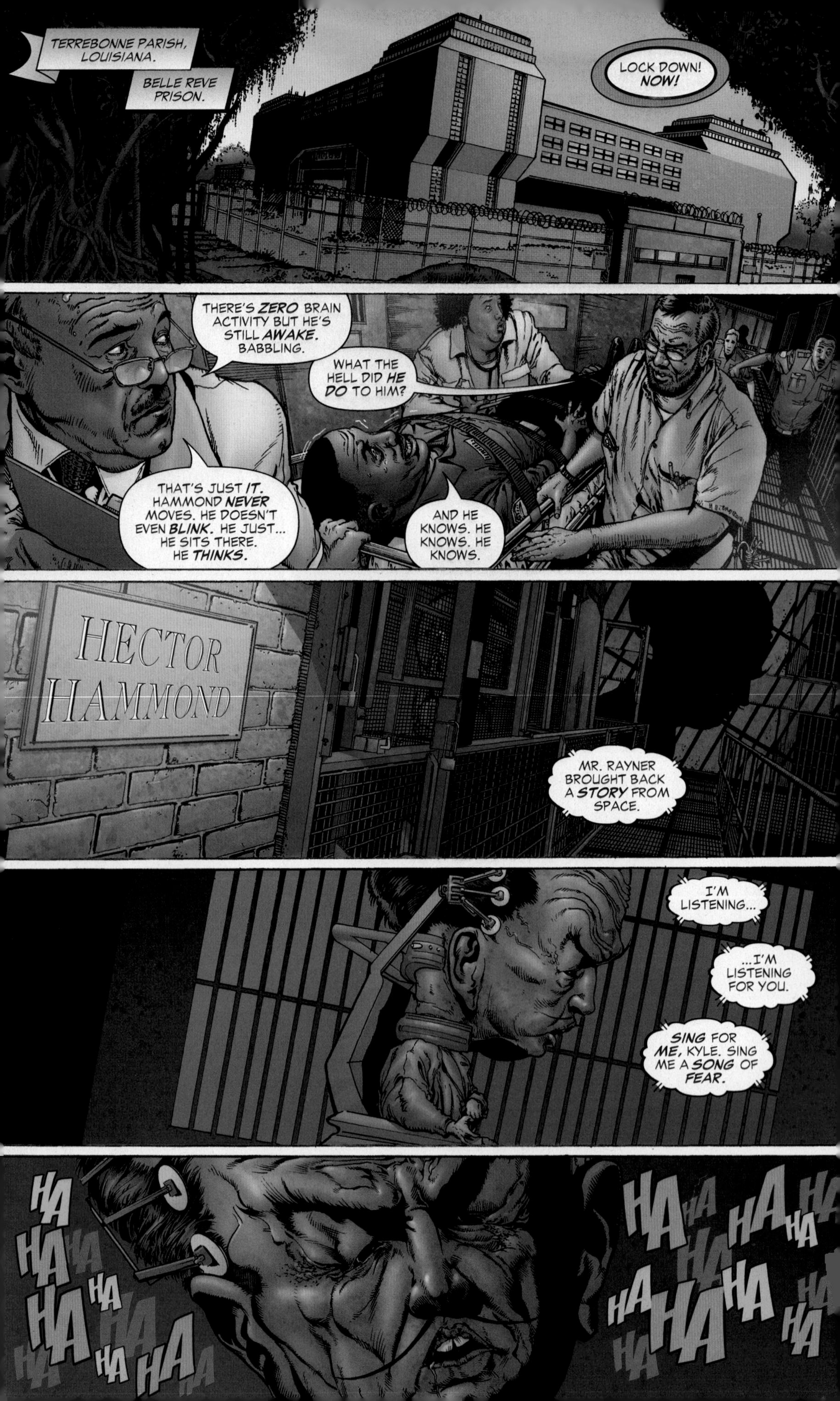
TERREBONNE PARISH, LOUISIANA.
BELLE REVE PRISON.
LOCK DOWN! NOW!
THERE'S ZERO BRAIN ACTIVITY BUT HE'S STILL AWAKE. BABBLING.
WHAT THE HELL DID HE DO TO HIM?
THAT'S JUST IT. HAMMOND NEVER MOVES. HE DOESN'T EVEN BLINK. HE JUST... HE SITS THERE. HE THINKS.
AND HE KNOWS. HE KNOWS. HE KNOWS.
HECTOR HAMMOND
MR. RAYNER BROUGHT BACK A STORY FROM SPACE.
I'M LISTENING...
...I'M LISTENING FOR YOU.
SING FOR ME, KYLE. SING ME A SONG OF FEAR.
HA HA HA HA HA HA HA HA HA HA HA
HA HA HA HA HA HA HA HA HA HA HA HA HA HA

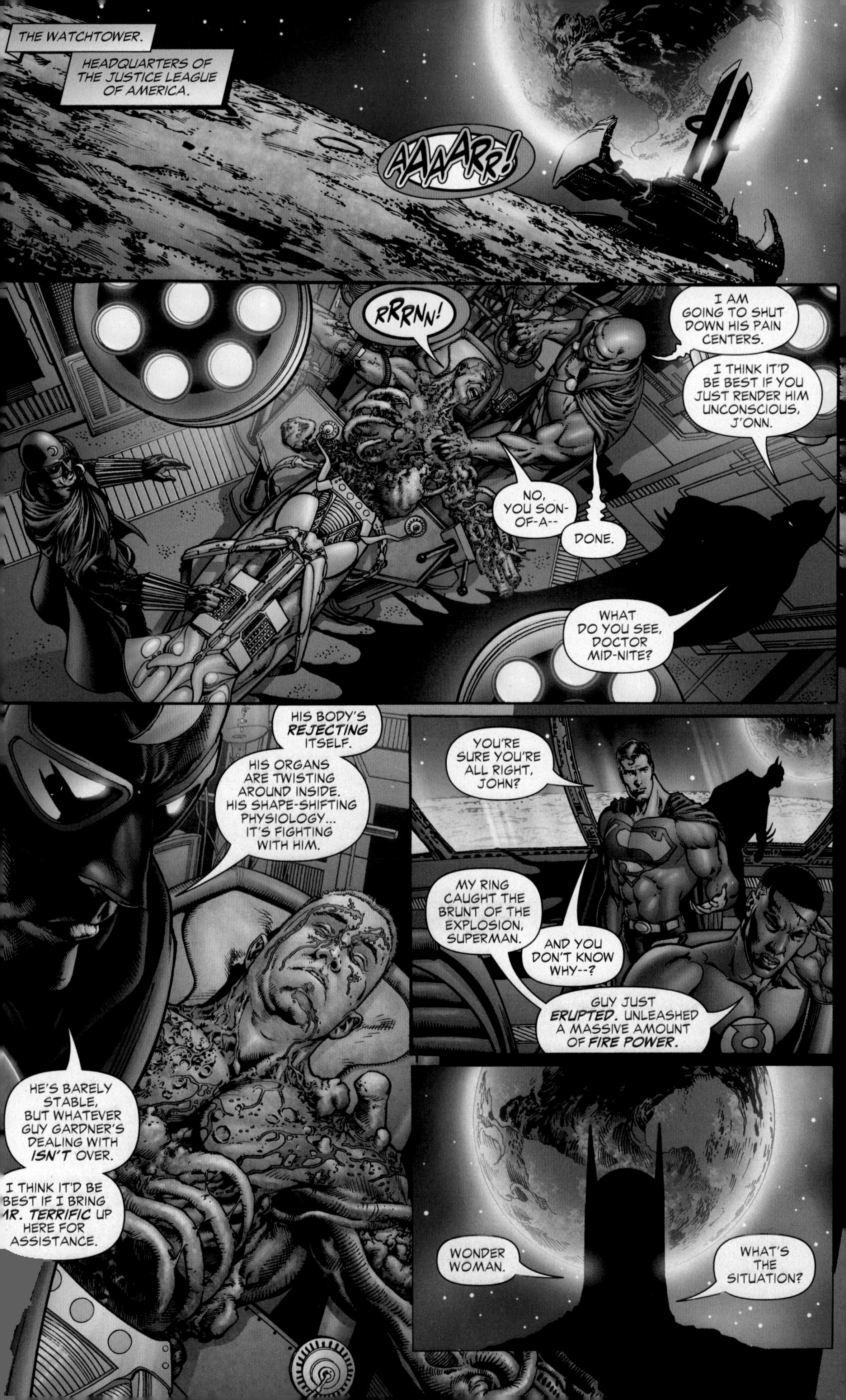
THE WATCHTOWER.
HEADQUARTERS OF THE JUSTICE LEAGUE OF AMERICA.
AAAARR!
RRRNN!
I AM GOING TO SHUT DOWN HIS PAIN CENTERS.
I THINK IT'D BE BEST IF YOU JUST RENDER HIM UNCONSCIOUS, J'ONN.
NO, YOU SON-OF-A--
DONE.
WHAT DO YOU SEE, DOCTOR MID-NITE?
HIS BODY'S REJECTING ITSELF.
HIS ORGANS ARE TWISTING AROUND INSIDE. HIS SHAPE-SHIFTING PHYSIOLOGY... IT'S FIGHTING WITH HIM.
HE'S BARELY STABLE, BUT WHATEVER GUY GARDNER'S DEALING WITH ISN'T OVER.
I THINK IT'D BE BEST IF I BRING MR. TERRIFIC UP HERE FOR ASSISTANCE.
YOU'RE SURE YOU'RE ALL RIGHT, JOHN?
MY RING CAUGHT THE BRUNT OF THE EXPLOSION, SUPERMAN.
AND YOU DON'T KNOW WHY--?
GUY JUST ERUPTED. UNLEASHED A MASSIVE AMOUNT OF FIRE POWER.
WONDER WOMAN.
WHAT'S THE SITUATION?

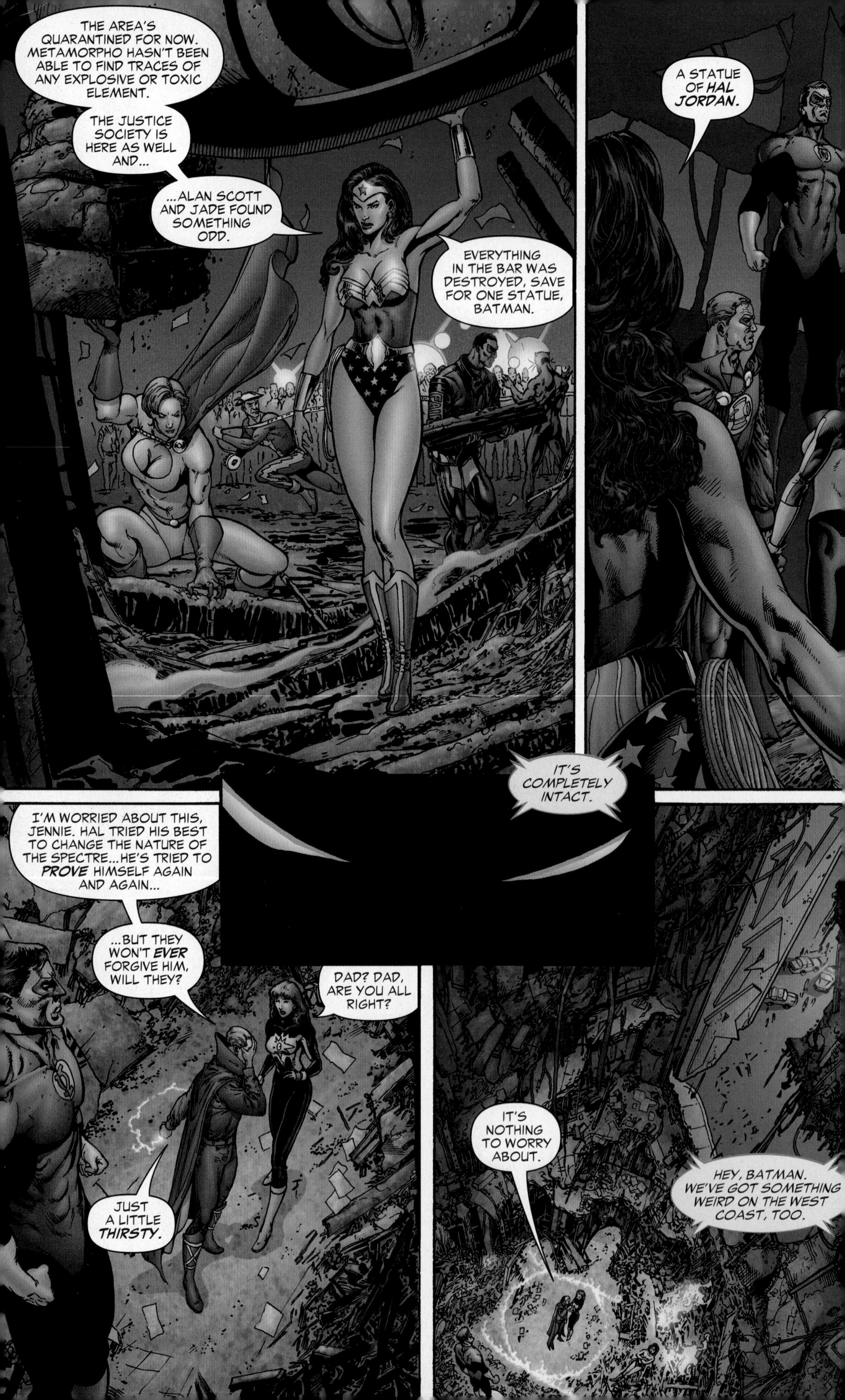
THE AREA'S QUARANTINED FOR NOW. METAMORPHO HASN'T BEEN ABLE TO FIND TRACES OF ANY EXPLOSIVE OR TOXIC ELEMENT.
THE JUSTICE SOCIETY IS HERE AS WELL AND...
...ALAN SCOTT AND JADE FOUND SOMETHING ODD.
EVERYTHING IN THE BAR WAS DESTROYED, SAVE FOR ONE STATUE, BATMAN.
A STATUE OF *HAL JORDAN.*
IT'S COMPLETELY INTACT.
I'M WORRIED ABOUT THIS, JENNIE. HAL TRIED HIS BEST TO CHANGE THE NATURE OF THE SPECTRE...HE'S TRIED TO *PROVE* HIMSELF AGAIN AND AGAIN...
...BUT THEY WON'T *EVER* FORGIVE HIM, WILL THEY?
DAD? DAD, ARE YOU ALL RIGHT?
JUST A LITTLE *THIRSTY.*
IT'S NOTHING TO WORRY ABOUT.
HEY, BATMAN. WE'VE GOT SOMETHING WEIRD ON THE WEST COAST, TOO.

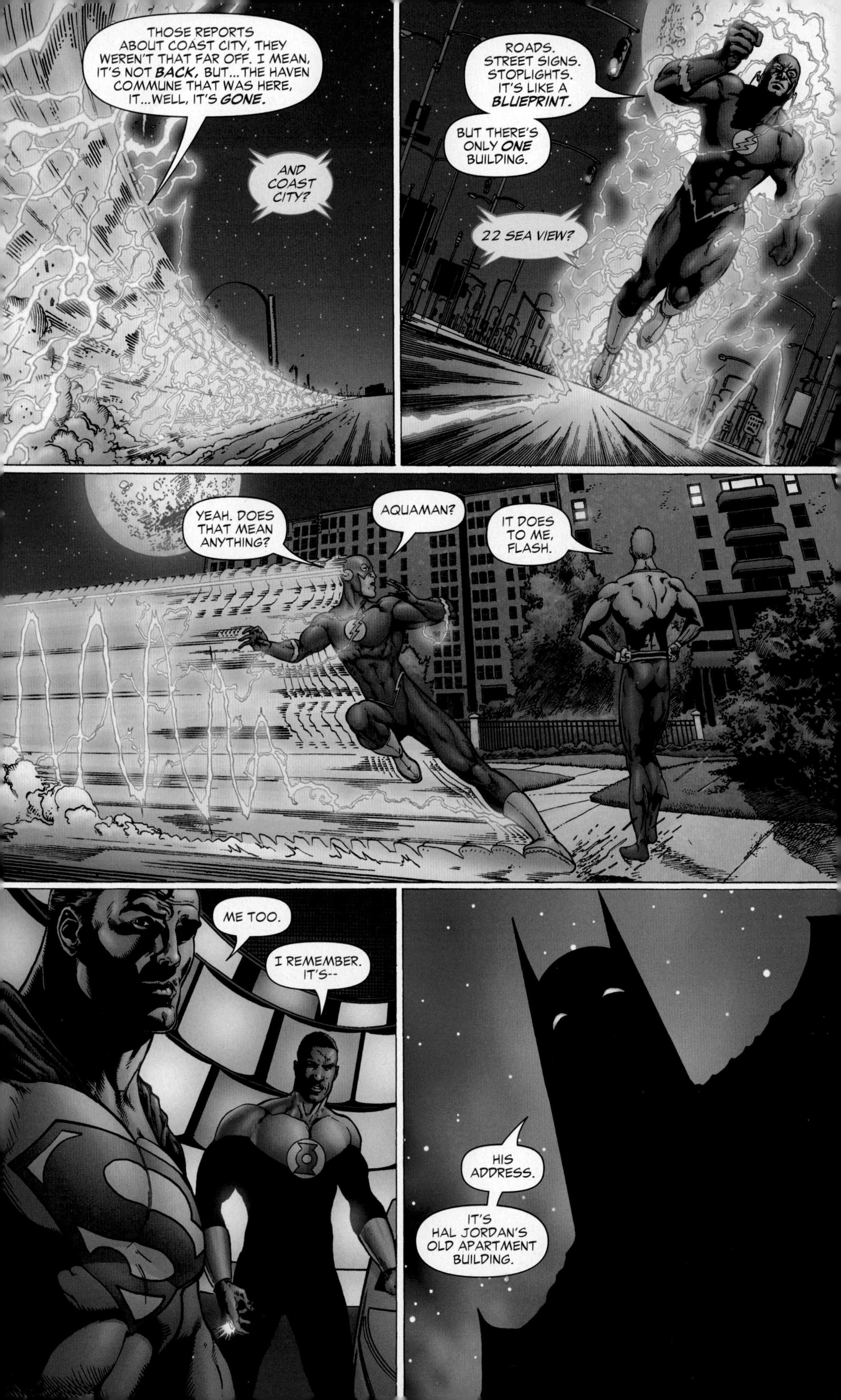
THOSE REPORTS ABOUT COAST CITY, THEY WEREN'T THAT FAR OFF. I MEAN, IT'S NOT BACK, BUT... THE HAVEN COMMUNE THAT WAS HERE, IT...WELL, IT'S GONE.
AND COAST CITY?
ROADS. STREET SIGNS. STOPLIGHTS. IT'S LIKE A BLUEPRINT.
BUT THERE'S ONLY ONE BUILDING.
22 SEA VIEW?
YEAH. DOES THAT MEAN ANYTHING?
AQUAMAN?
IT DOES TO ME, FLASH.
ME TOO.
I REMEMBER. IT'S--
HIS ADDRESS.
IT'S HAL JORDAN'S OLD APARTMENT BUILDING.

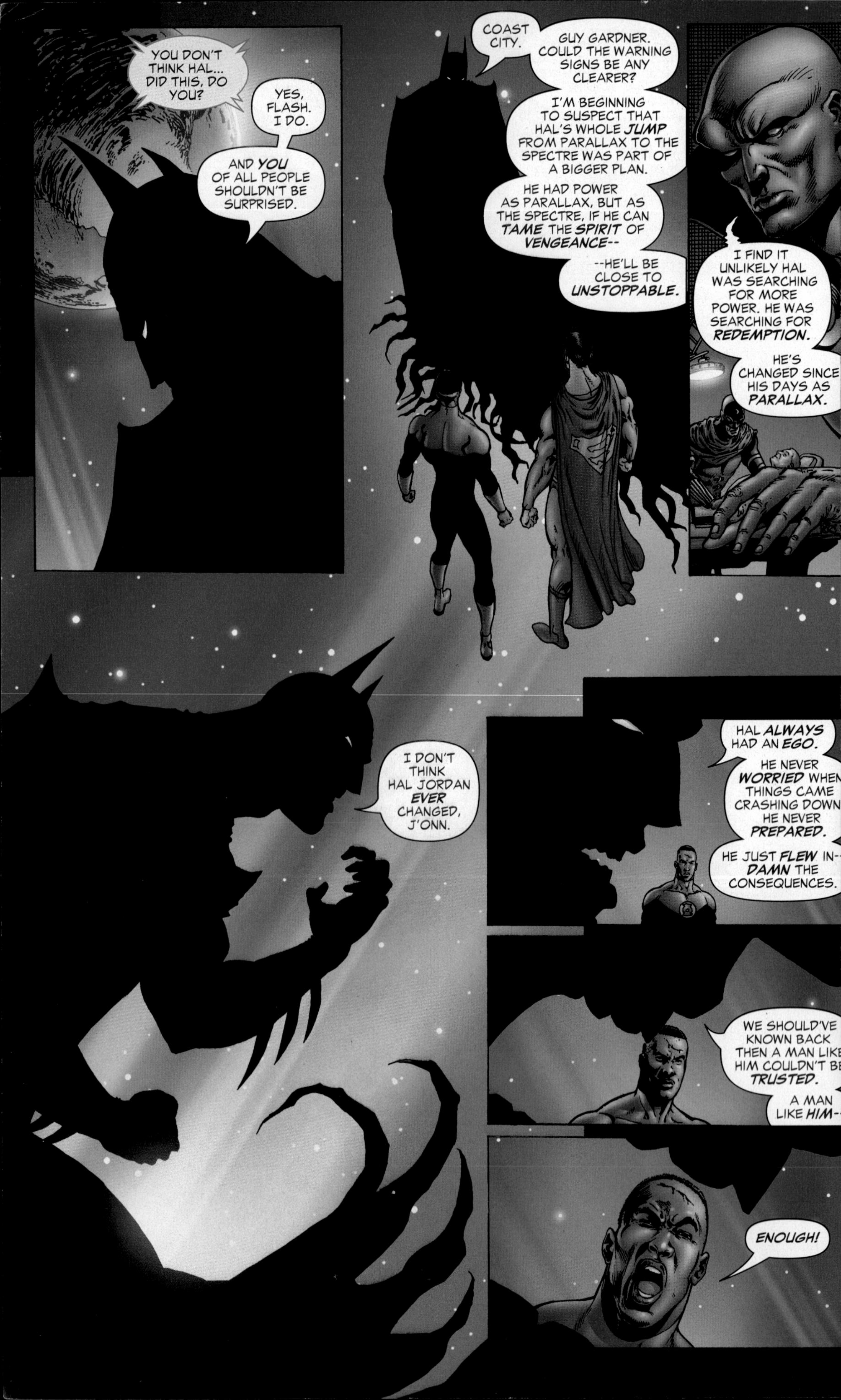

YOU DON'T THINK HAL... DID THIS, DO YOU?
YES, FLASH. I DO.
AND YOU OF ALL PEOPLE SHOULDN'T BE SURPRISED.
COAST CITY.
GUY GARDNER. COULD THE WARNING SIGNS BE ANY CLEARER?
I'M BEGINNING TO SUSPECT THAT HAL'S WHOLE JUMP FROM PARALLAX TO THE SPECTRE WAS PART OF A BIGGER PLAN.
HE HAD POWER AS PARALLAX, BUT AS THE SPECTRE, IF HE CAN TAME THE SPIRIT OF VENGEANCE--
--HE'LL BE CLOSE TO UNSTOPPABLE.
I FIND IT UNLIKELY HAL WAS SEARCHING FOR MORE POWER. HE WAS SEARCHING FOR REDEMPTION.
HE'S CHANGED SINCE HIS DAYS AS PARALLAX.
I DON'T THINK HAL JORDAN EVER CHANGED, J'ONN.
HAL ALWAYS HAD AN EGO.
HE NEVER WORRIED WHEN THINGS CAME CRASHING DOWN. HE NEVER PREPARED.
HE JUST FLEW IN-- DAMN THE CONSEQUENCES.
WE SHOULD'VE KNOWN BACK THEN A MAN LIKE HIM COULDN'T BE TRUSTED.
A MAN LIKE HIM--
ENOUGH!

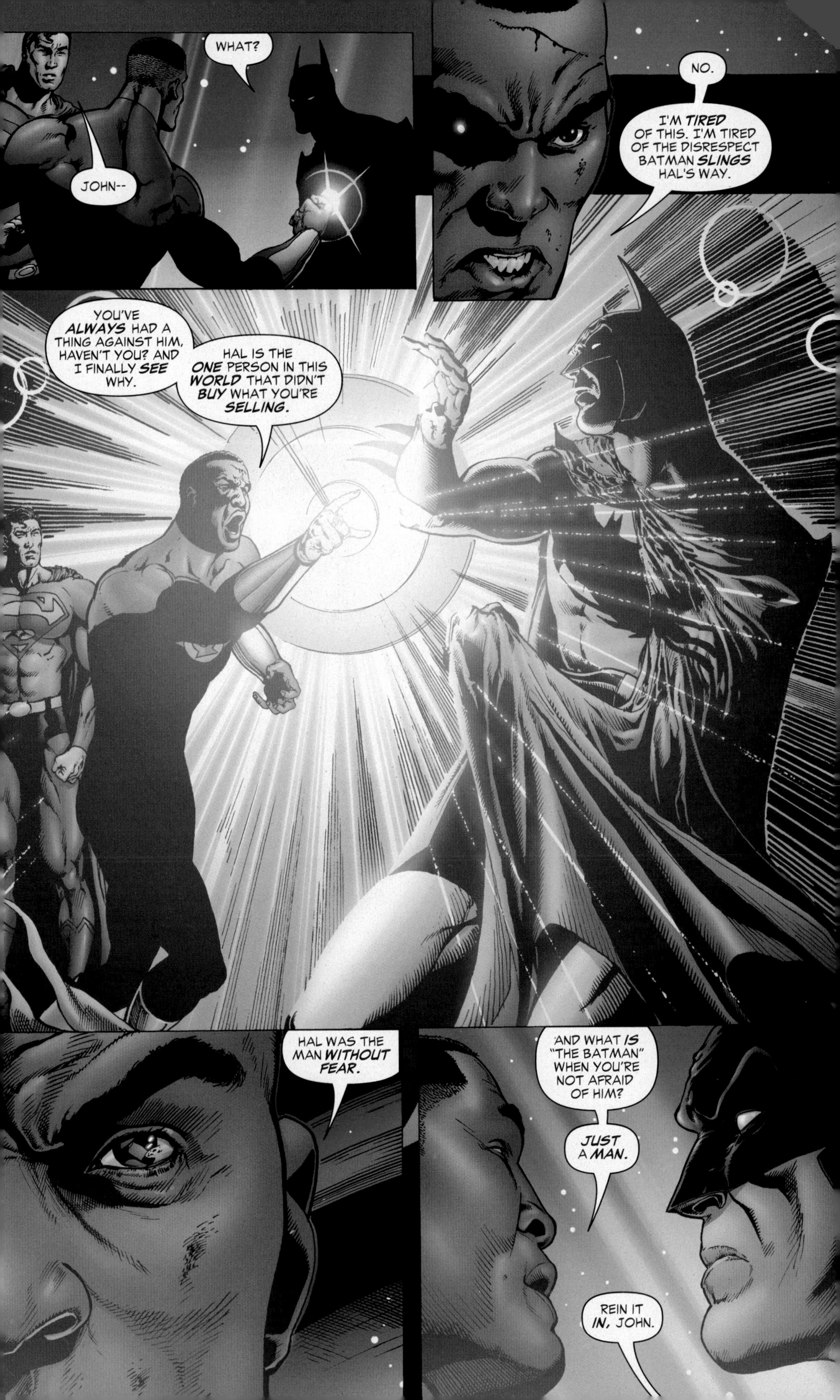
WHAT?
JOHN--
NO.
I'M TIRED OF THIS. I'M TIRED OF THE DISRESPECT BATMAN SLINGS HAL'S WAY.
YOU'VE ALWAYS HAD A THING AGAINST HIM, HAVEN'T YOU? AND I FINALLY SEE WHY.
HAL IS THE ONE PERSON IN THIS WORLD THAT DIDN'T BUY WHAT YOU'RE SELLING.
HAL WAS THE MAN WITHOUT FEAR.
AND WHAT IS "THE BATMAN" WHEN YOU'RE NOT AFRAID OF HIM?
JUST A MAN.
REIN IT IN, JOHN.

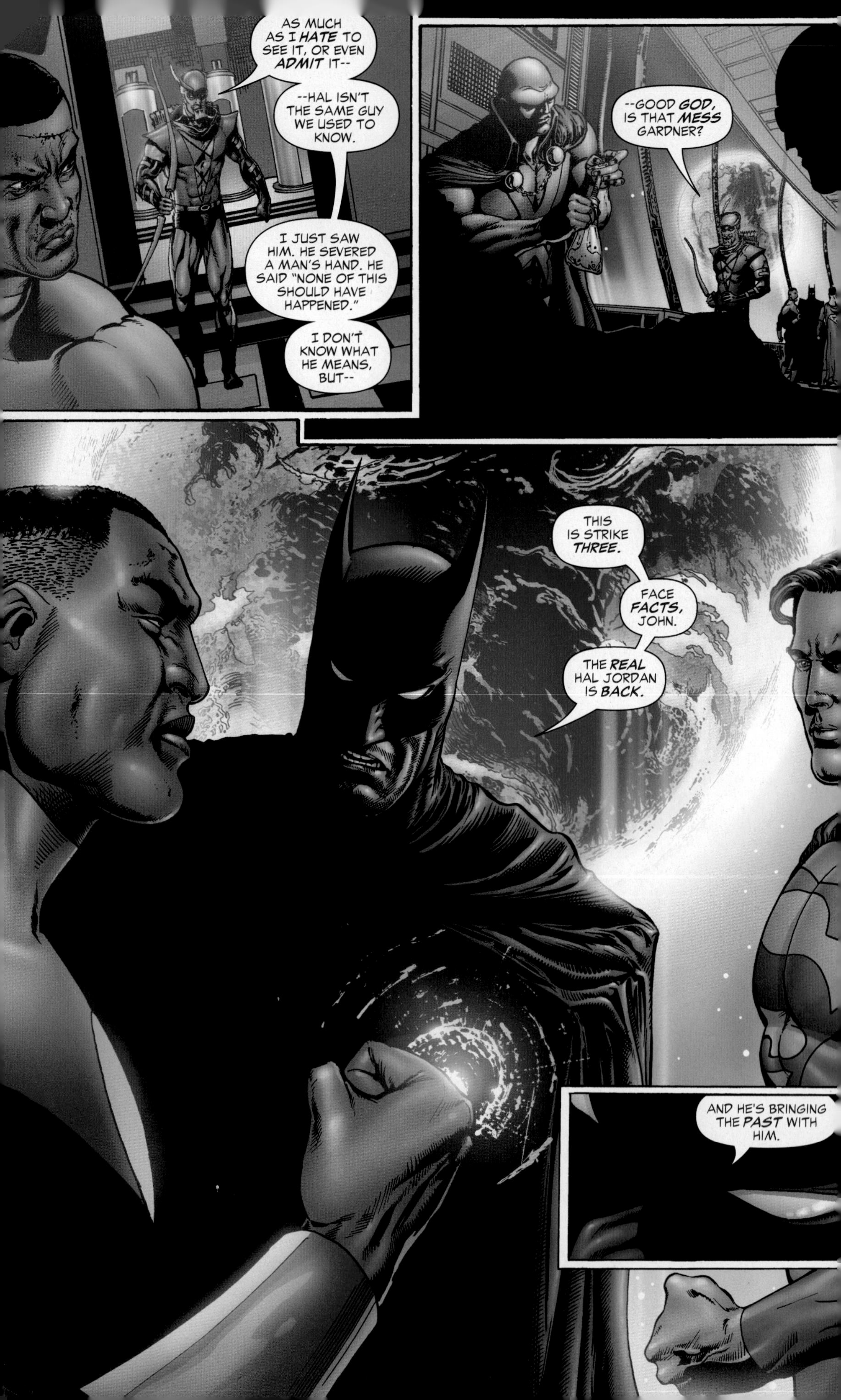
AS MUCH AS I HATE TO SEE IT, OR EVEN ADMIT IT--
--HAL ISN'T THE SAME GUY WE USED TO KNOW.
I JUST SAW HIM. HE SEVERED A MAN'S HAND. HE SAID "NONE OF THIS SHOULD HAVE HAPPENED."
I DON'T KNOW WHAT HE MEANS, BUT--
--GOOD GOD, IS THAT MESS GARDNER?
THIS IS STRIKE THREE.
FACE FACTS, JOHN.
THE REAL HAL JORDAN IS BACK.
AND HE'S BRINGING THE PAST WITH HIM.

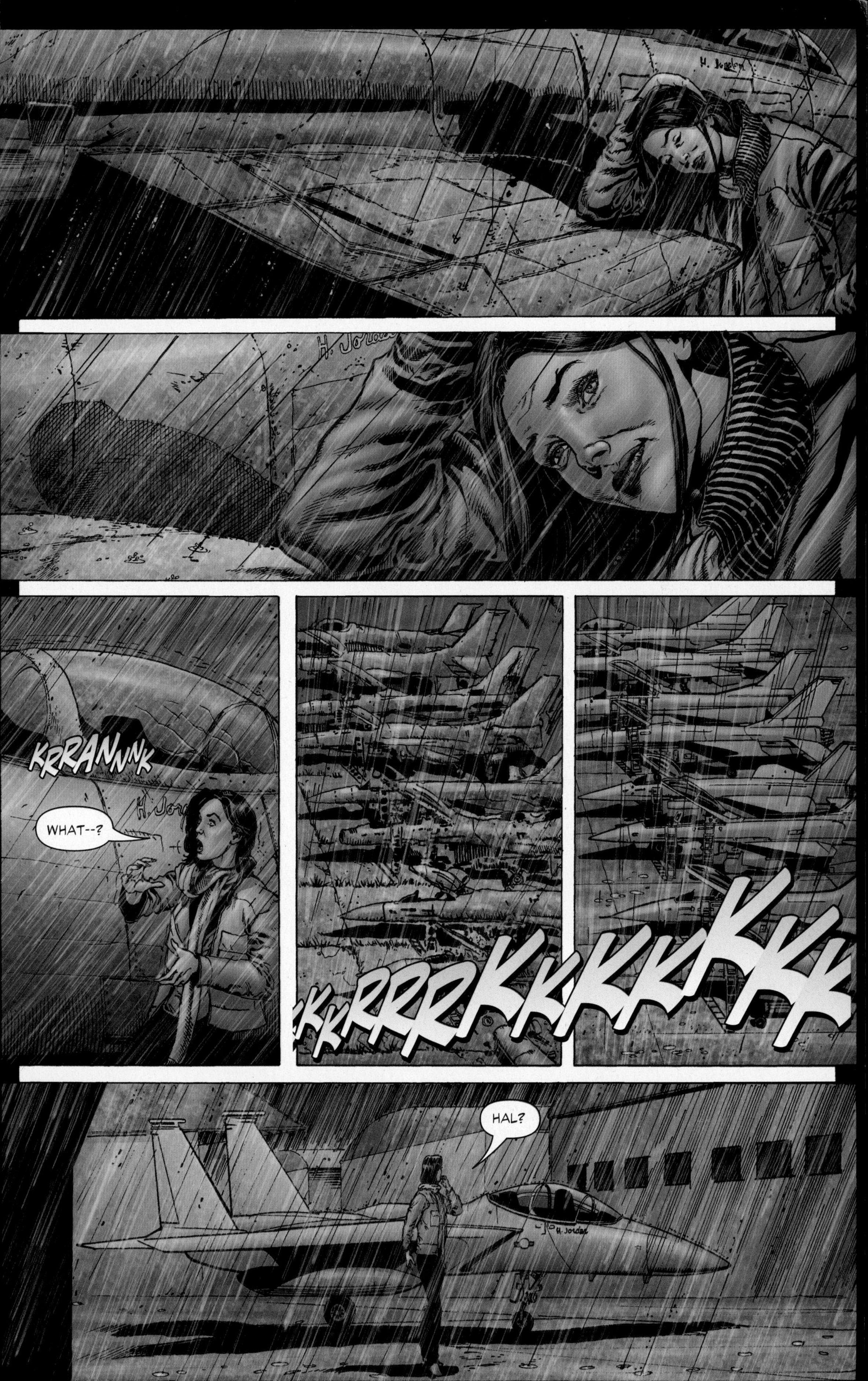
H. Jordan
KRRANNNK
WHAT--?
KKRRRKKKKKK
HAL?

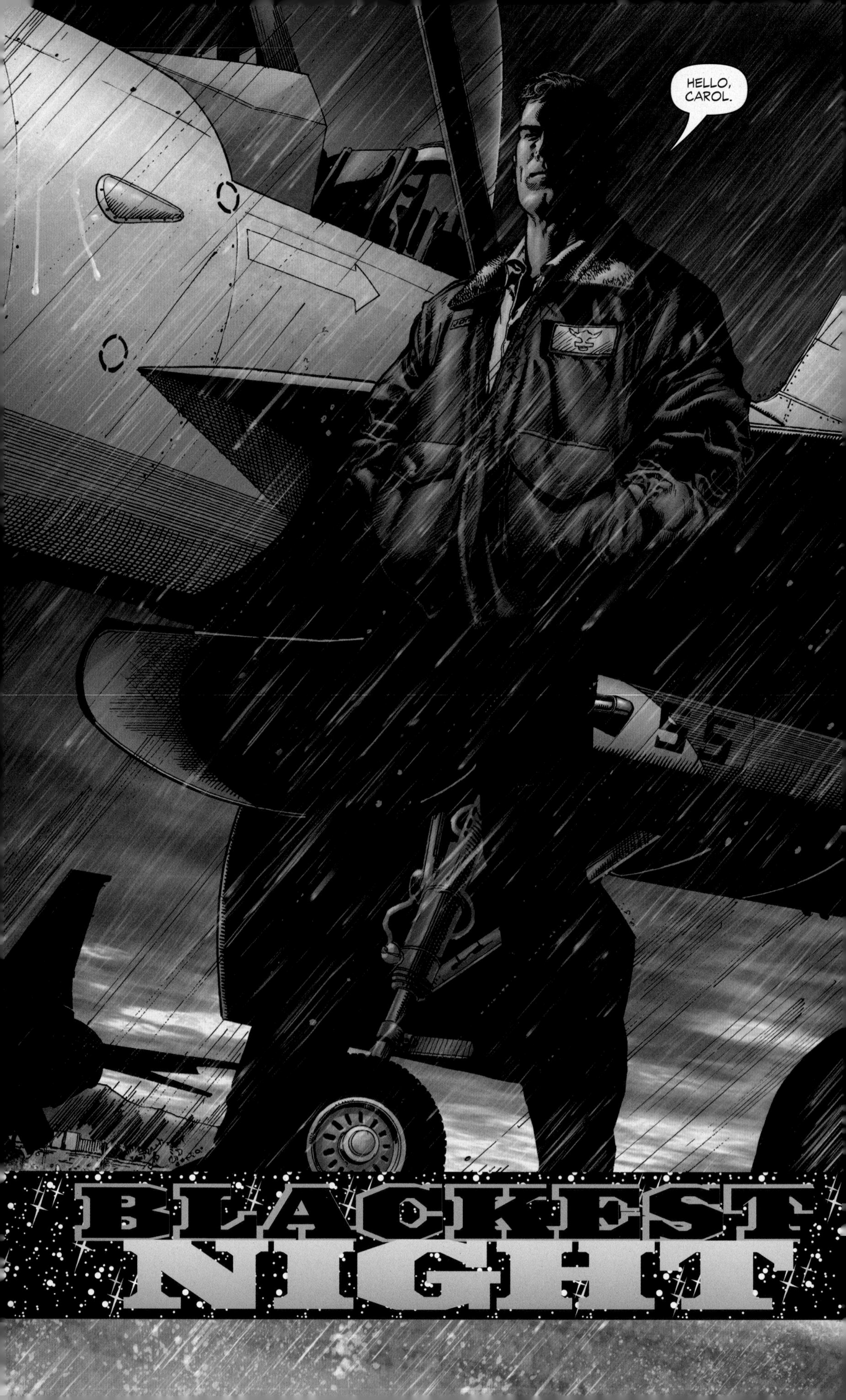
HELLO, CAROL.
BLACKEST NIGHT

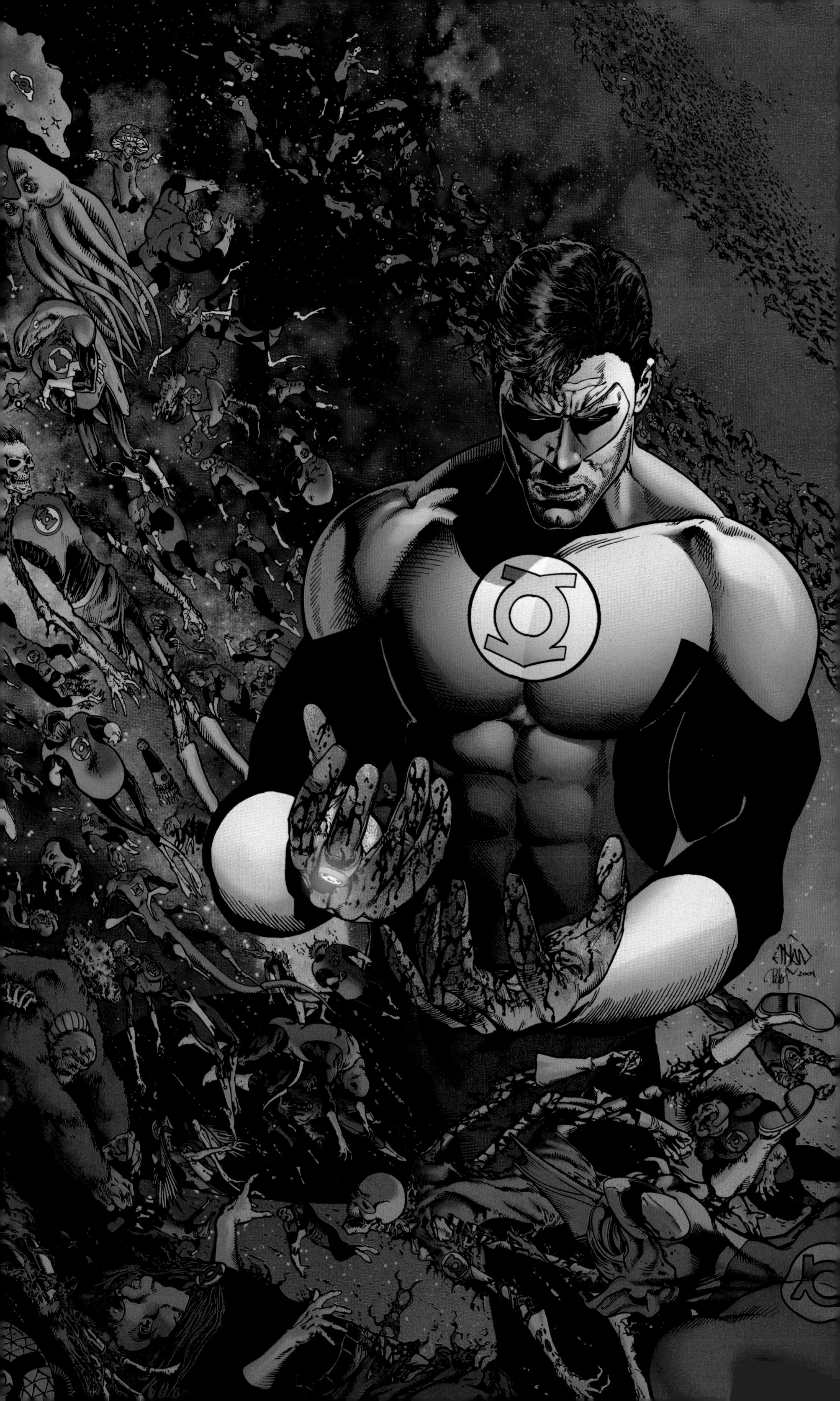

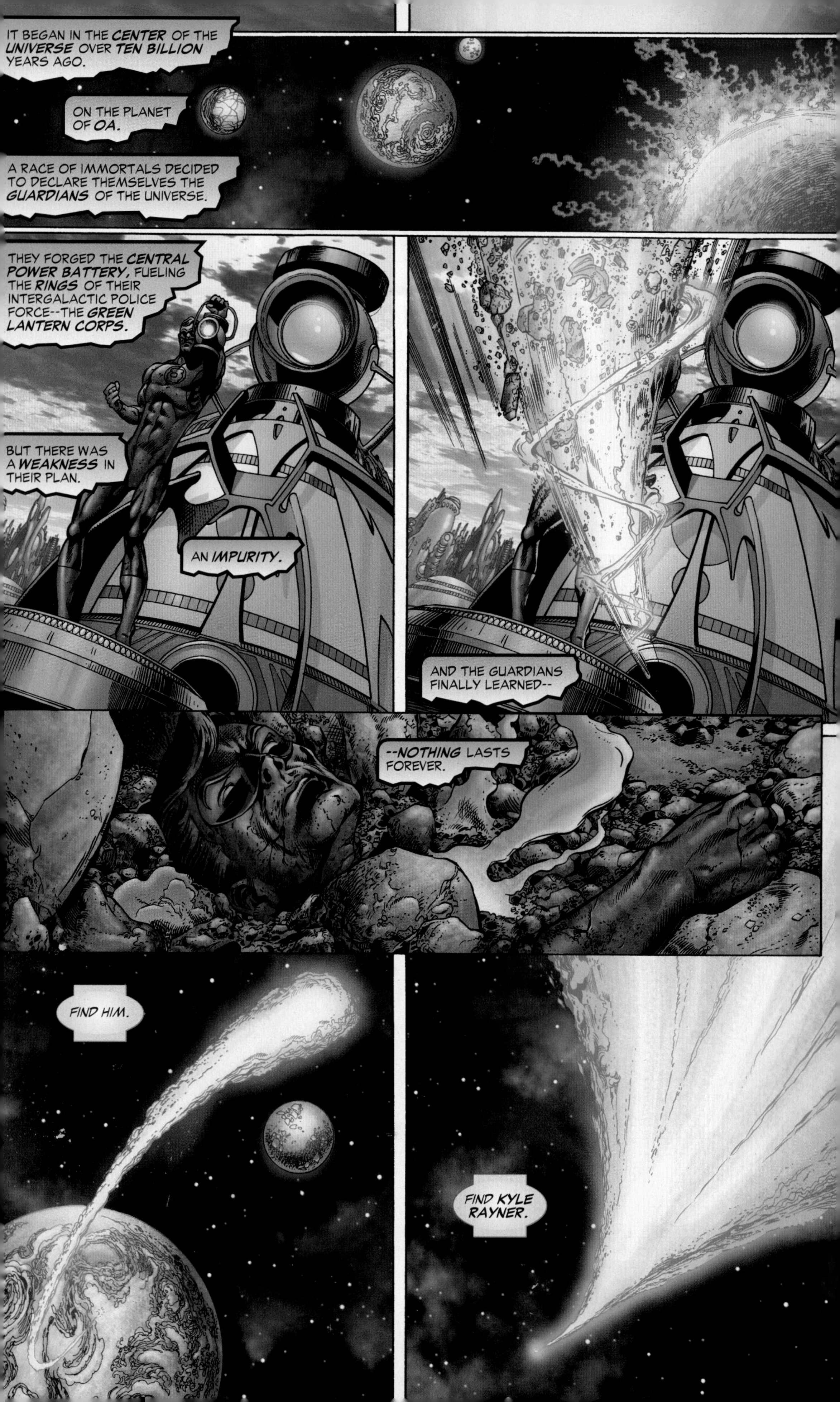

IT BEGAN IN THE CENTER OF THE UNIVERSE OVER TEN BILLION YEARS AGO.
ON THE PLANET OF OA.
A RACE OF IMMORTALS DECIDED TO DECLARE THEMSELVES THE GUARDIANS OF THE UNIVERSE.
THEY FORGED THE CENTRAL POWER BATTERY, FUELING THE RINGS OF THEIR INTERGALACTIC POLICE FORCE--THE GREEN LANTERN CORPS.
BUT THERE WAS A WEAKNESS IN THEIR PLAN.
AN IMPURITY.
AND THE GUARDIANS FINALLY LEARNED--
--NOTHING LASTS FOREVER.
FIND HIM.
FIND KYLE RAYNER.

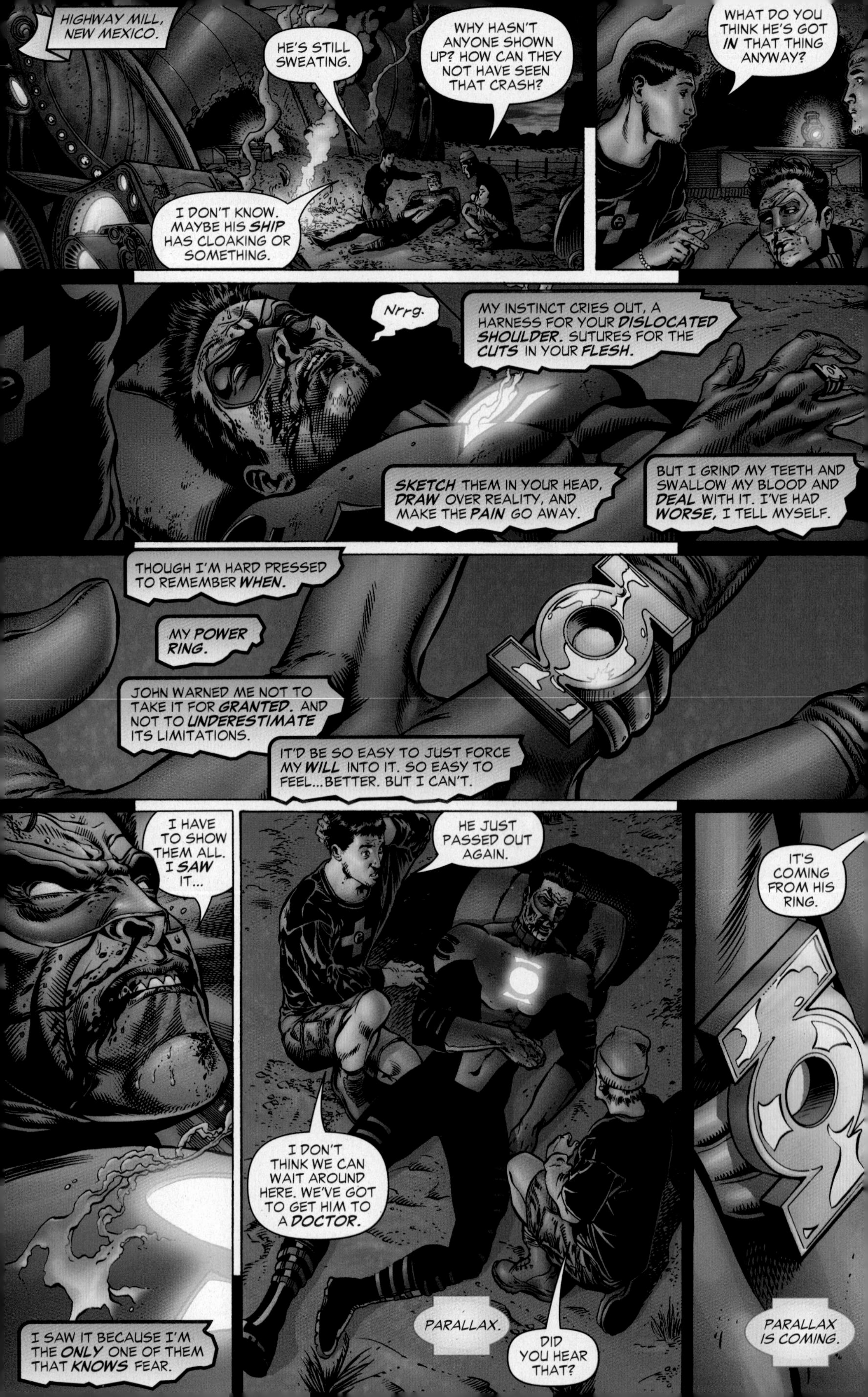
HIGHWAY MILL, NEW MEXICO.
HE'S STILL SWEATING.
WHY HASN'T ANYONE SHOWN UP? HOW CAN THEY NOT HAVE SEEN THAT CRASH?
I DON'T KNOW. MAYBE HIS SHIP HAS CLOAKING OR SOMETHING.
WHAT DO YOU THINK HE'S GOT IN THAT THING ANYWAY?
Nrrg.
MY INSTINCT CRIES OUT, A HARNESS FOR YOUR DISLOCATED SHOULDER. SUTURES FOR THE CUTS IN YOUR FLESH.
SKETCH THEM IN YOUR HEAD, DRAW OVER REALITY, AND MAKE THE PAIN GO AWAY.
BUT I GRIND MY TEETH AND SWALLOW MY BLOOD AND DEAL WITH IT. I'VE HAD WORSE, I TELL MYSELF.
THOUGH I'M HARD PRESSED TO REMEMBER WHEN.
MY POWER RING.
JOHN WARNED ME NOT TO TAKE IT FOR GRANTED. AND NOT TO UNDERESTIMATE ITS LIMITATIONS.
IT'D BE SO EASY TO JUST FORCE MY WILL INTO IT. SO EASY TO FEEL...BETTER. BUT I CAN'T.
I HAVE TO SHOW THEM ALL. I SAW IT...
I SAW IT BECAUSE I'M THE ONLY ONE OF THEM THAT KNOWS FEAR.
HE JUST PASSED OUT AGAIN.
I DON'T THINK WE CAN WAIT AROUND HERE. WE'VE GOT TO GET HIM TO A DOCTOR.
PARALLAX.
DID YOU HEAR THAT?
IT'S COMING FROM HIS RING.
PARALLAX IS COMING.

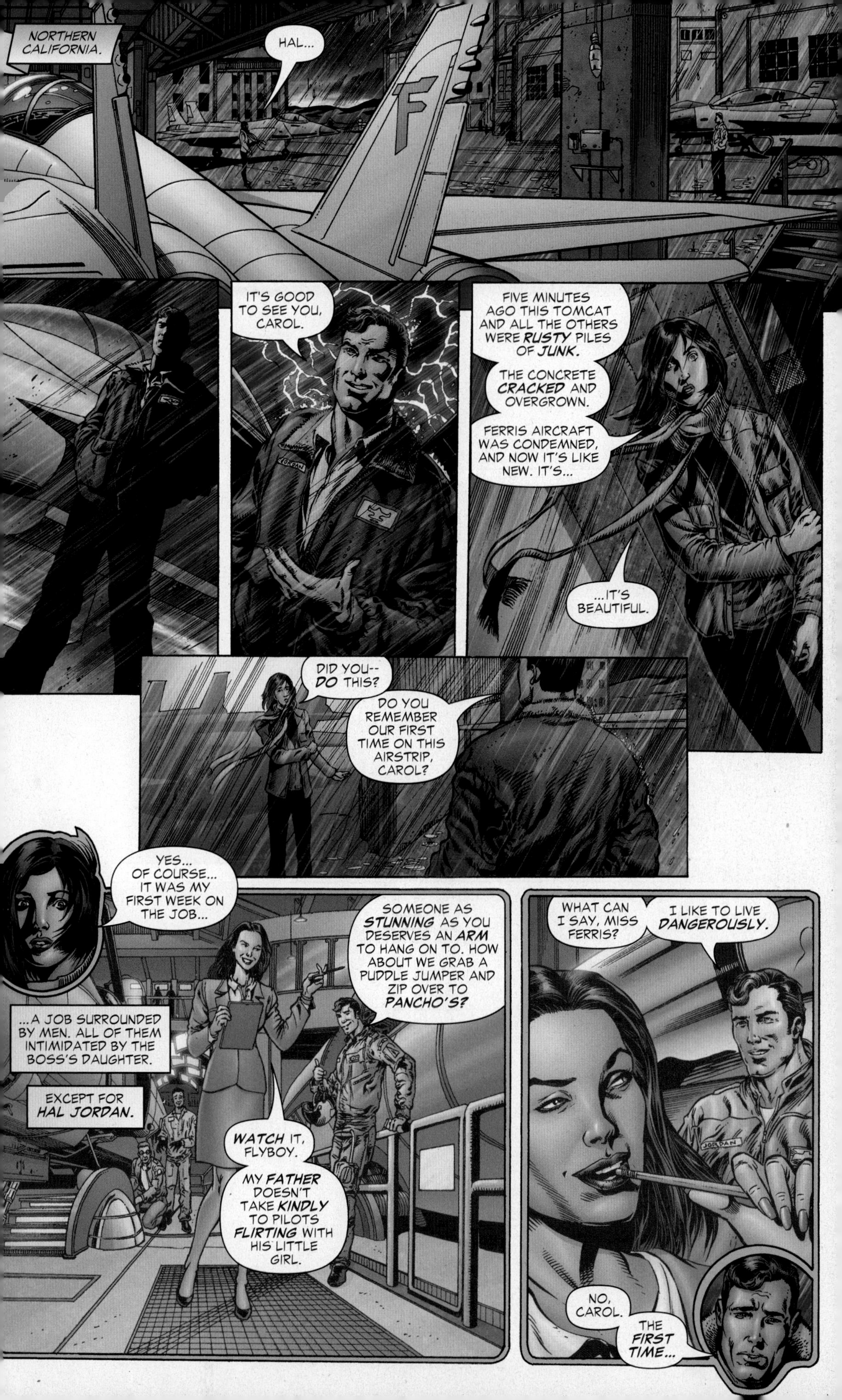
NORTHERN CALIFORNIA.
HAL...
IT'S GOOD TO SEE YOU, CAROL.
FIVE MINUTES AGO THIS TOMCAT AND ALL THE OTHERS WERE RUSTY PILES OF JUNK.
THE CONCRETE CRACKED AND OVERGROWN.
FERRIS AIRCRAFT WAS CONDEMNED, AND NOW IT'S LIKE NEW. IT'S...
...IT'S BEAUTIFUL.
DID YOU-- DO THIS?
DO YOU REMEMBER OUR FIRST TIME ON THIS AIRSTRIP, CAROL?
YES... OF COURSE... IT WAS MY FIRST WEEK ON THE JOB...
...A JOB SURROUNDED BY MEN. ALL OF THEM INTIMIDATED BY THE BOSS'S DAUGHTER.
EXCEPT FOR HAL JORDAN.
SOMEONE AS STUNNING AS YOU DESERVES AN ARM TO HANG ON TO. HOW ABOUT WE GRAB A PUDDLE JUMPER AND ZIP OVER TO PANCHO'S?
WATCH IT, FLYBOY.
MY FATHER DOESN'T TAKE KINDLY TO PILOTS FLIRTING WITH HIS LITTLE GIRL.
WHAT CAN I SAY, MISS FERRIS?
I LIKE TO LIVE DANGEROUSLY.
NO, CAROL.
THE FIRST TIME...

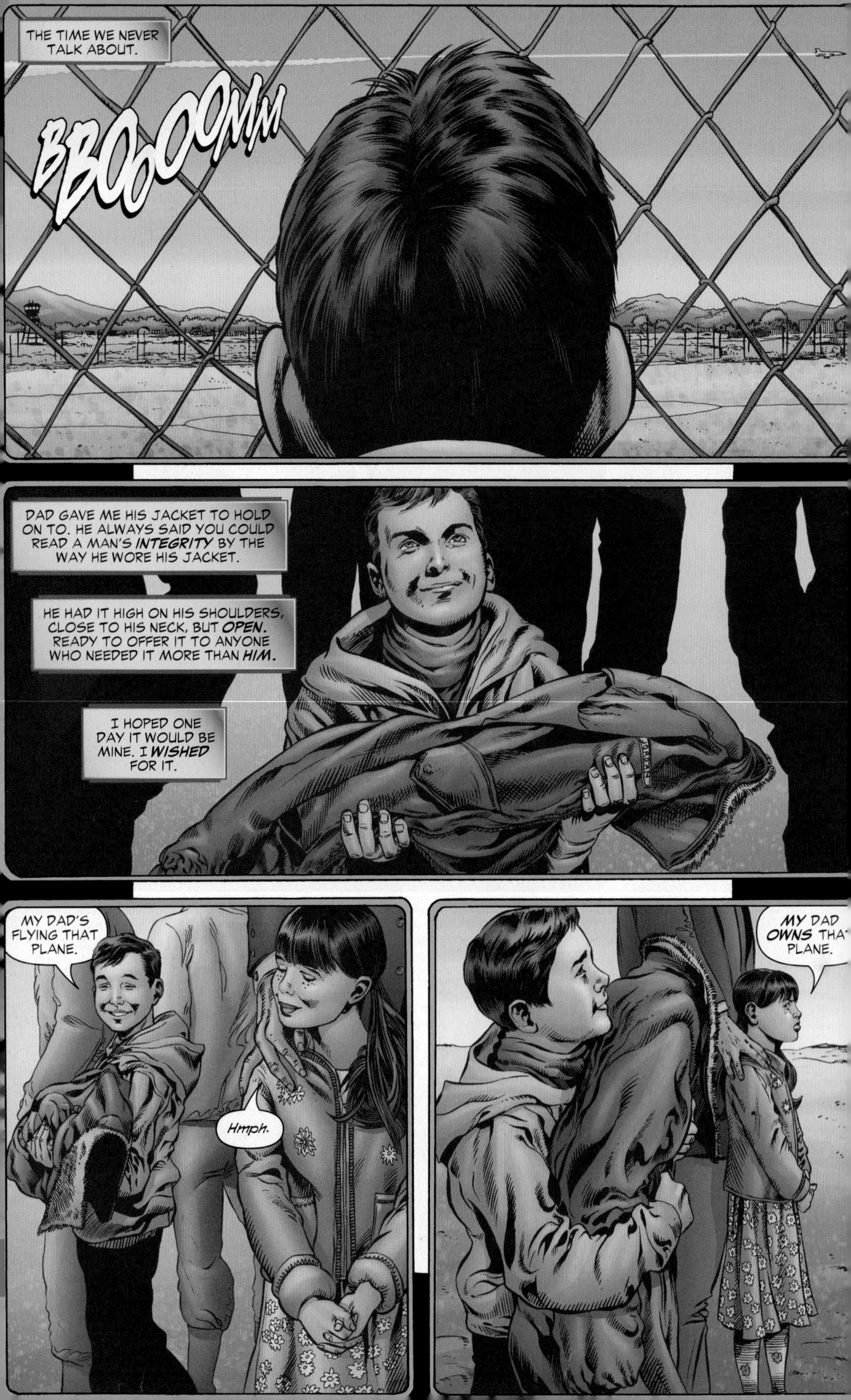
THE TIME WE NEVER TALK ABOUT.
BBOOOOMM
DAD GAVE ME HIS JACKET TO HOLD ON TO. HE ALWAYS SAID YOU COULD READ A MAN'S *INTEGRITY* BY THE WAY HE WORE HIS JACKET.
HE HAD IT HIGH ON HIS SHOULDERS, CLOSE TO HIS NECK, BUT *OPEN*. READY TO OFFER IT TO ANYONE WHO NEEDED IT MORE THAN *HIM*.
I HOPED ONE DAY IT WOULD BE MINE. I *WISHED* FOR IT.
JORDAN
MY DAD'S FLYING THAT PLANE.
Hmph.
MY DAD *OWNS* THAT PLANE.

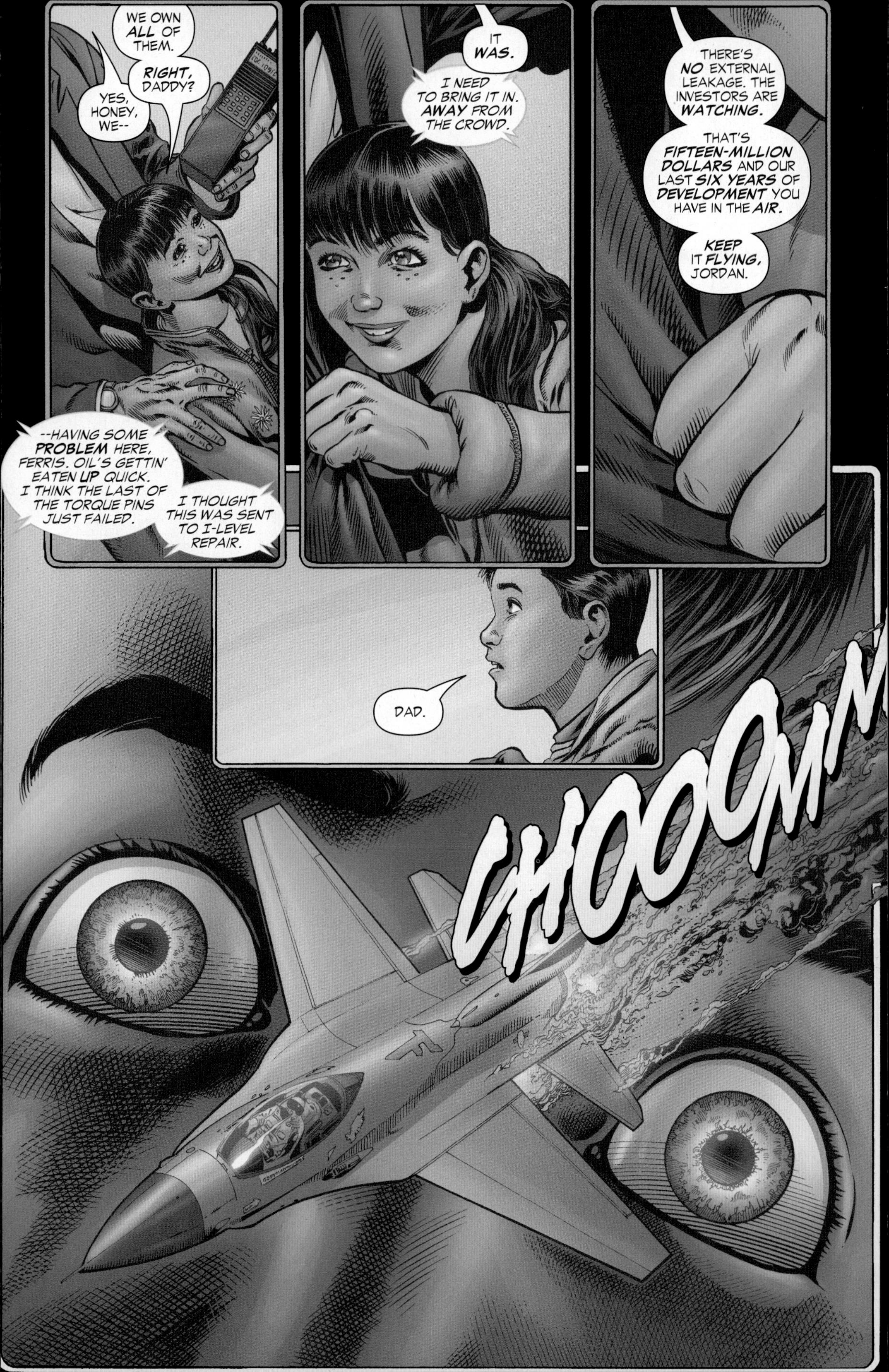

WE OWN ALL OF THEM.
RIGHT, DADDY?
YES, HONEY, WE--
--HAVING SOME PROBLEM HERE, FERRIS. OIL'S GETTIN' EATEN UP QUICK. I THINK THE LAST OF THE TORQUE PINS JUST FAILED.
I THOUGHT THIS WAS SENT TO I-LEVEL REPAIR.
IT WAS.
I NEED TO BRING IT IN. AWAY FROM THE CROWD.
THERE'S NO EXTERNAL LEAKAGE. THE INVESTORS ARE WATCHING.
THAT'S FIFTEEN-MILLION DOLLARS AND OUR LAST SIX YEARS OF DEVELOPMENT YOU HAVE IN THE AIR.
KEEP IT FLYING, JORDAN.
DAD.
CHOOOMM

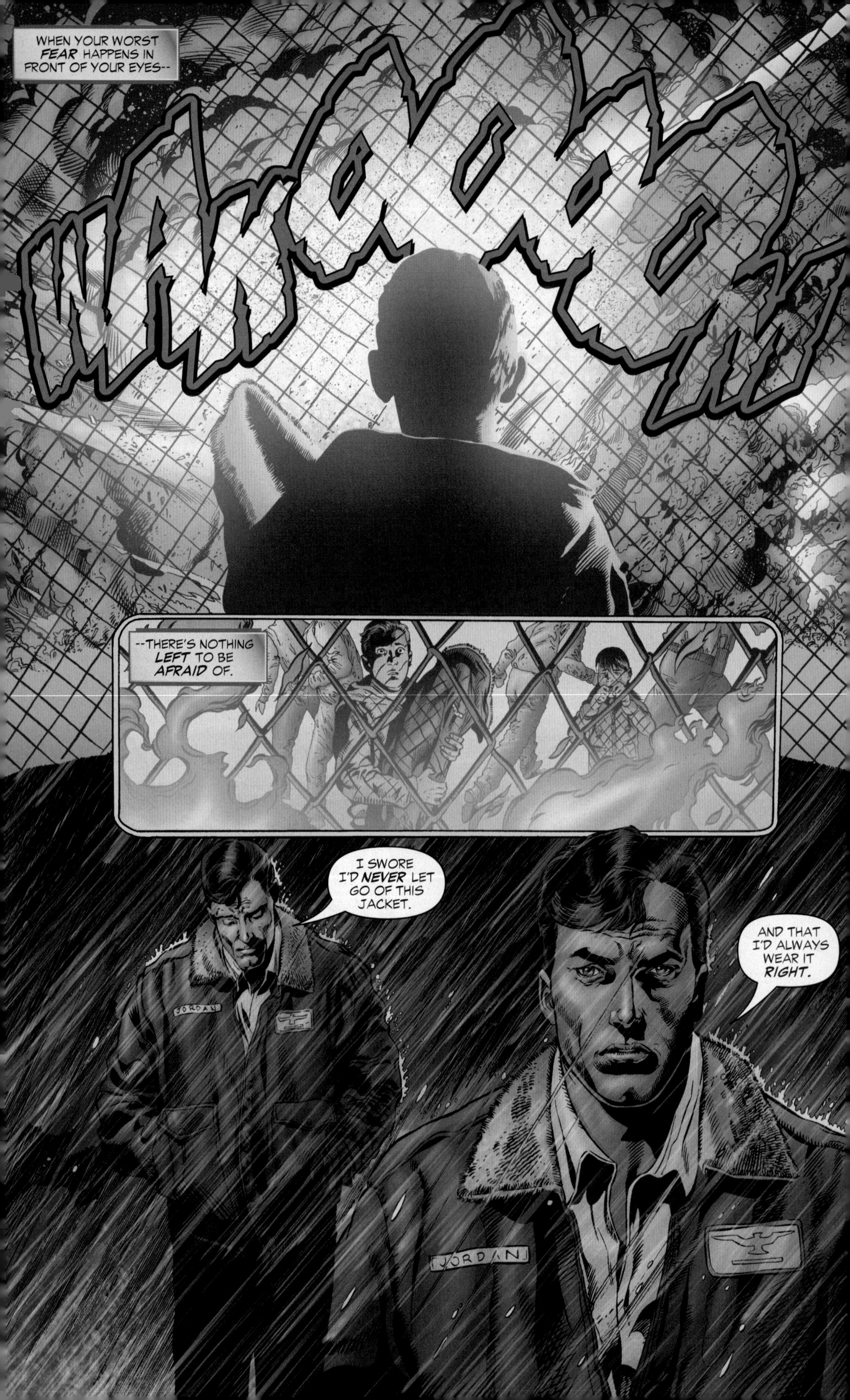
WHEN YOUR WORST FEAR HAPPENS IN FRONT OF YOUR EYES--
--THERE'S NOTHING LEFT TO BE AFRAID OF.
JORDAN
I SWORE I'D NEVER LET GO OF THIS JACKET.
AND THAT I'D ALWAYS WEAR IT RIGHT.
JORDAN

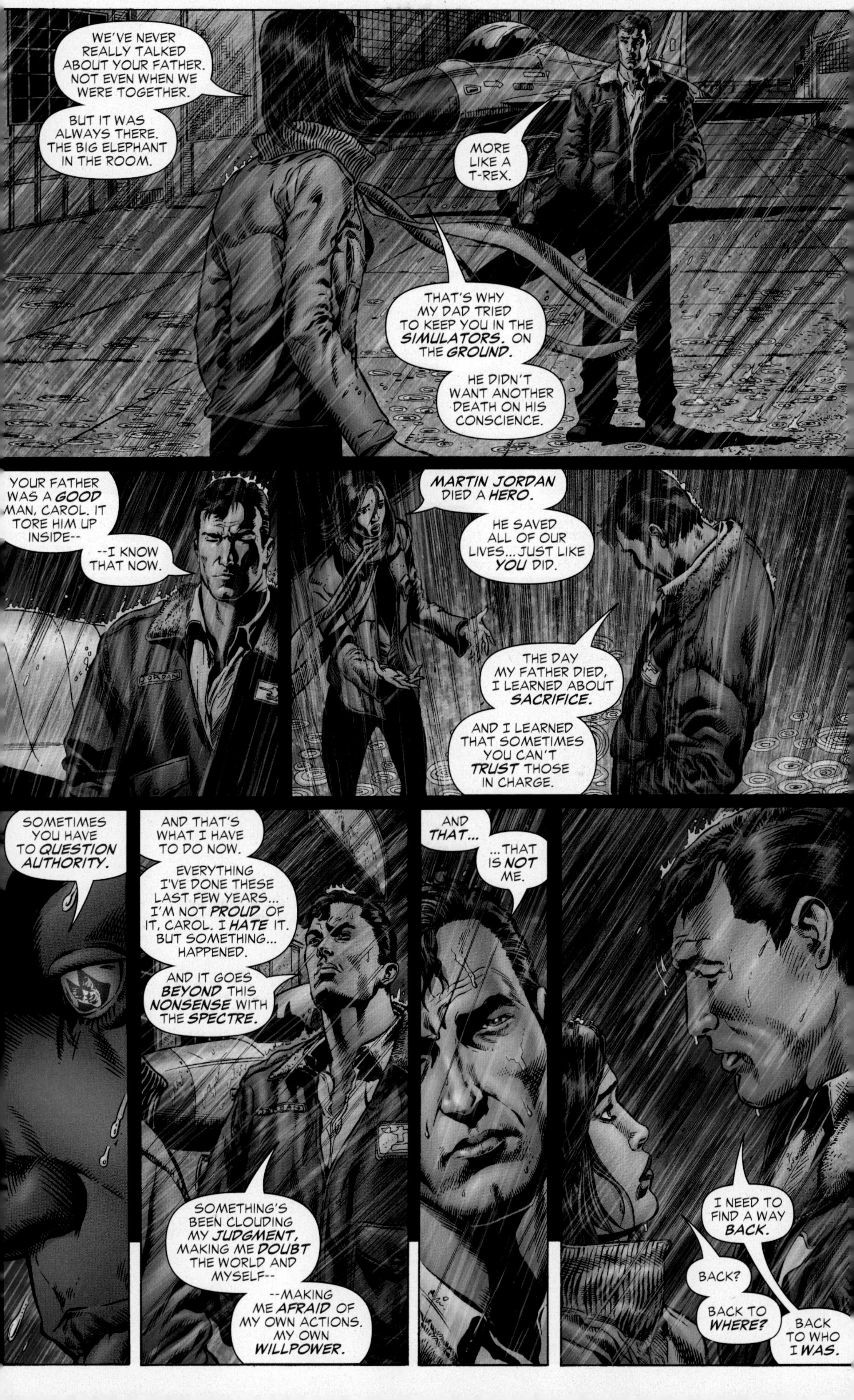

WE'VE NEVER REALLY TALKED ABOUT YOUR FATHER. NOT EVEN WHEN WE WERE TOGETHER.
BUT IT WAS ALWAYS THERE. THE BIG ELEPHANT IN THE ROOM.
MORE LIKE A T-REX.
THAT'S WHY MY DAD TRIED TO KEEP YOU IN THE SIMULATORS. ON THE GROUND.
HE DIDN'T WANT ANOTHER DEATH ON HIS CONSCIENCE.
YOUR FATHER WAS A GOOD MAN, CAROL. IT TORE HIM UP INSIDE--
--I KNOW THAT NOW.
MARTIN JORDAN DIED A HERO.
HE SAVED ALL OF OUR LIVES...JUST LIKE YOU DID.
THE DAY MY FATHER DIED, I LEARNED ABOUT SACRIFICE.
AND I LEARNED THAT SOMETIMES YOU CAN'T TRUST THOSE IN CHARGE.
SOMETIMES YOU HAVE TO QUESTION AUTHORITY.
AND THAT'S WHAT I HAVE TO DO NOW.
EVERYTHING I'VE DONE THESE LAST FEW YEARS... I'M NOT PROUD OF IT, CAROL. I HATE IT. BUT SOMETHING... HAPPENED.
AND IT GOES BEYOND THIS NONSENSE WITH THE SPECTRE.
SOMETHING'S BEEN CLOUDING MY JUDGMENT, MAKING ME DOUBT THE WORLD AND MYSELF--
--MAKING ME AFRAID OF MY OWN ACTIONS. MY OWN WILLPOWER.
AND THAT...
...THAT IS NOT ME.
I NEED TO FIND A WAY BACK.
BACK?
BACK TO WHERE?
BACK TO WHO I WAS.

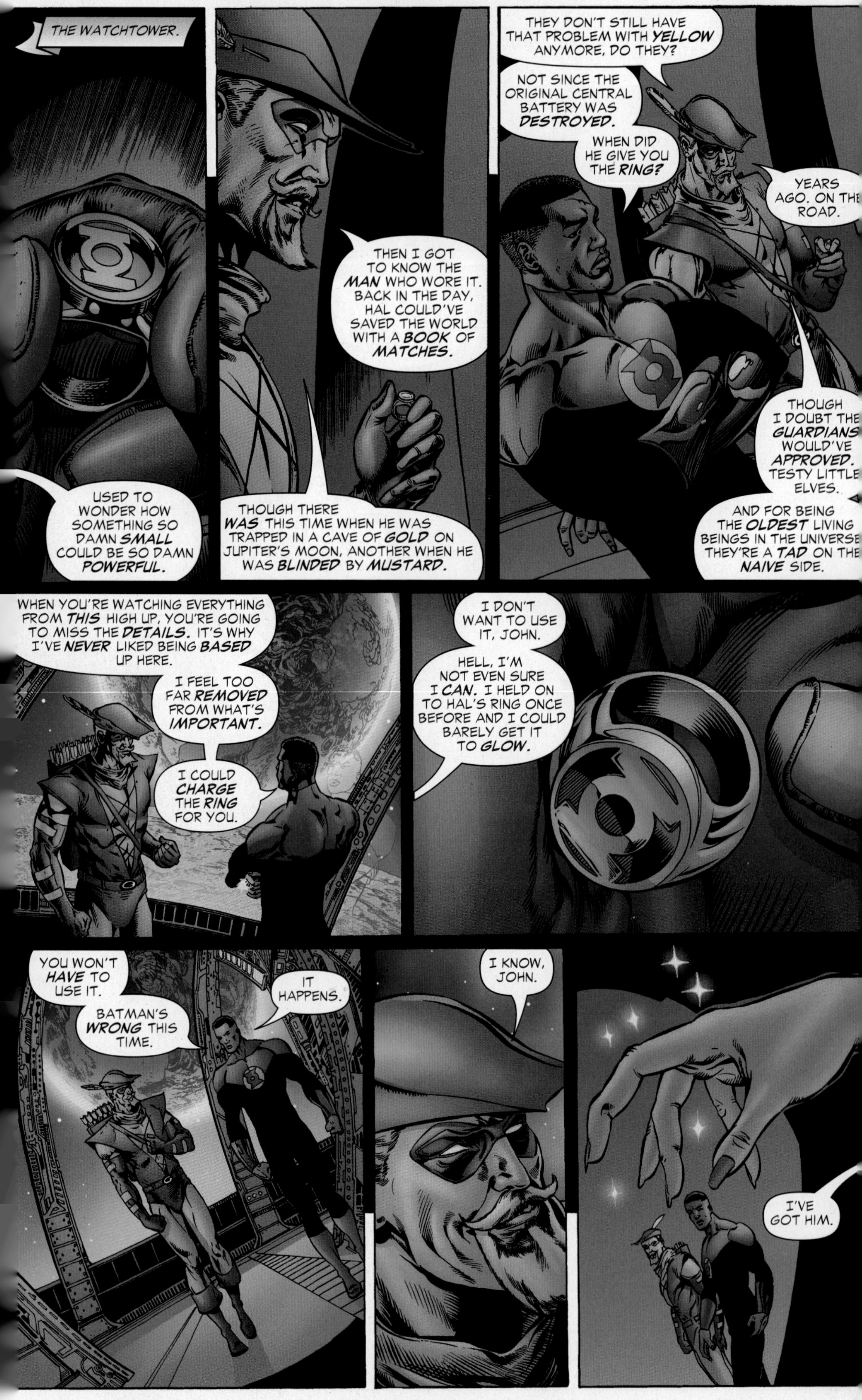
THE WATCHTOWER.
USED TO WONDER HOW SOMETHING SO DAMN SMALL COULD BE SO DAMN POWERFUL.
THEN I GOT TO KNOW THE MAN WHO WORE IT. BACK IN THE DAY, HAL COULD'VE SAVED THE WORLD WITH A BOOK OF MATCHES.
THOUGH THERE WAS THIS TIME WHEN HE WAS TRAPPED IN A CAVE OF GOLD ON JUPITER'S MOON, ANOTHER WHEN HE WAS BLINDED BY MUSTARD.
THEY DON'T STILL HAVE THAT PROBLEM WITH YELLOW ANYMORE, DO THEY?
NOT SINCE THE ORIGINAL CENTRAL BATTERY WAS DESTROYED.
WHEN DID HE GIVE YOU THE RING?
YEARS AGO. ON THE ROAD.
THOUGH I DOUBT THE GUARDIANS WOULD'VE APPROVED. TESTY LITTLE ELVES.
AND FOR BEING THE OLDEST LIVING BEINGS IN THE UNIVERSE THEY'RE A TAD ON THE NAIVE SIDE.
WHEN YOU'RE WATCHING EVERYTHING FROM THIS HIGH UP, YOU'RE GOING TO MISS THE DETAILS. IT'S WHY I'VE NEVER LIKED BEING BASED UP HERE.
I FEEL TOO FAR REMOVED FROM WHAT'S IMPORTANT.
I COULD CHARGE THE RING FOR YOU.
I DON'T WANT TO USE IT, JOHN.
HELL, I'M NOT EVEN SURE I CAN. I HELD ON TO HAL'S RING ONCE BEFORE AND I COULD BARELY GET IT TO GLOW.
YOU WON'T HAVE TO USE IT.
BATMAN'S WRONG THIS TIME.
IT HAPPENS.
I KNOW, JOHN.
I'VE GOT HIM.

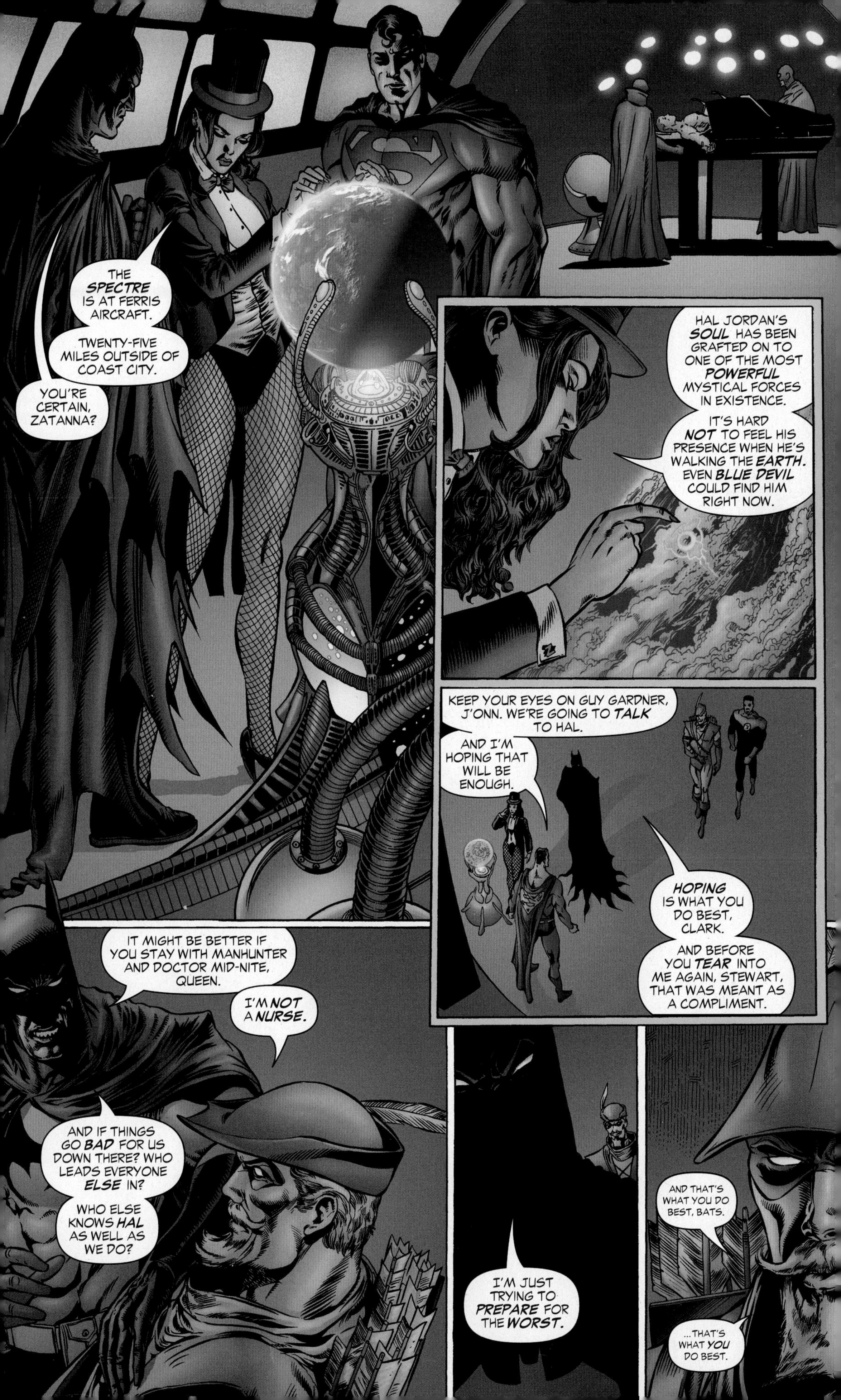
THE SPECTRE IS AT FERRIS AIRCRAFT.
TWENTY-FIVE MILES OUTSIDE OF COAST CITY.
YOU'RE CERTAIN, ZATANNA?
HAL JORDAN'S SOUL HAS BEEN GRAFTED ON TO ONE OF THE MOST POWERFUL MYSTICAL FORCES IN EXISTENCE.
IT'S HARD NOT TO FEEL HIS PRESENCE WHEN HE'S WALKING THE EARTH. EVEN BLUE DEVIL COULD FIND HIM RIGHT NOW.
KEEP YOUR EYES ON GUY GARDNER, J'ONN. WE'RE GOING TO TALK TO HAL.
AND I'M HOPING THAT WILL BE ENOUGH.
HOPING IS WHAT YOU DO BEST, CLARK.
AND BEFORE YOU TEAR INTO ME AGAIN, STEWART, THAT WAS MEANT AS A COMPLIMENT.
IT MIGHT BE BETTER IF YOU STAY WITH MANHUNTER AND DOCTOR MID-NITE, QUEEN.
I'M NOT A NURSE.
AND IF THINGS GO BAD FOR US DOWN THERE? WHO LEADS EVERYONE ELSE IN?
WHO ELSE KNOWS HAL AS WELL AS WE DO?
I'M JUST TRYING TO PREPARE FOR THE WORST.
AND THAT'S WHAT YOU DO BEST, BATS.
...THAT'S WHAT YOU DO BEST.

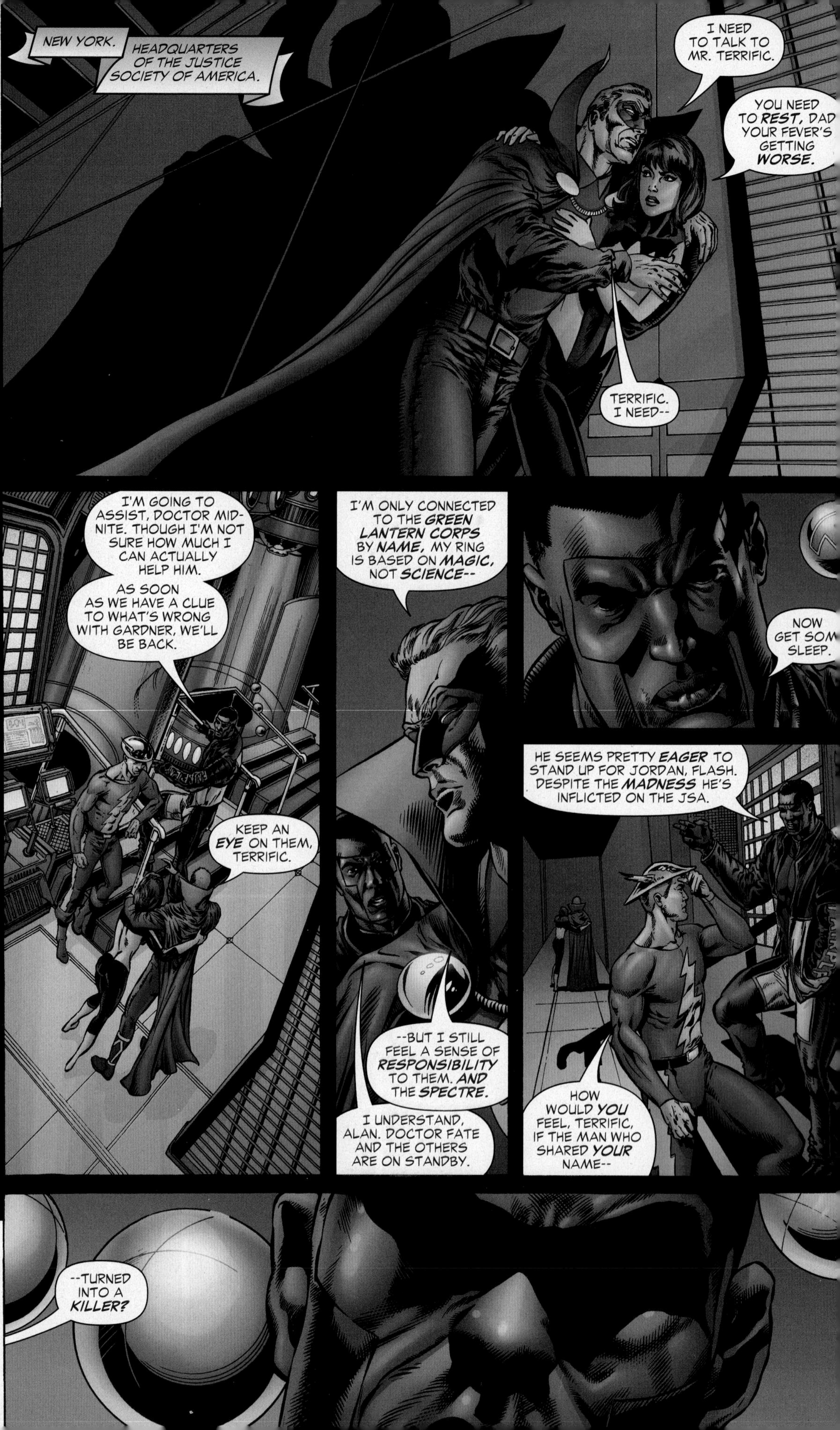
NEW YORK.
HEADQUARTERS OF THE JUSTICE SOCIETY OF AMERICA.
I NEED TO TALK TO MR. TERRIFIC.
YOU NEED TO REST, DAD YOUR FEVER'S GETTING WORSE.
TERRIFIC. I NEED--
I'M GOING TO ASSIST, DOCTOR MID-NITE. THOUGH I'M NOT SURE HOW MUCH I CAN ACTUALLY HELP HIM.
AS SOON AS WE HAVE A CLUE TO WHAT'S WRONG WITH GARDNER, WE'LL BE BACK.
KEEP AN EYE ON THEM, TERRIFIC.
I'M ONLY CONNECTED TO THE GREEN LANTERN CORPS BY NAME. MY RING IS BASED ON MAGIC, NOT SCIENCE--
--BUT I STILL FEEL A SENSE OF RESPONSIBILITY TO THEM. AND THE SPECTRE.
I UNDERSTAND, ALAN. DOCTOR FATE AND THE OTHERS ARE ON STANDBY.
NOW GET SOM SLEEP.
HE SEEMS PRETTY EAGER TO STAND UP FOR JORDAN, FLASH. DESPITE THE MADNESS HE'S INFLICTED ON THE JSA.
HOW WOULD YOU FEEL, TERRIFIC, IF THE MAN WHO SHARED YOUR NAME--
--TURNED INTO A KILLER?

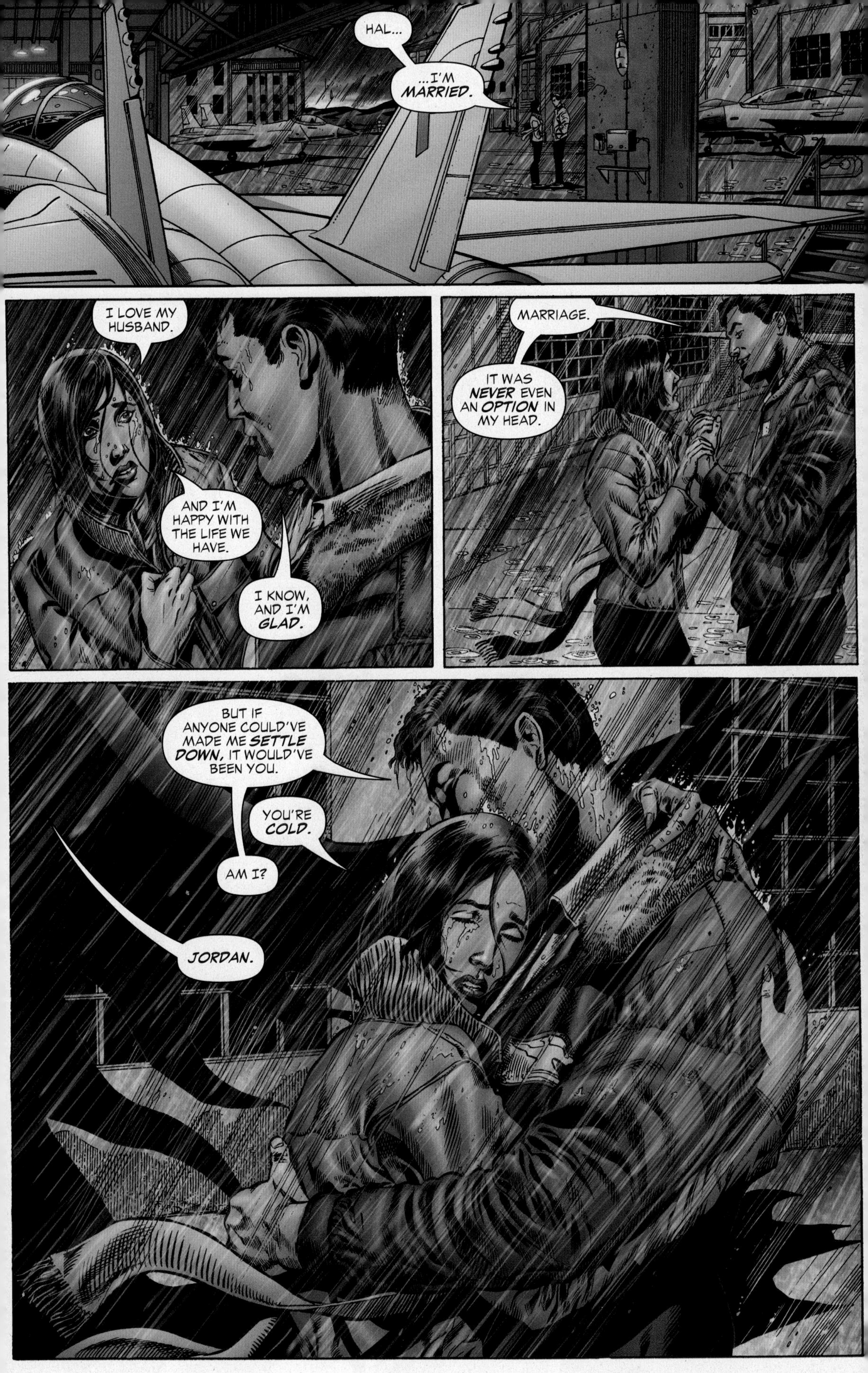
HAL...
...I'M MARRIED.
I LOVE MY HUSBAND.
AND I'M HAPPY WITH THE LIFE WE HAVE.
I KNOW, AND I'M GLAD.
MARRIAGE.
IT WAS NEVER EVEN AN OPTION IN MY HEAD.
BUT IF ANYONE COULD'VE MADE ME SETTLE DOWN, IT WOULD'VE BEEN YOU.
YOU'RE COLD.
AM I?
JORDAN.

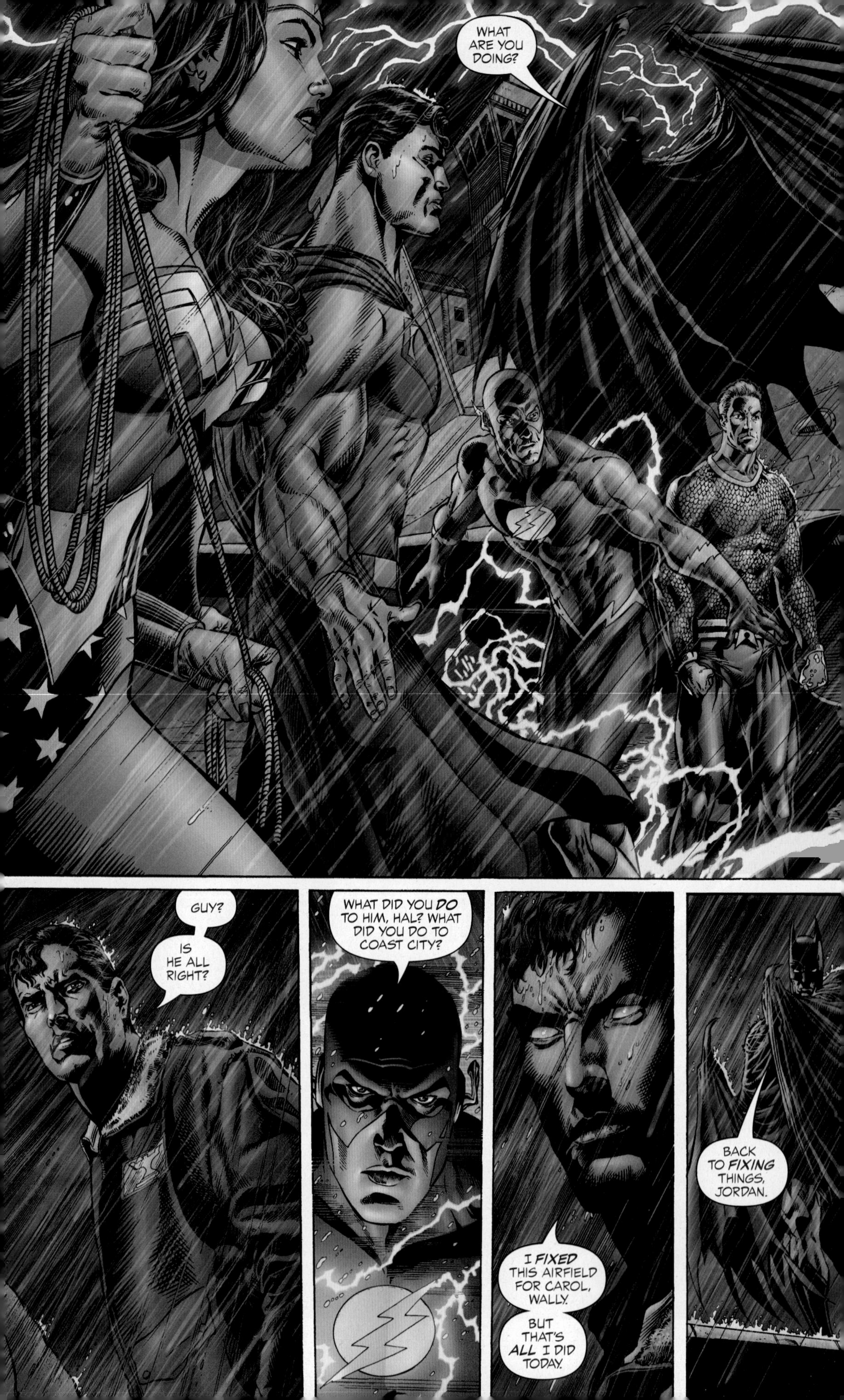
WHAT ARE YOU DOING?
GUY?
IS HE ALL RIGHT?
WHAT DID YOU DO TO HIM, HAL? WHAT DID YOU DO TO COAST CITY?
I FIXED THIS AIRFIELD FOR CAROL, WALLY.
BUT THAT'S ALL I DID TODAY.
BACK TO FIXING THINGS, JORDAN.

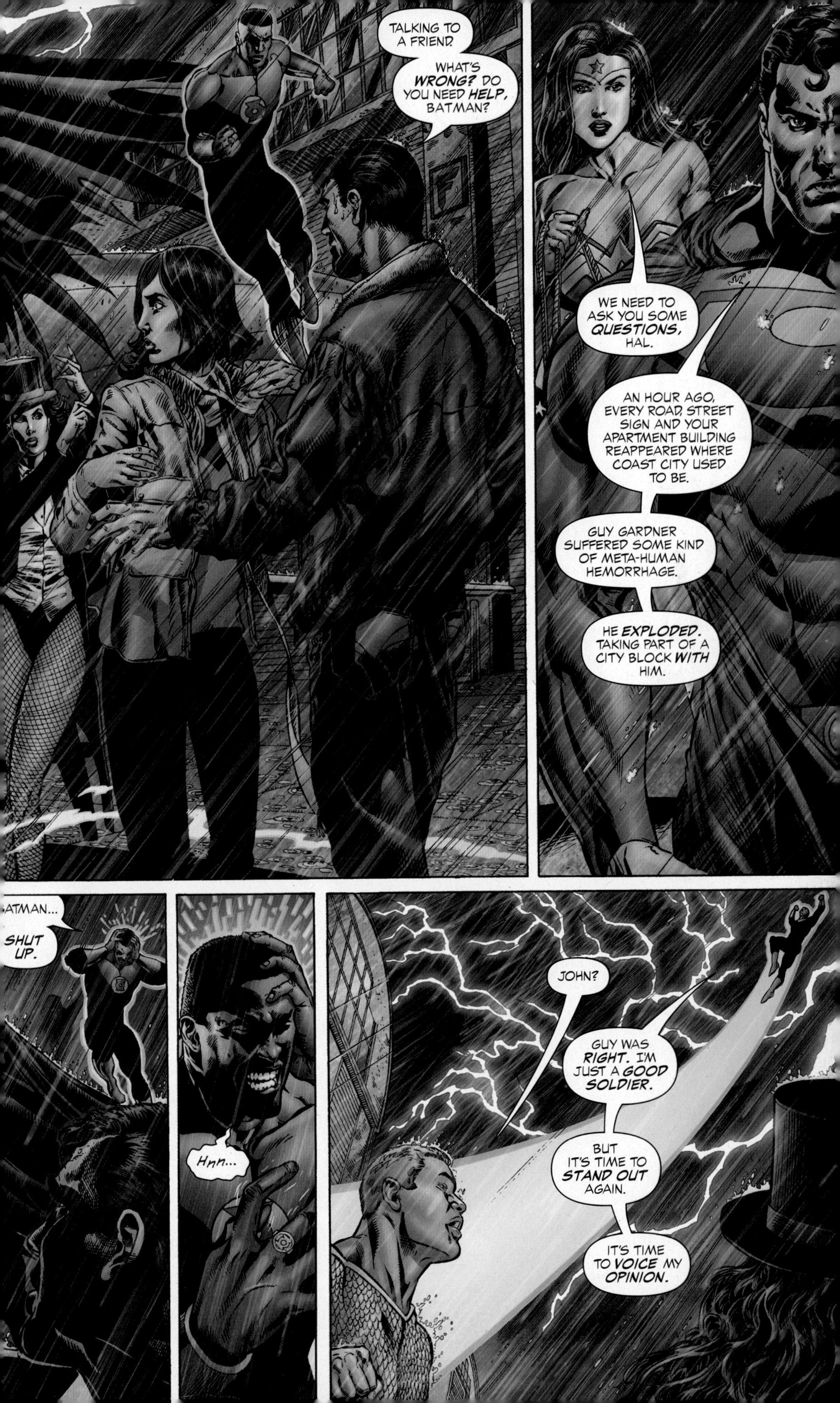
TALKING TO A FRIEND.
WHAT'S WRONG? DO YOU NEED HELP, BATMAN?
WE NEED TO ASK YOU SOME QUESTIONS, HAL.
AN HOUR AGO, EVERY ROAD, STREET SIGN AND YOUR APARTMENT BUILDING REAPPEARED WHERE COAST CITY USED TO BE.
GUY GARDNER SUFFERED SOME KIND OF META-HUMAN HEMORRHAGE.
HE EXPLODED. TAKING PART OF A CITY BLOCK WITH HIM.
ATMAN...
SHUT UP.
Hnn...
JOHN?
GUY WAS RIGHT. I'M JUST A GOOD SOLDIER.
BUT IT'S TIME TO STAND OUT AGAIN.
IT'S TIME TO VOICE MY OPINION.

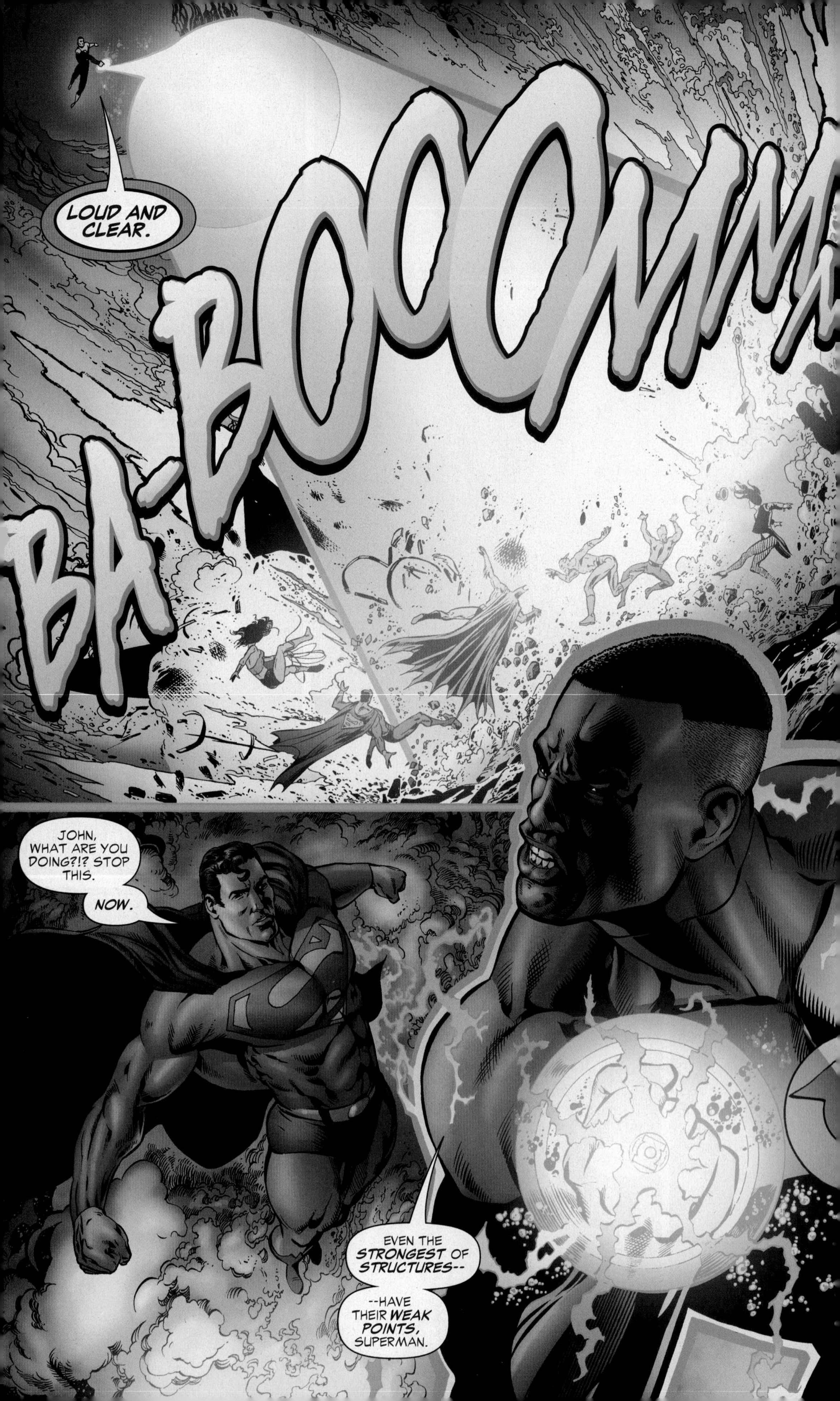
LOUD AND CLEAR.
BA-BOOOMM
JOHN, WHAT ARE YOU DOING?!? STOP THIS.
NOW.
EVEN THE STRONGEST OF STRUCTURES--
--HAVE THEIR WEAK POINTS, SUPERMAN.

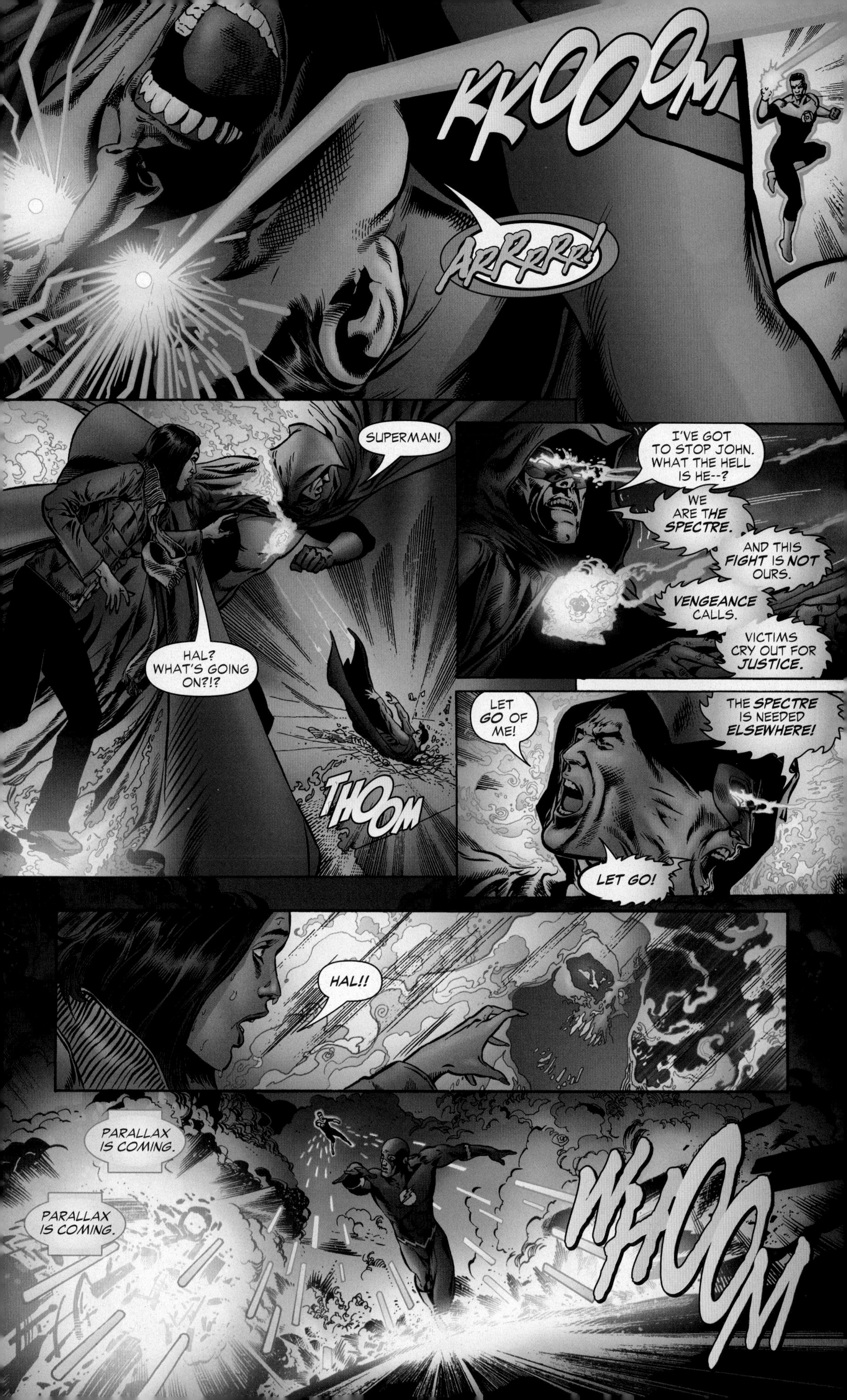
KKOOOOM
ARRRRR!
SUPERMAN!
HAL? WHAT'S GOING ON?!?
THOOM
I'VE GOT TO STOP JOHN. WHAT THE HELL IS HE--?
WE ARE THE SPECTRE.
AND THIS FIGHT IS NOT OURS.
VENGEANCE CALLS.
VICTIMS CRY OUT FOR JUSTICE.
LET GO OF ME!
THE SPECTRE IS NEEDED ELSEWHERE!
LET GO!
HAL!!
PARALLAX IS COMING.
PARALLAX IS COMING.
WHOOOM

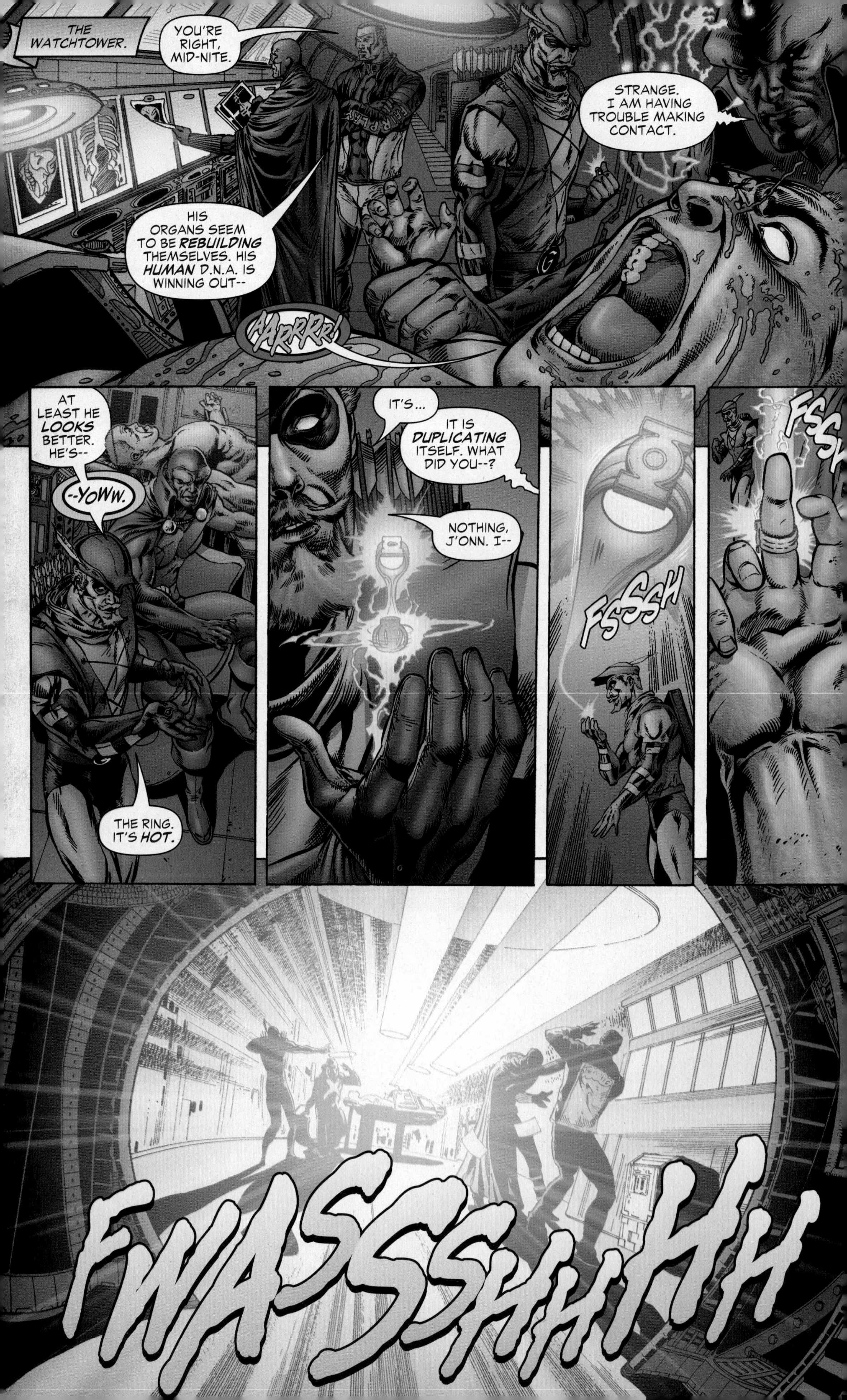

THE WATCHTOWER.
YOU'RE RIGHT, MID-NITE.
HIS ORGANS SEEM TO BE REBUILDING THEMSELVES. HIS HUMAN D.N.A. IS WINNING OUT--
STRANGE. I AM HAVING TROUBLE MAKING CONTACT.
AARRRR!
AT LEAST HE LOOKS BETTER. HE'S--
--YOWW.
THE RING. IT'S HOT.
IT'S...
IT IS DUPLICATING ITSELF. WHAT DID YOU--?
NOTHING, J'ONN. I--
FSSSH
FWASSSHHHH

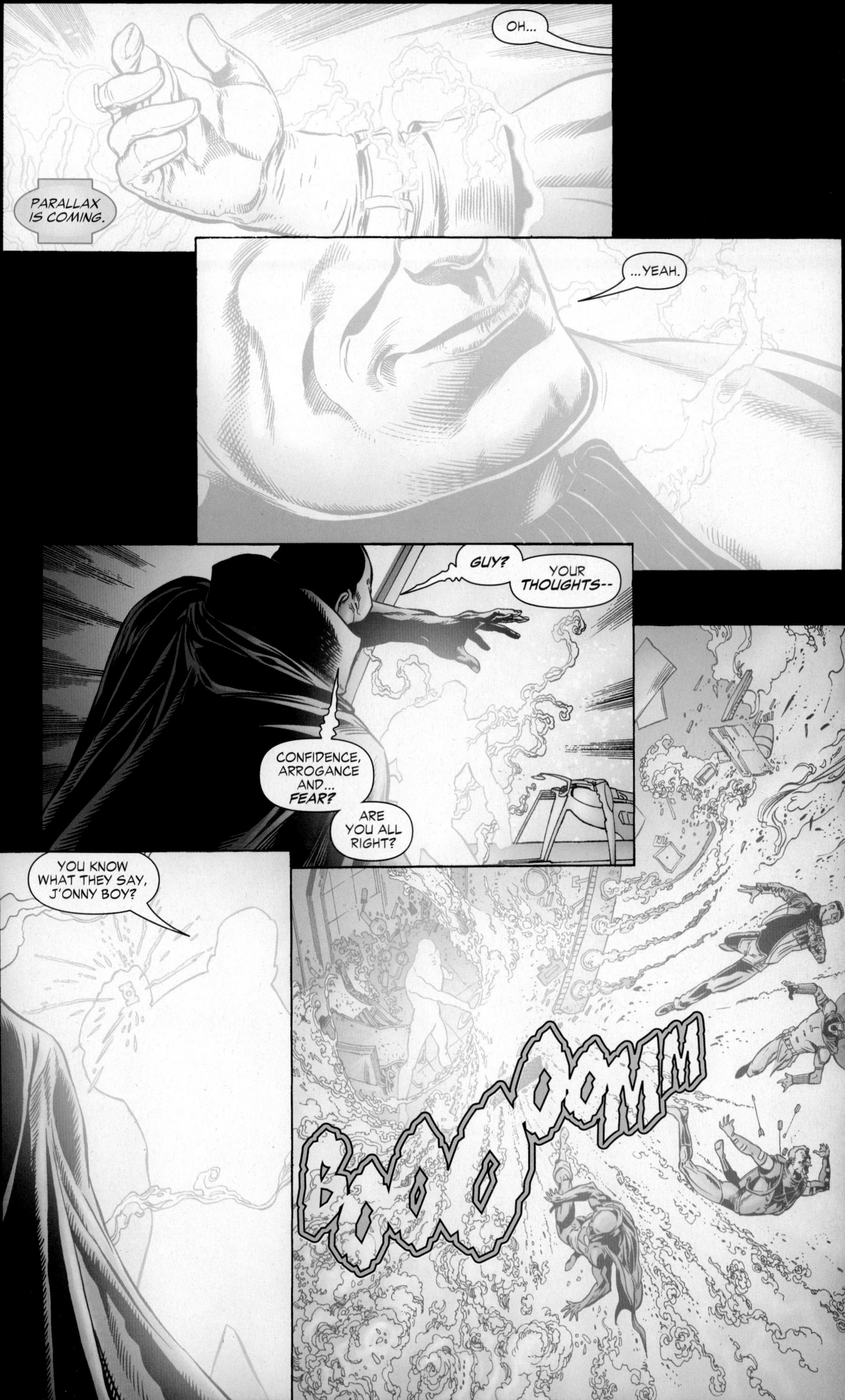
OH...
PARALLAX IS COMING.
...YEAH.
GUY?
YOUR THOUGHTS--
CONFIDENCE, ARROGANCE AND... FEAR?
ARE YOU ALL RIGHT?
YOU KNOW WHAT THEY SAY, J'ONNY BOY?
BOOOOMM

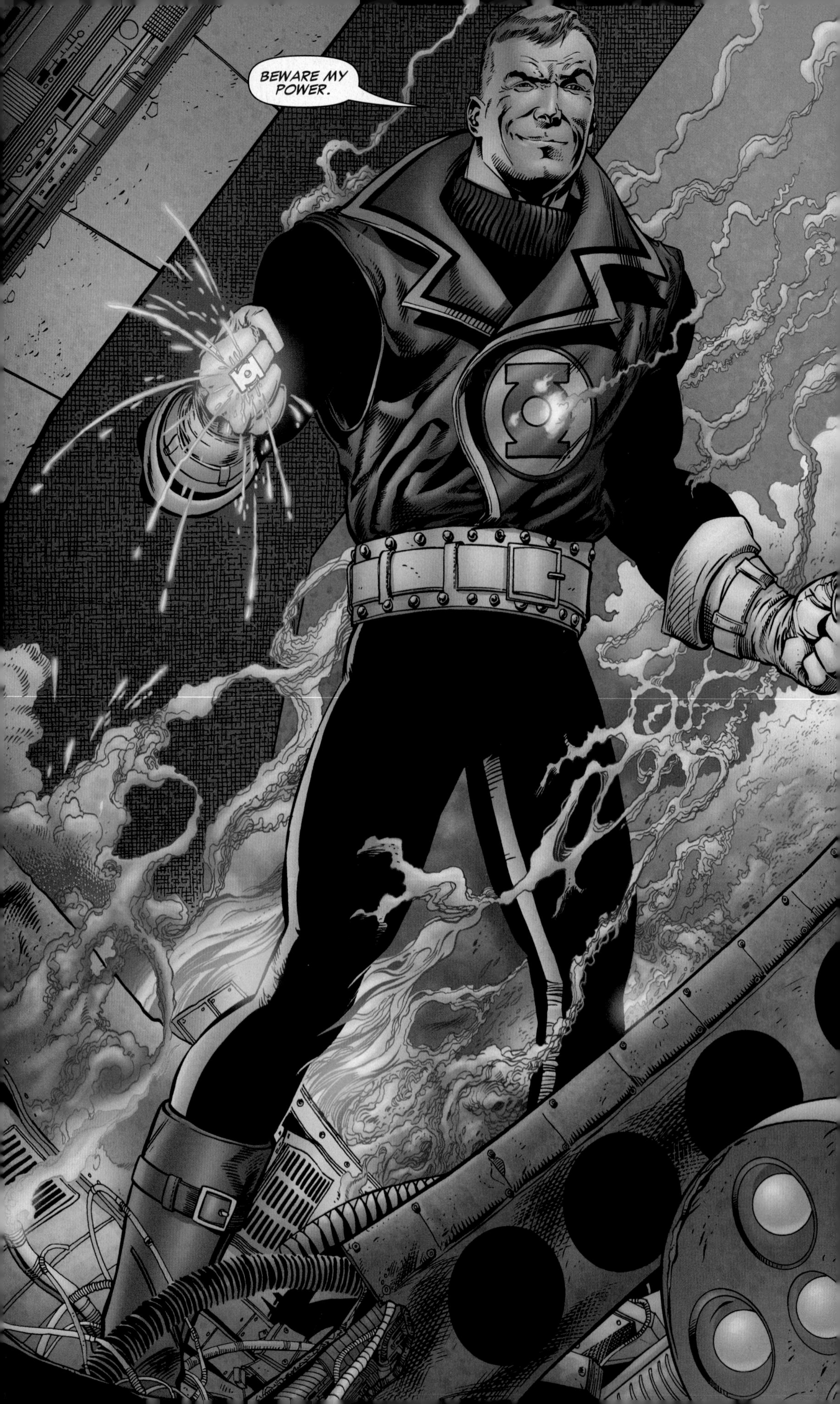
BEWARE MY POWER.

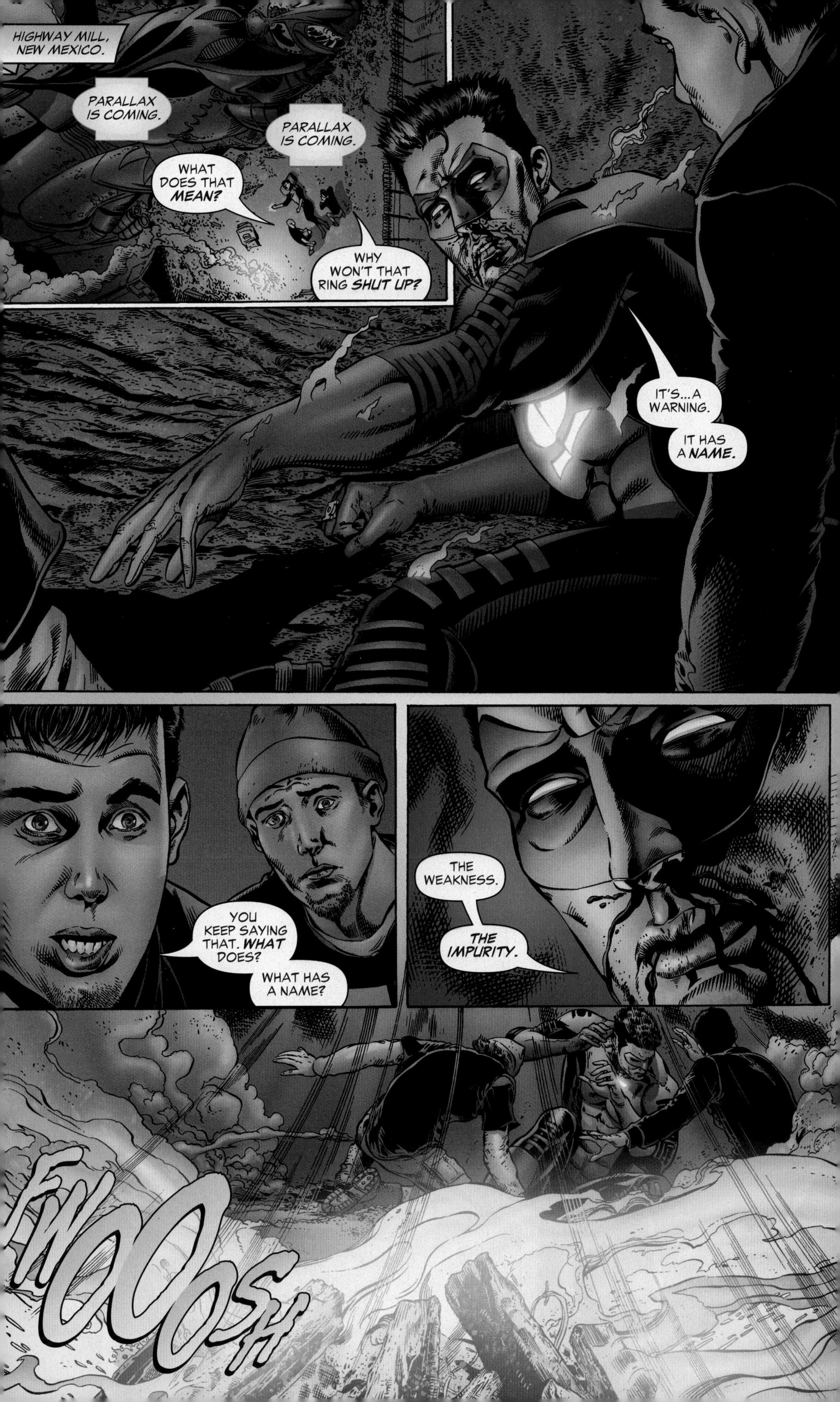
HIGHWAY MILL, NEW MEXICO.
PARALLAX IS COMING.
PARALLAX IS COMING.
WHAT DOES THAT MEAN?
WHY WON'T THAT RING SHUT UP?
IT'S...A WARNING.
IT HAS A NAME.
YOU KEEP SAYING THAT. WHAT DOES?
WHAT HAS A NAME?
THE WEAKNESS.
THE IMPURITY.
FWOOOSH

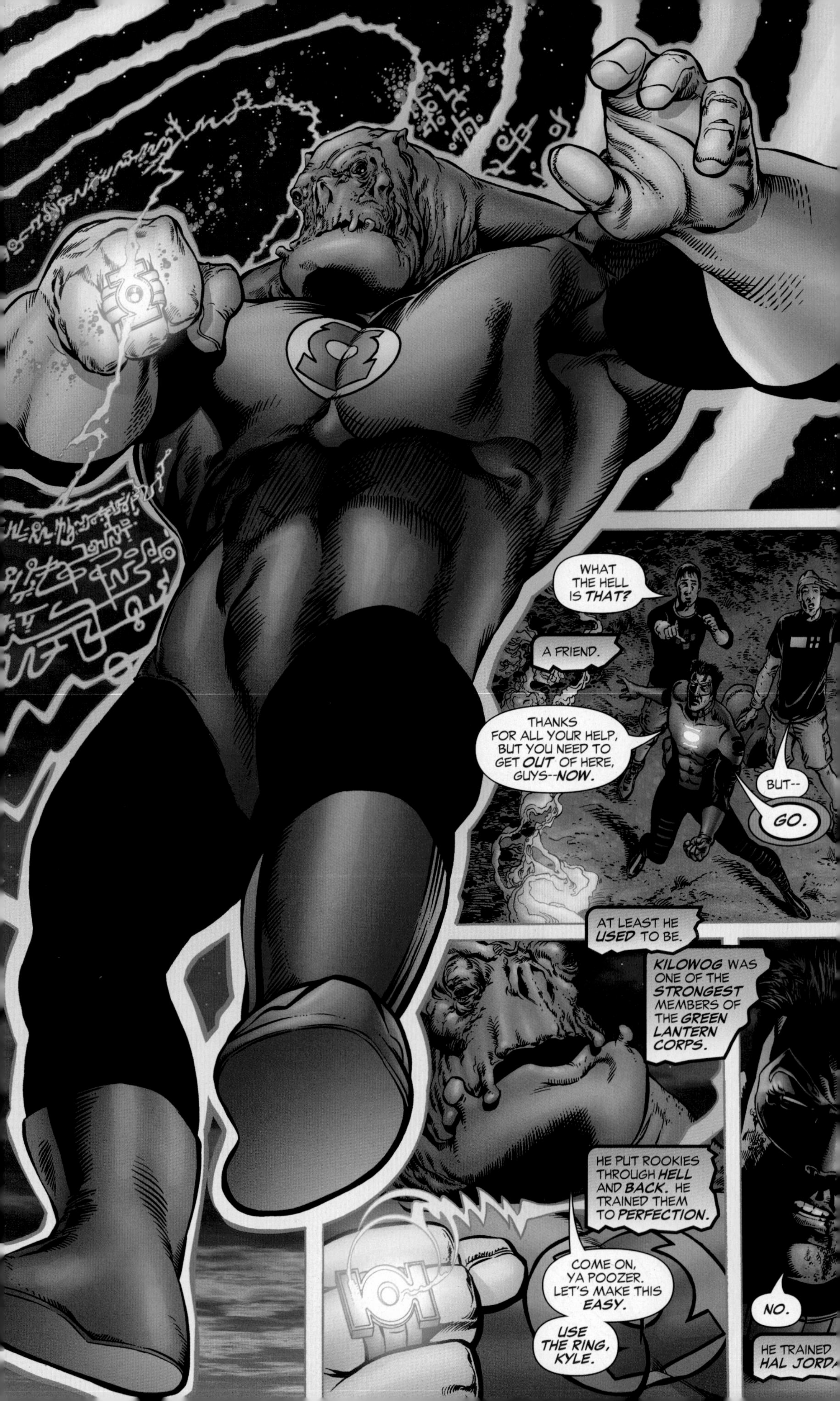

WHAT THE HELL IS THAT?
A FRIEND.
THANKS FOR ALL YOUR HELP, BUT YOU NEED TO GET OUT OF HERE, GUYS--NOW.
BUT--
GO.
AT LEAST HE USED TO BE.
KILOWOG WAS ONE OF THE STRONGEST MEMBERS OF THE GREEN LANTERN CORPS.
HE PUT ROOKIES THROUGH HELL AND BACK. HE TRAINED THEM TO PERFECTION.
COME ON, YA POOZER. LET'S MAKE THIS EASY.
USE THE RING, KYLE.
NO.
HE TRAINED HAL JORD

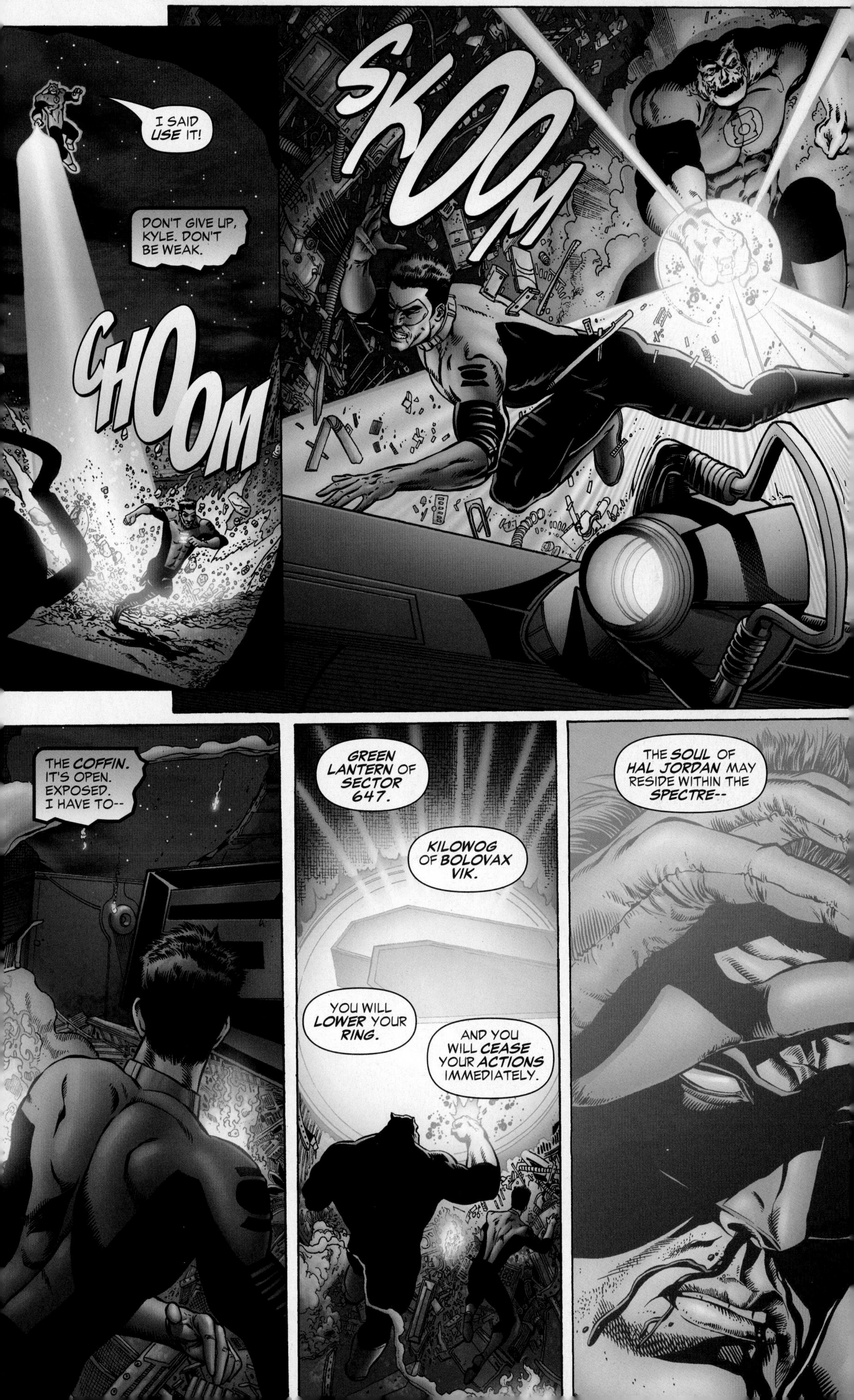
I SAID USE IT!
DON'T GIVE UP, KYLE. DON'T BE WEAK.
CHOOOM
SKOOM
THE COFFIN. IT'S OPEN. EXPOSED. I HAVE TO--
GREEN LANTERN OF SECTOR 647.
KILOWOG OF BOLOVAX VIK.
YOU WILL LOWER YOUR RING.
AND YOU WILL CEASE YOUR ACTIONS IMMEDIATELY.
THE SOUL OF HAL JORDAN MAY RESIDE WITHIN THE SPECTRE--

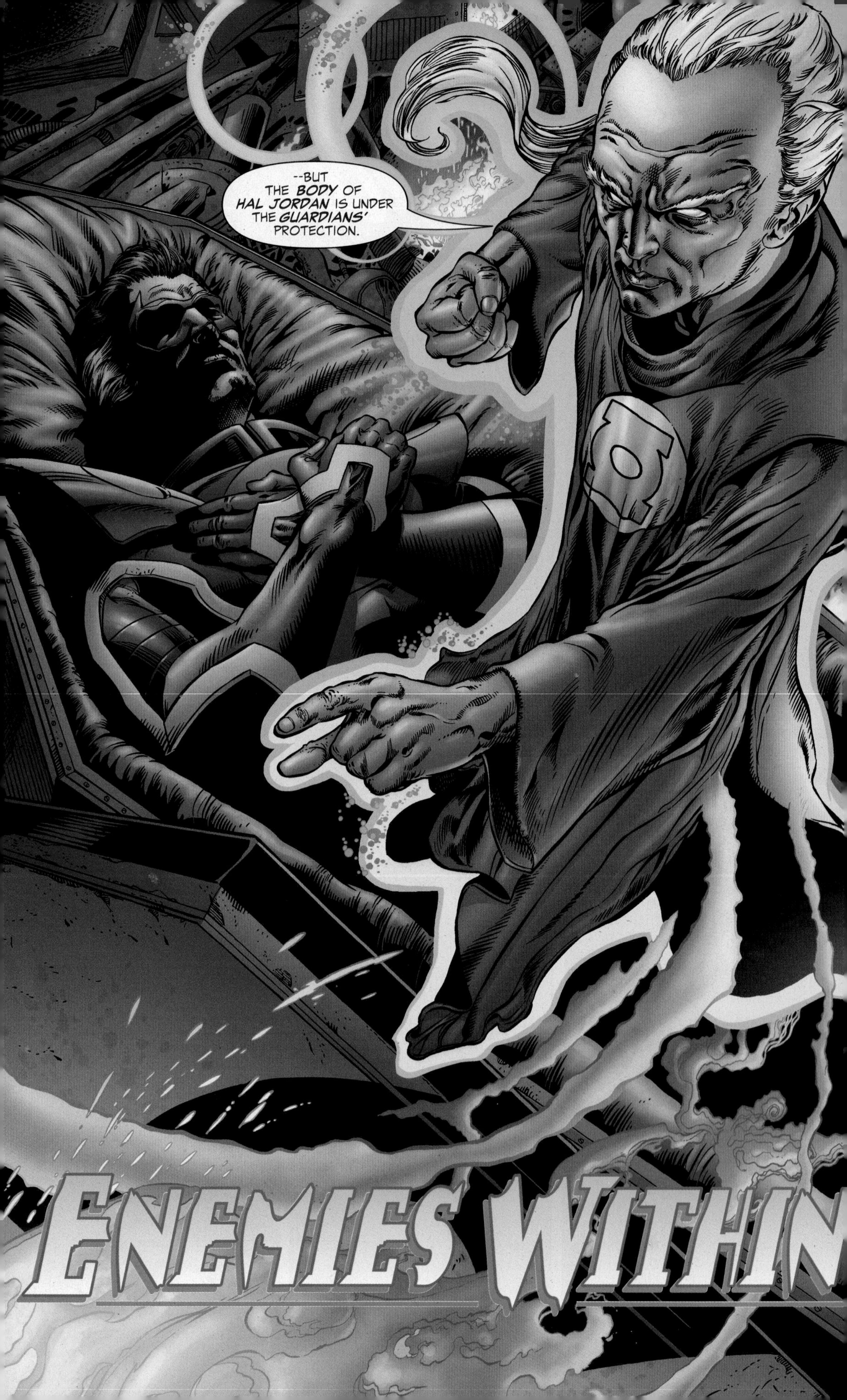
--BUT THE BODY OF HAL JORDAN IS UNDER THE GUARDIANS' PROTECTION.
ENEMIES WITHIN

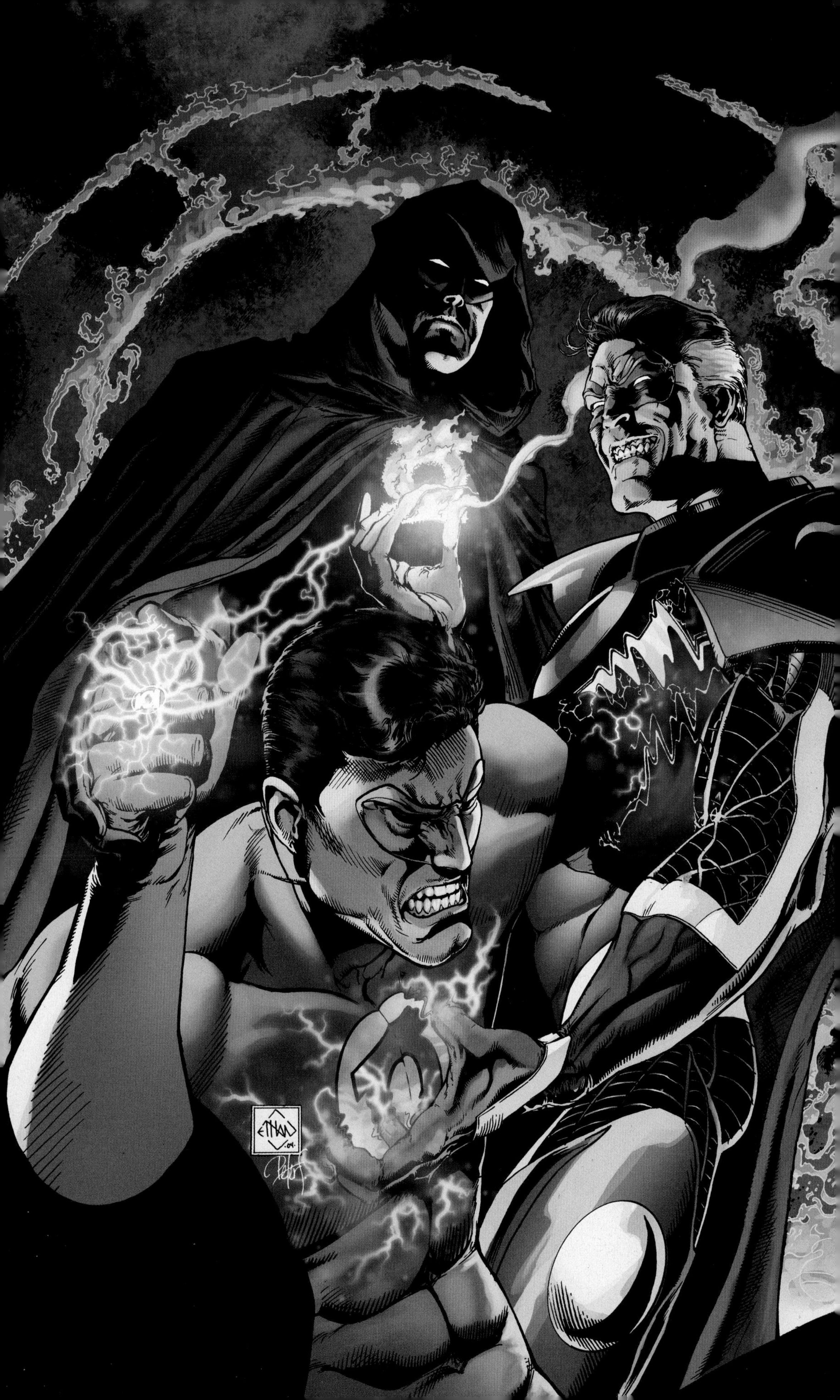

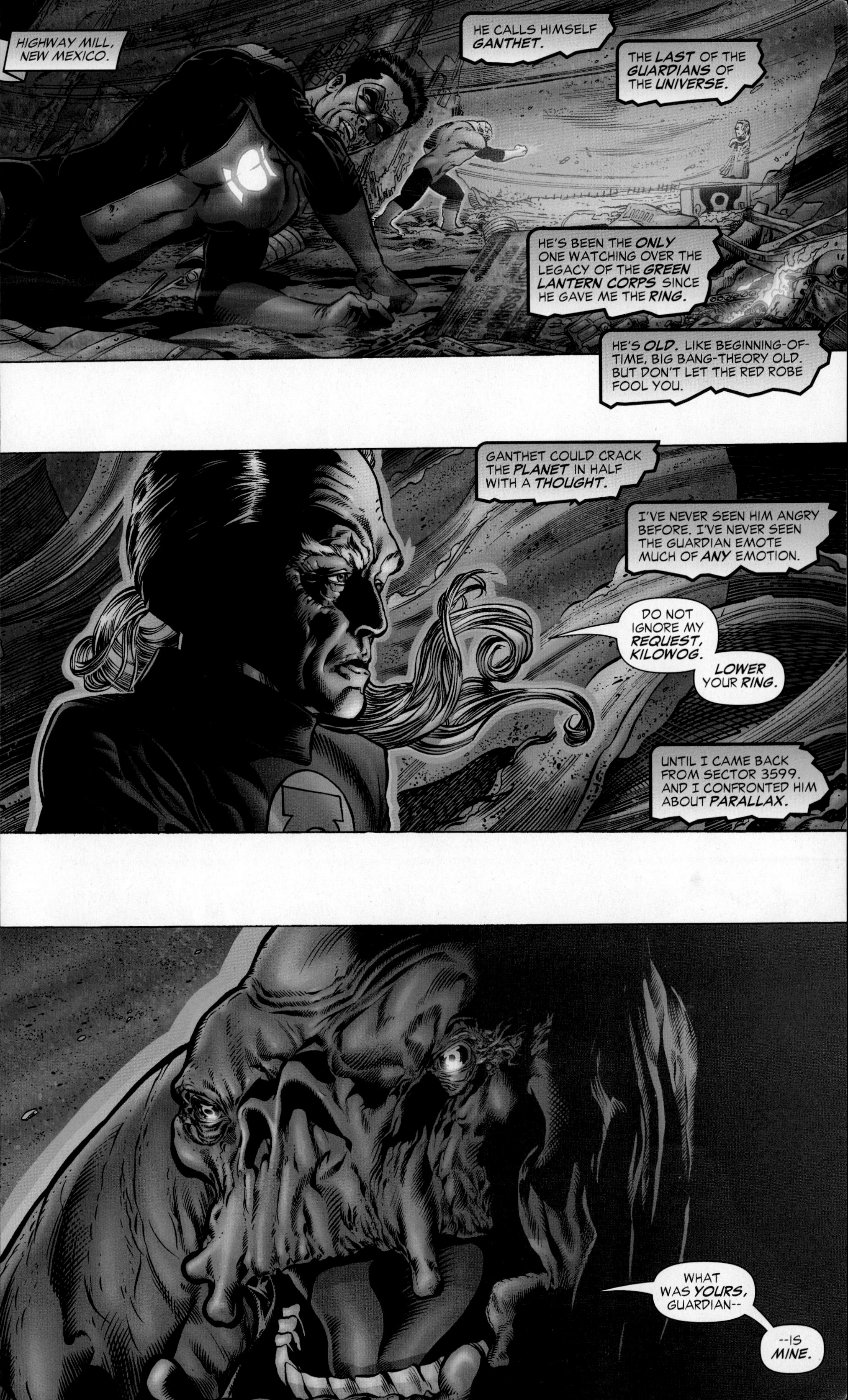
HIGHWAY MILL, NEW MEXICO.
HE CALLS HIMSELF GANTHET.
THE LAST OF THE GUARDIANS OF THE UNIVERSE.
HE'S BEEN THE ONLY ONE WATCHING OVER THE LEGACY OF THE GREEN LANTERN CORPS SINCE HE GAVE ME THE RING.
HE'S OLD. LIKE BEGINNING-OF-TIME, BIG BANG-THEORY OLD. BUT DON'T LET THE RED ROBE FOOL YOU.
GANTHET COULD CRACK THE PLANET IN HALF WITH A THOUGHT.
I'VE NEVER SEEN HIM ANGRY BEFORE. I'VE NEVER SEEN THE GUARDIAN EMOTE MUCH OF ANY EMOTION.
DO NOT IGNORE MY REQUEST, KILOWOG.
LOWER YOUR RING.
UNTIL I CAME BACK FROM SECTOR 3599. AND I CONFRONTED HIM ABOUT PARALLAX.
WHAT WAS YOURS, GUARDIAN--
--IS MINE.

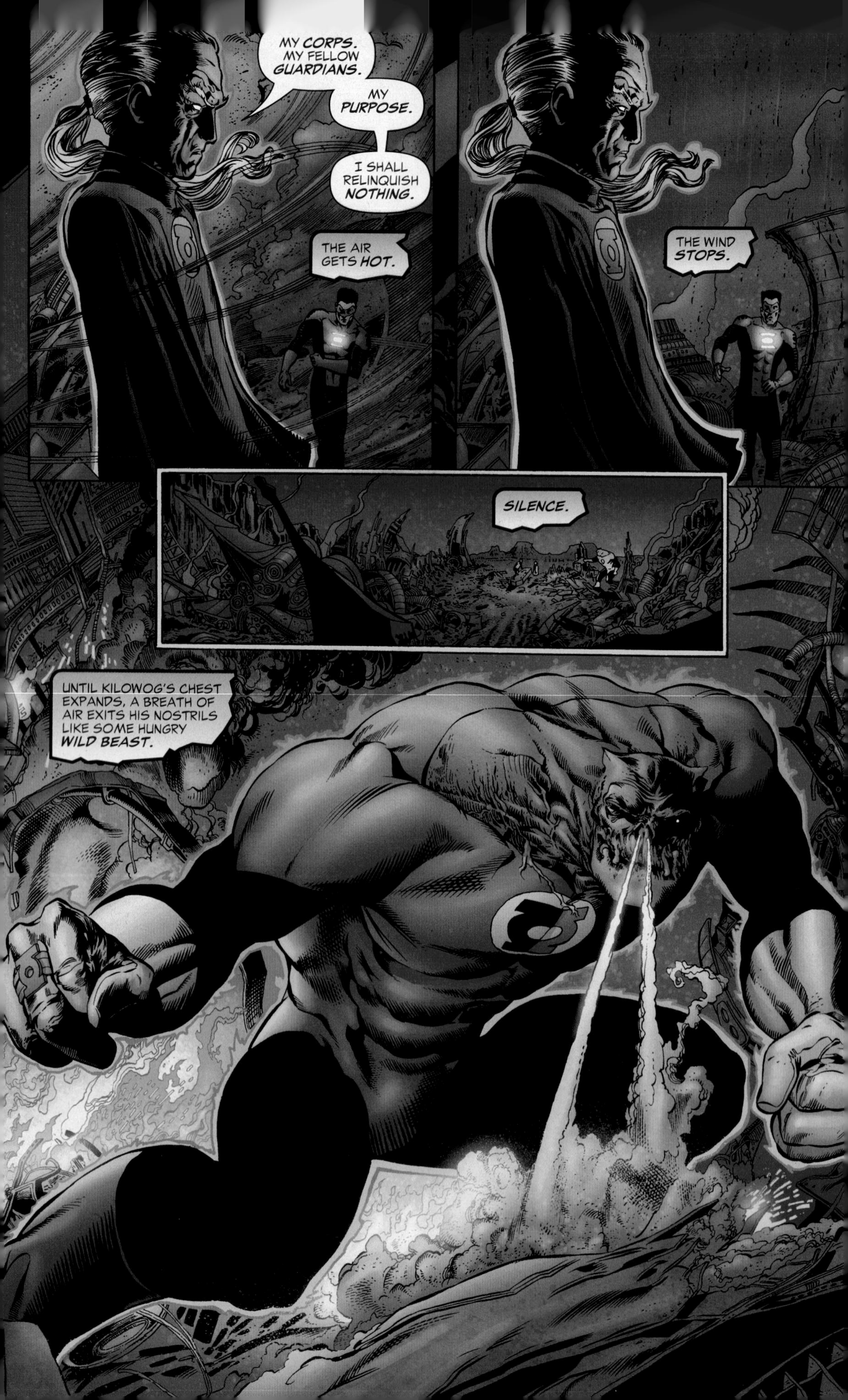
MY CORPS. MY FELLOW GUARDIANS.
MY PURPOSE.
I SHALL RELINQUISH NOTHING.
THE AIR GETS HOT.
THE WIND STOPS.
SILENCE.
UNTIL KILOWOG'S CHEST EXPANDS, A BREATH OF AIR EXITS HIS NOSTRILS LIKE SOME HUNGRY WILD BEAST.

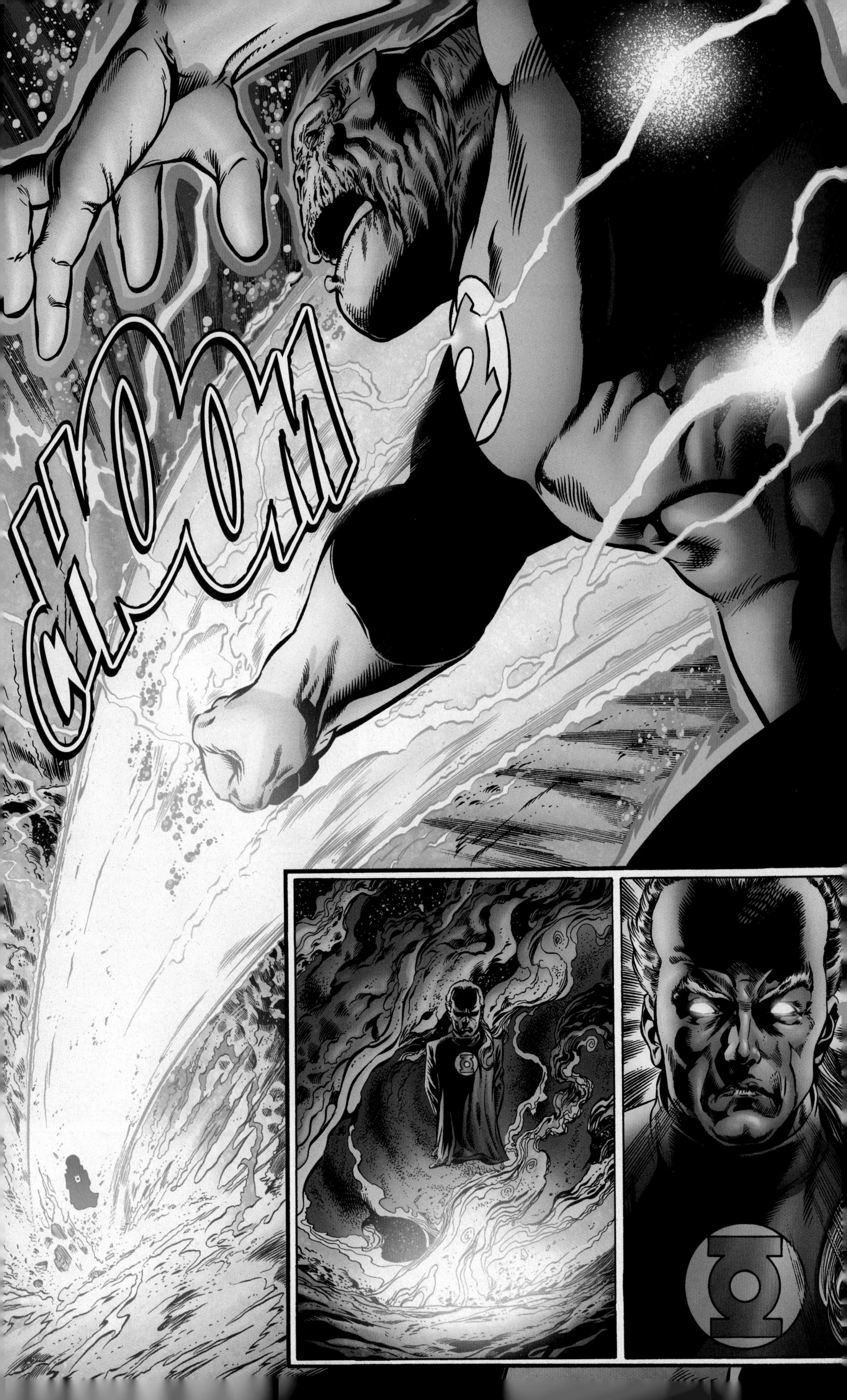
CHOOM

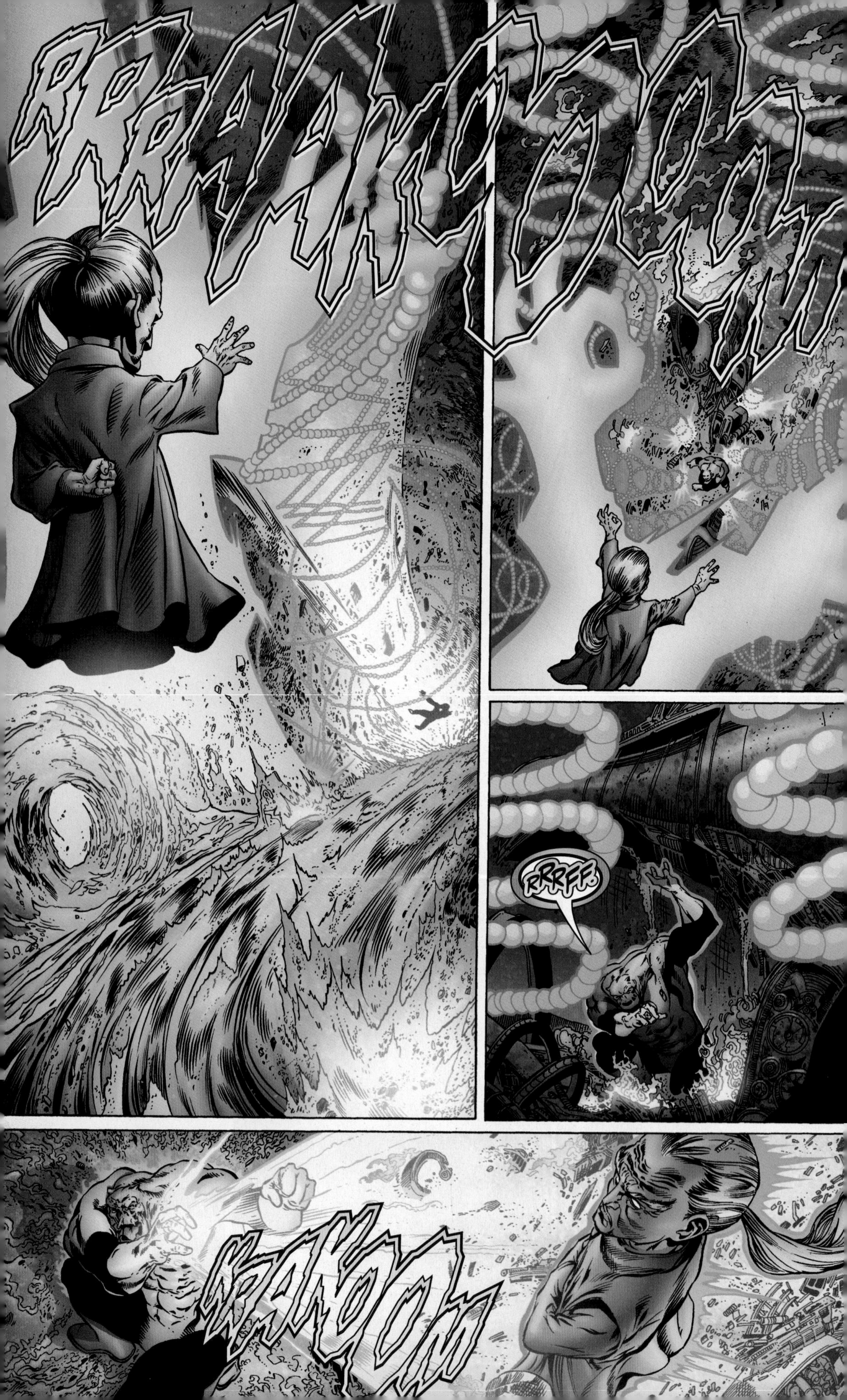
RRRFF.

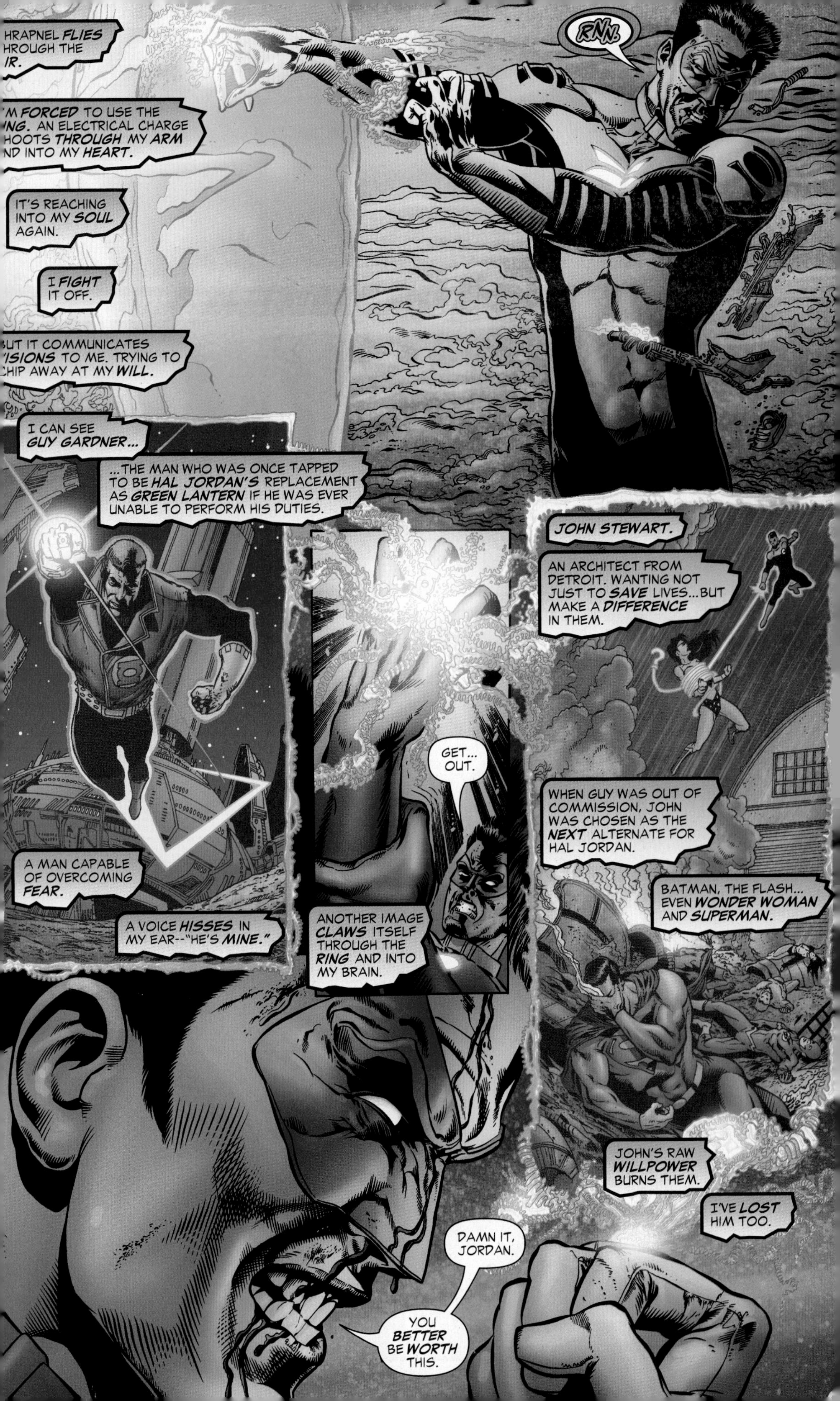

HRAPNEL FLIES
HROUGH THE
IR.
RNN.
'M FORCED TO USE THE
NG. AN ELECTRICAL CHARGE
HOOTS THROUGH MY ARM
ND INTO MY HEART.
IT'S REACHING INTO MY SOUL AGAIN.
I FIGHT IT OFF.
UT IT COMMUNICATES
ISIONS TO ME. TRYING TO
HIP AWAY AT MY WILL.
I CAN SEE GUY GARDNER...
...THE MAN WHO WAS ONCE TAPPED TO BE HAL JORDAN'S REPLACEMENT AS GREEN LANTERN IF HE WAS EVER UNABLE TO PERFORM HIS DUTIES.
A MAN CAPABLE OF OVERCOMING FEAR.
A VOICE HISSES IN MY EAR--"HE'S MINE."
GET... OUT.
ANOTHER IMAGE CLAWS ITSELF THROUGH THE RING AND INTO MY BRAIN.
JOHN STEWART.
AN ARCHITECT FROM DETROIT. WANTING NOT JUST TO SAVE LIVES...BUT MAKE A DIFFERENCE IN THEM.
WHEN GUY WAS OUT OF COMMISSION, JOHN WAS CHOSEN AS THE NEXT ALTERNATE FOR HAL JORDAN.
BATMAN, THE FLASH... EVEN WONDER WOMAN AND SUPERMAN.
JOHN'S RAW WILLPOWER BURNS THEM.
I'VE LOST HIM TOO.
DAMN IT, JORDAN.
YOU BETTER BE WORTH THIS.

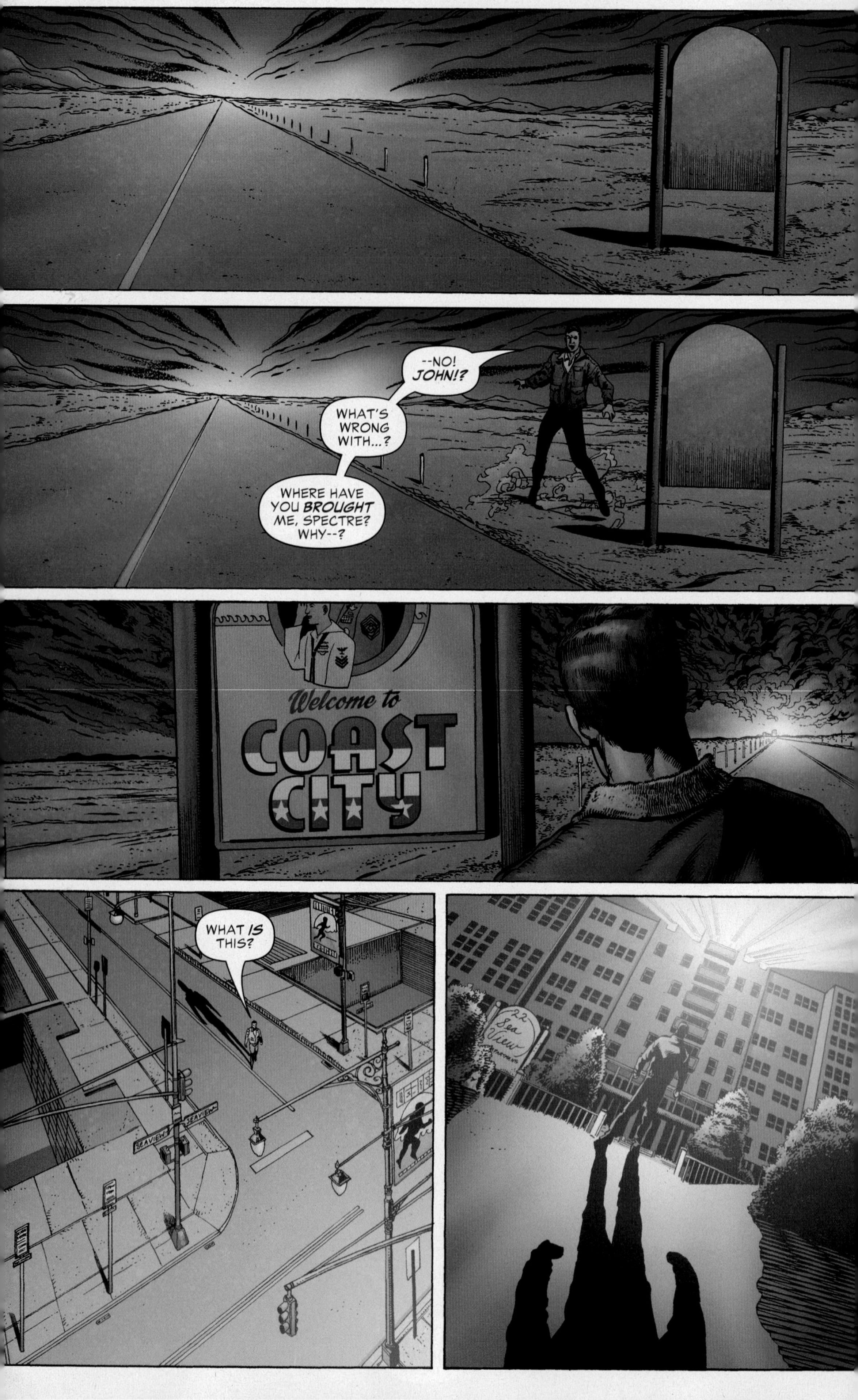

--NO! JOHN!?
WHAT'S WRONG WITH...?
WHERE HAVE YOU BROUGHT ME, SPECTRE? WHY--?
Welcome to
COAST CITY
WHAT IS THIS?
SEAVIEW
SEAVIEW
22 Sea View

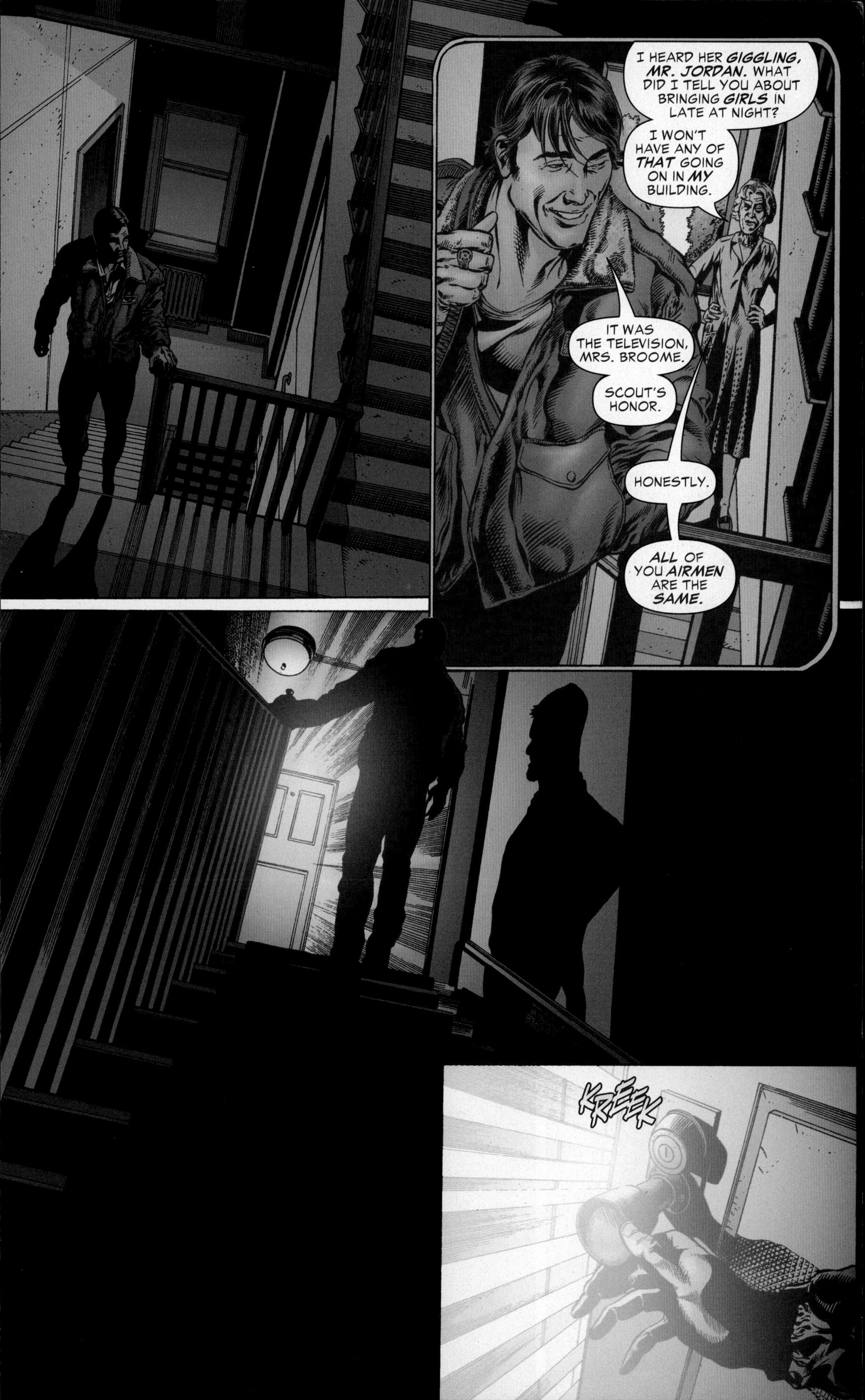
I HEARD HER GIGGLING, MR. JORDAN. WHAT DID I TELL YOU ABOUT BRINGING GIRLS IN LATE AT NIGHT?
I WON'T HAVE ANY OF THAT GOING ON IN MY BUILDING.
IT WAS THE TELEVISION, MRS. BROOME.
SCOUT'S HONOR.
HONESTLY.
ALL OF YOU AIRMEN ARE THE SAME.
KREEK

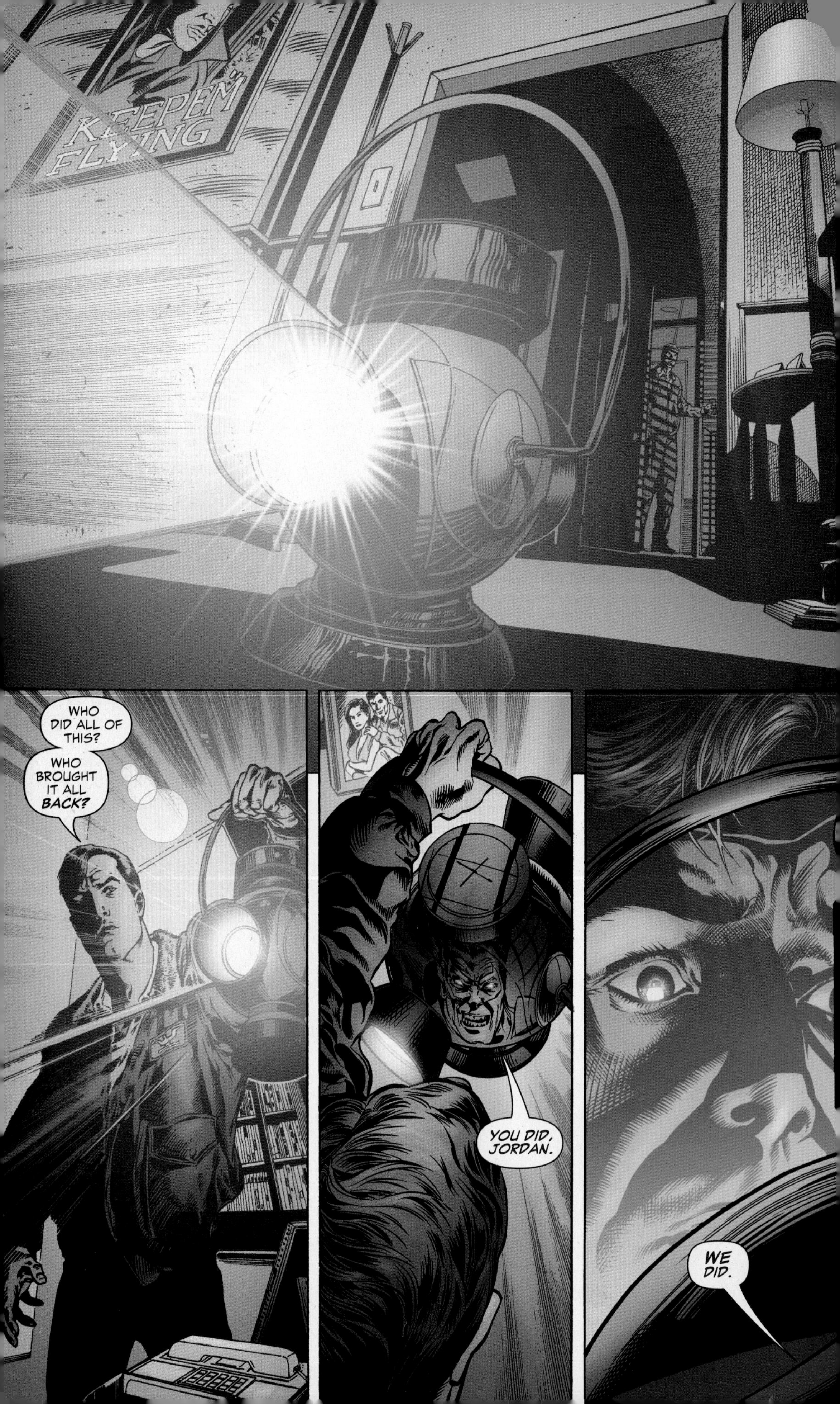
KEEP 'EM FLYING
WHO DID ALL OF THIS?
WHO BROUGHT IT ALL BACK?
YOU DID, JORDAN.
WE DID.

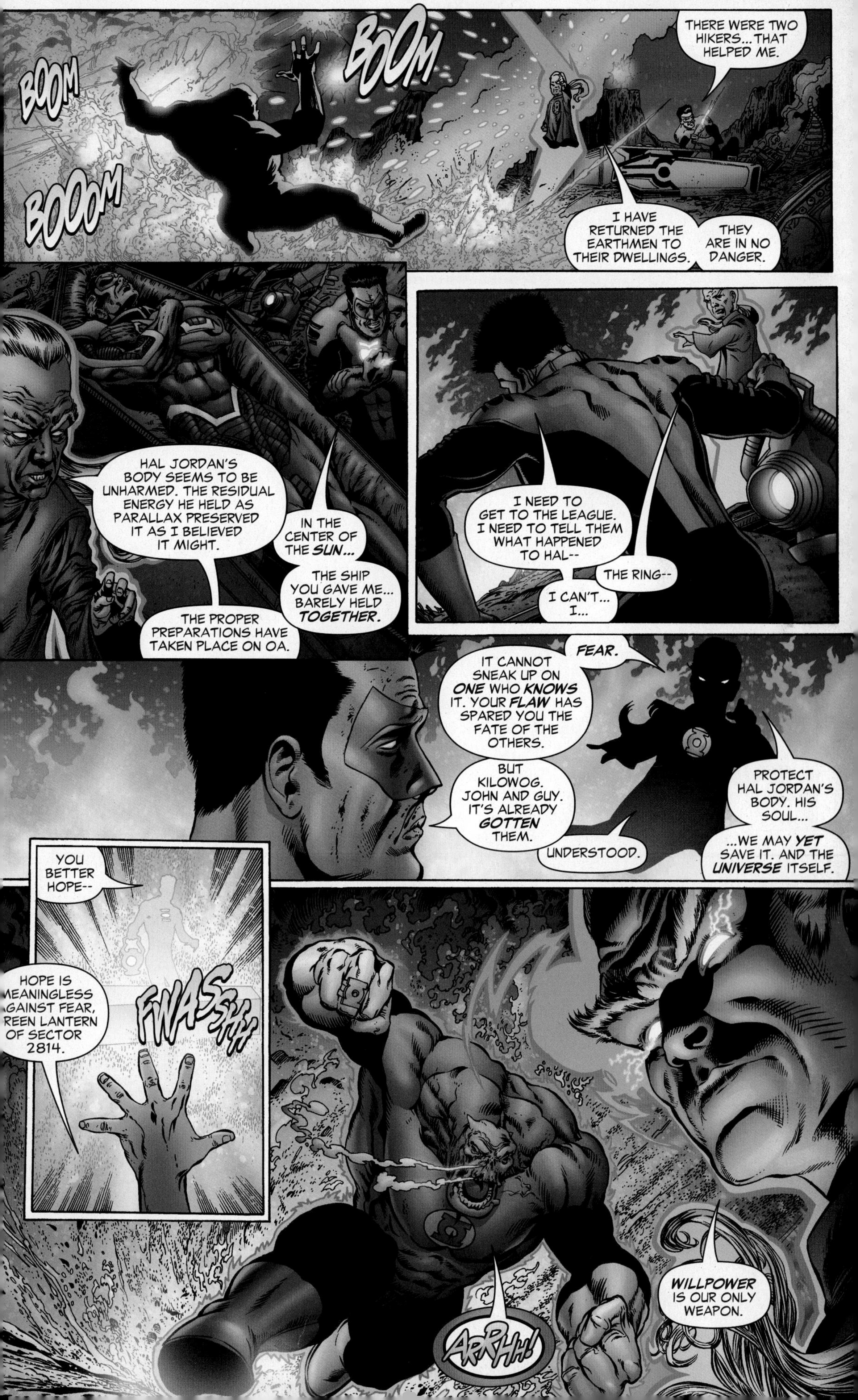
BOOM
BOOOM
BOOM
THERE WERE TWO HIKERS...THAT HELPED ME.
I HAVE RETURNED THE EARTHMEN TO THEIR DWELLINGS.
THEY ARE IN NO DANGER.
HAL JORDAN'S BODY SEEMS TO BE UNHARMED. THE RESIDUAL ENERGY HE HELD AS PARALLAX PRESERVED IT AS I BELIEVED IT MIGHT.
THE PROPER PREPARATIONS HAVE TAKEN PLACE ON OA.
IN THE CENTER OF THE SUN...
THE SHIP YOU GAVE ME... BARELY HELD TOGETHER.
I NEED TO GET TO THE LEAGUE. I NEED TO TELL THEM WHAT HAPPENED TO HAL--
THE RING--
I CAN'T... I...
FEAR.
IT CANNOT SNEAK UP ON ONE WHO KNOWS IT. YOUR FLAW HAS SPARED YOU THE FATE OF THE OTHERS.
BUT KILOWOG. JOHN AND GUY. IT'S ALREADY GOTTEN THEM.
UNDERSTOOD.
PROTECT HAL JORDAN'S BODY. HIS SOUL...
...WE MAY YET SAVE IT. AND THE UNIVERSE ITSELF.
YOU BETTER HOPE--
HOPE IS MEANINGLESS AGAINST FEAR, REEN LANTERN OF SECTOR 2814.
FWASSHH
WILLPOWER IS OUR ONLY WEAPON.
ARRHH!

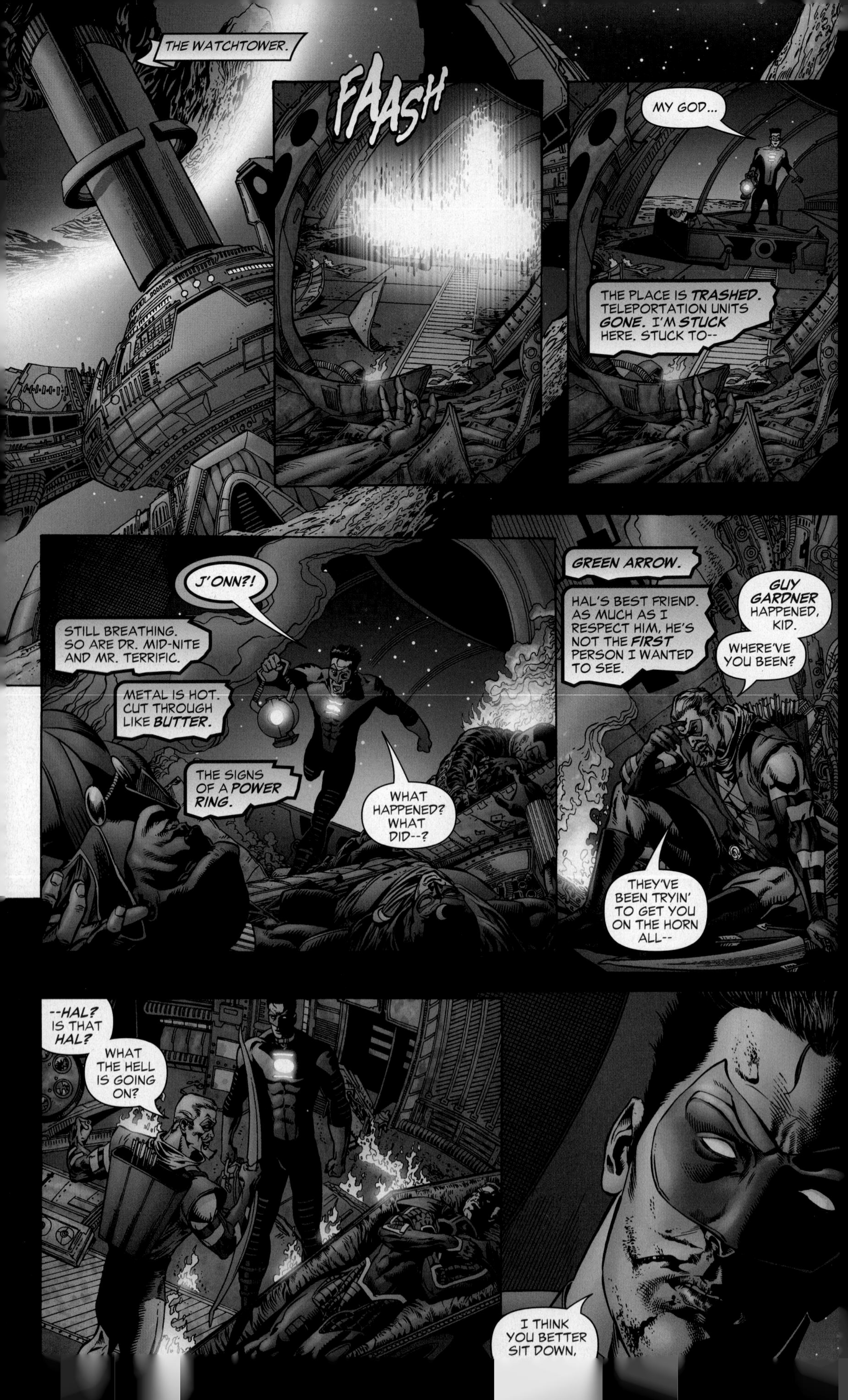
THE WATCHTOWER.
FAASH
MY GOD...
THE PLACE IS TRASHED. TELEPORTATION UNITS GONE. I'M STUCK HERE. STUCK TO--
J'ONN?!
STILL BREATHING. SO ARE DR. MID-NITE AND MR. TERRIFIC.
METAL IS HOT. CUT THROUGH LIKE BUTTER.
THE SIGNS OF A POWER RING.
WHAT HAPPENED? WHAT DID--?
GREEN ARROW.
HAL'S BEST FRIEND. AS MUCH AS I RESPECT HIM, HE'S NOT THE FIRST PERSON I WANTED TO SEE.
GUY GARDNER HAPPENED, KID.
WHERE'VE YOU BEEN?
THEY'VE BEEN TRYIN' TO GET YOU ON THE HORN ALL--
--HAL? IS THAT HAL?
WHAT THE HELL IS GOING ON?
I THINK YOU BETTER SIT DOWN,

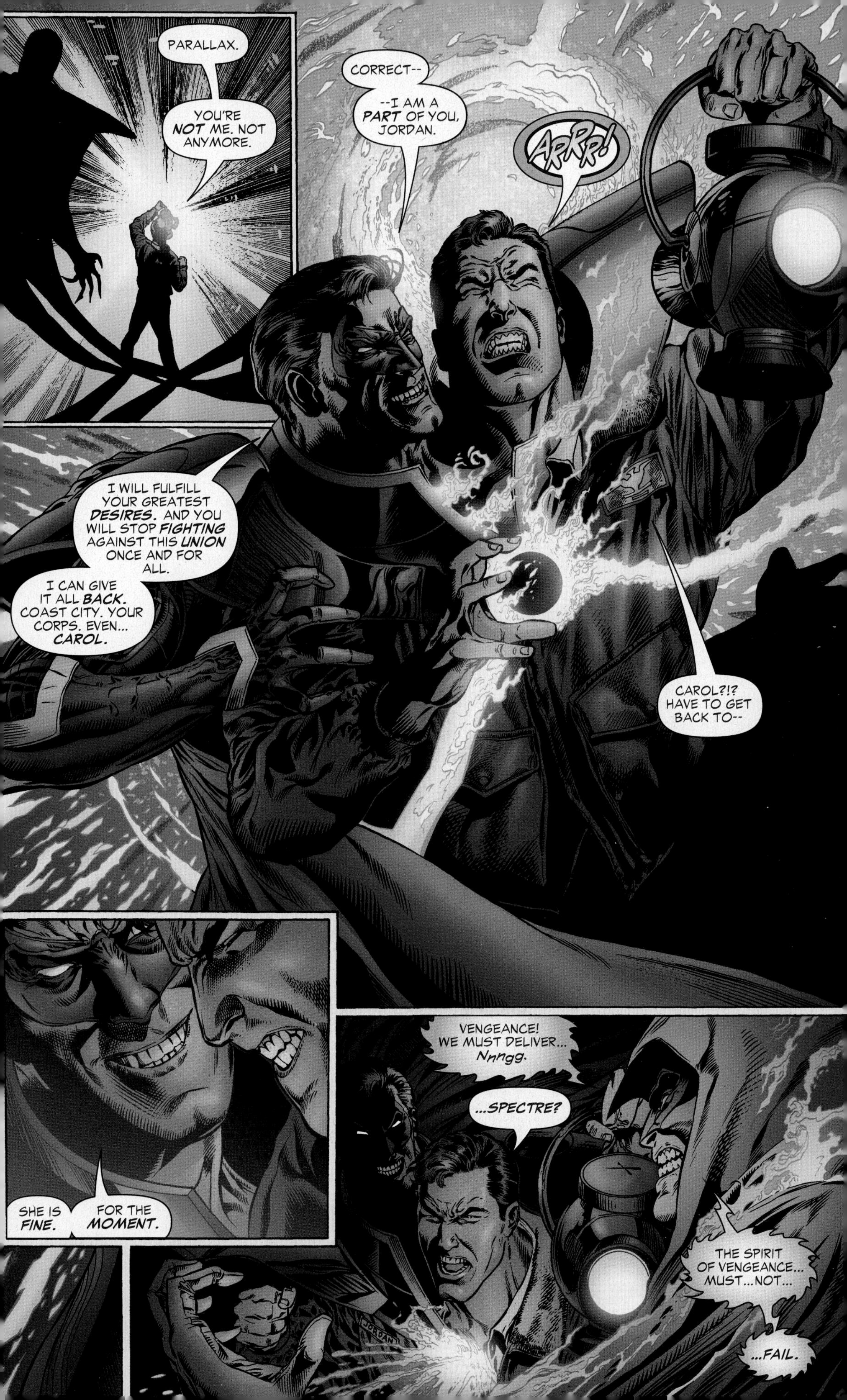
PARALLAX.
YOU'RE NOT ME. NOT ANYMORE.
CORRECT--
--I AM A PART OF YOU, JORDAN.
ARRR!
I WILL FULFILL YOUR GREATEST DESIRES. AND YOU WILL STOP FIGHTING AGAINST THIS UNION ONCE AND FOR ALL.
I CAN GIVE IT ALL BACK. COAST CITY. YOUR CORPS. EVEN... CAROL.
CAROL?!? HAVE TO GET BACK TO--
SHE IS FINE.
FOR THE MOMENT.
VENGEANCE! WE MUST DELIVER... Nnngg.
...SPECTRE?
THE SPIRIT OF VENGEANCE... MUST...NOT...
...FAIL.

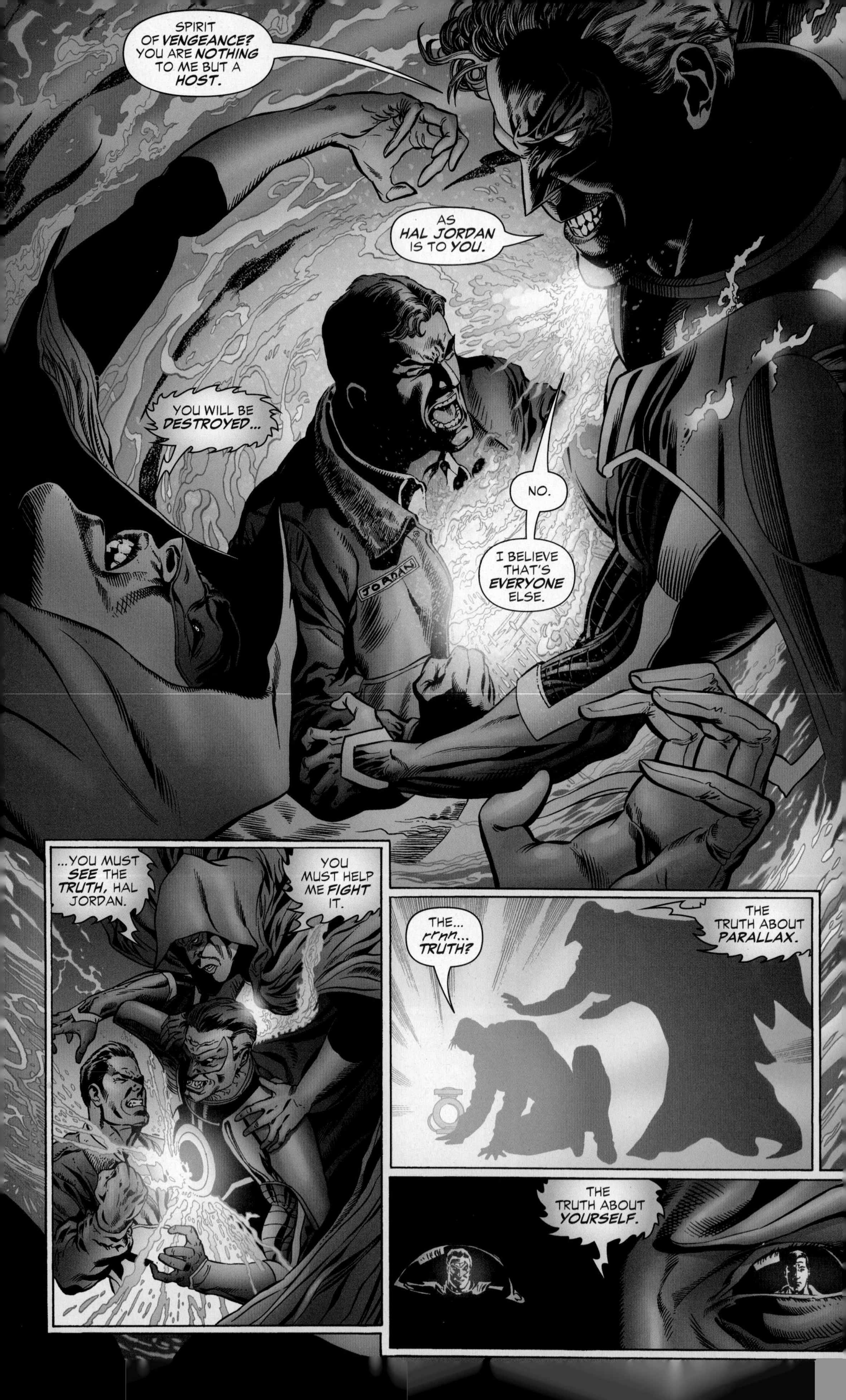
SPIRIT OF VENGEANCE? YOU ARE NOTHING TO ME BUT A HOST.
AS HAL JORDAN IS TO YOU.
YOU WILL BE DESTROYED...
NO.
I BELIEVE THAT'S EVERYONE ELSE.
JORDAN
...YOU MUST SEE THE TRUTH, HAL JORDAN.
YOU MUST HELP ME FIGHT IT.
THE... rrnn... TRUTH?
THE TRUTH ABOUT PARALLAX.
THE TRUTH ABOUT YOURSELF.

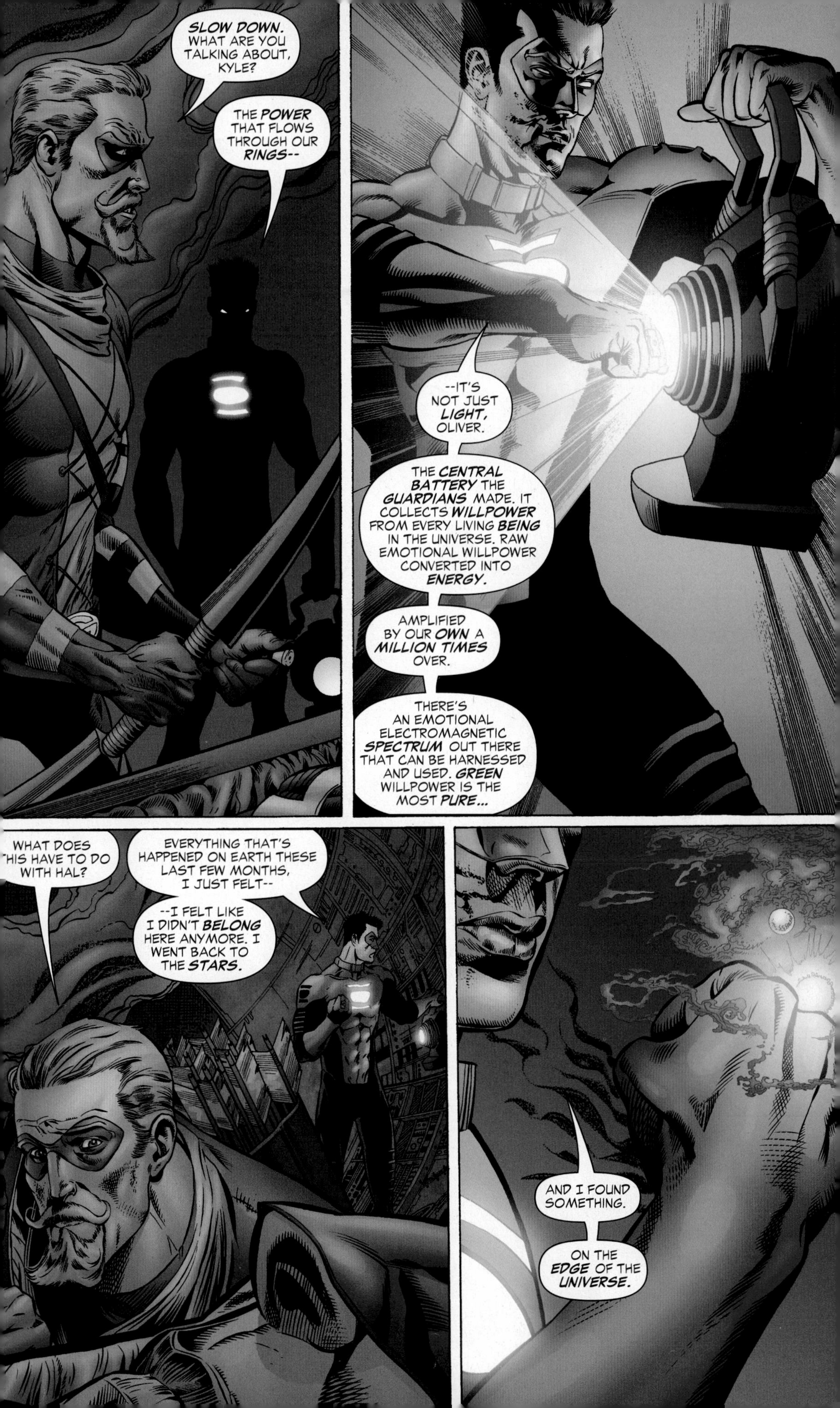
SLOW DOWN. WHAT ARE YOU TALKING ABOUT, KYLE?
THE POWER THAT FLOWS THROUGH OUR RINGS--
--IT'S NOT JUST LIGHT, OLIVER.
THE CENTRAL BATTERY THE GUARDIANS MADE. IT COLLECTS WILLPOWER FROM EVERY LIVING BEING IN THE UNIVERSE. RAW EMOTIONAL WILLPOWER CONVERTED INTO ENERGY.
AMPLIFIED BY OUR OWN A MILLION TIMES OVER.
THERE'S AN EMOTIONAL ELECTROMAGNETIC SPECTRUM OUT THERE THAT CAN BE HARNESSED AND USED. GREEN WILLPOWER IS THE MOST PURE...
WHAT DOES THIS HAVE TO DO WITH HAL?
EVERYTHING THAT'S HAPPENED ON EARTH THESE LAST FEW MONTHS, I JUST FELT--
--I FELT LIKE I DIDN'T BELONG HERE ANYMORE. I WENT BACK TO THE STARS.
AND I FOUND SOMETHING.
ON THE EDGE OF THE UNIVERSE.

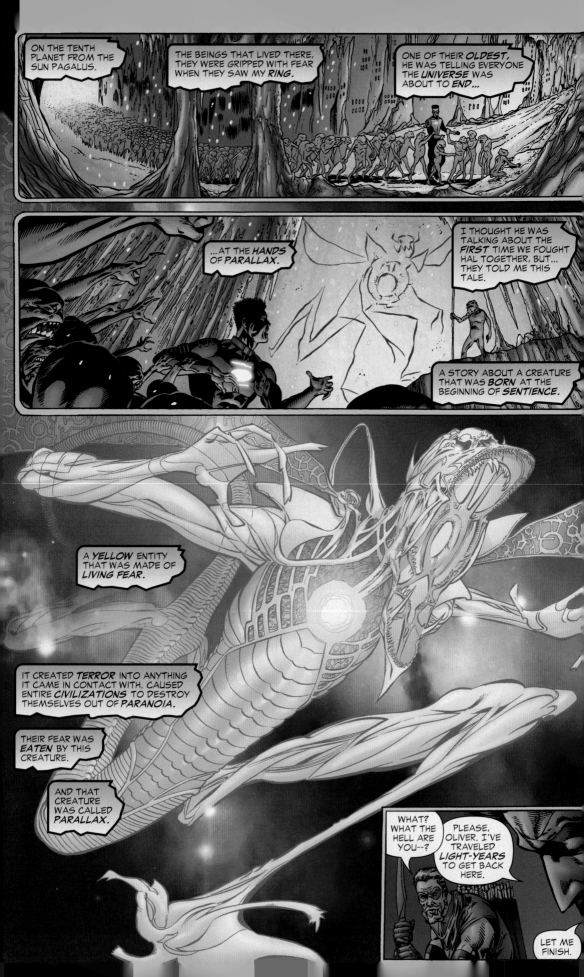

ON THE TENTH PLANET FROM THE SUN PAGALUS.

THE BEINGS THAT LIVED THERE, THEY WERE GRIPPED WITH FEAR WHEN THEY SAW MY *RING*.

ONE OF THEIR *OLDEST*, HE WAS TELLING EVERYONE THE *UNIVERSE* WAS ABOUT TO *END*...

...AT THE *HANDS* OF *PARALLAX*.

I THOUGHT HE WAS TALKING ABOUT THE *FIRST* TIME WE FOUGHT HAL TOGETHER, BUT... THEY TOLD ME THIS TALE.

A STORY ABOUT A CREATURE THAT WAS *BORN* AT THE BEGINNING OF *SENTIENCE*.

A *YELLOW* ENTITY THAT WAS MADE OF *LIVING FEAR*.

IT CREATED *TERROR* INTO ANYTHING IT CAME IN CONTACT WITH. CAUSED ENTIRE *CIVILIZATIONS* TO DESTROY THEMSELVES OUT OF *PARANOIA*.

THEIR FEAR WAS *EATEN* BY THIS CREATURE.

AND THAT CREATURE WAS CALLED *PARALLAX*.

WHAT? WHAT THE HELL ARE YOU--?

PLEASE, OLIVER. I'VE TRAVELED *LIGHT-YEARS* TO GET BACK HERE.

LET ME FINISH.

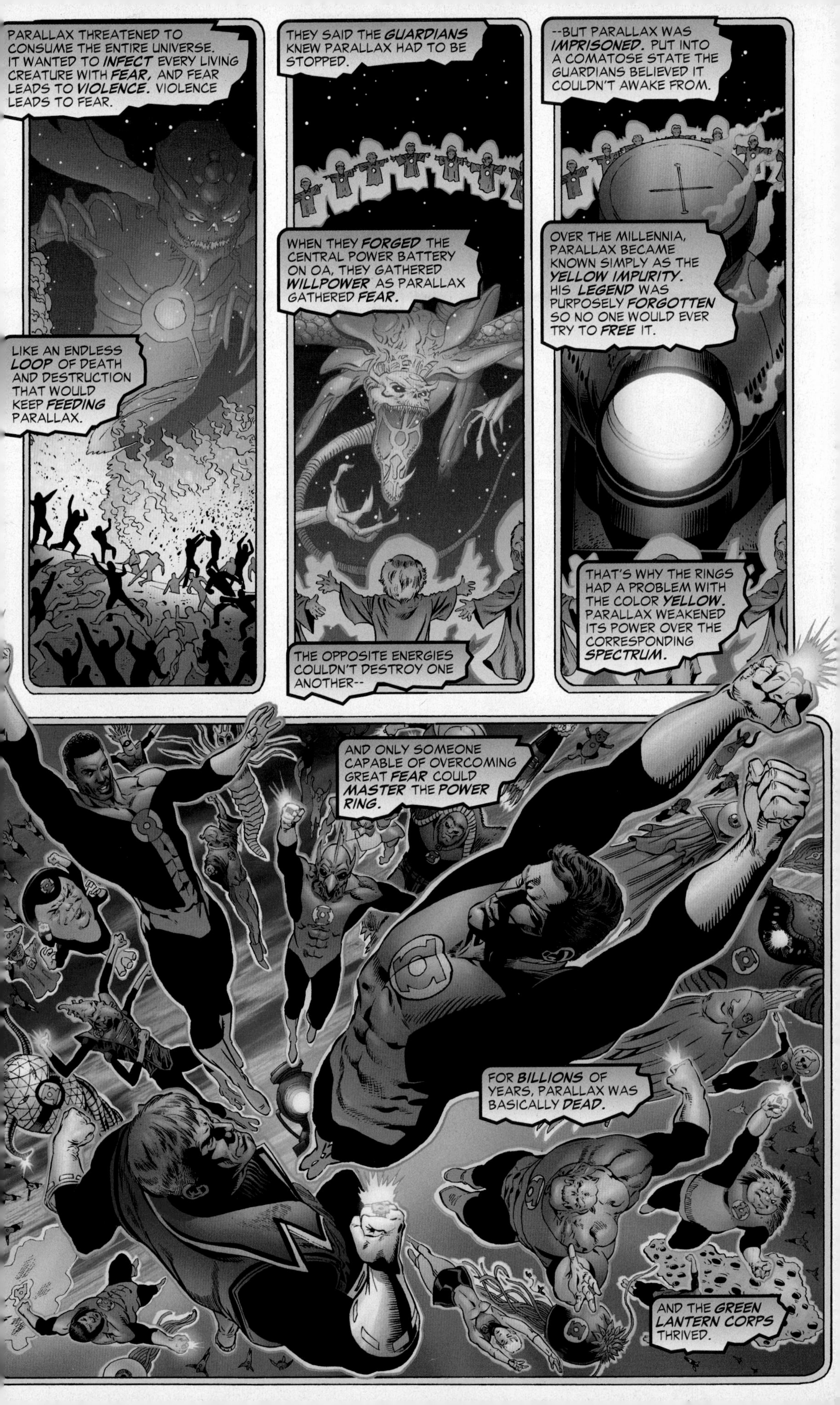
PARALLAX THREATENED TO CONSUME THE ENTIRE UNIVERSE. IT WANTED TO INFECT EVERY LIVING CREATURE WITH FEAR, AND FEAR LEADS TO VIOLENCE. VIOLENCE LEADS TO FEAR.
LIKE AN ENDLESS LOOP OF DEATH AND DESTRUCTION THAT WOULD KEEP FEEDING PARALLAX.
THEY SAID THE GUARDIANS KNEW PARALLAX HAD TO BE STOPPED.
WHEN THEY FORGED THE CENTRAL POWER BATTERY ON OA, THEY GATHERED WILLPOWER AS PARALLAX GATHERED FEAR.
THE OPPOSITE ENERGIES COULDN'T DESTROY ONE ANOTHER--
--BUT PARALLAX WAS IMPRISONED. PUT INTO A COMATOSE STATE THE GUARDIANS BELIEVED IT COULDN'T AWAKE FROM.
OVER THE MILLENNIA, PARALLAX BECAME KNOWN SIMPLY AS THE YELLOW IMPURITY. HIS LEGEND WAS PURPOSELY FORGOTTEN SO NO ONE WOULD EVER TRY TO FREE IT.
THAT'S WHY THE RINGS HAD A PROBLEM WITH THE COLOR YELLOW. PARALLAX WEAKENED ITS POWER OVER THE CORRESPONDING SPECTRUM.
AND ONLY SOMEONE CAPABLE OF OVERCOMING GREAT FEAR COULD MASTER THE POWER RING.
FOR BILLIONS OF YEARS, PARALLAX WAS BASICALLY DEAD.
AND THE GREEN LANTERN CORPS THRIVED.

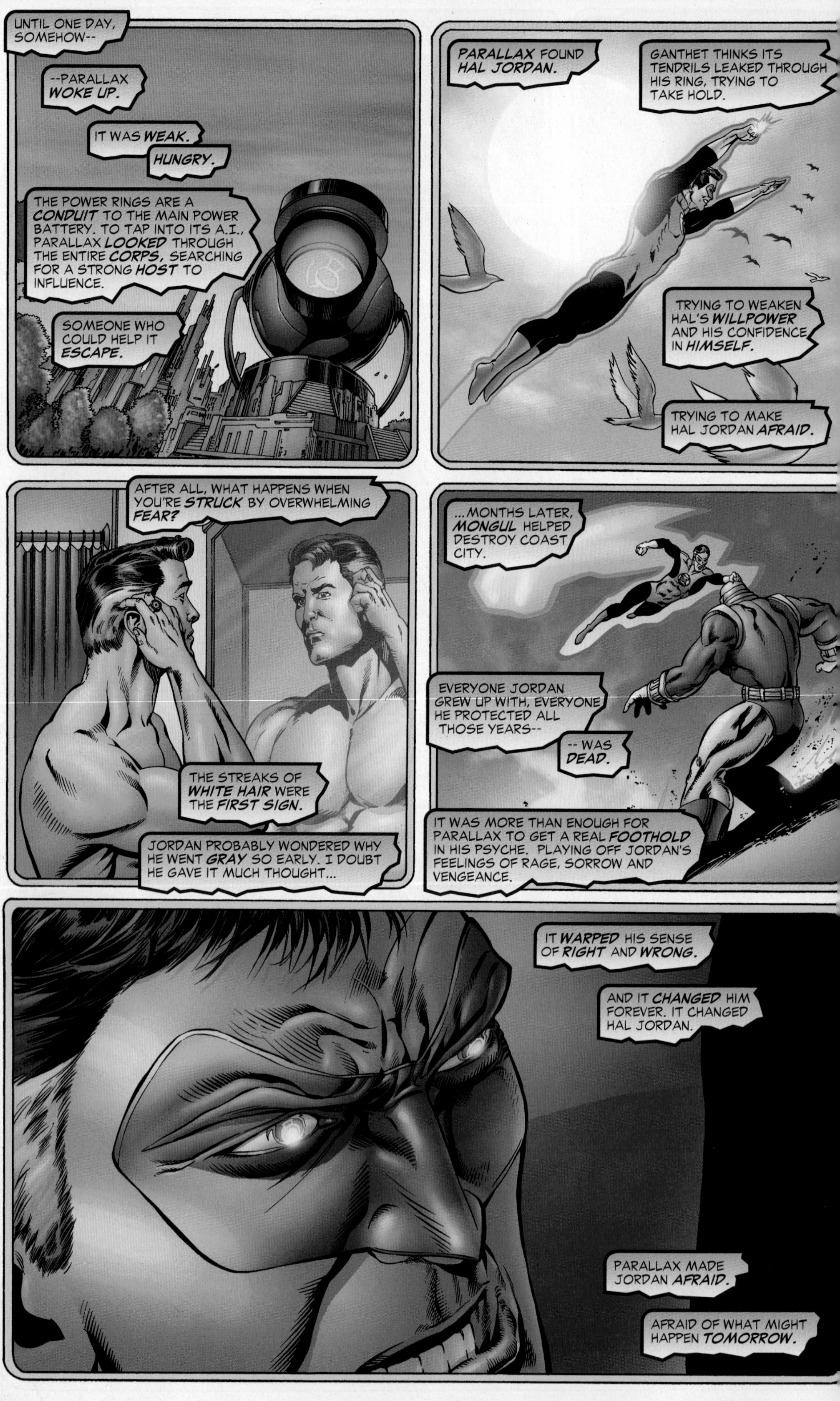
UNTIL ONE DAY, SOMEHOW--
--PARALLAX WOKE UP.
IT WAS WEAK.
HUNGRY.
THE POWER RINGS ARE A CONDUIT TO THE MAIN POWER BATTERY. TO TAP INTO ITS A.I., PARALLAX LOOKED THROUGH THE ENTIRE CORPS, SEARCHING FOR A STRONG HOST TO INFLUENCE.
SOMEONE WHO COULD HELP IT ESCAPE.
PARALLAX FOUND HAL JORDAN.
GANTHET THINKS ITS TENDRILS LEAKED THROUGH HIS RING, TRYING TO TAKE HOLD.
TRYING TO WEAKEN HAL'S WILLPOWER AND HIS CONFIDENCE IN HIMSELF.
TRYING TO MAKE HAL JORDAN AFRAID.
AFTER ALL, WHAT HAPPENS WHEN YOU'RE STRUCK BY OVERWHELMING FEAR?
THE STREAKS OF WHITE HAIR WERE THE FIRST SIGN.
JORDAN PROBABLY WONDERED WHY HE WENT GRAY SO EARLY. I DOUBT HE GAVE IT MUCH THOUGHT...
...MONTHS LATER, MONGUL HELPED DESTROY COAST CITY.
EVERYONE JORDAN GREW UP WITH, EVERYONE HE PROTECTED ALL THOSE YEARS--
-- WAS DEAD.
IT WAS MORE THAN ENOUGH FOR PARALLAX TO GET A REAL FOOTHOLD IN HIS PSYCHE. PLAYING OFF JORDAN'S FEELINGS OF RAGE, SORROW AND VENGEANCE.
IT WARPED HIS SENSE OF RIGHT AND WRONG.
AND IT CHANGED HIM FOREVER. IT CHANGED HAL JORDAN.
PARALLAX MADE JORDAN AFRAID.
AFRAID OF WHAT MIGHT HAPPEN TOMORROW.

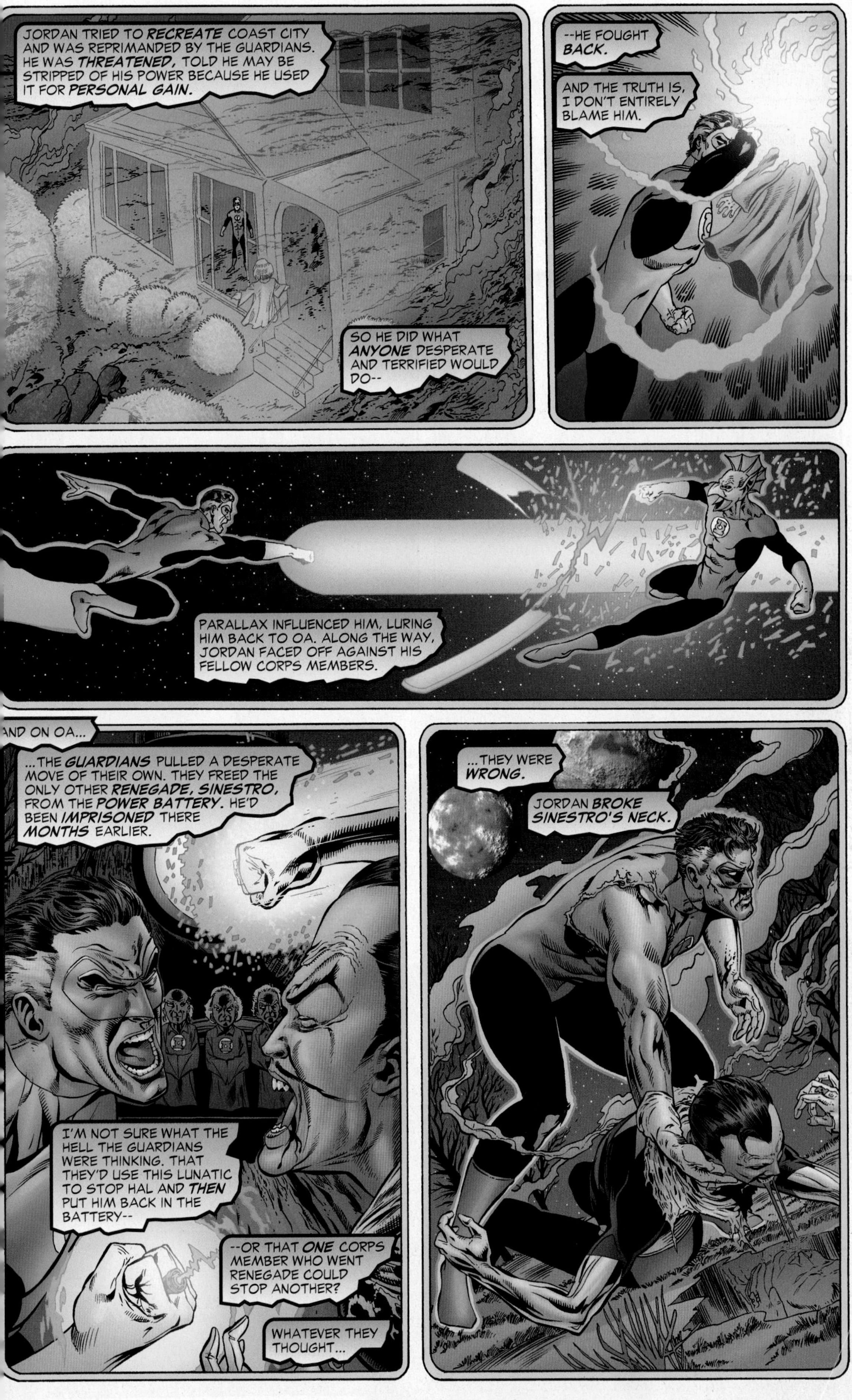

JORDAN TRIED TO RECREATE COAST CITY AND WAS REPRIMANDED BY THE GUARDIANS. HE WAS THREATENED, TOLD HE MAY BE STRIPPED OF HIS POWER BECAUSE HE USED IT FOR PERSONAL GAIN.
SO HE DID WHAT ANYONE DESPERATE AND TERRIFIED WOULD DO--
--HE FOUGHT BACK.
AND THE TRUTH IS, I DON'T ENTIRELY BLAME HIM.
PARALLAX INFLUENCED HIM, LURING HIM BACK TO OA. ALONG THE WAY, JORDAN FACED OFF AGAINST HIS FELLOW CORPS MEMBERS.
AND ON OA...
...THE GUARDIANS PULLED A DESPERATE MOVE OF THEIR OWN. THEY FREED THE ONLY OTHER RENEGADE, SINESTRO, FROM THE POWER BATTERY. HE'D BEEN IMPRISONED THERE MONTHS EARLIER.
I'M NOT SURE WHAT THE HELL THE GUARDIANS WERE THINKING. THAT THEY'D USE THIS LUNATIC TO STOP HAL AND THEN PUT HIM BACK IN THE BATTERY--
--OR THAT ONE CORPS MEMBER WHO WENT RENEGADE COULD STOP ANOTHER?
WHATEVER THEY THOUGHT...
...THEY WERE WRONG.
JORDAN BROKE SINESTRO'S NECK.

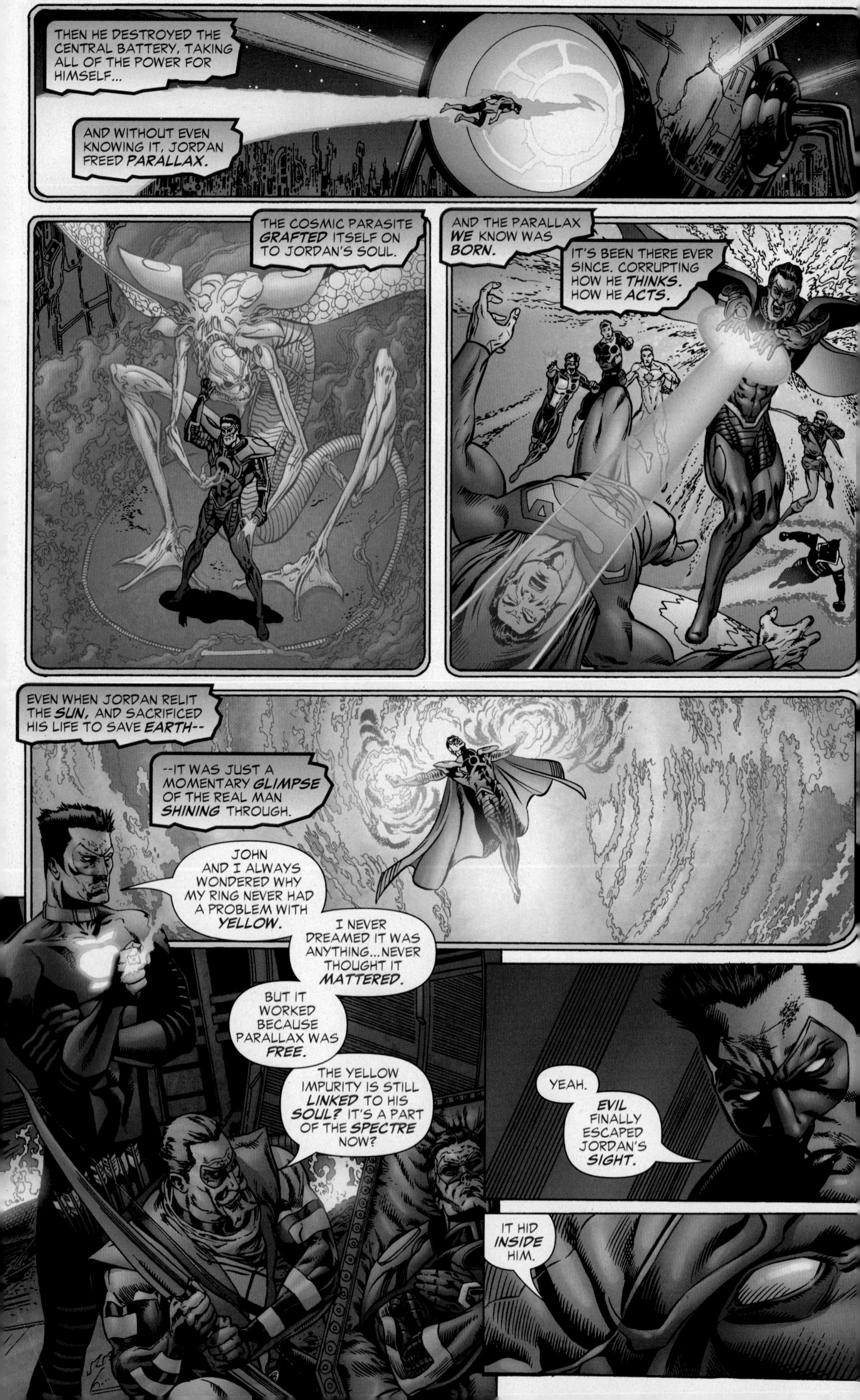
THEN HE DESTROYED THE CENTRAL BATTERY, TAKING ALL OF THE POWER FOR HIMSELF...
AND WITHOUT EVEN KNOWING IT, JORDAN FREED PARALLAX.
THE COSMIC PARASITE GRAFTED ITSELF ON TO JORDAN'S SOUL.
AND THE PARALLAX WE KNOW WAS BORN.
IT'S BEEN THERE EVER SINCE. CORRUPTING HOW HE THINKS. HOW HE ACTS.
EVEN WHEN JORDAN RELIT THE SUN, AND SACRIFICED HIS LIFE TO SAVE EARTH--
--IT WAS JUST A MOMENTARY GLIMPSE OF THE REAL MAN SHINING THROUGH.
JOHN AND I ALWAYS WONDERED WHY MY RING NEVER HAD A PROBLEM WITH YELLOW.
I NEVER DREAMED IT WAS ANYTHING...NEVER THOUGHT IT MATTERED.
BUT IT WORKED BECAUSE PARALLAX WAS FREE.
THE YELLOW IMPURITY IS STILL LINKED TO HIS SOUL? IT'S A PART OF THE SPECTRE NOW?
YEAH.
EVIL FINALLY ESCAPED JORDAN'S SIGHT.
IT HID INSIDE HIM.

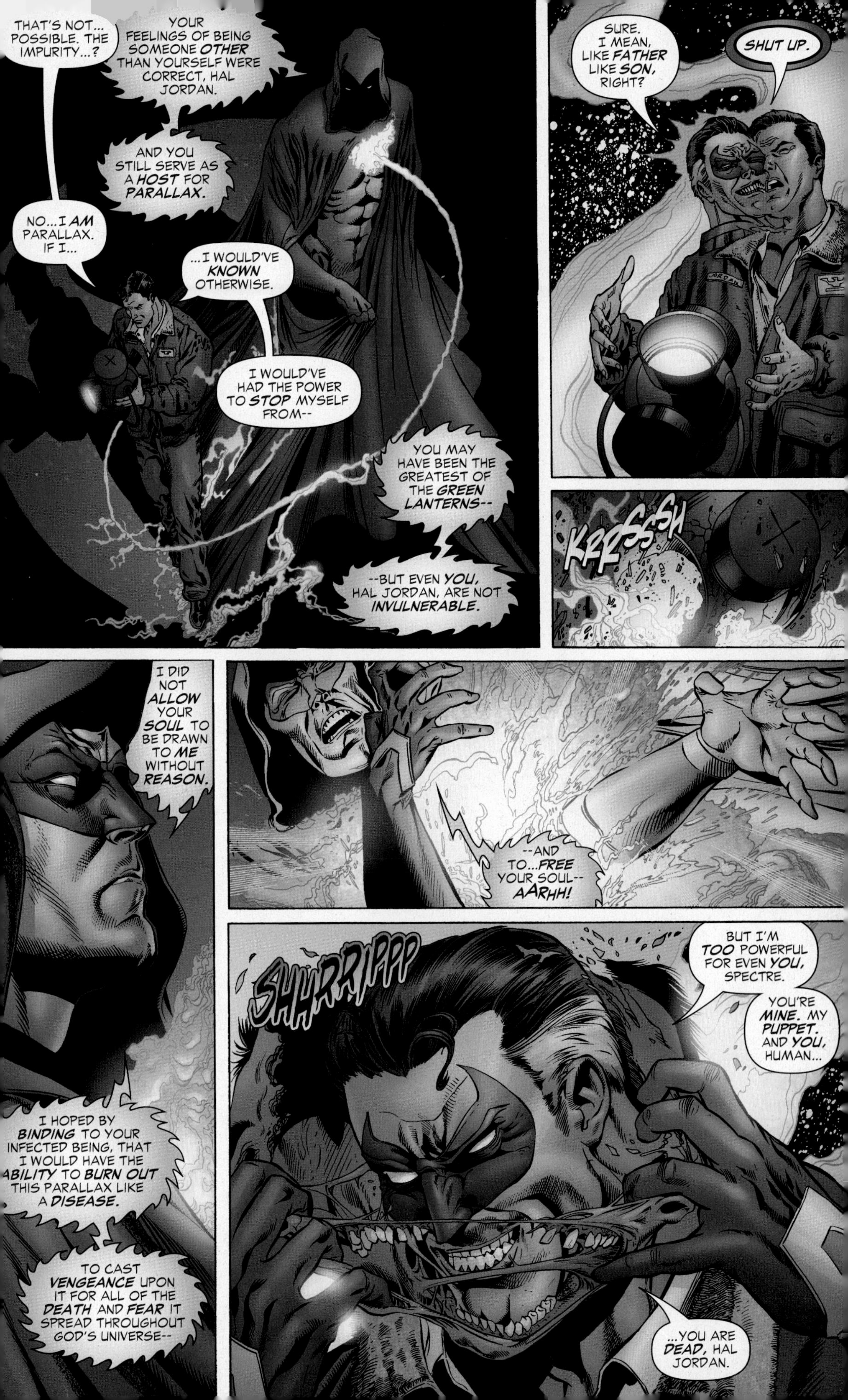
THAT'S NOT... POSSIBLE. THE IMPURITY...?
YOUR FEELINGS OF BEING SOMEONE OTHER THAN YOURSELF WERE CORRECT, HAL JORDAN.
AND YOU STILL SERVE AS A HOST FOR PARALLAX.
NO...I AM PARALLAX. IF I...
...I WOULD'VE KNOWN OTHERWISE.
I WOULD'VE HAD THE POWER TO STOP MYSELF FROM--
YOU MAY HAVE BEEN THE GREATEST OF THE GREEN LANTERNS--
--BUT EVEN YOU, HAL JORDAN, ARE NOT INVULNERABLE.
SURE. I MEAN, LIKE FATHER LIKE SON, RIGHT?
SHUT UP.
KRRSSSH
I DID NOT ALLOW YOUR SOUL TO BE DRAWN TO ME WITHOUT REASON.
I HOPED BY BINDING TO YOUR INFECTED BEING, THAT I WOULD HAVE THE ABILITY TO BURN OUT THIS PARALLAX LIKE A DISEASE.
TO CAST VENGEANCE UPON IT FOR ALL OF THE DEATH AND FEAR IT SPREAD THROUGHOUT GOD'S UNIVERSE--
--AND TO...FREE YOUR SOUL--AARHH!
SHHRRIPPP
BUT I'M TOO POWERFUL FOR EVEN YOU, SPECTRE.
YOU'RE MINE. MY PUPPET. AND YOU, HUMAN...
...YOU ARE DEAD, HAL JORDAN.

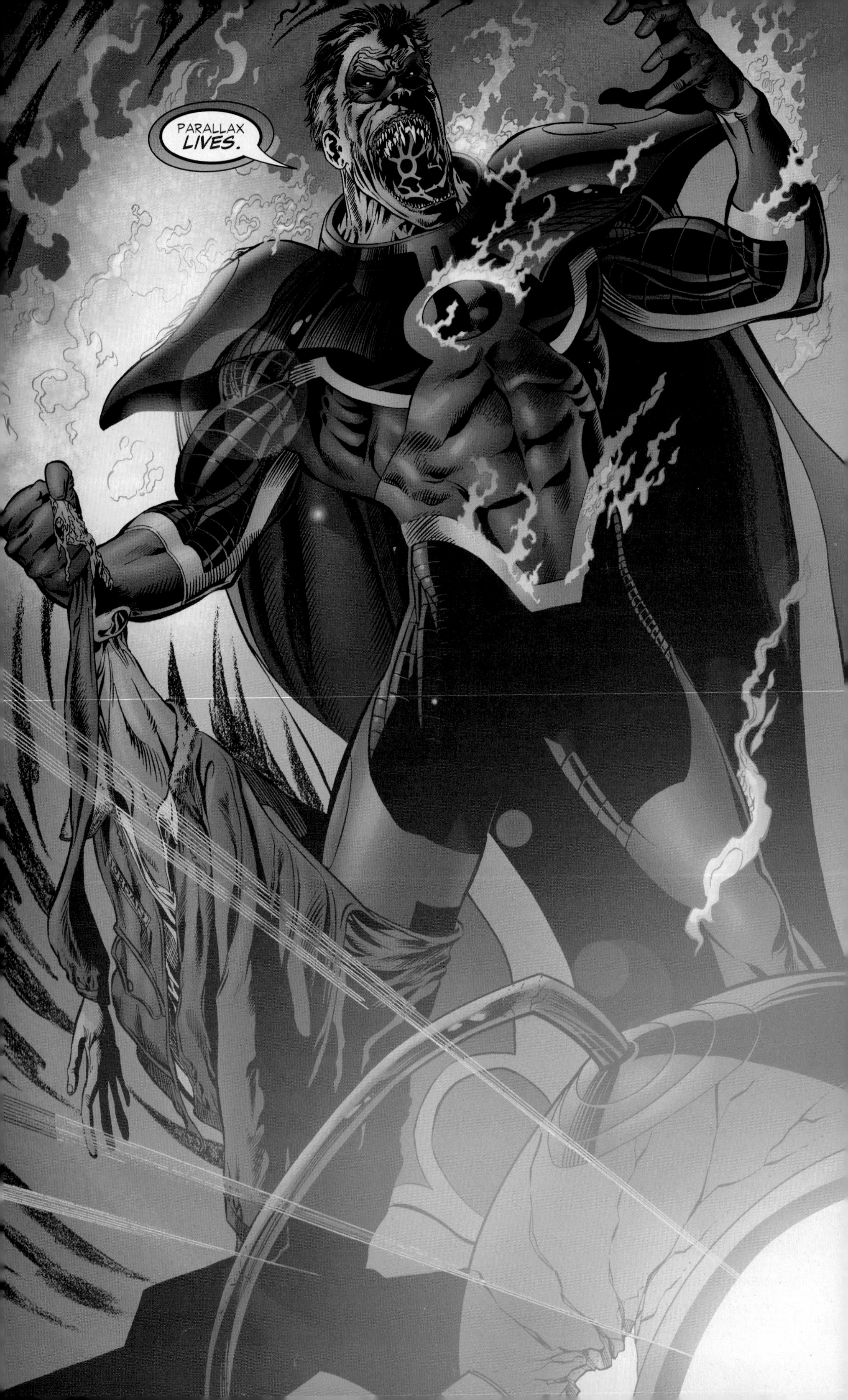
PARALLAX LIVES.

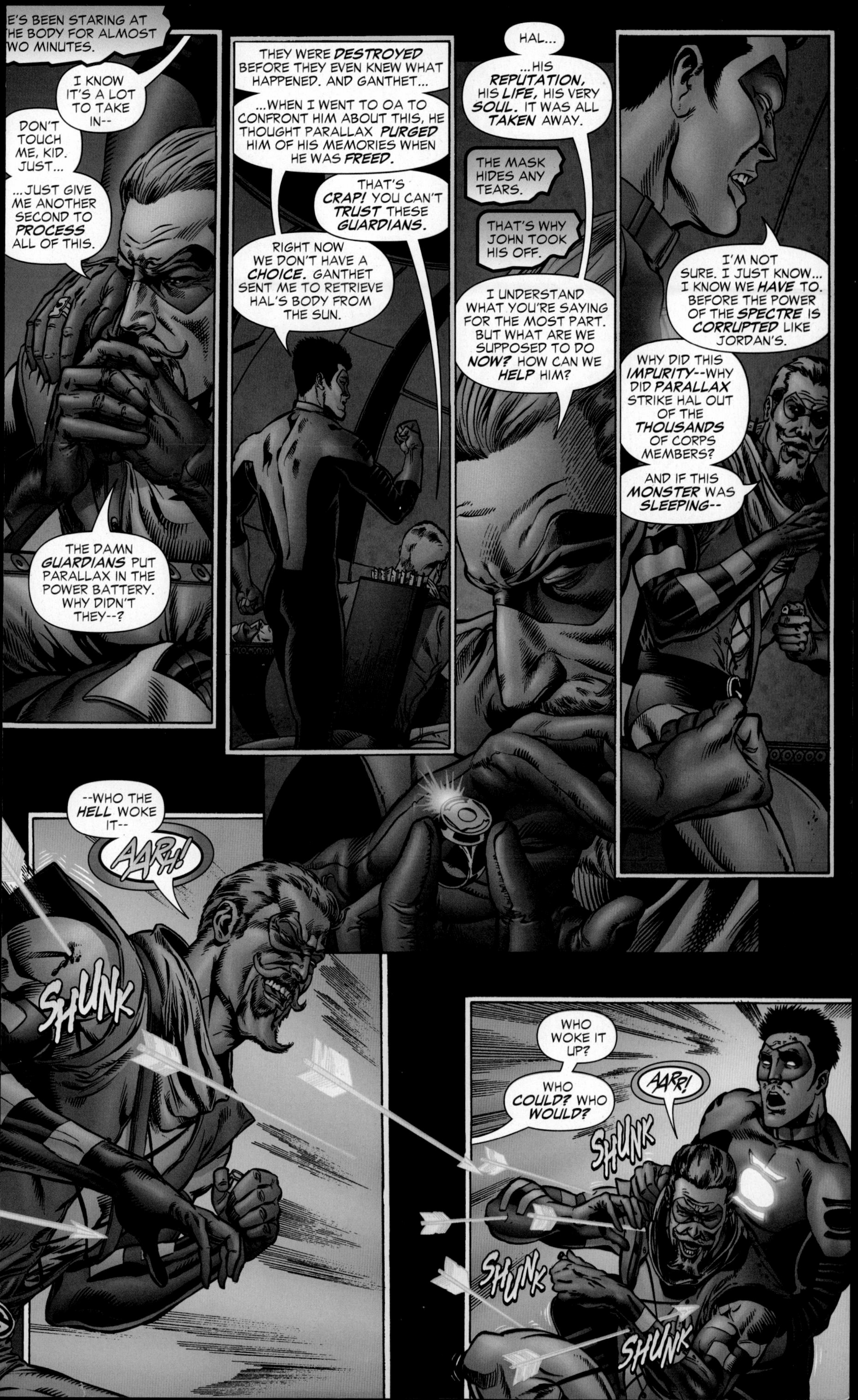

E'S BEEN STARING AT HE BODY FOR ALMOST WO MINUTES.
I KNOW IT'S A LOT TO TAKE IN--
DON'T TOUCH ME, KID. JUST...
...JUST GIVE ME ANOTHER SECOND TO PROCESS ALL OF THIS.
THE DAMN GUARDIANS PUT PARALLAX IN THE POWER BATTERY. WHY DIDN'T THEY--?
THEY WERE DESTROYED BEFORE THEY EVEN KNEW WHAT HAPPENED. AND GANTHET...
...WHEN I WENT TO OA TO CONFRONT HIM ABOUT THIS, HE THOUGHT PARALLAX PURGED HIM OF HIS MEMORIES WHEN HE WAS FREED.
THAT'S CRAP! YOU CAN'T TRUST THESE GUARDIANS.
RIGHT NOW WE DON'T HAVE A CHOICE. GANTHET SENT ME TO RETRIEVE HAL'S BODY FROM THE SUN.
HAL...
...HIS REPUTATION, HIS LIFE, HIS VERY SOUL. IT WAS ALL TAKEN AWAY.
THE MASK HIDES ANY TEARS.
THAT'S WHY JOHN TOOK HIS OFF.
I UNDERSTAND WHAT YOU'RE SAYING FOR THE MOST PART. BUT WHAT ARE WE SUPPOSED TO DO NOW? HOW CAN WE HELP HIM?
I'M NOT SURE. I JUST KNOW... I KNOW WE HAVE TO. BEFORE THE POWER OF THE SPECTRE IS CORRUPTED LIKE JORDAN'S.
WHY DID THIS IMPURITY--WHY DID PARALLAX STRIKE HAL OUT OF THE THOUSANDS OF CORPS MEMBERS?
AND IF THIS MONSTER WAS SLEEPING--
--WHO THE HELL WOKE IT--
AARH!
SHUNK
WHO WOKE IT UP?
WHO COULD? WHO WOULD?
AARR!
SHUNK
SHUNK
SHUNK

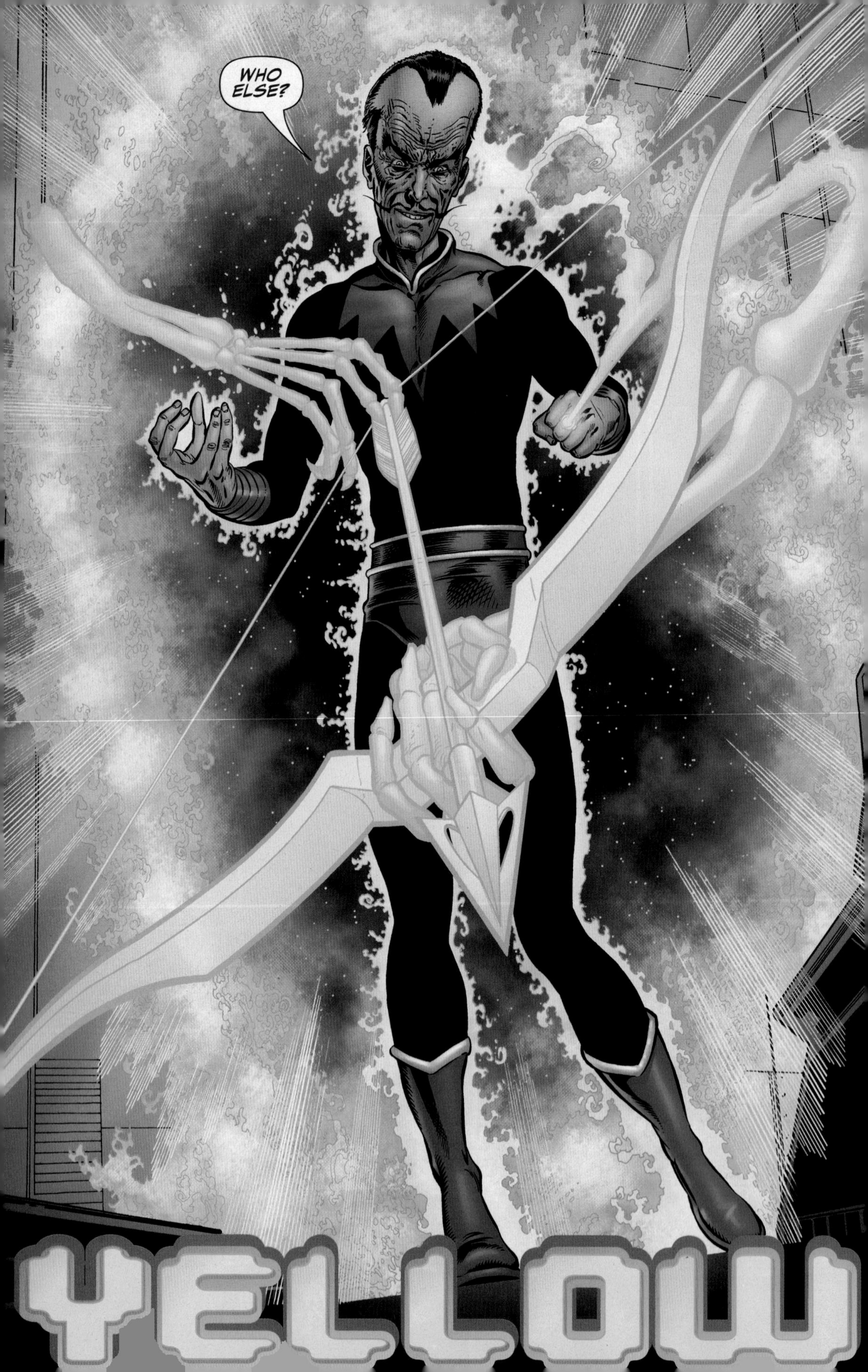
WHO ELSE?
YELLOW

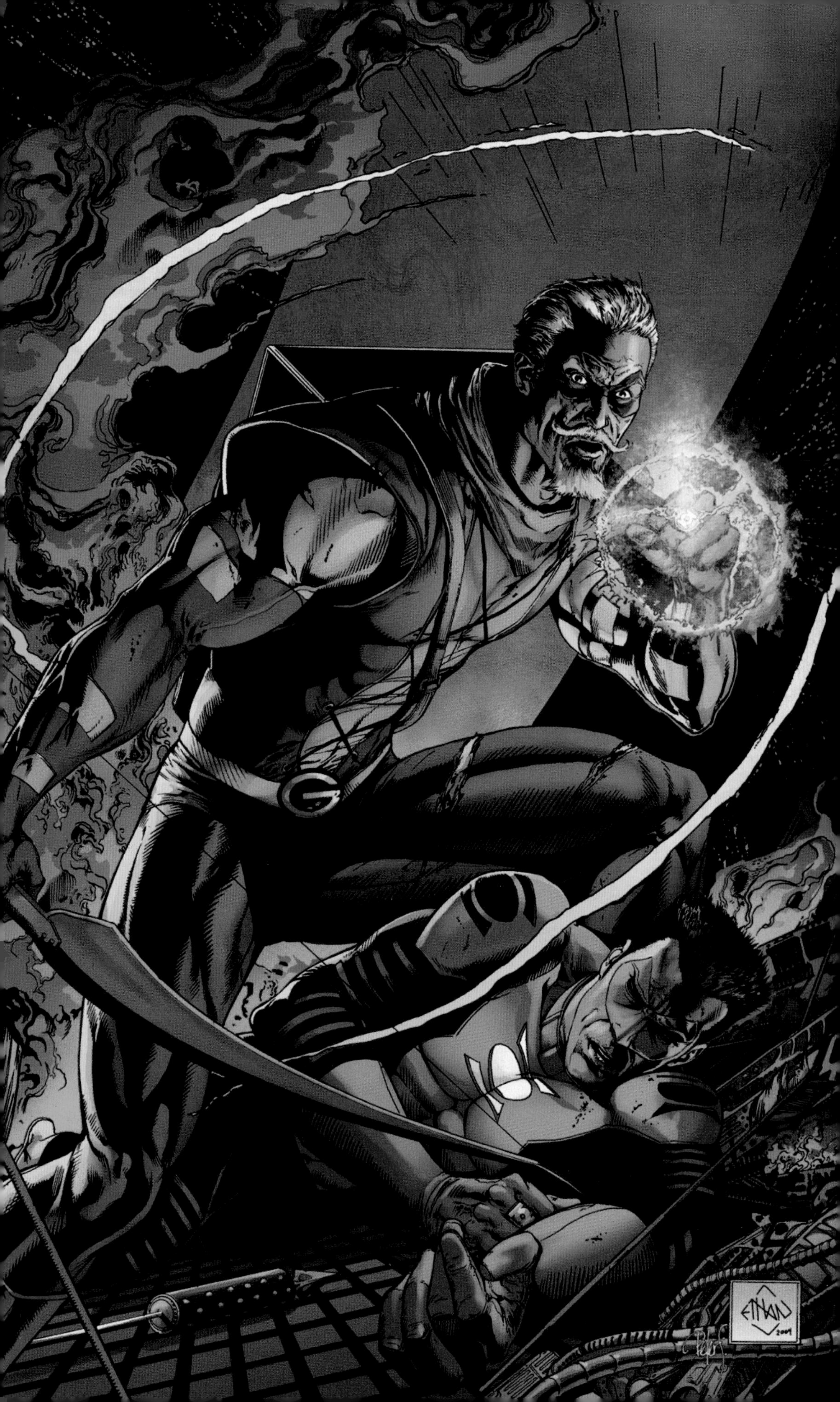

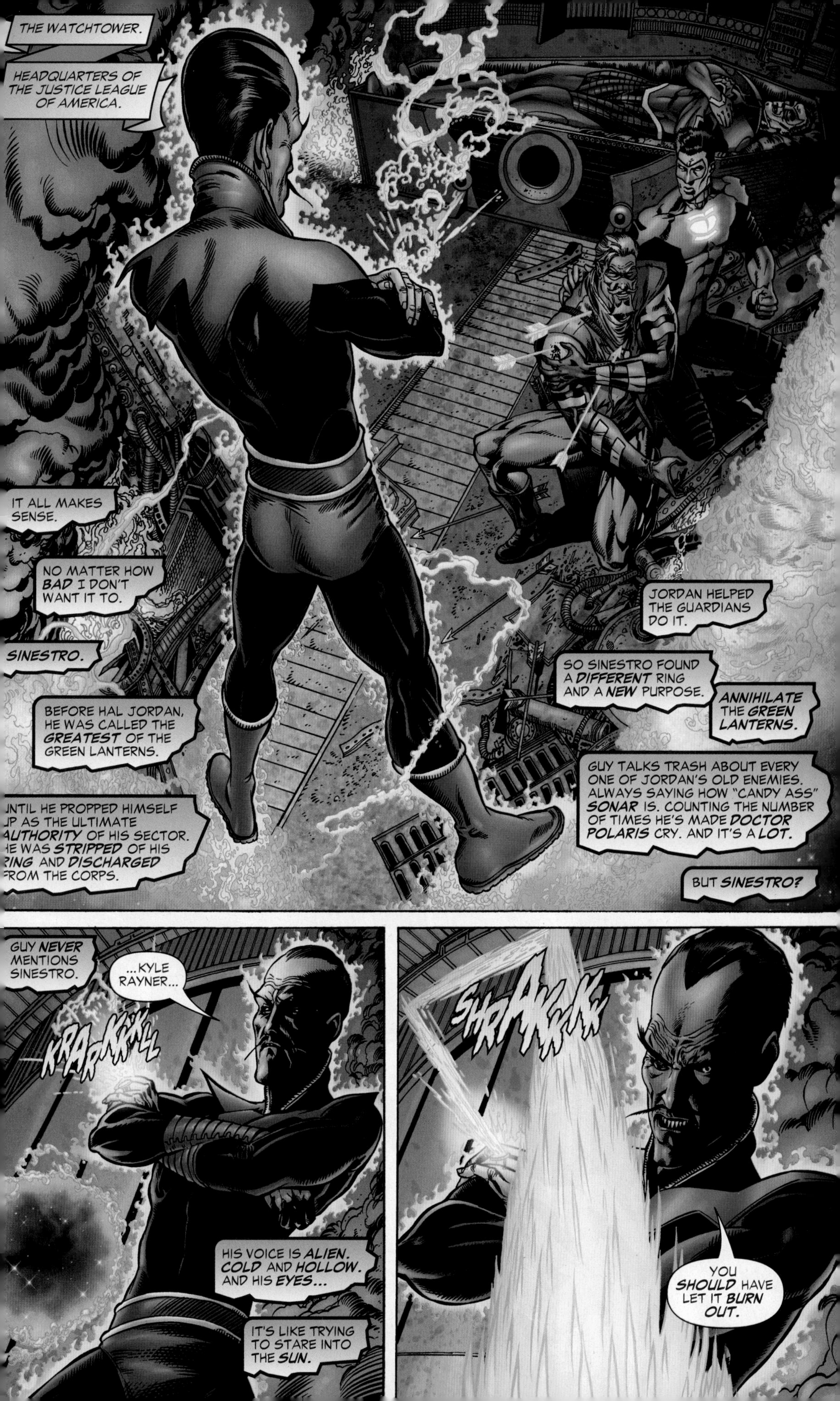
THE WATCHTOWER.
HEADQUARTERS OF THE JUSTICE LEAGUE OF AMERICA.
IT ALL MAKES SENSE.
NO MATTER HOW BAD I DON'T WANT IT TO.
SINESTRO.
BEFORE HAL JORDAN, HE WAS CALLED THE GREATEST OF THE GREEN LANTERNS.
UNTIL HE PROPPED HIMSELF UP AS THE ULTIMATE AUTHORITY OF HIS SECTOR. HE WAS STRIPPED OF HIS RING AND DISCHARGED FROM THE CORPS.
JORDAN HELPED THE GUARDIANS DO IT.
SO SINESTRO FOUND A DIFFERENT RING AND A NEW PURPOSE.
ANNIHILATE THE GREEN LANTERNS.
GUY TALKS TRASH ABOUT EVERY ONE OF JORDAN'S OLD ENEMIES. ALWAYS SAYING HOW "CANDY ASS" SONAR IS. COUNTING THE NUMBER OF TIMES HE'S MADE DOCTOR POLARIS CRY. AND IT'S A LOT.
BUT SINESTRO?
GUY NEVER MENTIONS SINESTRO.
...KYLE RAYNER...
KRAKKKLL
HIS VOICE IS ALIEN. COLD AND HOLLOW. AND HIS EYES...
IT'S LIKE TRYING TO STARE INTO THE SUN.
SHRAKKK
YOU SHOULD HAVE LET IT BURN OUT.

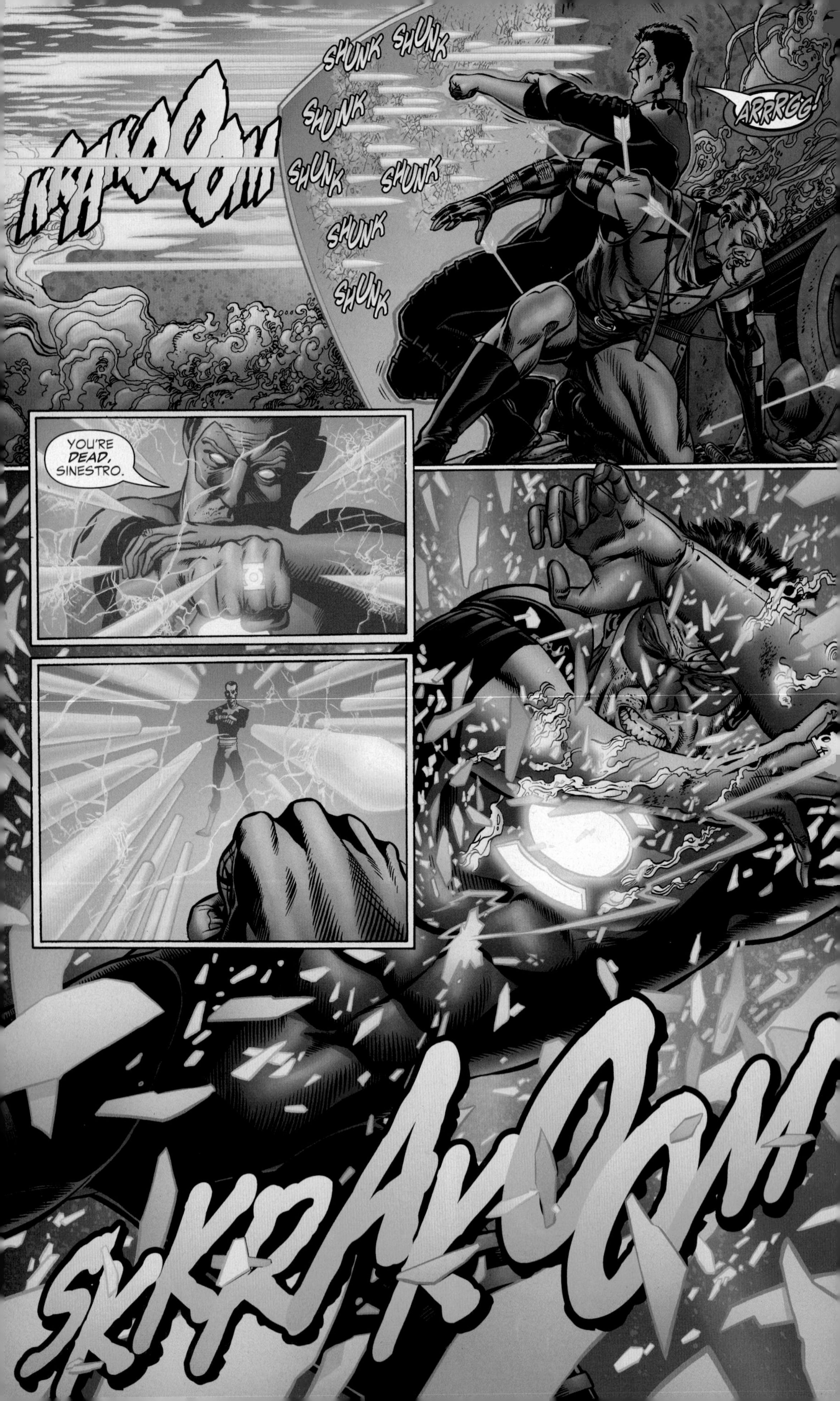

KRAKOOM
SHUNK SHUNK
SHUNK
SHUNK
SHUNK
SHUNK
SHUNK
ARRRGG!
YOU'RE DEAD, SINESTRO.
SKRAKOOM

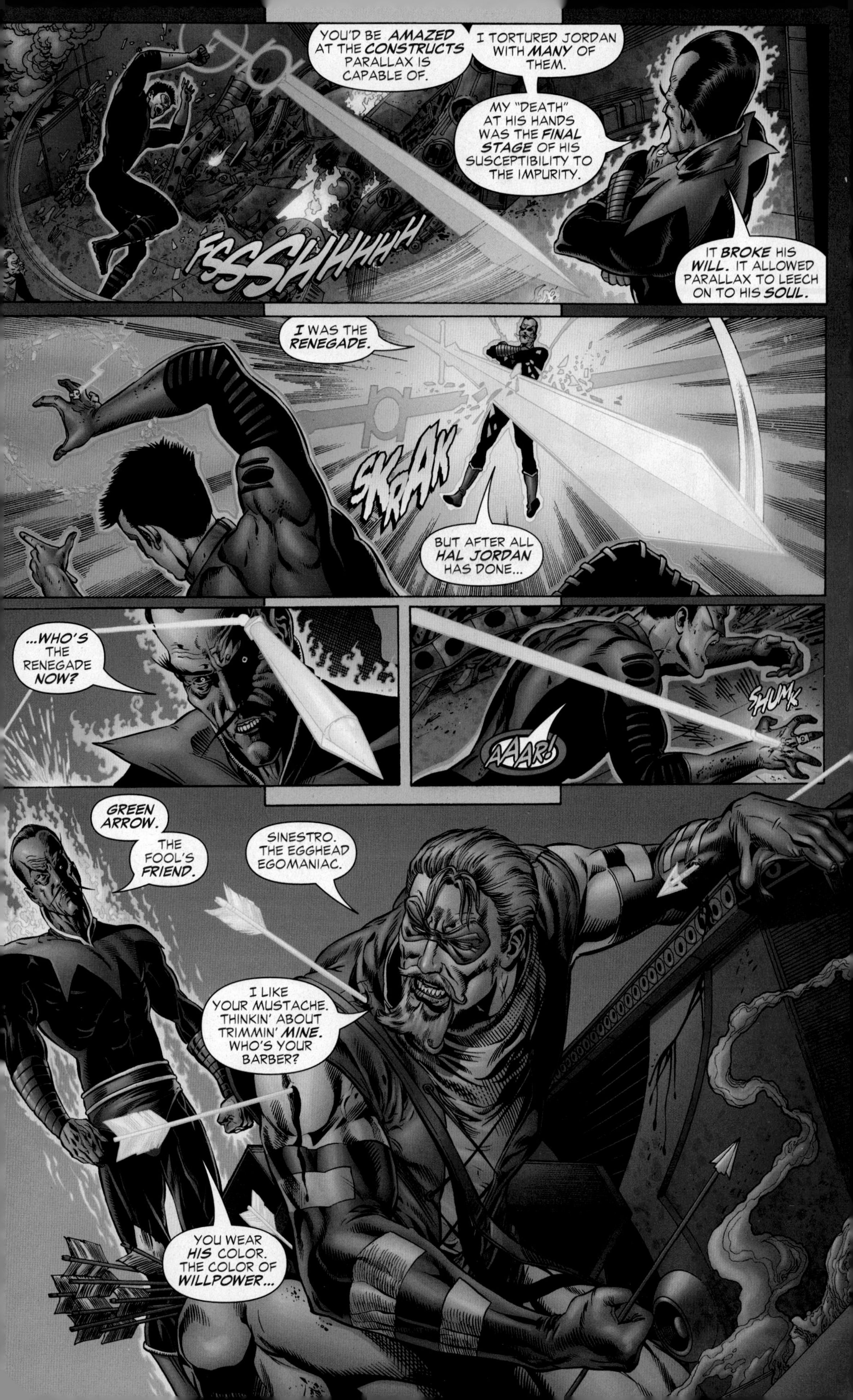

YOU'D BE AMAZED AT THE CONSTRUCTS PARALLAX IS CAPABLE OF.
I TORTURED JORDAN WITH MANY OF THEM.
MY "DEATH" AT HIS HANDS WAS THE FINAL STAGE OF HIS SUSCEPTIBILITY TO THE IMPURITY.
FSSSHHHHH
IT BROKE HIS WILL. IT ALLOWED PARALLAX TO LEECH ON TO HIS SOUL.
I WAS THE RENEGADE.
SKRAK
BUT AFTER ALL HAL JORDAN HAS DONE...
...WHO'S THE RENEGADE NOW?
SHUNK
AAAR!
GREEN ARROW.
THE FOOL'S FRIEND.
SINESTRO. THE EGGHEAD EGOMANIAC.
I LIKE YOUR MUSTACHE. THINKIN' ABOUT TRIMMIN' MINE. WHO'S YOUR BARBER?
YOU WEAR HIS COLOR. THE COLOR OF WILLPOWER...

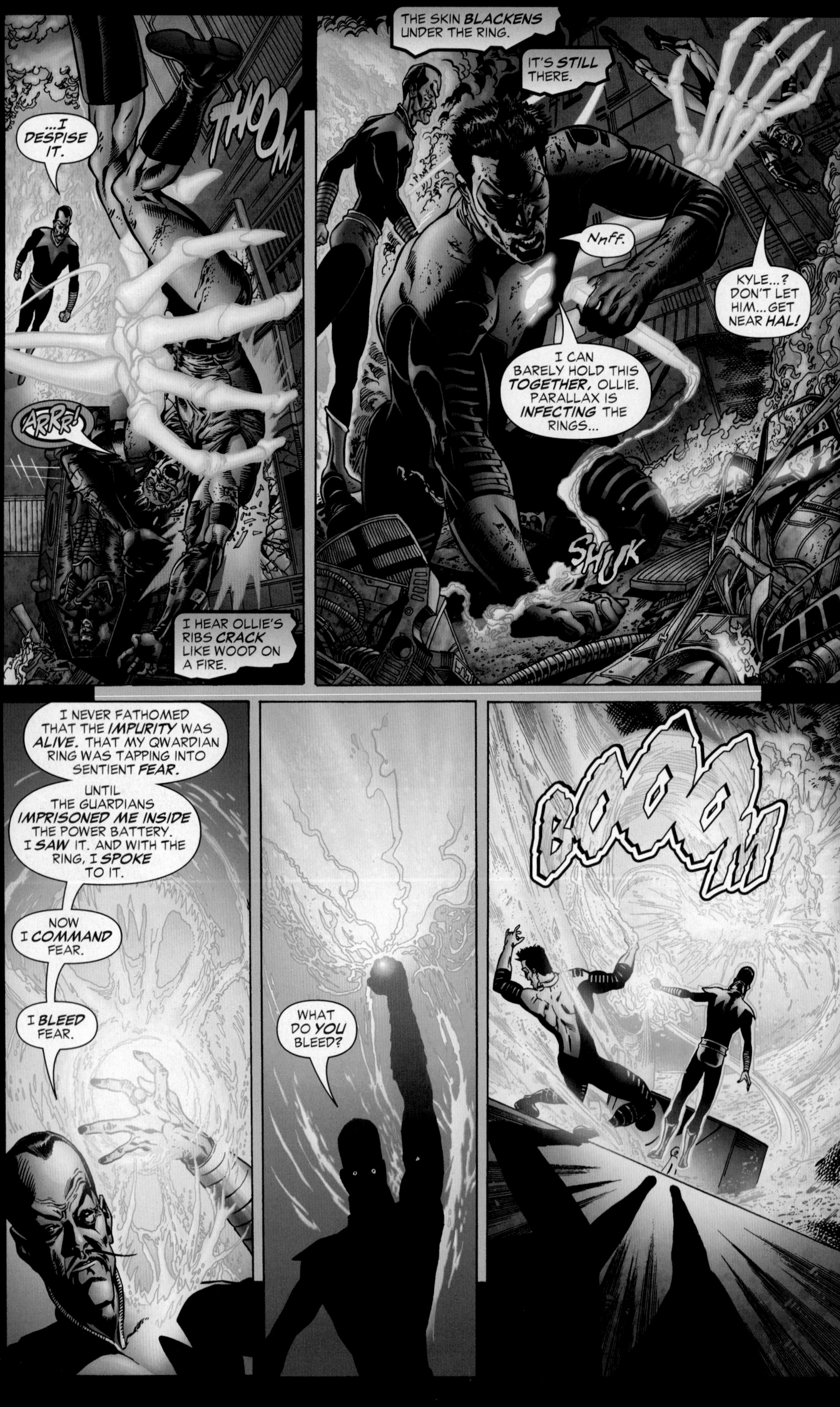
...I DESPISE IT.
THOOM
ARRR!
I HEAR OLLIE'S RIBS CRACK LIKE WOOD ON A FIRE.
THE SKIN BLACKENS UNDER THE RING.
IT'S STILL THERE.
Nnff.
I CAN BARELY HOLD THIS TOGETHER, OLLIE. PARALLAX IS INFECTING THE RINGS...
KYLE...? DON'T LET HIM...GET NEAR HAL!
SHUK
I NEVER FATHOMED THAT THE IMPURITY WAS ALIVE. THAT MY QWARDIAN RING WAS TAPPING INTO SENTIENT FEAR.
UNTIL THE GUARDIANS IMPRISONED ME INSIDE THE POWER BATTERY. I SAW IT. AND WITH THE RING, I SPOKE TO IT.
NOW I COMMAND FEAR.
I BLEED FEAR.
WHAT DO YOU BLEED?
BOOOM

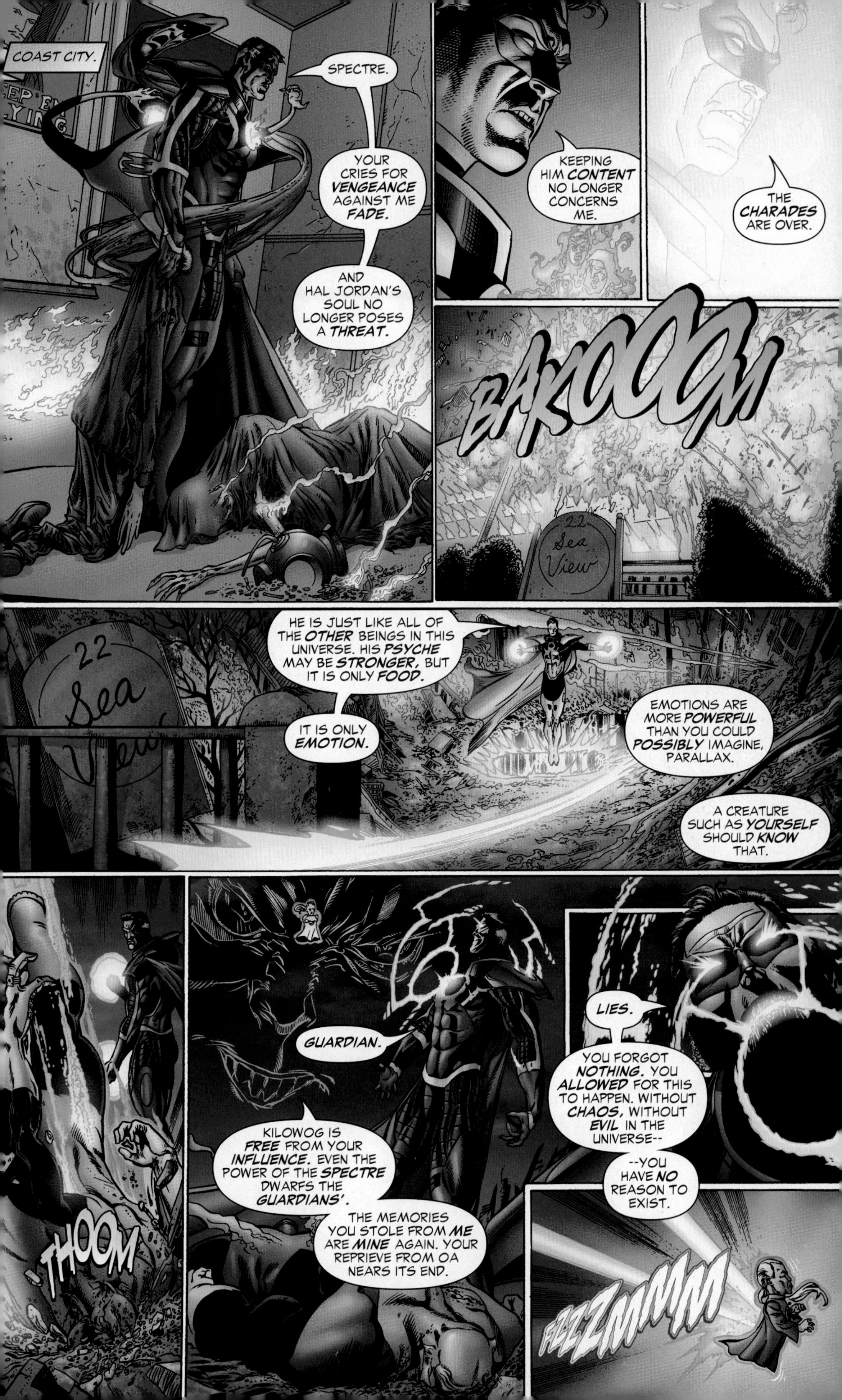
COAST CITY.
SPECTRE.
YOUR CRIES FOR VENGEANCE AGAINST ME FADE.
AND HAL JORDAN'S SOUL NO LONGER POSES A THREAT.
KEEPING HIM CONTENT NO LONGER CONCERNS ME.
THE CHARADES ARE OVER.
BAKOOOM
22 Sea View
HE IS JUST LIKE ALL OF THE OTHER BEINGS IN THIS UNIVERSE. HIS PSYCHE MAY BE STRONGER, BUT IT IS ONLY FOOD.
IT IS ONLY EMOTION.
EMOTIONS ARE MORE POWERFUL THAN YOU COULD POSSIBLY IMAGINE, PARALLAX.
A CREATURE SUCH AS YOURSELF SHOULD KNOW THAT.
THOOM
GUARDIAN.
KILOWOG IS FREE FROM YOUR INFLUENCE. EVEN THE POWER OF THE SPECTRE DWARFS THE GUARDIANS'.
THE MEMORIES YOU STOLE FROM ME ARE MINE AGAIN. YOUR REPRIEVE FROM OA NEARS ITS END.
LIES.
YOU FORGOT NOTHING. YOU ALLOWED FOR THIS TO HAPPEN. WITHOUT CHAOS, WITHOUT EVIL IN THE UNIVERSE--
--YOU HAVE NO REASON TO EXIST.
FZZZMMMM

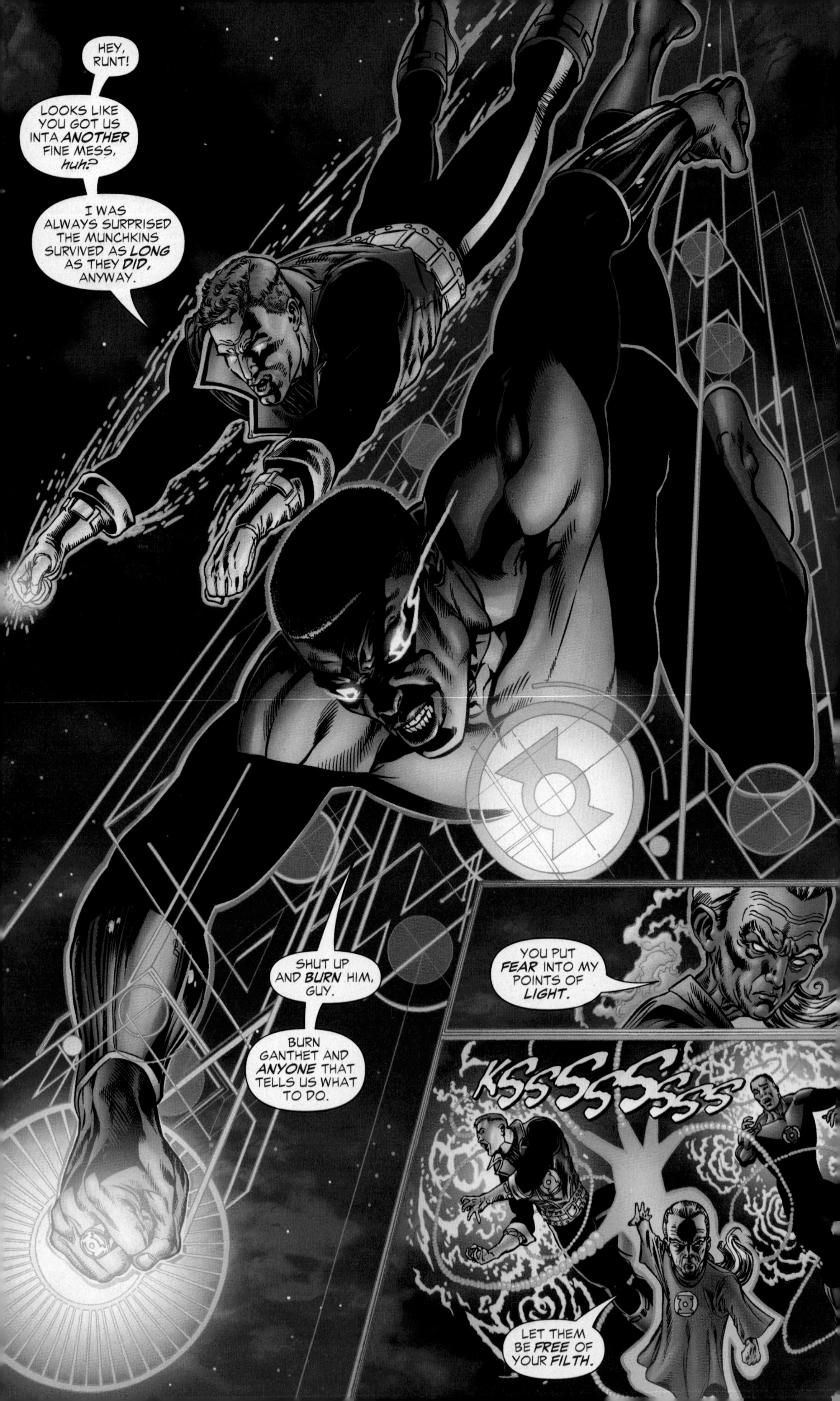
HEY, RUNT!
LOOKS LIKE YOU GOT US INTA ANOTHER FINE MESS, huh?
I WAS ALWAYS SURPRISED THE MUNCHKINS SURVIVED AS LONG AS THEY DID, ANYWAY.
SHUT UP AND BURN HIM, GUY.
BURN GANTHET AND ANYONE THAT TELLS US WHAT TO DO.
YOU PUT FEAR INTO MY POINTS OF LIGHT.
KSSSSSSSSS
LET THEM BE FREE OF YOUR FILTH.

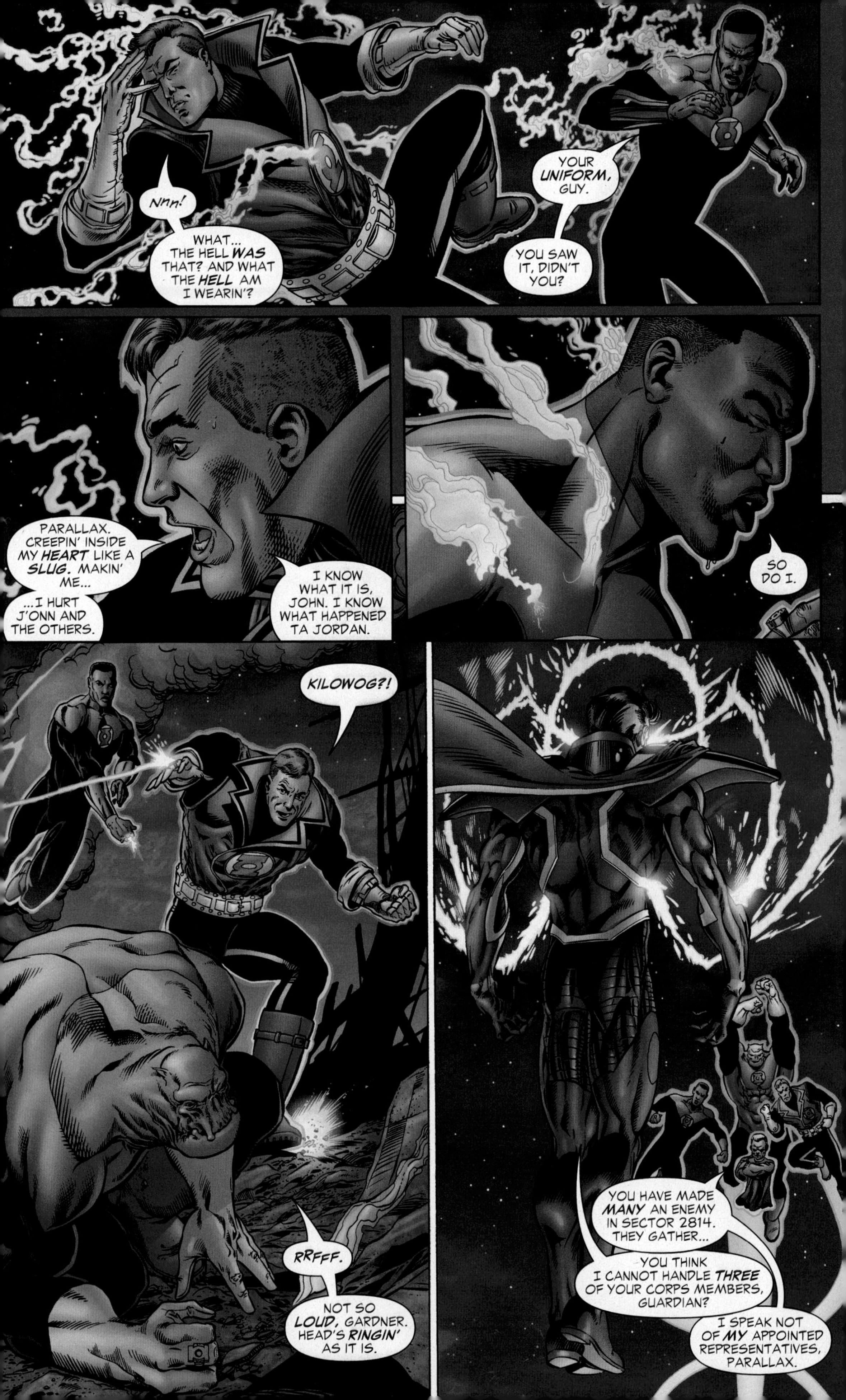
Nnn!
WHAT... THE HELL WAS THAT? AND WHAT THE HELL AM I WEARIN'?
YOUR UNIFORM, GUY.
YOU SAW IT, DIDN'T YOU?
PARALLAX. CREEPIN' INSIDE MY HEART LIKE A SLUG. MAKIN' ME...
...I HURT J'ONN AND THE OTHERS.
I KNOW WHAT IT IS, JOHN. I KNOW WHAT HAPPENED TA JORDAN.
SO DO I.
KILOWOG?!
RRFFF.
NOT SO LOUD, GARDNER. HEAD'S RINGIN' AS IT IS.
YOU HAVE MADE MANY AN ENEMY IN SECTOR 2814. THEY GATHER...
-YOU THINK I CANNOT HANDLE THREE OF YOUR CORPS MEMBERS, GUARDIAN?
I SPEAK NOT OF MY APPOINTED REPRESENTATIVES, PARALLAX.

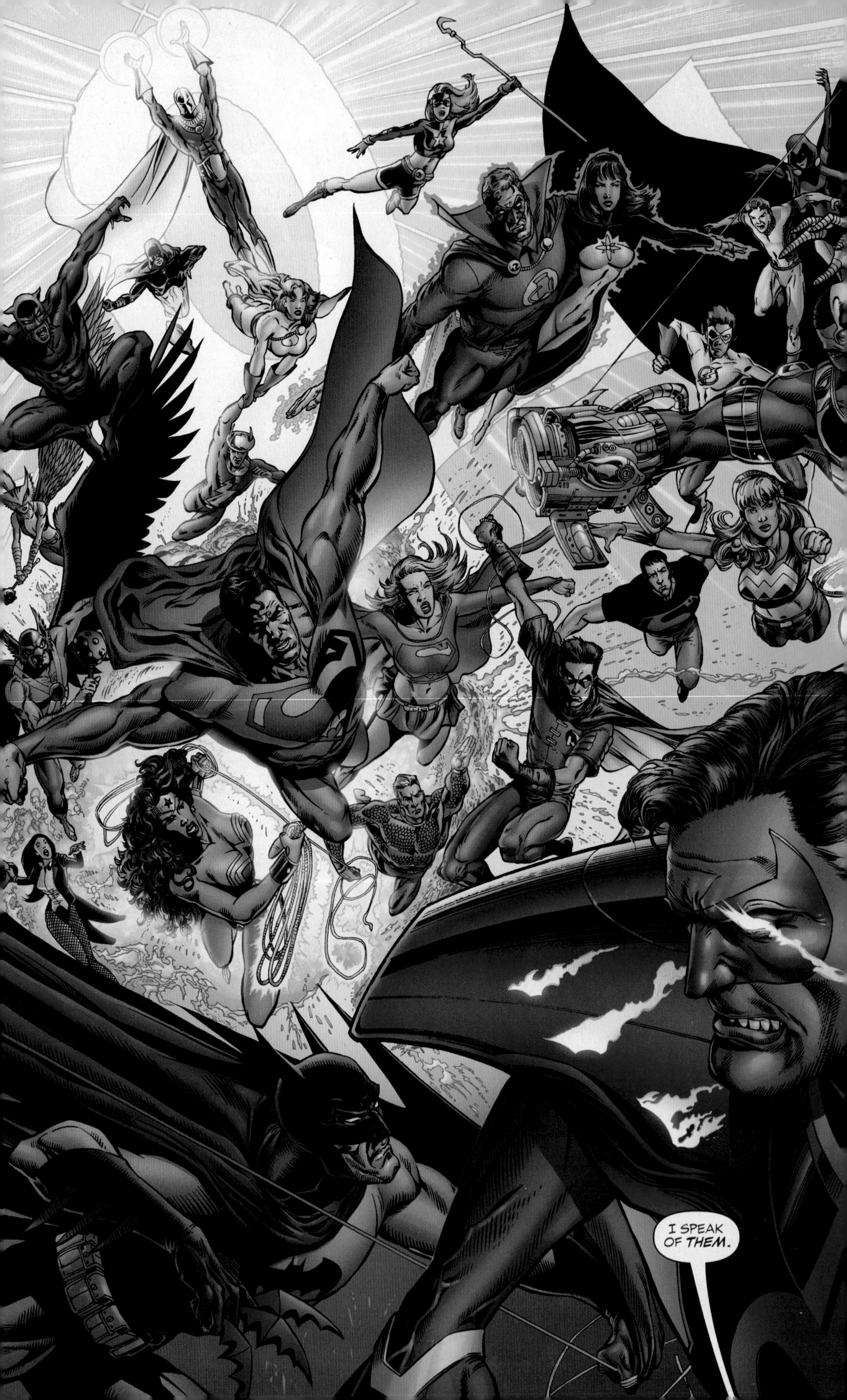
I SPEAK OF THEM.

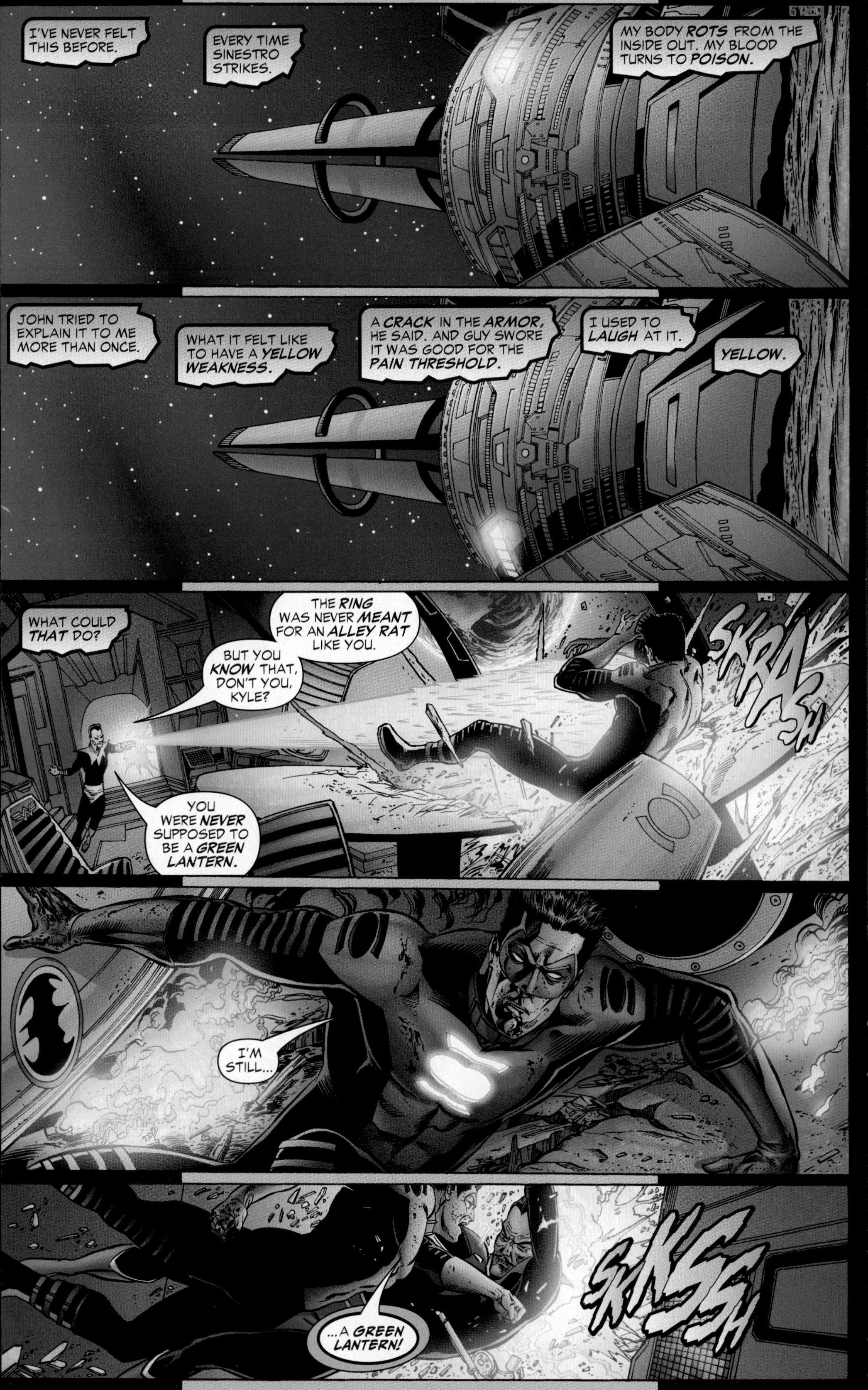
I'VE NEVER FELT THIS BEFORE.
EVERY TIME SINESTRO STRIKES.
MY BODY ROTS FROM THE INSIDE OUT. MY BLOOD TURNS TO POISON.
JOHN TRIED TO EXPLAIN IT TO ME MORE THAN ONCE.
WHAT IT FELT LIKE TO HAVE A YELLOW WEAKNESS.
A CRACK IN THE ARMOR, HE SAID. AND GUY SWORE IT WAS GOOD FOR THE PAIN THRESHOLD.
I USED TO LAUGH AT IT.
YELLOW.
WHAT COULD THAT DO?
THE RING WAS NEVER MEANT FOR AN ALLEY RAT LIKE YOU.
BUT YOU KNOW THAT, DON'T YOU, KYLE?
YOU WERE NEVER SUPPOSED TO BE A GREEN LANTERN.
SKRASH
I'M STILL...
...A GREEN LANTERN!
SKKSSH

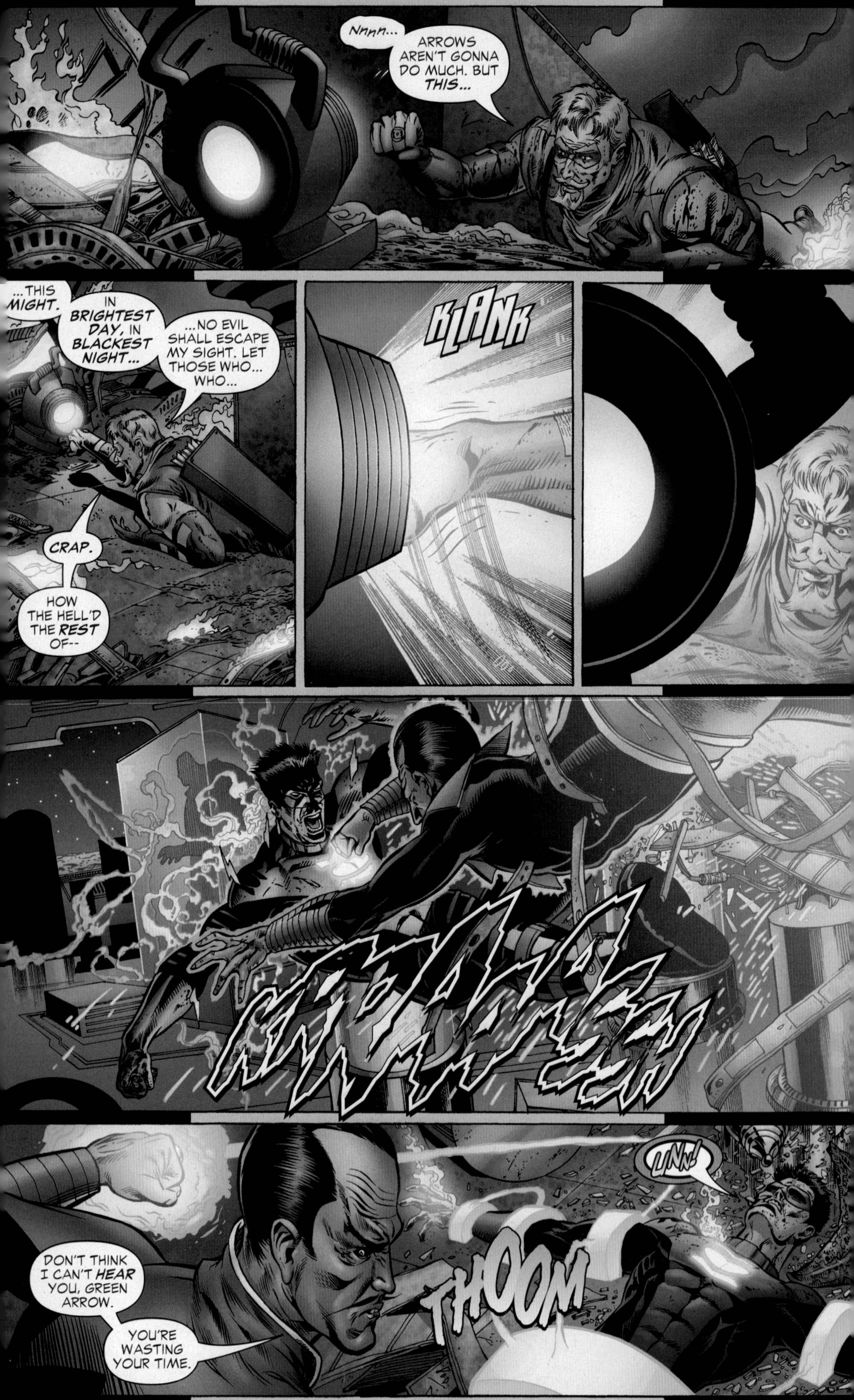
Nnnn...
ARROWS AREN'T GONNA DO MUCH. BUT THIS...
...THIS MIGHT.
IN BRIGHTEST DAY, IN BLACKEST NIGHT...
...NO EVIL SHALL ESCAPE MY SIGHT. LET THOSE WHO... WHO...
CRAP.
HOW THE HELL'D THE REST OF--
KLANK
UNN!
THOOM
DON'T THINK I CAN'T HEAR YOU, GREEN ARROW.
YOU'RE WASTING YOUR TIME.

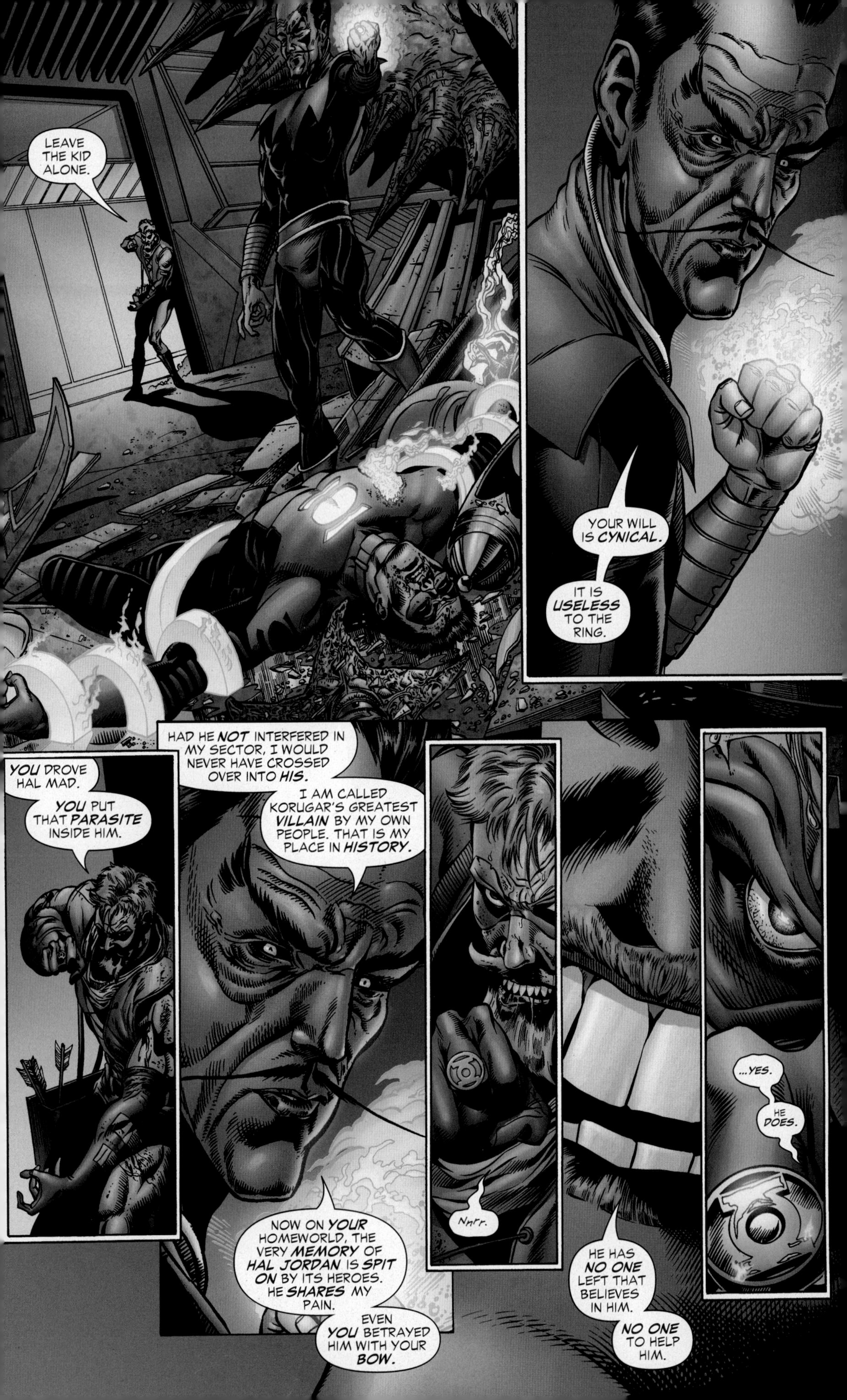
LEAVE THE KID ALONE.
YOUR WILL IS CYNICAL.
IT IS USELESS TO THE RING.
YOU DROVE HAL MAD.
YOU PUT THAT PARASITE INSIDE HIM.
HAD HE NOT INTERFERED IN MY SECTOR, I WOULD NEVER HAVE CROSSED OVER INTO HIS.
I AM CALLED KORUGAR'S GREATEST VILLAIN BY MY OWN PEOPLE. THAT IS MY PLACE IN HISTORY.
NOW ON YOUR HOMEWORLD, THE VERY MEMORY OF HAL JORDAN IS SPIT ON BY ITS HEROES. HE SHARES MY PAIN.
EVEN YOU BETRAYED HIM WITH YOUR BOW.
Nnrr.
HE HAS NO ONE LEFT THAT BELIEVES IN HIM.
NO ONE TO HELP HIM.
...YES.
HE DOES.

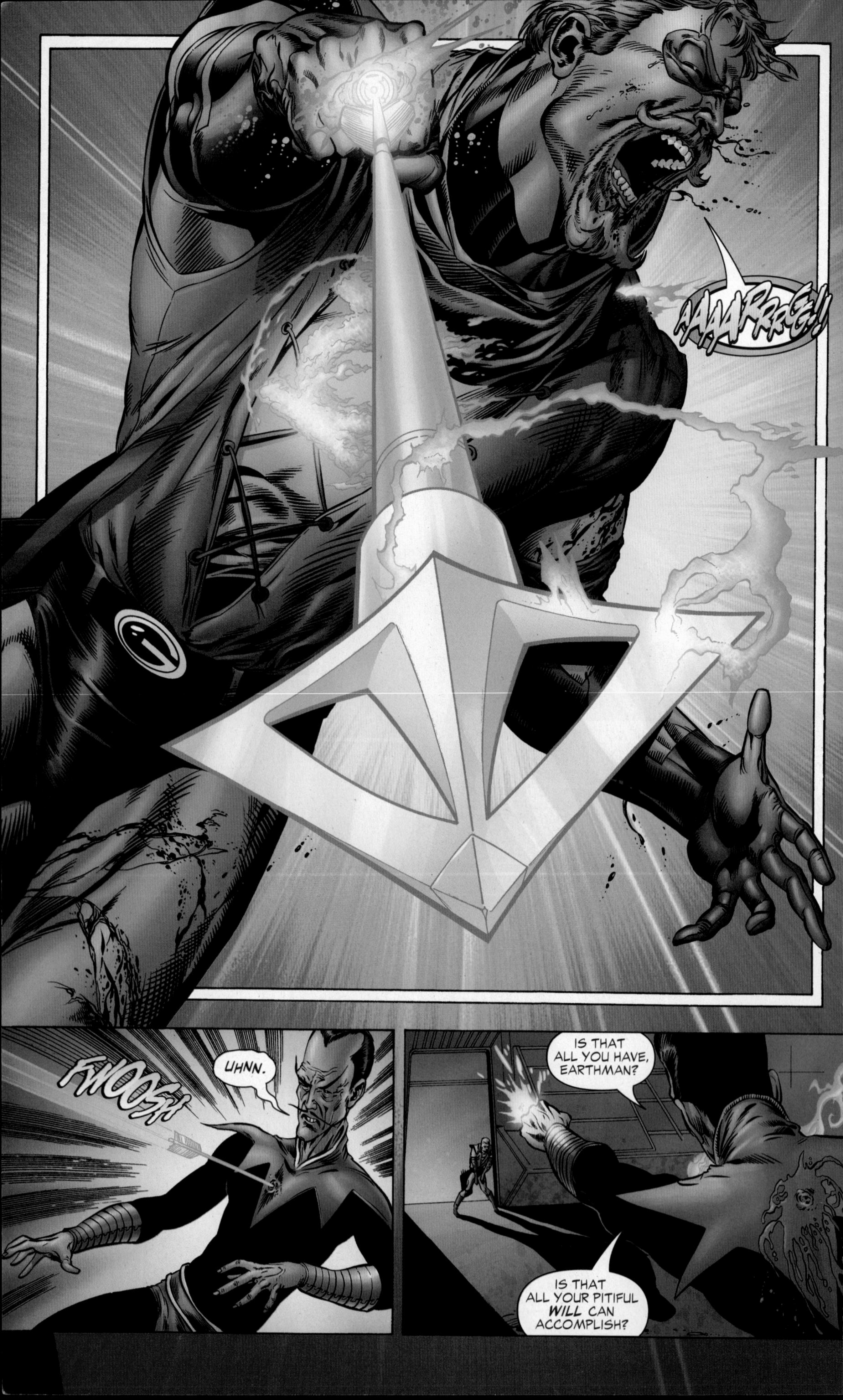
AAAARRRG!!
FWOOSH
UHNN.
IS THAT ALL YOU HAVE, EARTHMAN?
IS THAT ALL YOUR PITIFUL WILL CAN ACCOMPLISH?

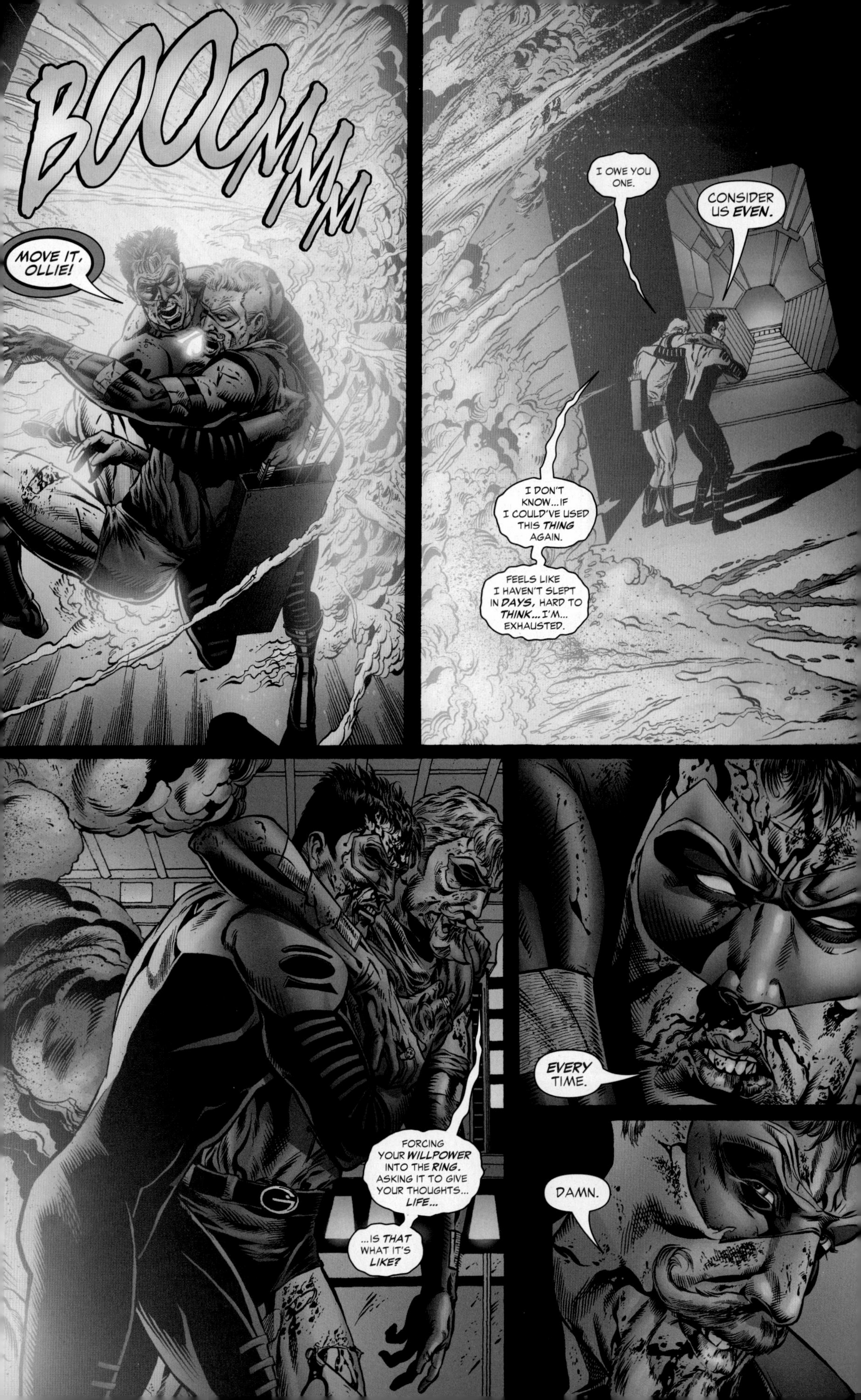
BOOOMMM
MOVE IT, OLLIE!
I OWE YOU ONE.
CONSIDER US EVEN.
I DON'T KNOW...IF I COULD'VE USED THIS THING AGAIN.
FEELS LIKE I HAVEN'T SLEPT IN DAYS, HARD TO THINK... I'M... EXHAUSTED.
FORCING YOUR WILLPOWER INTO THE RING. ASKING IT TO GIVE YOUR THOUGHTS... LIFE...
...IS THAT WHAT IT'S LIKE?
EVERY TIME.
DAMN.

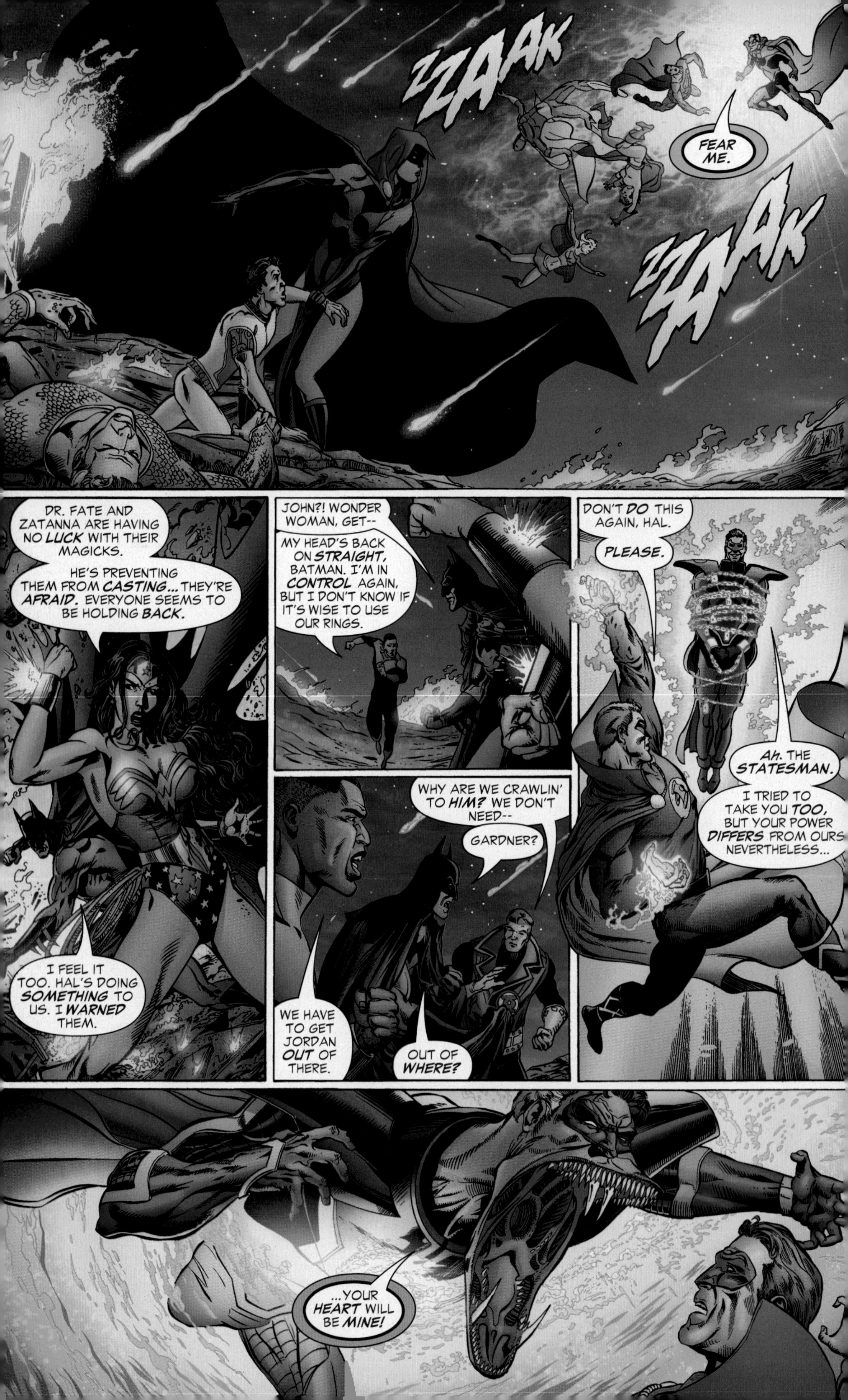
ZZAAK
FEAR ME.
ZZAAK
DR. FATE AND ZATANNA ARE HAVING NO LUCK WITH THEIR MAGICKS.
HE'S PREVENTING THEM FROM CASTING... THEY'RE AFRAID. EVERYONE SEEMS TO BE HOLDING BACK.
I FEEL IT TOO. HAL'S DOING SOMETHING TO US. I WARNED THEM.
JOHN?! WONDER WOMAN, GET--
MY HEAD'S BACK ON STRAIGHT, BATMAN. I'M IN CONTROL AGAIN, BUT I DON'T KNOW IF IT'S WISE TO USE OUR RINGS.
WHY ARE WE CRAWLIN' TO HIM? WE DON'T NEED--
GARDNER?
WE HAVE TO GET JORDAN OUT OF THERE.
OUT OF WHERE?
DON'T DO THIS AGAIN, HAL.
PLEASE.
Ah. THE STATESMAN.
I TRIED TO TAKE YOU TOO, BUT YOUR POWER DIFFERS FROM OURS NEVERTHELESS...
...YOUR HEART WILL BE MINE!

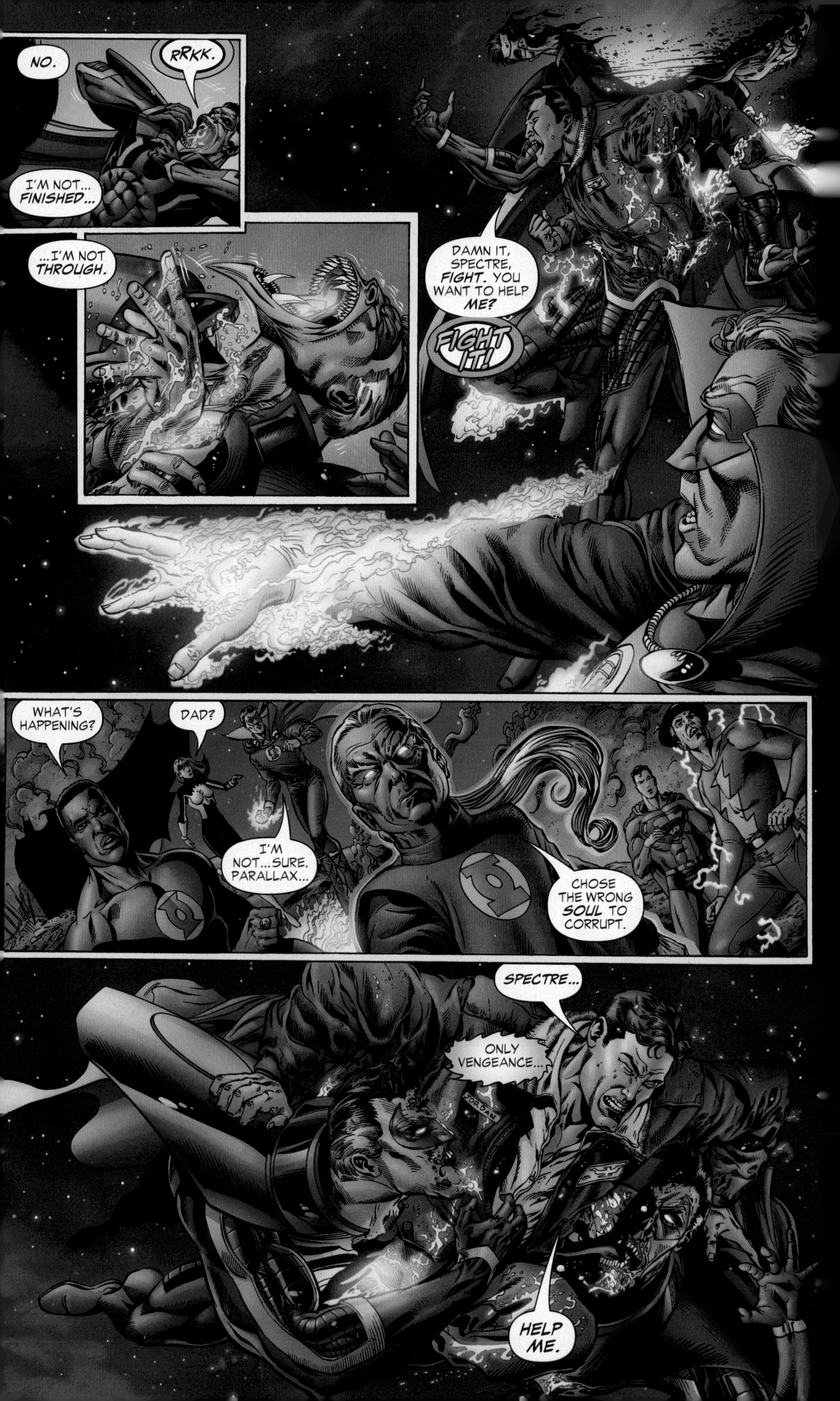
NO.
RRKK.
I'M NOT... FINISHED...
...I'M NOT THROUGH.
DAMN IT, SPECTRE, FIGHT. YOU WANT TO HELP ME?
FIGHT IT!
WHAT'S HAPPENING?
DAD?
I'M NOT...SURE. PARALLAX...
CHOSE THE WRONG SOUL TO CORRUPT.
SPECTRE...
ONLY VENGEANCE...
HELP ME.

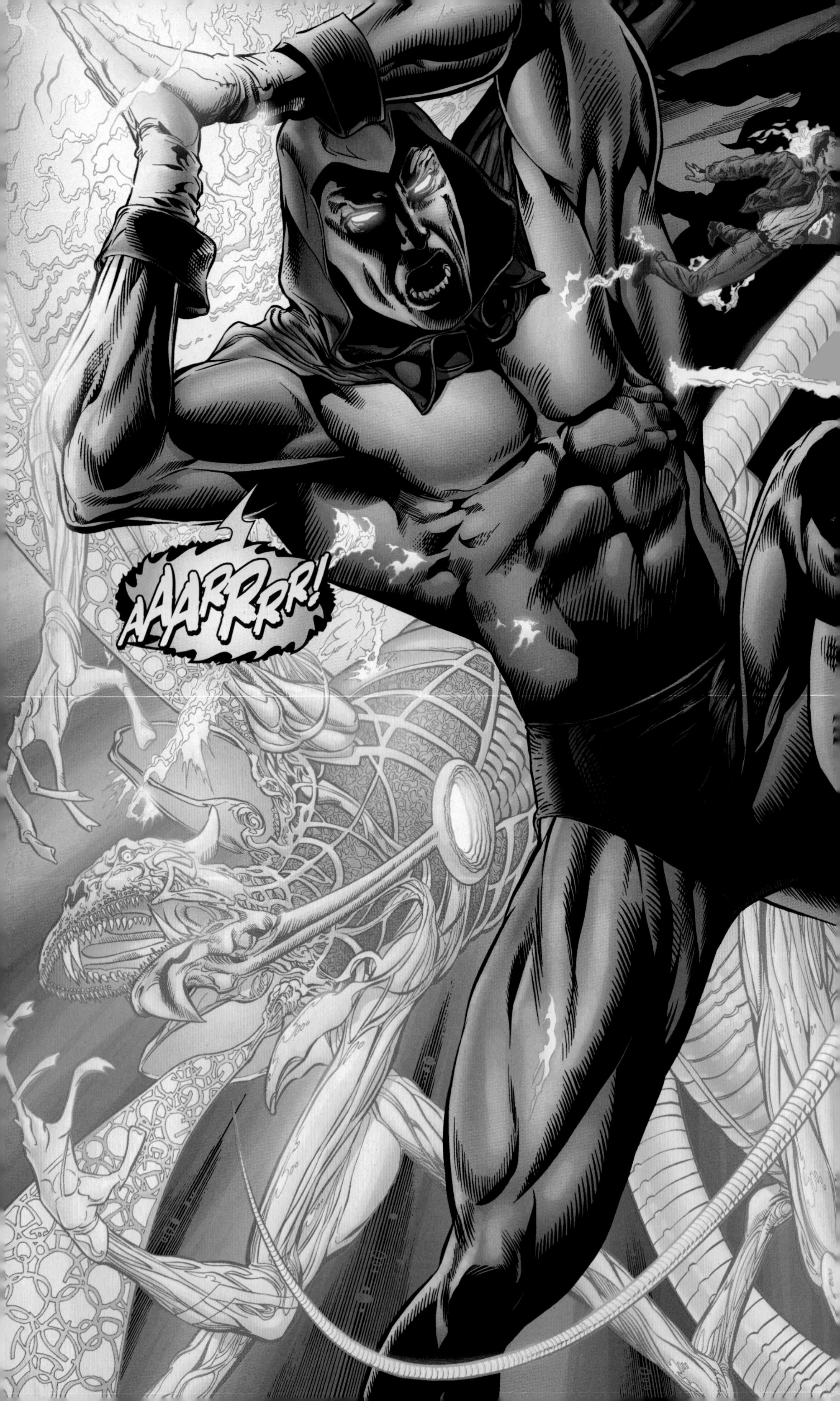
AAARRRR!

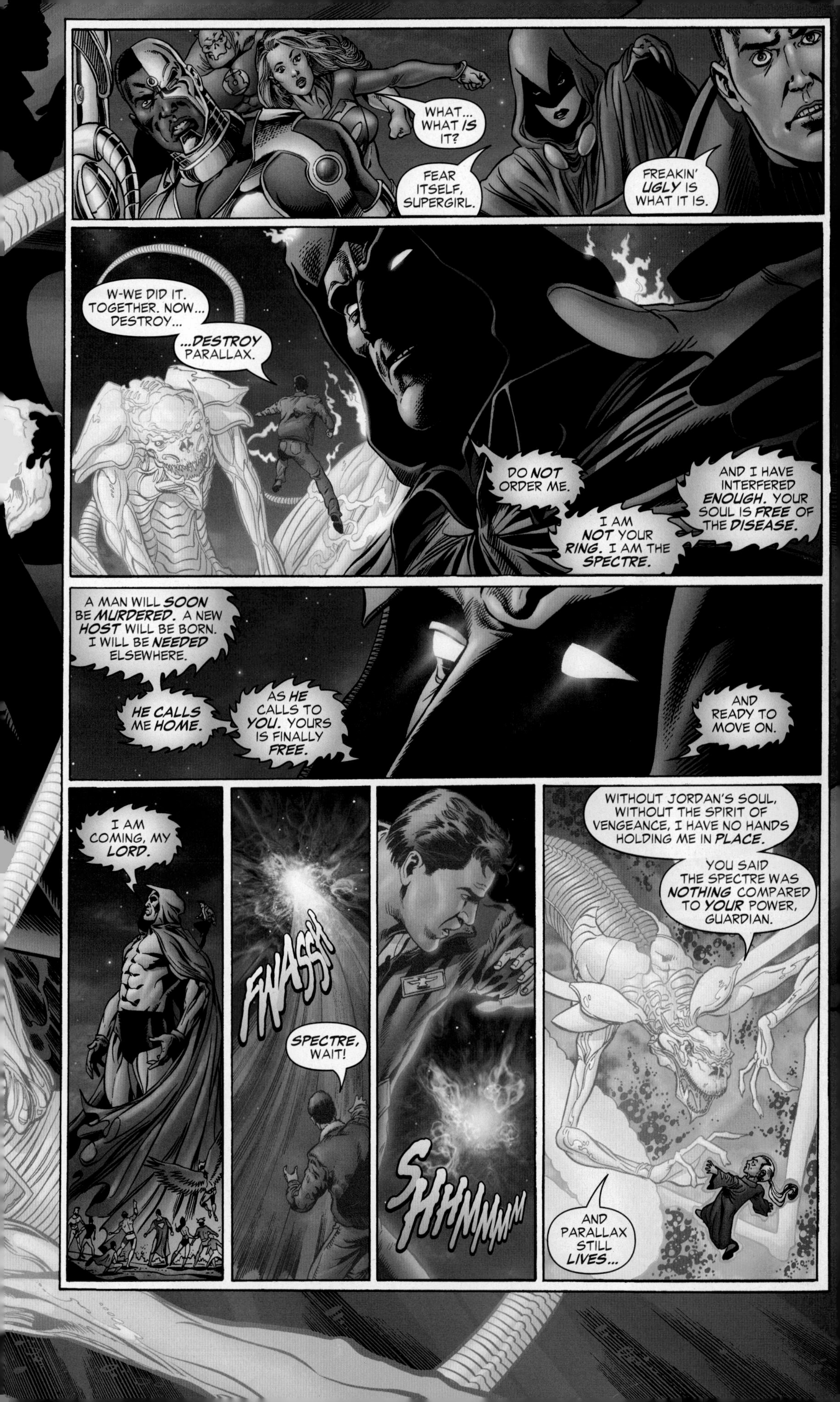
WHAT... WHAT IS IT?
FEAR ITSELF, SUPERGIRL.
FREAKIN' UGLY IS WHAT IT IS.
W-WE DID IT. TOGETHER. NOW... DESTROY...
...DESTROY PARALLAX.
DO NOT ORDER ME.
I AM NOT YOUR RING. I AM THE SPECTRE.
AND I HAVE INTERFERED ENOUGH. YOUR SOUL IS FREE OF THE DISEASE.
A MAN WILL SOON BE MURDERED. A NEW HOST WILL BE BORN. I WILL BE NEEDED ELSEWHERE.
HE CALLS ME HOME.
AS HE CALLS TO YOU. YOURS IS FINALLY FREE.
AND READY TO MOVE ON.
I AM COMING, MY LORD.
FWASSH
SPECTRE, WAIT!
SHHMMMM
WITHOUT JORDAN'S SOUL, WITHOUT THE SPIRIT OF VENGEANCE, I HAVE NO HANDS HOLDING ME IN PLACE.
YOU SAID THE SPECTRE WAS NOTHING COMPARED TO YOUR POWER, GUARDIAN.
AND PARALLAX STILL LIVES...

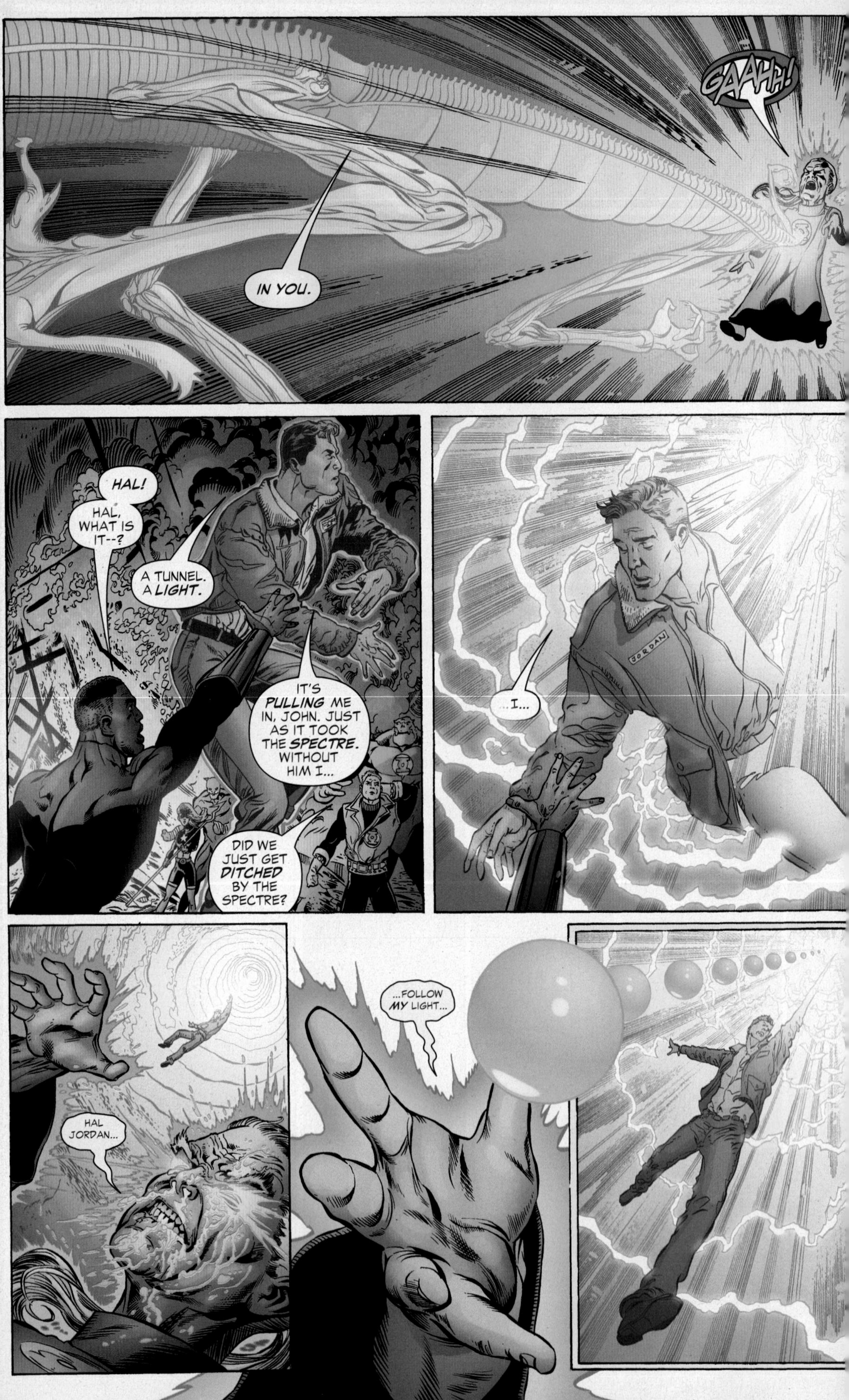

GAAHH!
IN YOU.
HAL!
HAL, WHAT IS IT--?
A TUNNEL. A LIGHT.
IT'S PULLING ME IN, JOHN. JUST AS IT TOOK THE SPECTRE. WITHOUT HIM I...
DID WE JUST GET DITCHED BY THE SPECTRE?
JORDAN
...I...
...FOLLOW MY LIGHT...
HAL JORDAN...

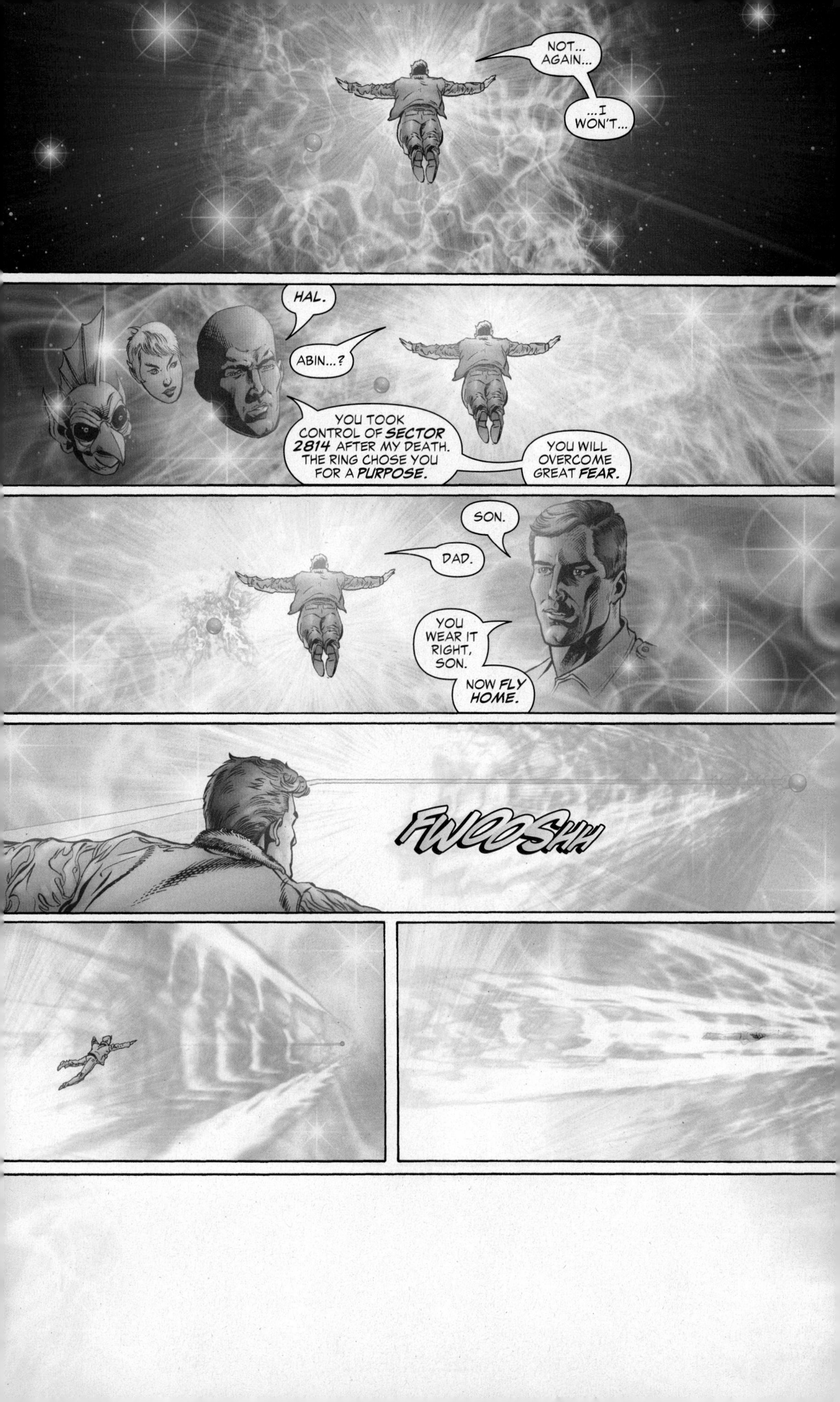
NOT... AGAIN...
...I WON'T...
HAL.
ABIN...?
YOU TOOK CONTROL OF SECTOR 2814 AFTER MY DEATH. THE RING CHOSE YOU FOR A PURPOSE.
YOU WILL OVERCOME GREAT FEAR.
SON.
DAD.
YOU WEAR IT RIGHT, SON.
NOW FLY HOME.
FWOOSHH

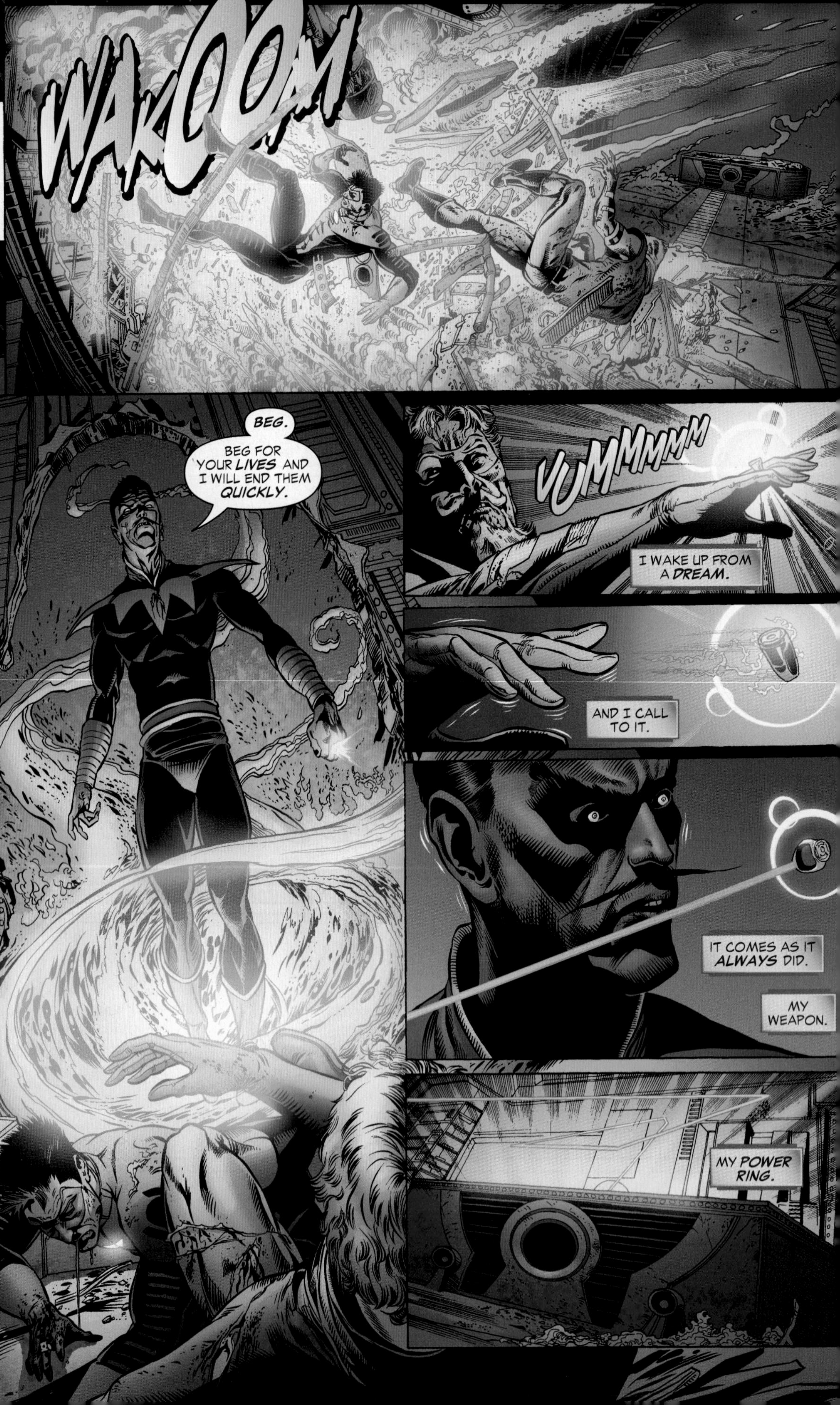
WAKOOM
BEG.
BEG FOR YOUR LIVES AND I WILL END THEM QUICKLY.
VUMMMMMM
I WAKE UP FROM A DREAM.
AND I CALL TO IT.
IT COMES AS IT ALWAYS DID.
MY WEAPON.
MY POWER RING.

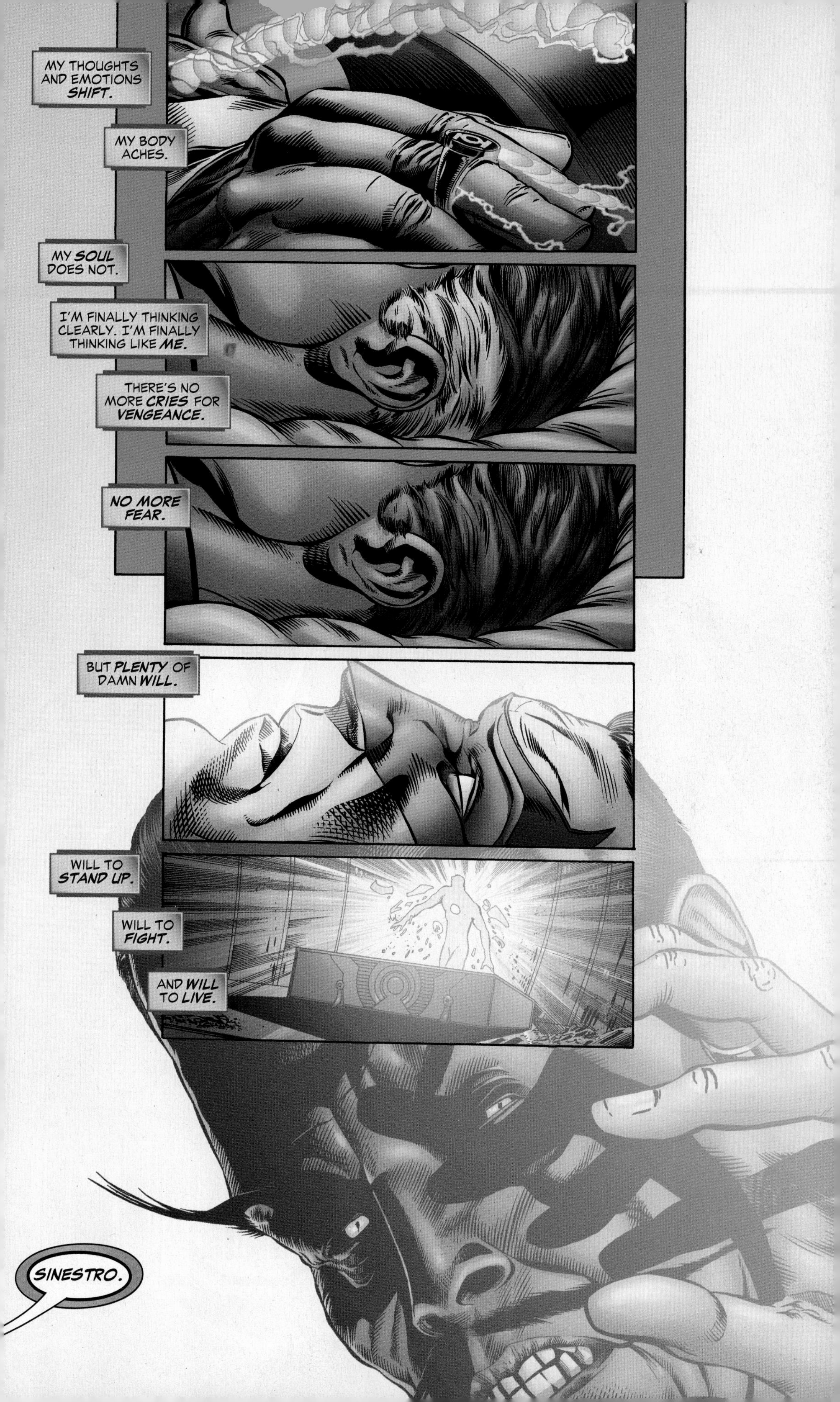
MY THOUGHTS AND EMOTIONS SHIFT.
MY BODY ACHES.
MY SOUL DOES NOT.
I'M FINALLY THINKING CLEARLY. I'M FINALLY THINKING LIKE ME.
THERE'S NO MORE CRIES FOR VENGEANCE.
NO MORE FEAR.
BUT PLENTY OF DAMN WILL.
WILL TO STAND UP.
WILL TO FIGHT.
AND WILL TO LIVE.
SINESTRO.

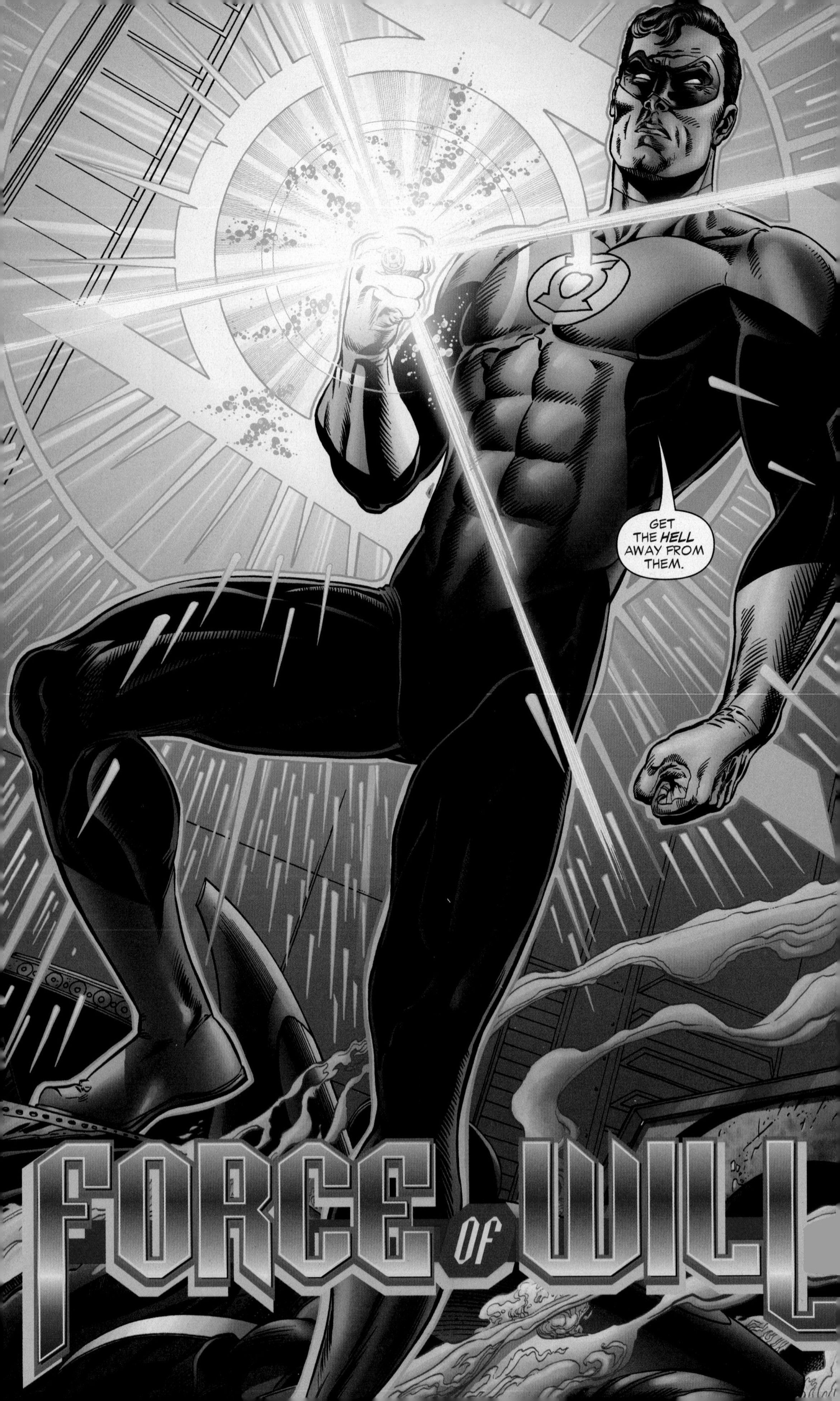
GET THE HELL AWAY FROM THEM.
FORCE OF WILL

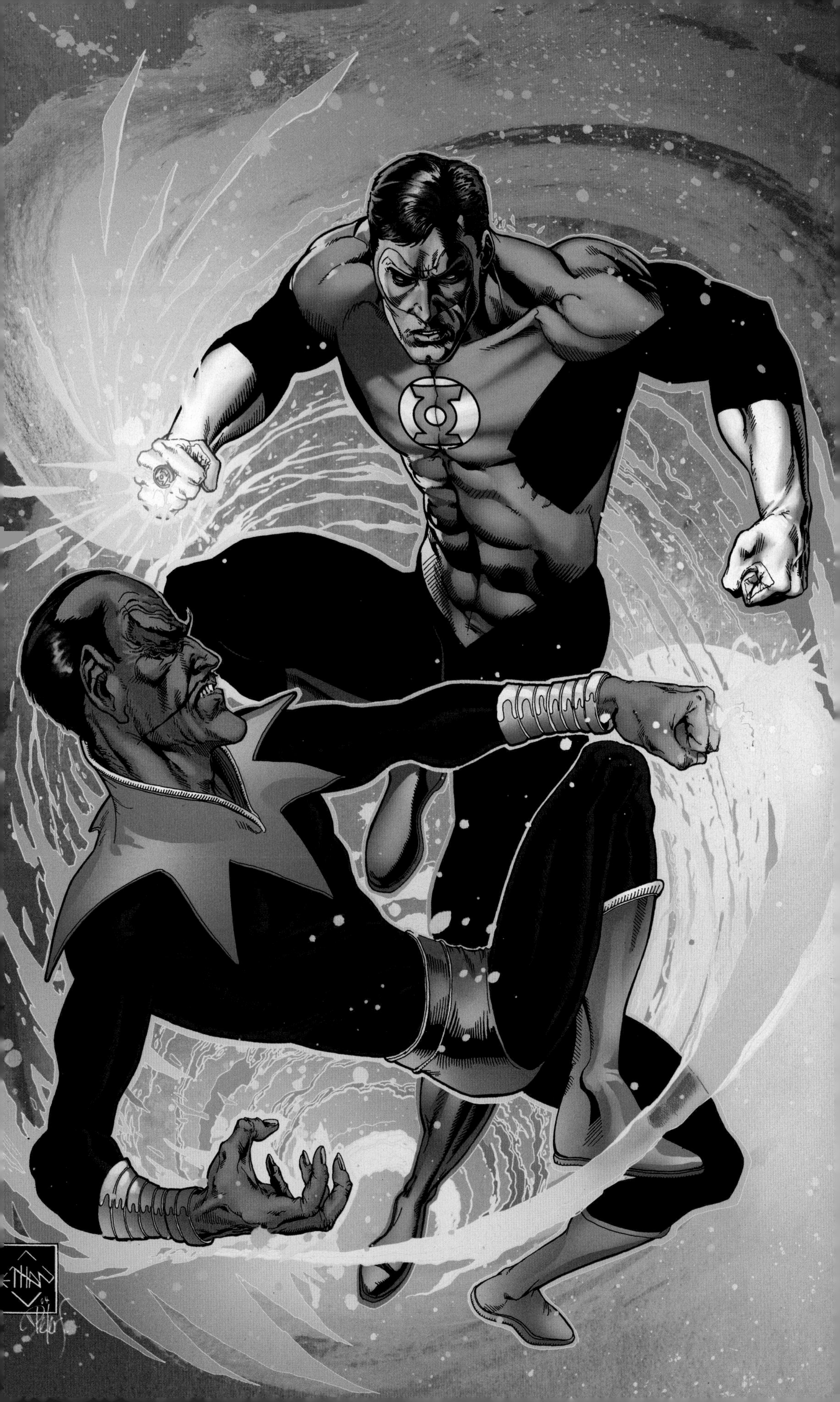

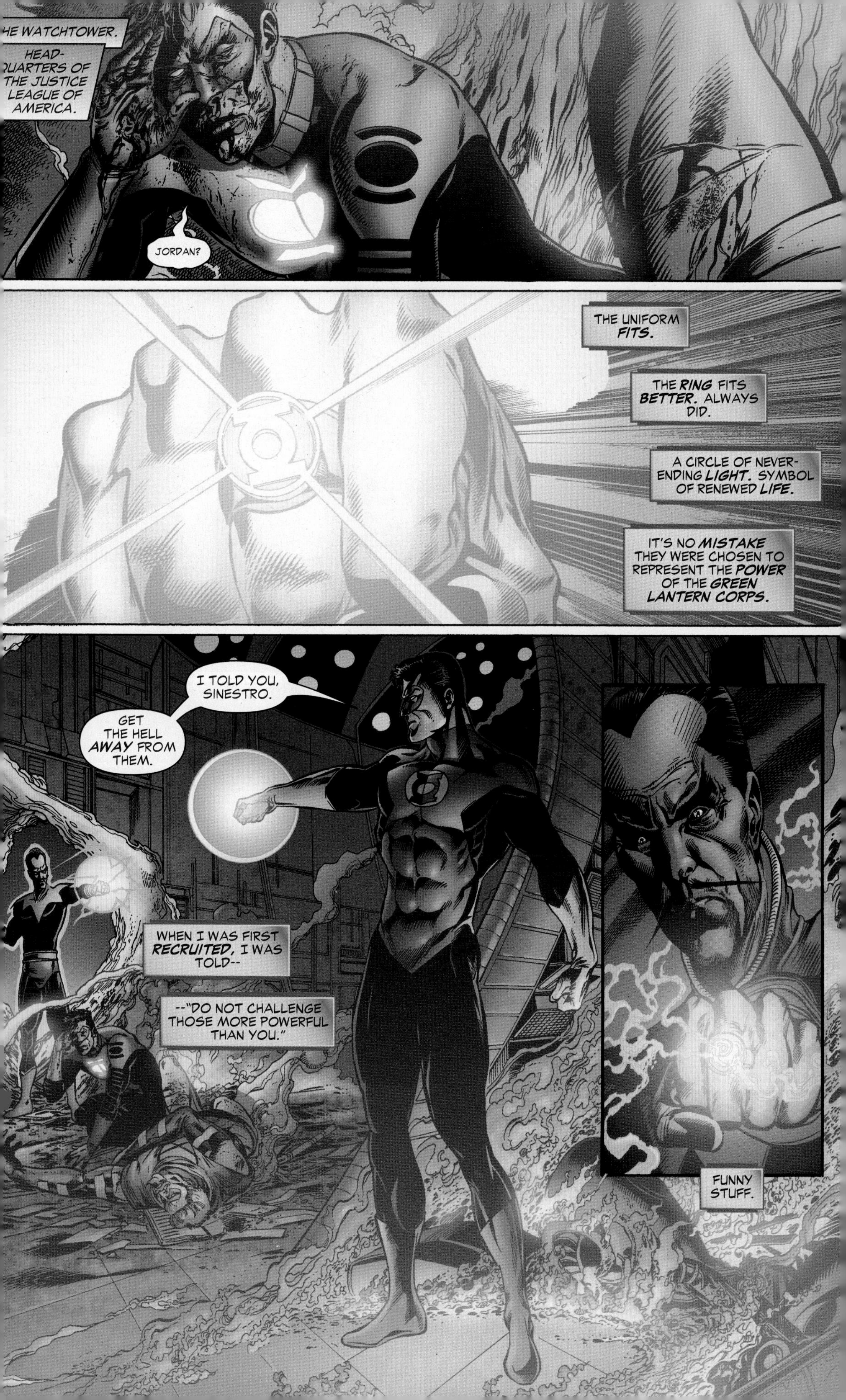
HE WATCHTOWER.
HEAD-QUARTERS OF THE JUSTICE LEAGUE OF AMERICA.
JORDAN?
THE UNIFORM FITS.
THE RING FITS BETTER. ALWAYS DID.
A CIRCLE OF NEVER-ENDING LIGHT. SYMBOL OF RENEWED LIFE.
IT'S NO MISTAKE THEY WERE CHOSEN TO REPRESENT THE POWER OF THE GREEN LANTERN CORPS.
I TOLD YOU, SINESTRO.
GET THE HELL AWAY FROM THEM.
WHEN I WAS FIRST RECRUITED, I WAS TOLD--
--"DO NOT CHALLENGE THOSE MORE POWERFUL THAN YOU."
FUNNY STUFF.

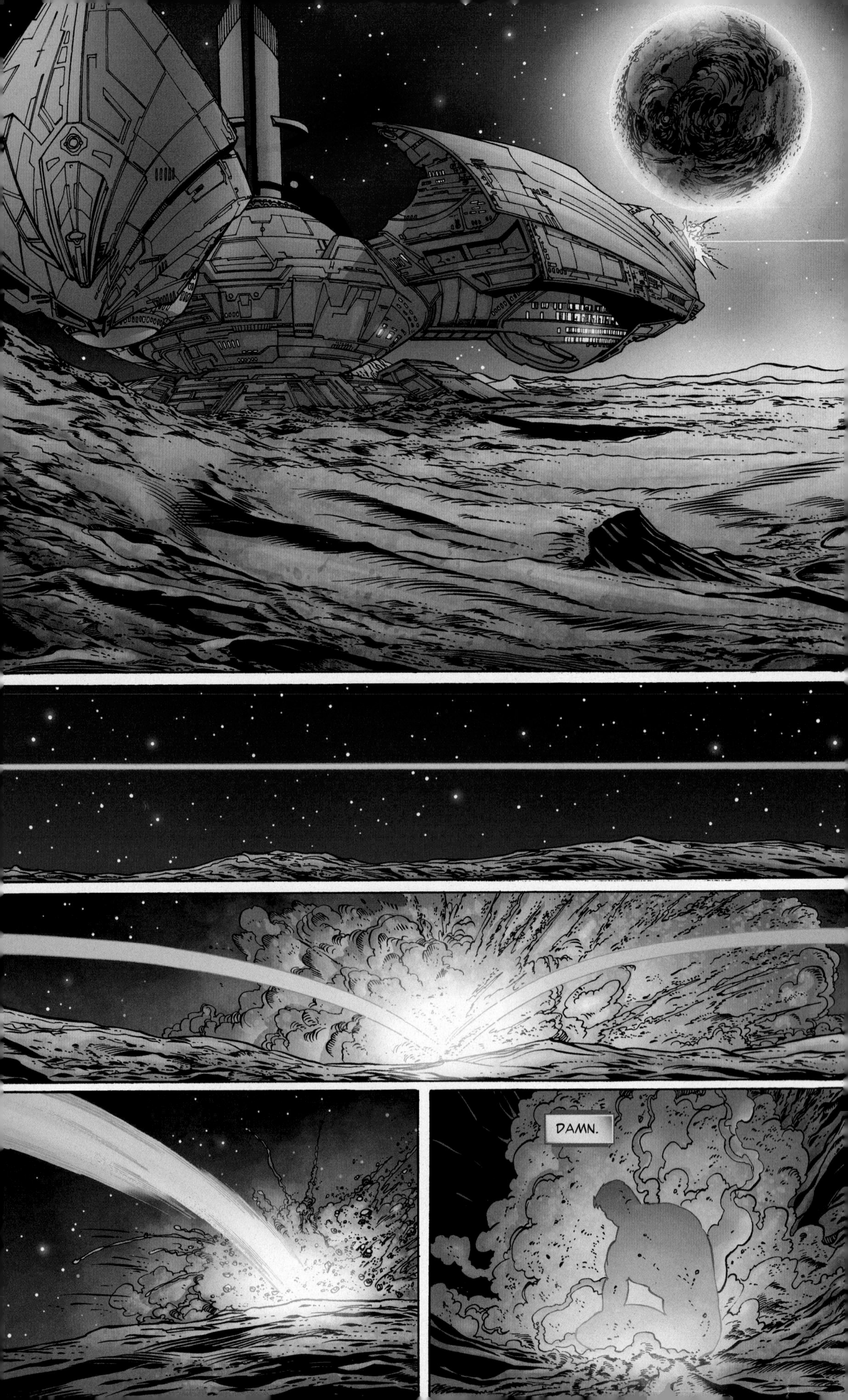
DAMN.

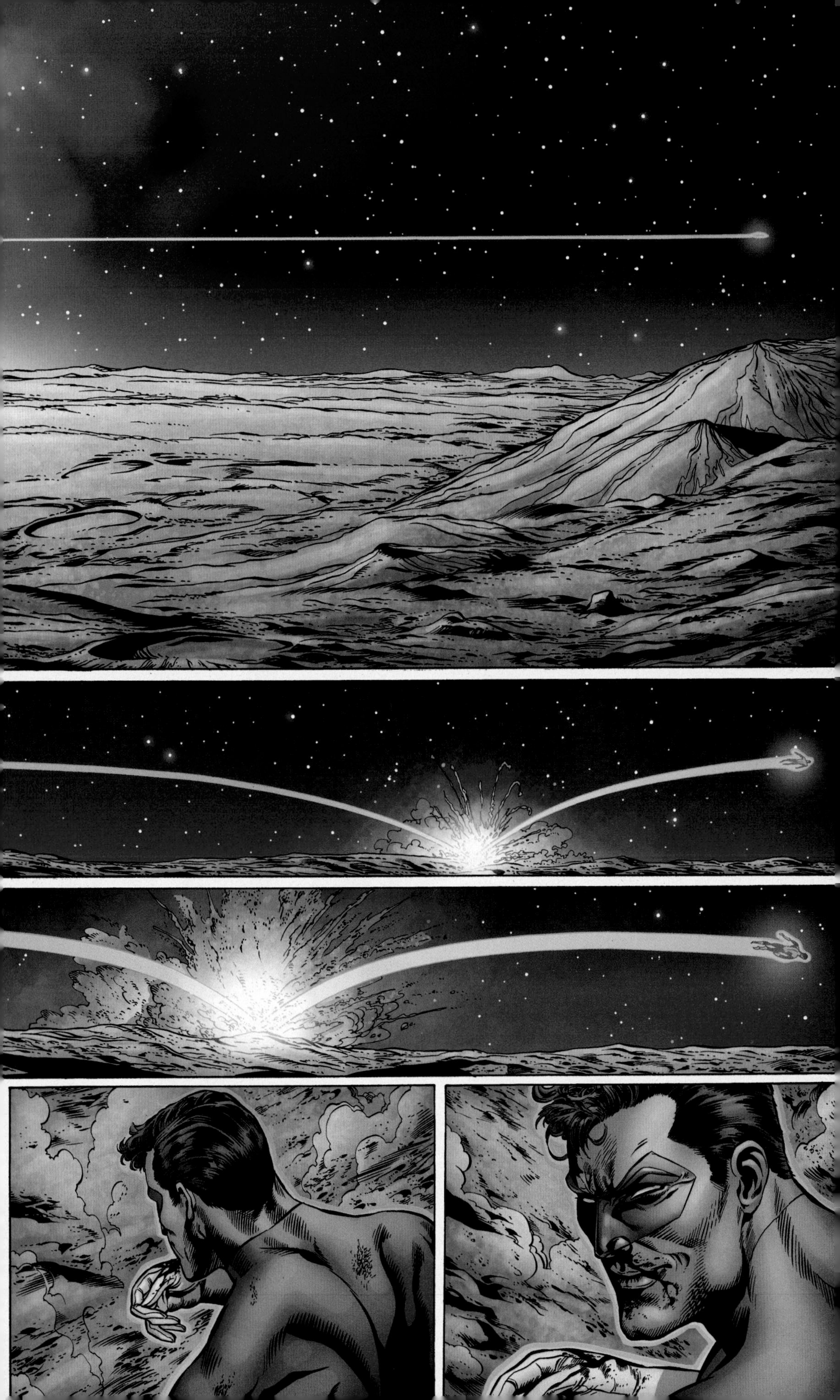

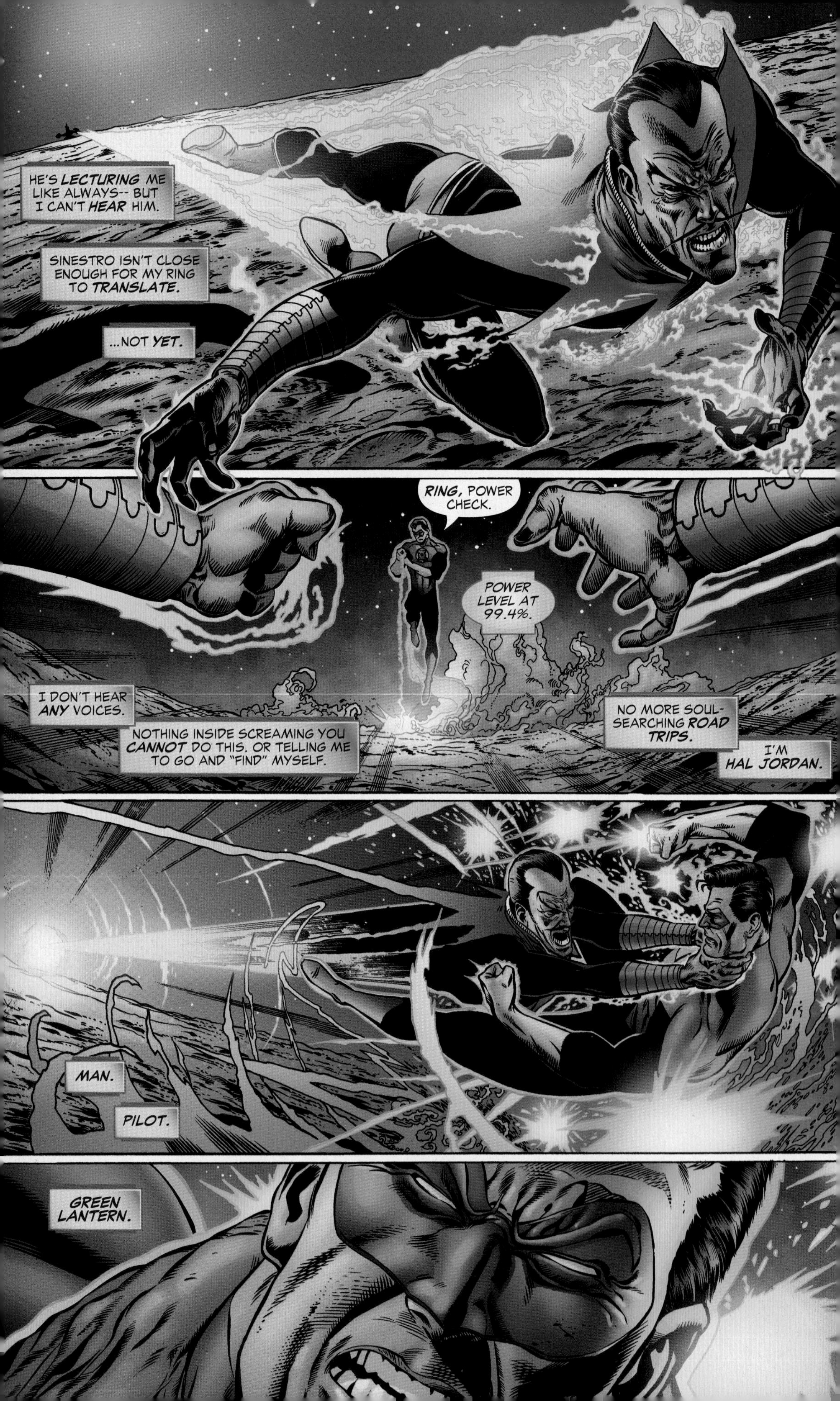
HE'S LECTURING ME LIKE ALWAYS-- BUT I CAN'T HEAR HIM.
SINESTRO ISN'T CLOSE ENOUGH FOR MY RING TO TRANSLATE.
...NOT YET.
RING, POWER CHECK.
POWER LEVEL AT 99.4%.
I DON'T HEAR ANY VOICES.
NOTHING INSIDE SCREAMING YOU CANNOT DO THIS. OR TELLING ME TO GO AND "FIND" MYSELF.
NO MORE SOUL-SEARCHING ROAD TRIPS.
I'M HAL JORDAN.
MAN.
PILOT.
GREEN LANTERN.

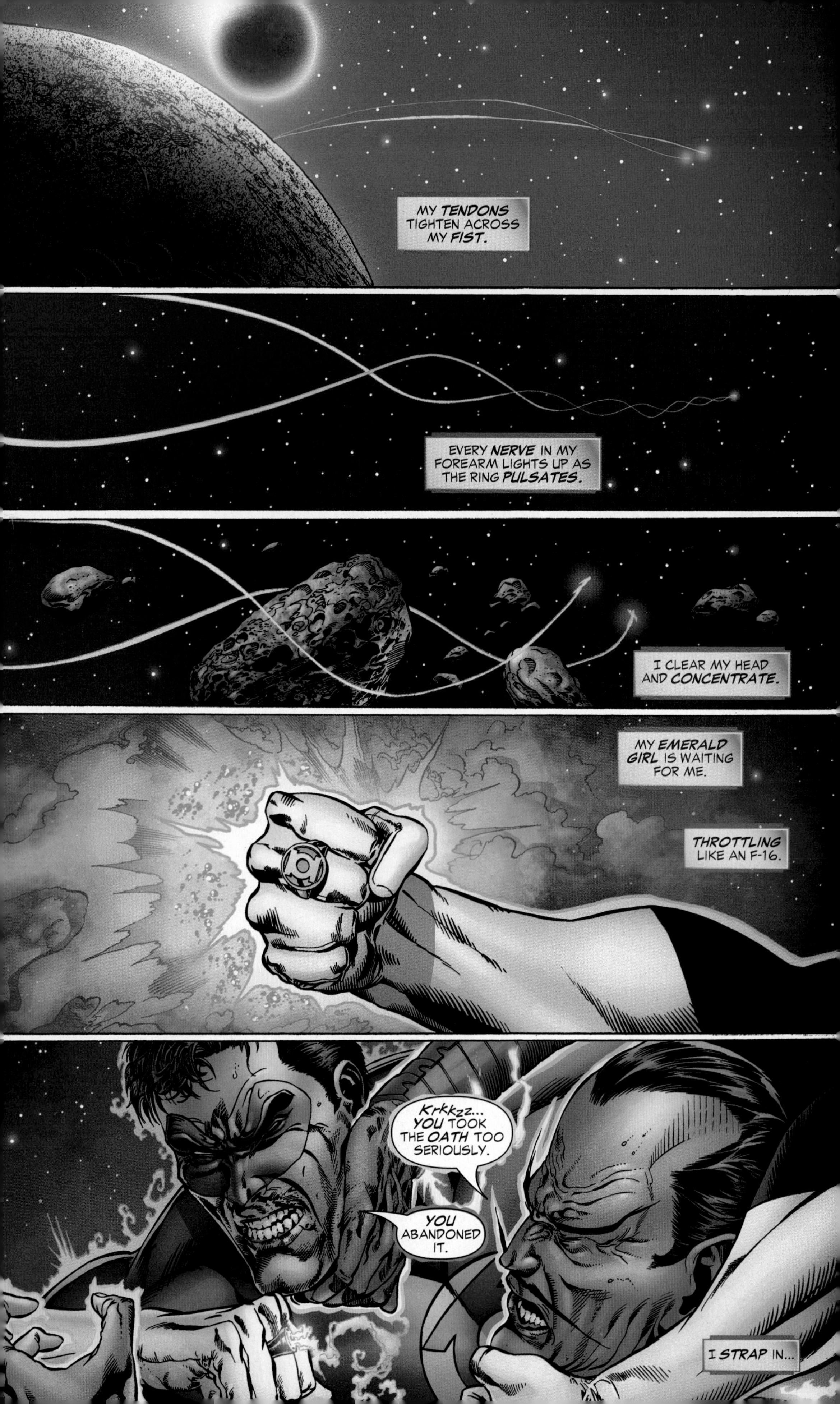
MY TENDONS TIGHTEN ACROSS MY FIST.
EVERY NERVE IN MY FOREARM LIGHTS UP AS THE RING PULSATES.
I CLEAR MY HEAD AND CONCENTRATE.
MY EMERALD GIRL IS WAITING FOR ME.
THROTTLING LIKE AN F-16.
Krkkzz... YOU TOOK THE OATH TOO SERIOUSLY.
YOU ABANDONED IT.
I STRAP IN...

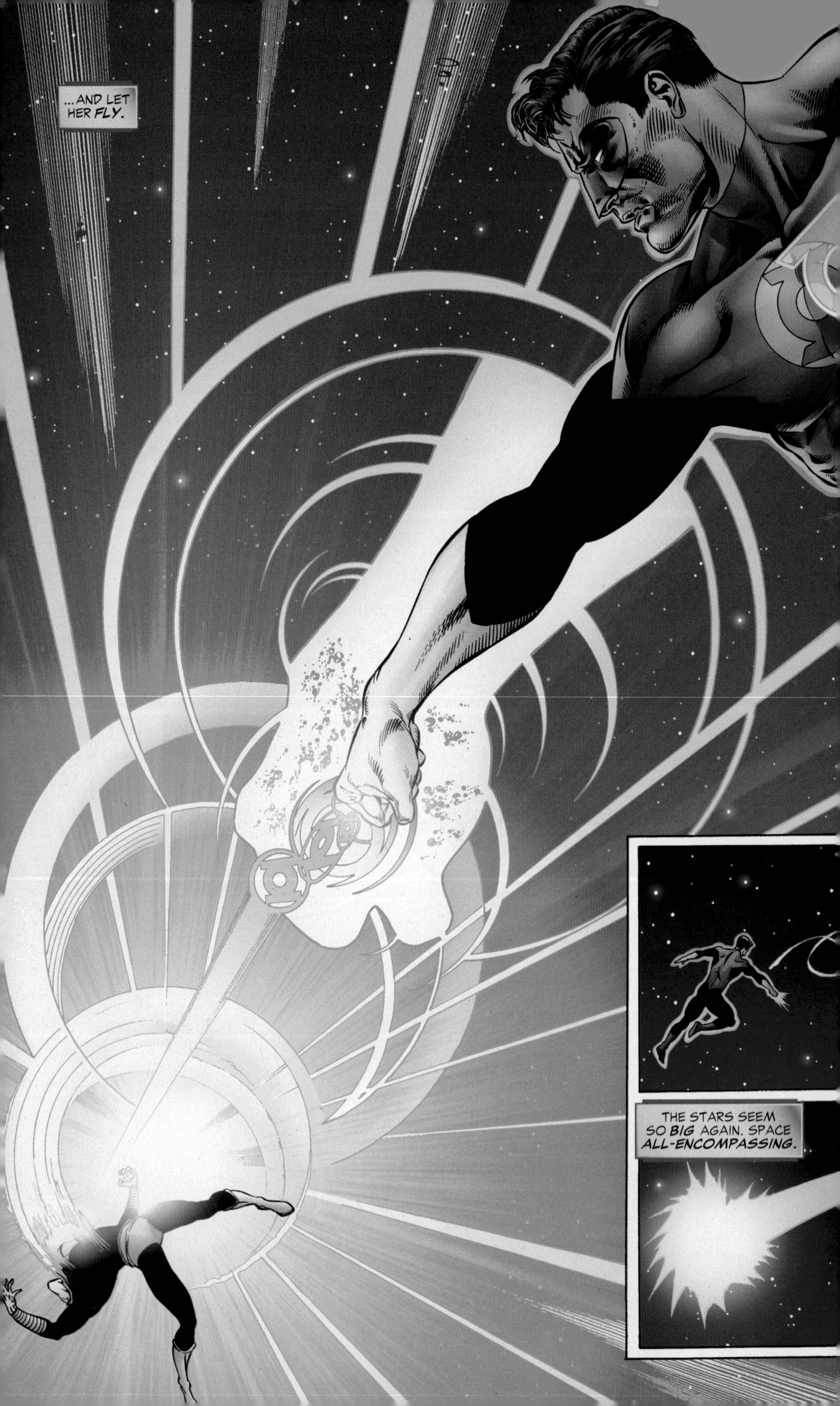
...AND LET HER FLY.
THE STARS SEEM SO BIG AGAIN. SPACE ALL-ENCOMPASSING.

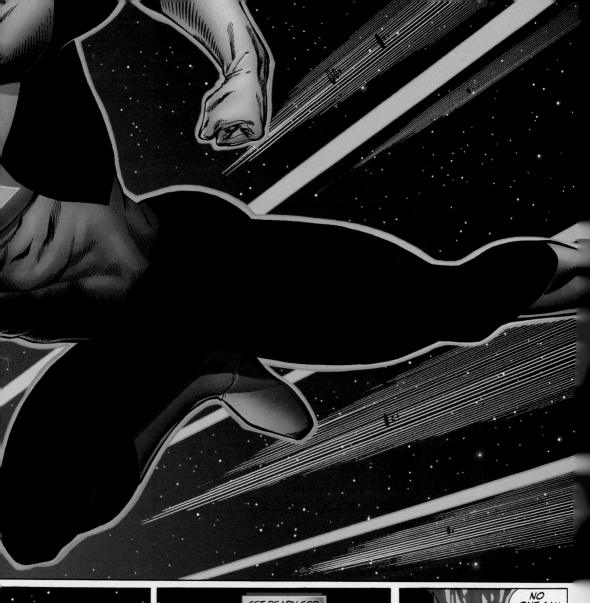

I PREP THE RING.

GET READY FOR ANOTHER SPIN.

THE OATH ABANDONED ME. YOU ALL DID.

WHEN YOU RIPPED KORUGAR FROM MY HANDS YOU LEFT IT IN CHAOS. UNDER THE CARE OF A NAIVE CHILD.

KATMA TUI COULD NOT REPLACE ME.

NO ONE CAN REPLACE ME.

KORUGAR'S TRUE PROTECTOR WILL HAVE HIS JUSTICE.

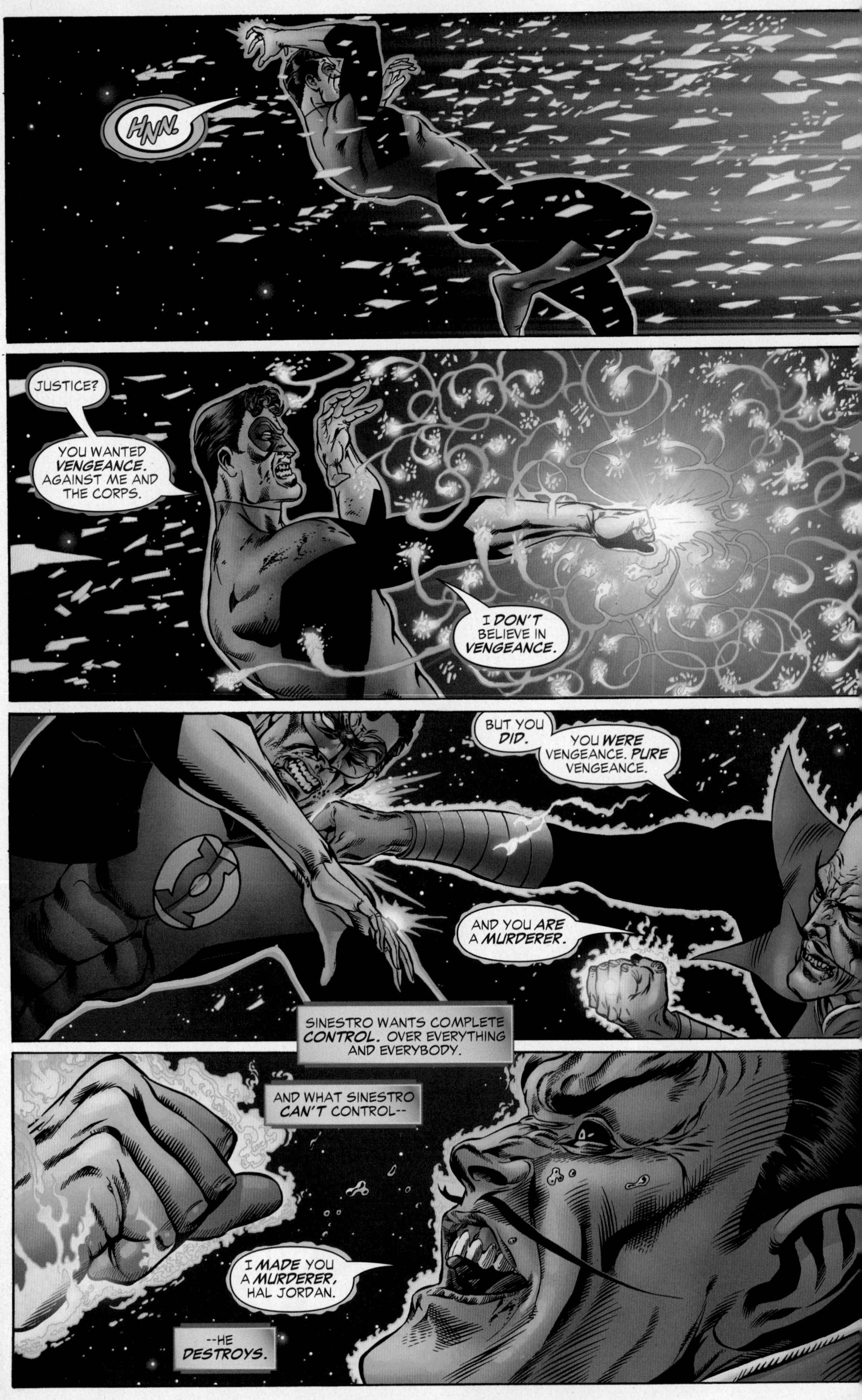

HNN.
JUSTICE?
YOU WANTED VENGEANCE. AGAINST ME AND THE CORPS.
I DON'T BELIEVE IN VENGEANCE.
BUT YOU DID.
YOU WERE VENGEANCE. PURE VENGEANCE.
AND YOU ARE A MURDERER.
SINESTRO WANTS COMPLETE CONTROL. OVER EVERYTHING AND EVERYBODY.
AND WHAT SINESTRO CAN'T CONTROL--
I MADE YOU A MURDERER, HAL JORDAN.
--HE DESTROYS.

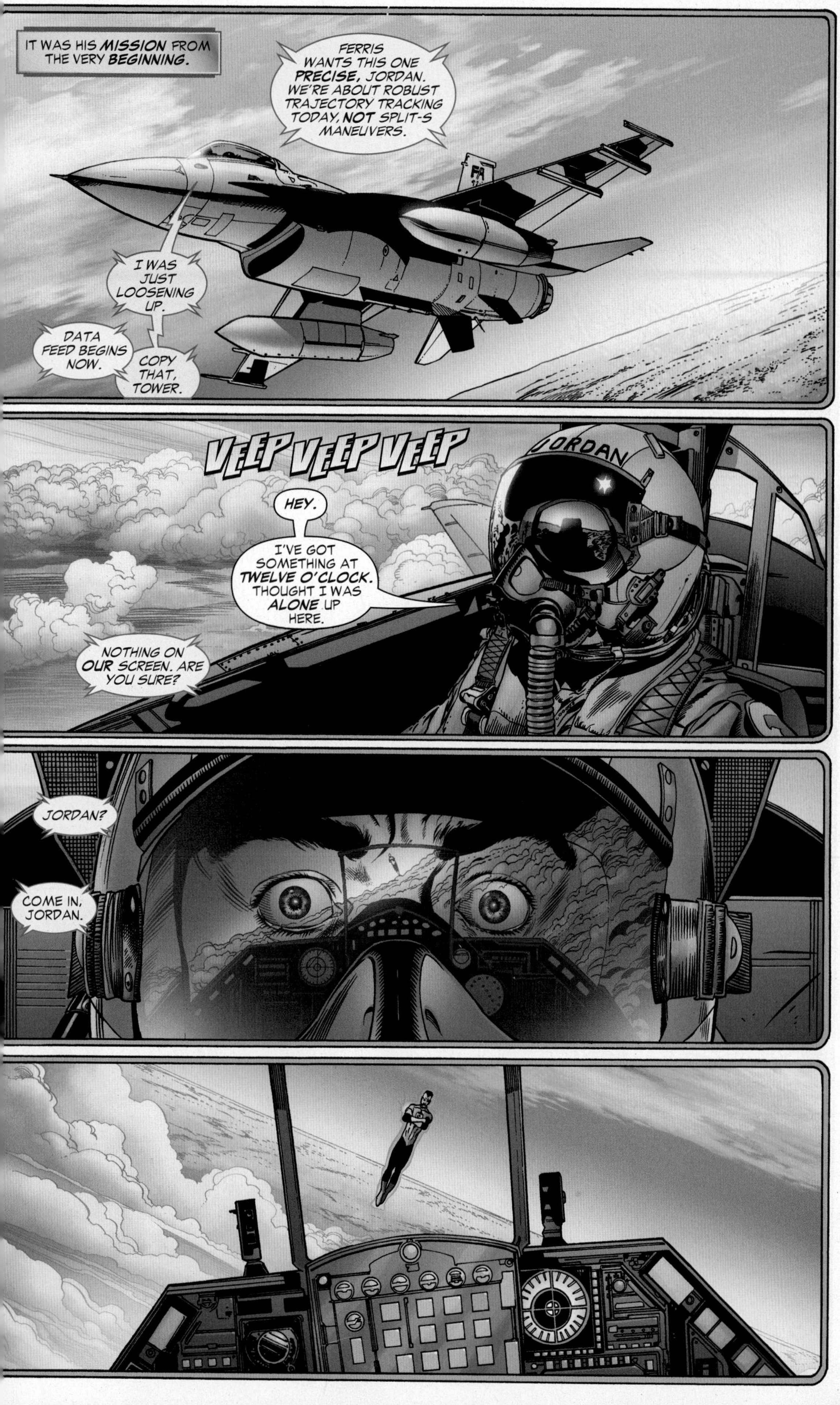
IT WAS HIS MISSION FROM THE VERY BEGINNING.
FERRIS WANTS THIS ONE PRECISE, JORDAN. WE'RE ABOUT ROBUST TRAJECTORY TRACKING TODAY, NOT SPLIT-S MANEUVERS.
I WAS JUST LOOSENING UP.
DATA FEED BEGINS NOW.
COPY THAT, TOWER.
VEEP VEEP VEEP
JORDAN
HEY.
I'VE GOT SOMETHING AT TWELVE O'CLOCK. THOUGHT I WAS ALONE UP HERE.
NOTHING ON OUR SCREEN. ARE YOU SURE?
JORDAN?
COME IN, JORDAN.

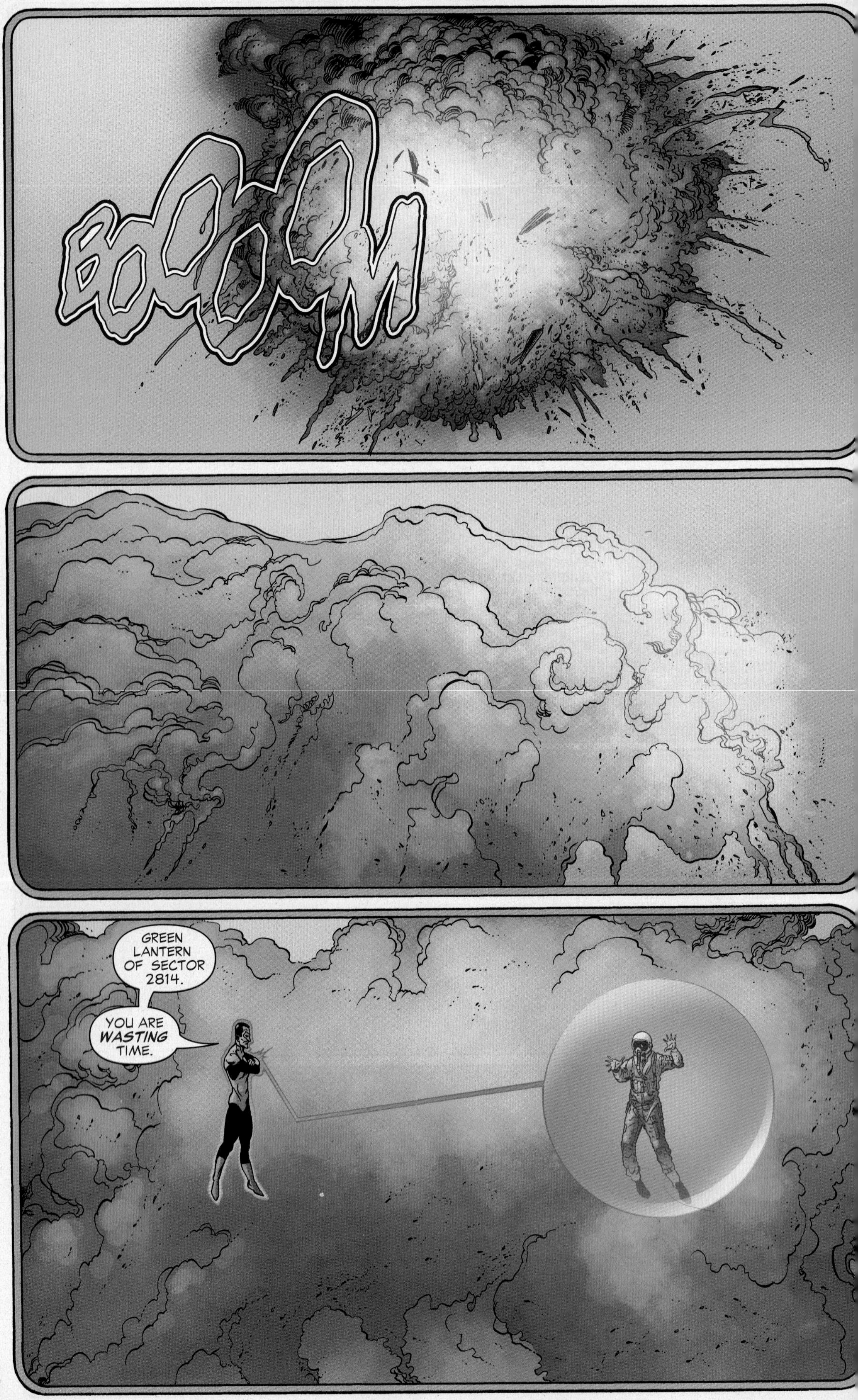
BOOOOM
GREEN LANTERN OF SECTOR 2814.
YOU ARE WASTING TIME.

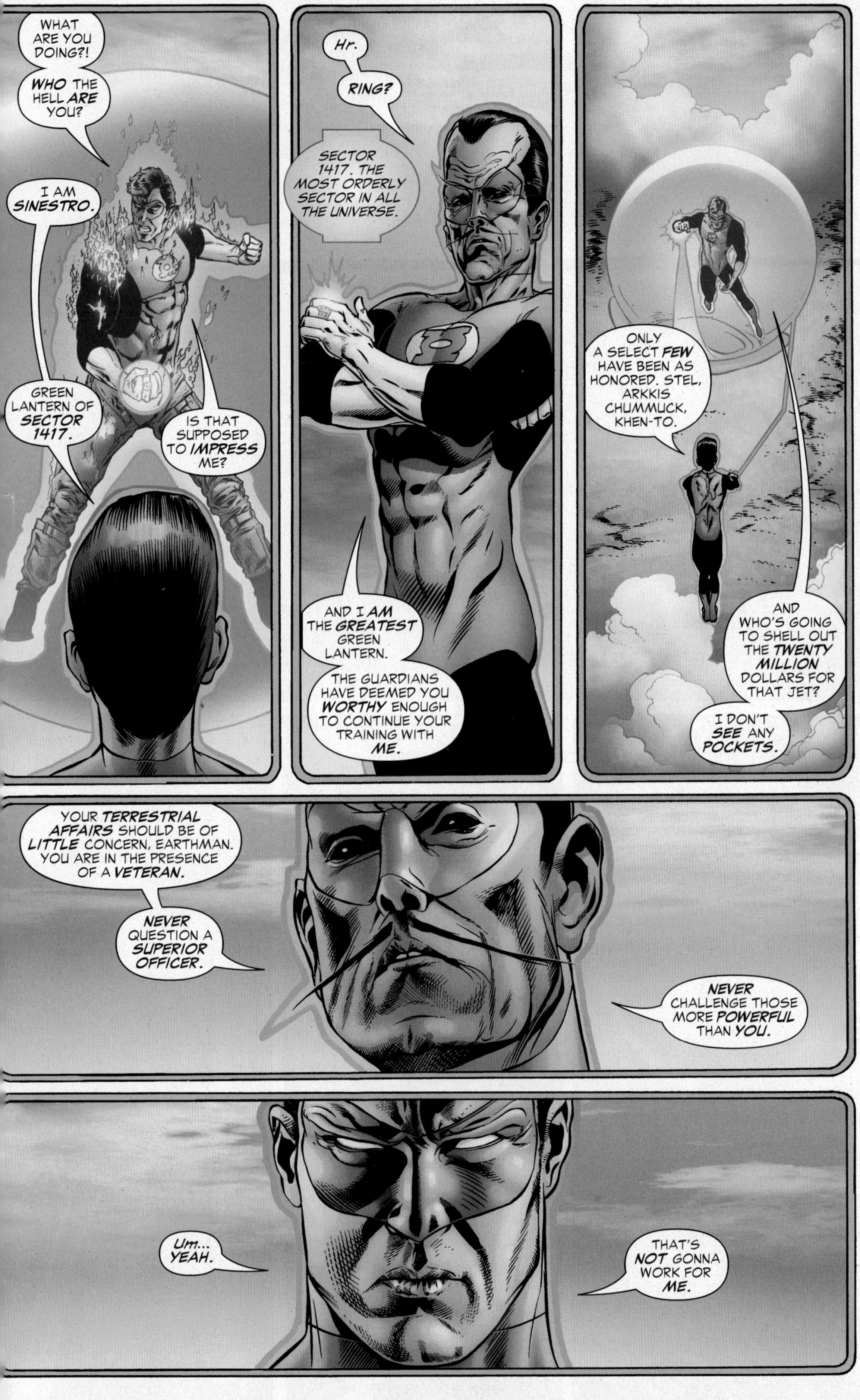
WHAT ARE YOU DOING?!
WHO THE HELL ARE YOU?
I AM SINESTRO.
GREEN LANTERN OF SECTOR 1417.
IS THAT SUPPOSED TO IMPRESS ME?
Hr.
RING?
SECTOR 1417. THE MOST ORDERLY SECTOR IN ALL THE UNIVERSE.
AND I AM THE GREATEST GREEN LANTERN.
THE GUARDIANS HAVE DEEMED YOU WORTHY ENOUGH TO CONTINUE YOUR TRAINING WITH ME.
ONLY A SELECT FEW HAVE BEEN AS HONORED. STEL, ARKKIS CHUMMUCK, KHEN-TO.
AND WHO'S GOING TO SHELL OUT THE TWENTY MILLION DOLLARS FOR THAT JET?
I DON'T SEE ANY POCKETS.
YOUR TERRESTRIAL AFFAIRS SHOULD BE OF LITTLE CONCERN, EARTHMAN. YOU ARE IN THE PRESENCE OF A VETERAN.
NEVER QUESTION A SUPERIOR OFFICER.
NEVER CHALLENGE THOSE MORE POWERFUL THAN YOU.
Um... YEAH.
THAT'S NOT GONNA WORK FOR ME.

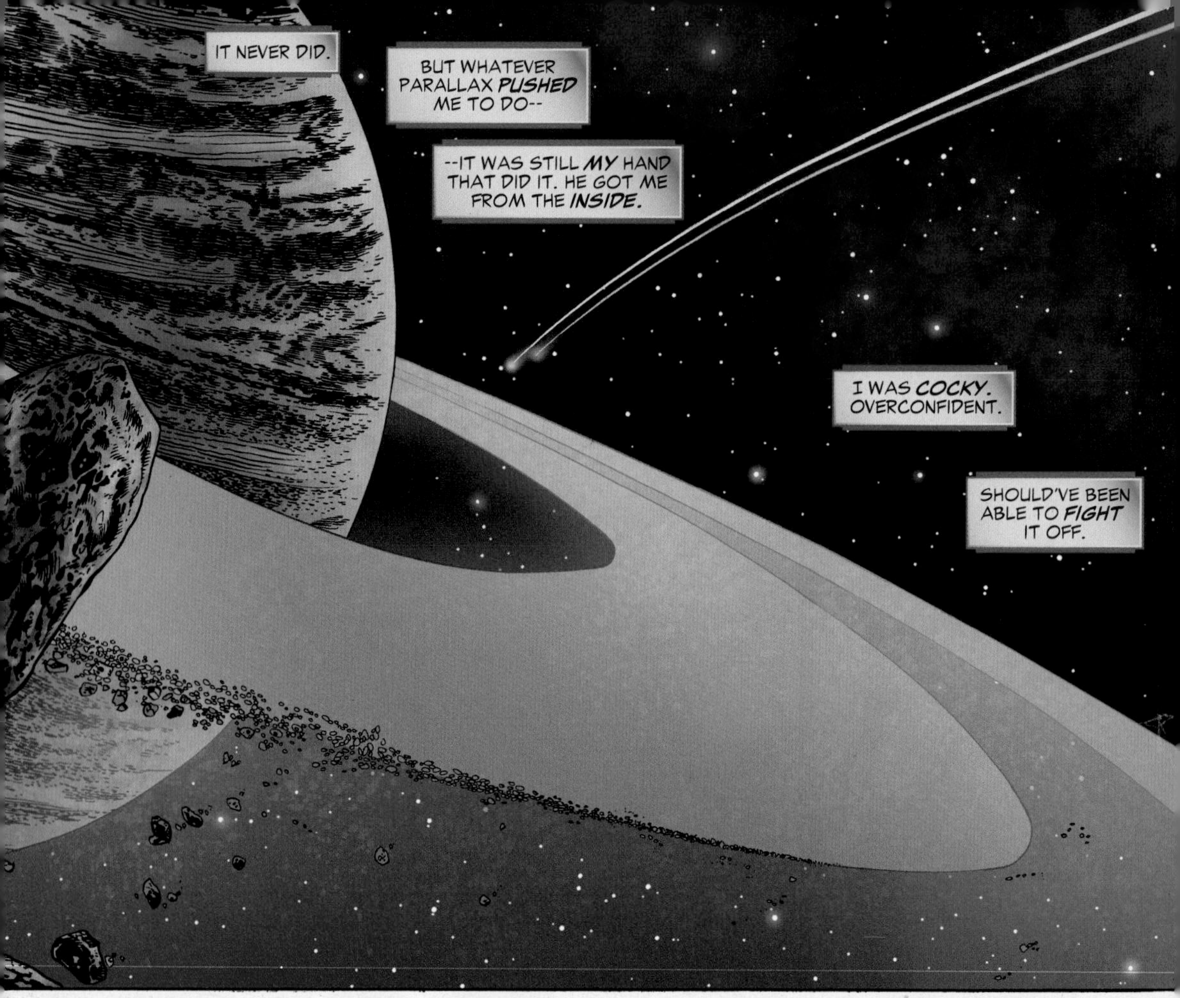
IT NEVER DID.
BUT WHATEVER PARALLAX PUSHED ME TO DO--
--IT WAS STILL MY HAND THAT DID IT. HE GOT ME FROM THE INSIDE.
I WAS COCKY. OVERCONFIDENT.
SHOULD'VE BEEN ABLE TO FIGHT IT OFF.

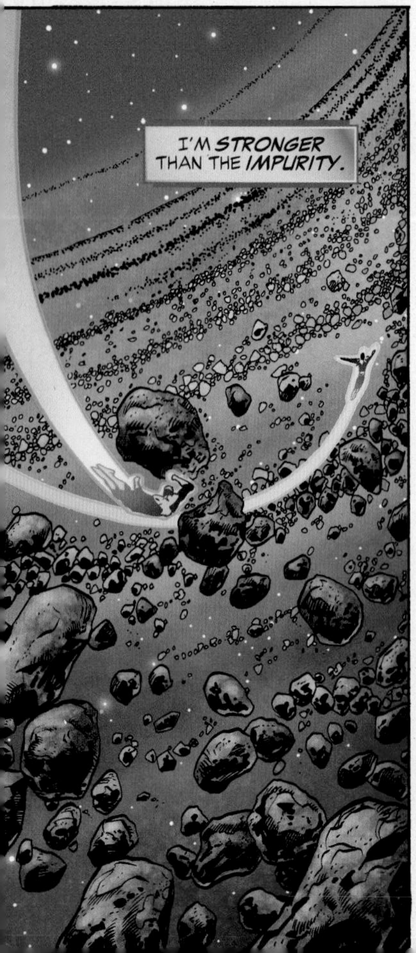
I'M STRONGER THAN THE IMPURITY.

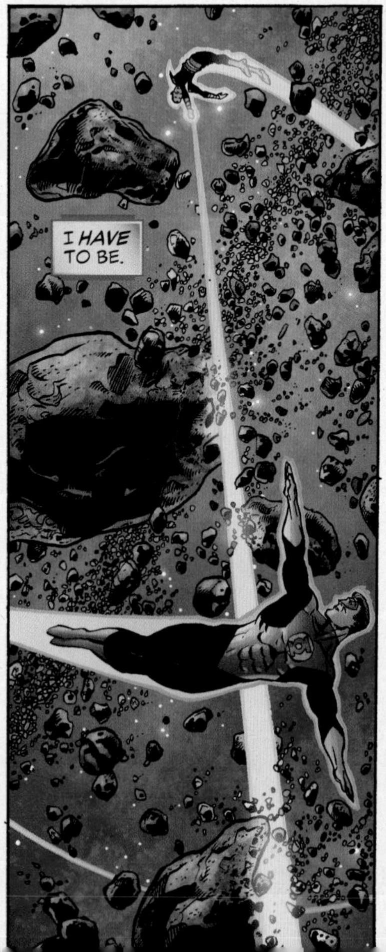
I HAVE TO BE.

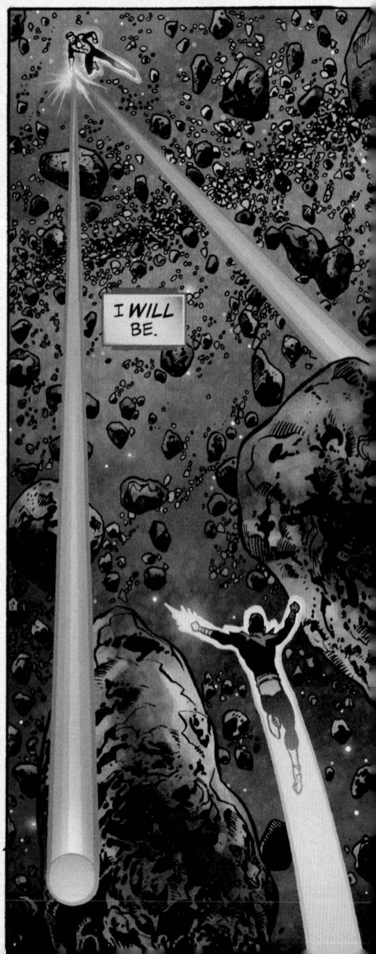
I WILL BE.

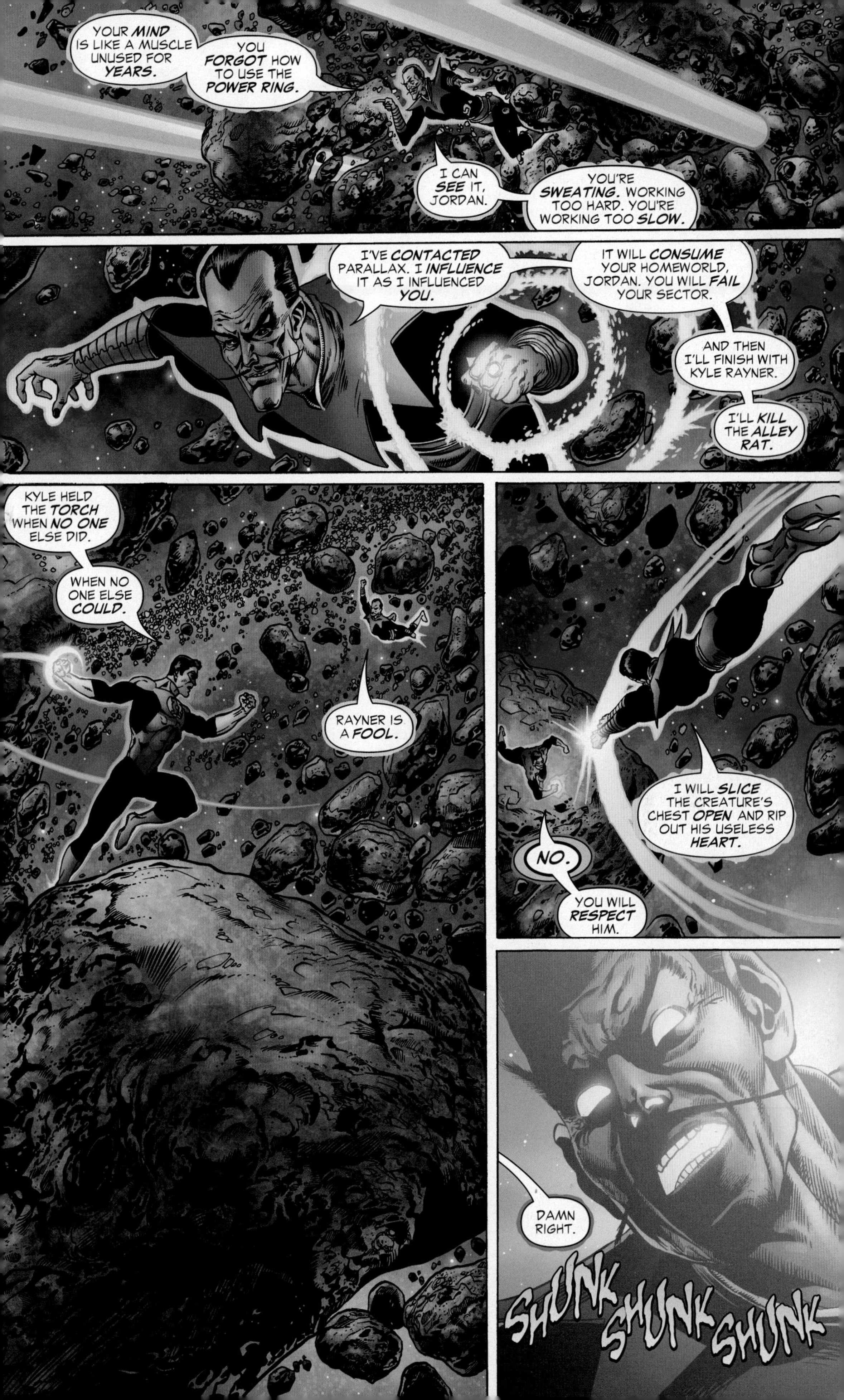
YOUR MIND IS LIKE A MUSCLE UNUSED FOR YEARS.
YOU FORGOT HOW TO USE THE POWER RING.
I CAN SEE IT, JORDAN.
YOU'RE SWEATING. WORKING TOO HARD. YOU'RE WORKING TOO SLOW.
I'VE CONTACTED PARALLAX. I INFLUENCE IT AS I INFLUENCED YOU.
IT WILL CONSUME YOUR HOMEWORLD, JORDAN. YOU WILL FAIL YOUR SECTOR.
AND THEN I'LL FINISH WITH KYLE RAYNER.
I'LL KILL THE ALLEY RAT.
KYLE HELD THE TORCH WHEN NO ONE ELSE DID.
WHEN NO ONE ELSE COULD.
RAYNER IS A FOOL.
I WILL SLICE THE CREATURE'S CHEST OPEN AND RIP OUT HIS USELESS HEART.
NO.
YOU WILL RESPECT HIM.
DAMN RIGHT.
SHUNK SHUNK SHUNK

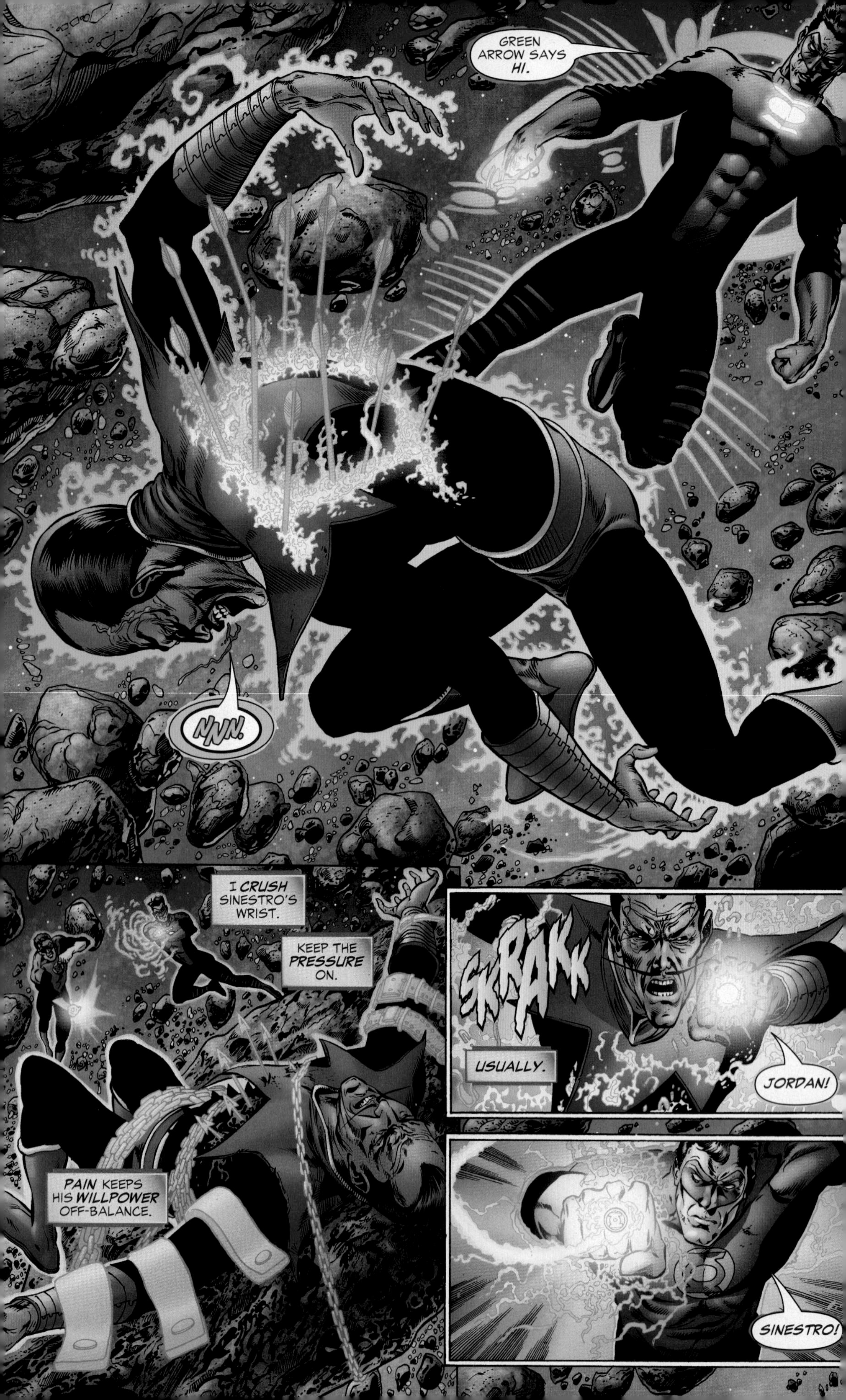
GREEN ARROW SAYS HI.
NNN.
I CRUSH SINESTRO'S WRIST.
KEEP THE PRESSURE ON.
PAIN KEEPS HIS WILLPOWER OFF-BALANCE.
SKRAKK
USUALLY.
JORDAN!
SINESTRO!

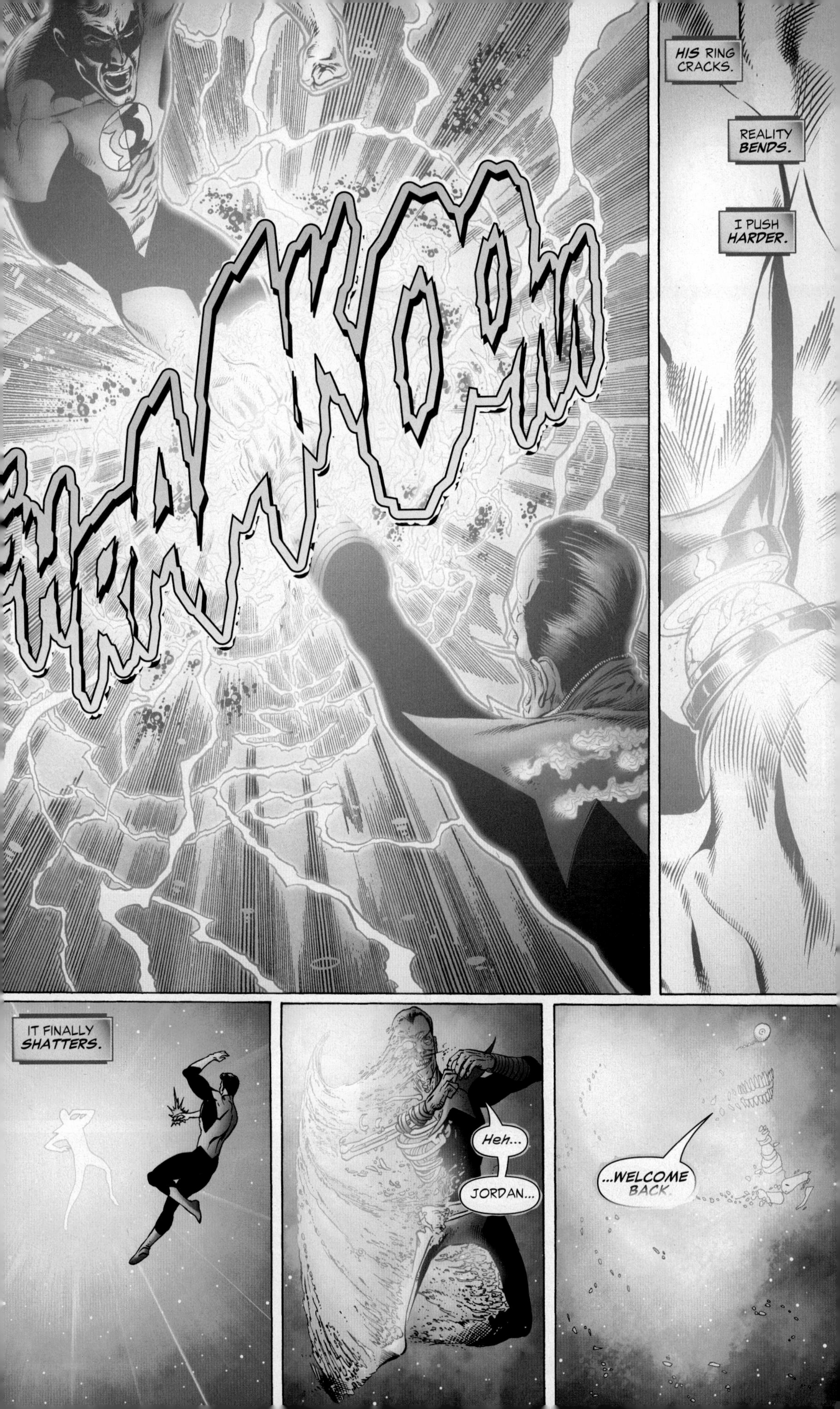
THAKOOM
HIS RING CRACKS.
REALITY BENDS.
I PUSH HARDER.
IT FINALLY SHATTERS.
Heh...
JORDAN...
...WELCOME BACK.

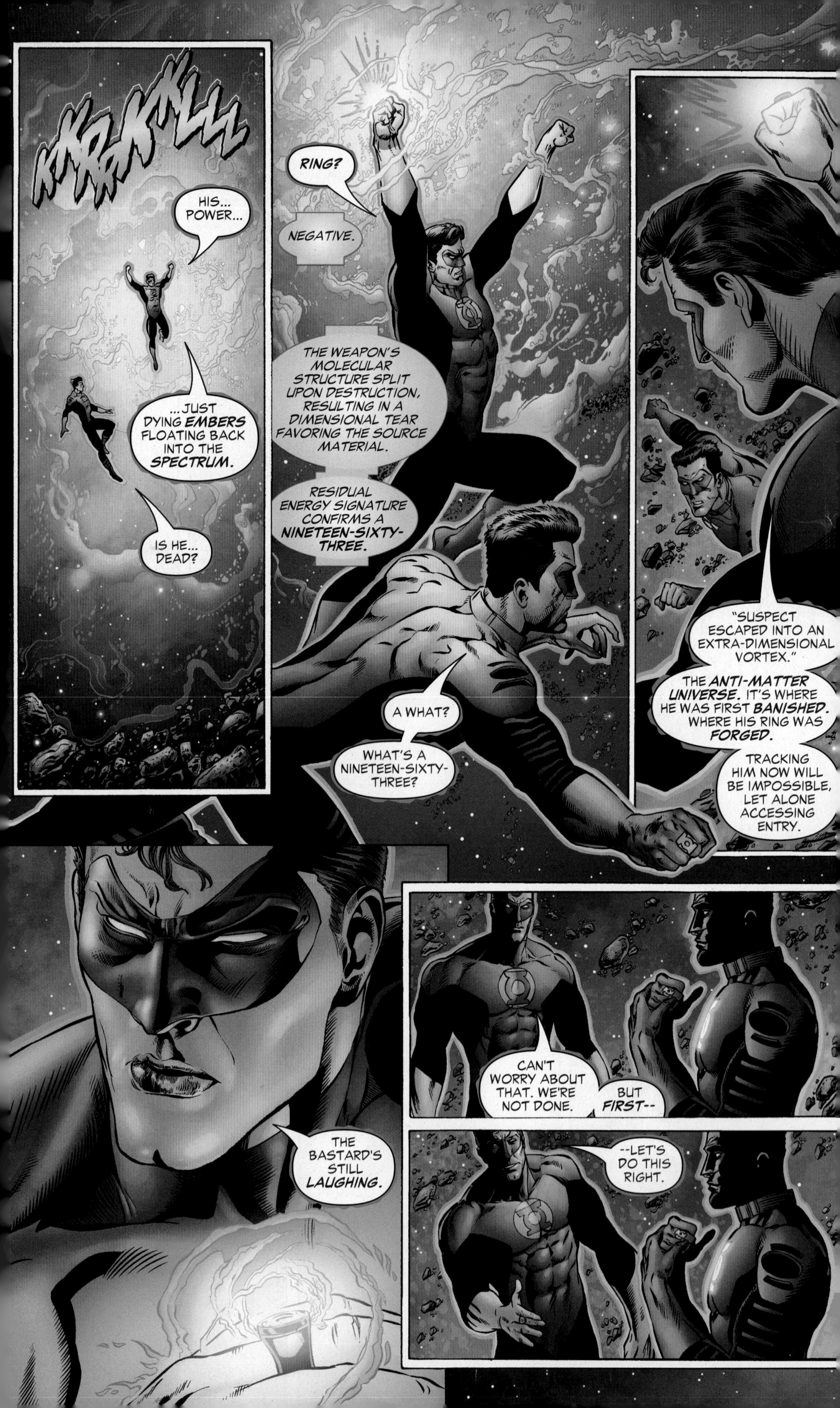
KKRAKKLLL
HIS... POWER...
...JUST DYING EMBERS FLOATING BACK INTO THE SPECTRUM.
IS HE... DEAD?
RING?
NEGATIVE.
THE WEAPON'S MOLECULAR STRUCTURE SPLIT UPON DESTRUCTION, RESULTING IN A DIMENSIONAL TEAR FAVORING THE SOURCE MATERIAL.
RESIDUAL ENERGY SIGNATURE CONFIRMS A NINETEEN-SIXTY-THREE.
A WHAT?
WHAT'S A NINETEEN-SIXTY-THREE?
"SUSPECT ESCAPED INTO AN EXTRA-DIMENSIONAL VORTEX."
THE ANTI-MATTER UNIVERSE. IT'S WHERE HE WAS FIRST BANISHED. WHERE HIS RING WAS FORGED.
TRACKING HIM NOW WILL BE IMPOSSIBLE, LET ALONE ACCESSING ENTRY.
THE BASTARD'S STILL LAUGHING.
CAN'T WORRY ABOUT THAT. WE'RE NOT DONE.
BUT FIRST--
--LET'S DO THIS RIGHT.

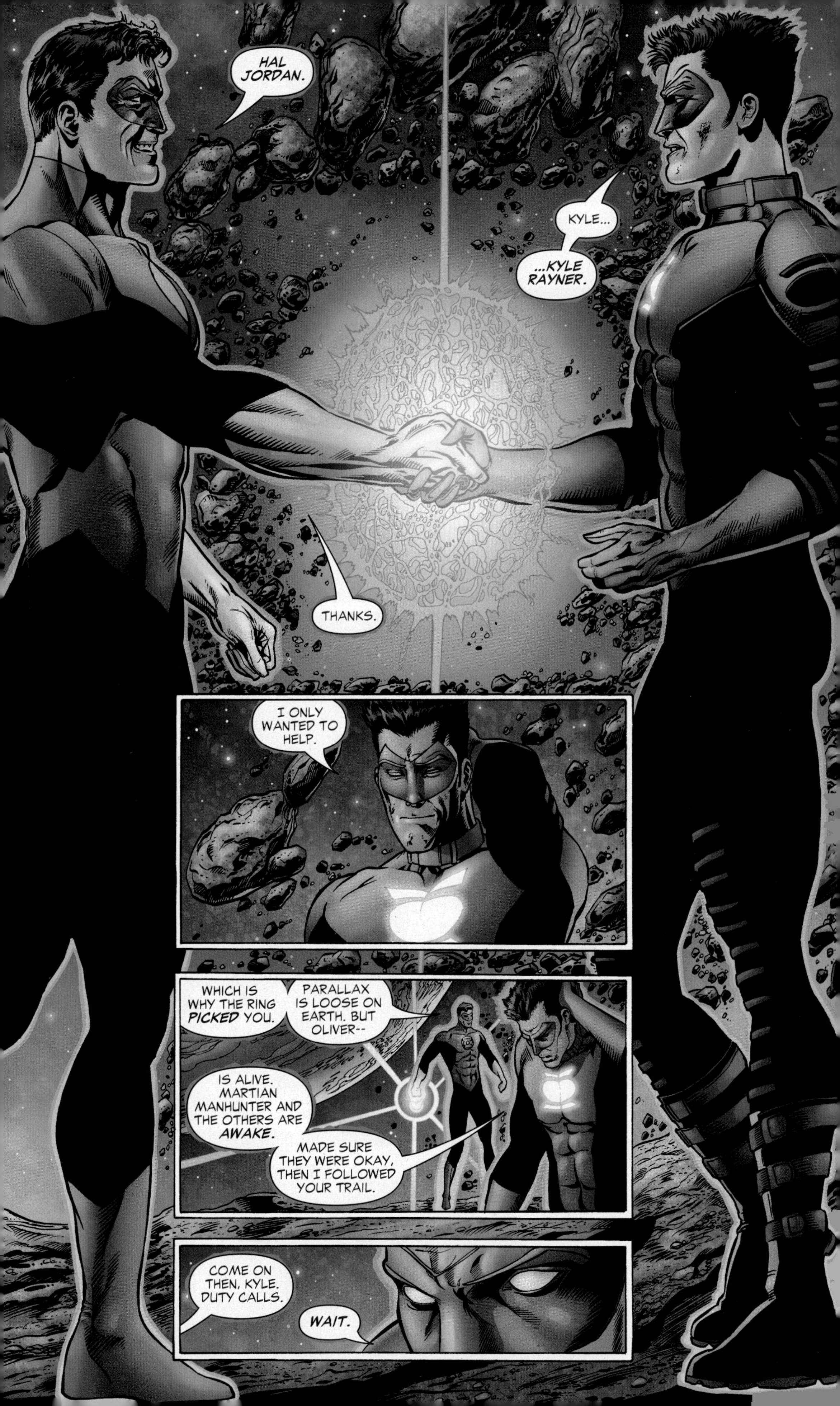
HAL JORDAN.
KYLE...
...KYLE RAYNER.
THANKS.
I ONLY WANTED TO HELP.
WHICH IS WHY THE RING PICKED YOU.
PARALLAX IS LOOSE ON EARTH. BUT OLIVER--
IS ALIVE. MARTIAN MANHUNTER AND THE OTHERS ARE AWAKE.
MADE SURE THEY WERE OKAY, THEN I FOLLOWED YOUR TRAIL.
COME ON THEN, KYLE. DUTY CALLS.
WAIT.

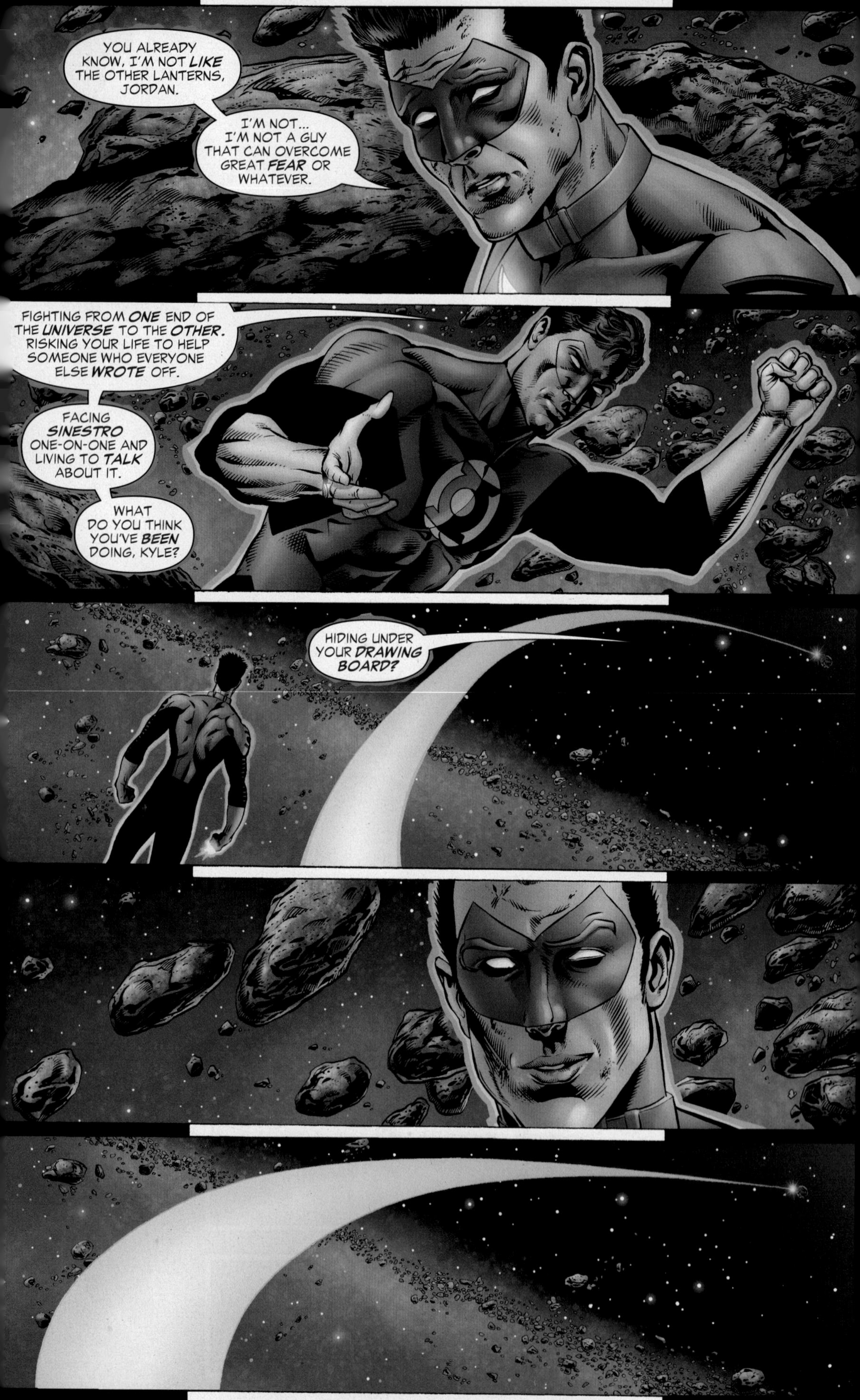
YOU ALREADY KNOW, I'M NOT LIKE THE OTHER LANTERNS, JORDAN.
I'M NOT... I'M NOT A GUY THAT CAN OVERCOME GREAT FEAR OR WHATEVER.
FIGHTING FROM ONE END OF THE UNIVERSE TO THE OTHER. RISKING YOUR LIFE TO HELP SOMEONE WHO EVERYONE ELSE WROTE OFF.
FACING SINESTRO ONE-ON-ONE AND LIVING TO TALK ABOUT IT.
WHAT DO YOU THINK YOU'VE BEEN DOING, KYLE?
HIDING UNDER YOUR DRAWING BOARD?

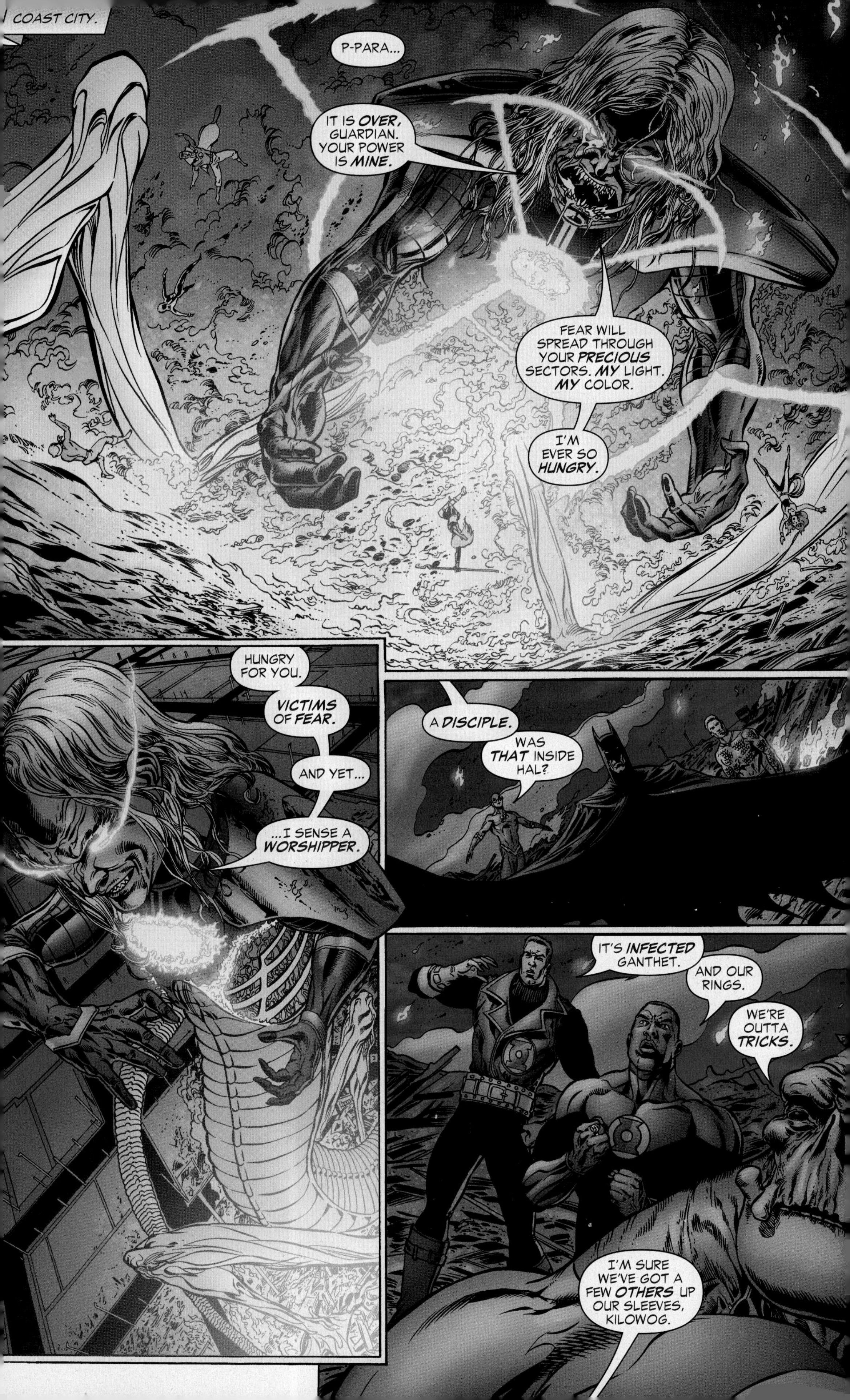
COAST CITY.
P-PARA...
IT IS OVER, GUARDIAN. YOUR POWER IS MINE.
FEAR WILL SPREAD THROUGH YOUR PRECIOUS SECTORS. MY LIGHT. MY COLOR.
I'M EVER SO HUNGRY.
HUNGRY FOR YOU.
VICTIMS OF FEAR.
AND YET...
...I SENSE A WORSHIPPER.
A DISCIPLE.
WAS THAT INSIDE HAL?
IT'S INFECTED GANTHET.
AND OUR RINGS.
WE'RE OUTTA TRICKS.
I'M SURE WE'VE GOT A FEW OTHERS UP OUR SLEEVES, KILOWOG.

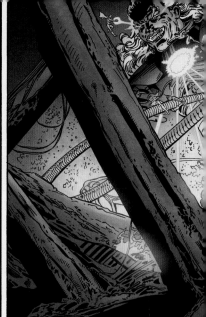

POLISH OFF YOUR RINGS AND STAND TOGETHER.

REMEMBER FEAR AND YOU CAN SHAKE OFF PARALLAX.

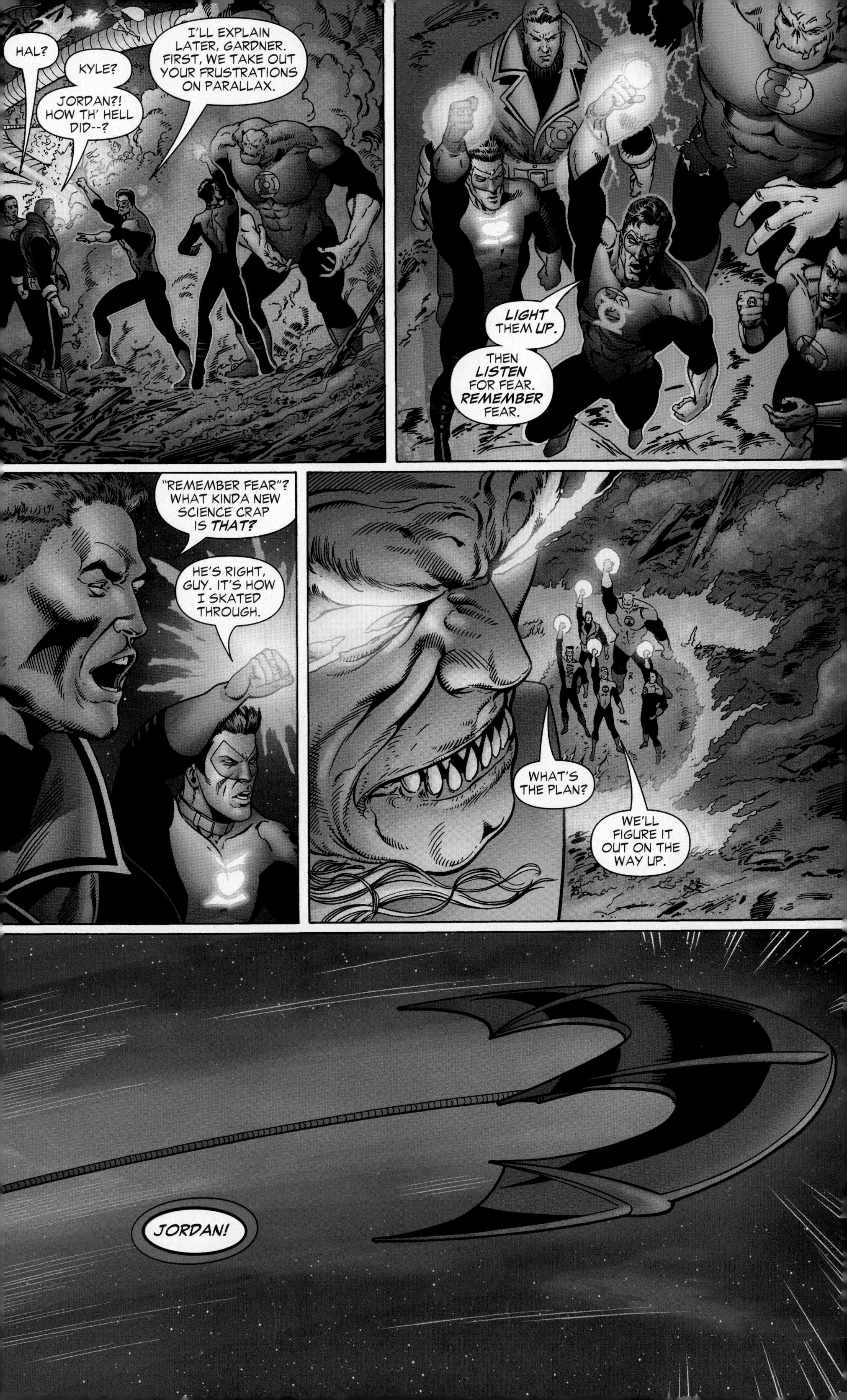
HAL?
KYLE?
JORDAN?! HOW TH' HELL DID--?
I'LL EXPLAIN LATER, GARDNER. FIRST, WE TAKE OUT YOUR FRUSTRATIONS ON PARALLAX.
LIGHT THEM UP.
THEN LISTEN FOR FEAR. REMEMBER FEAR.
"REMEMBER FEAR"? WHAT KINDA NEW SCIENCE CRAP IS THAT?
HE'S RIGHT, GUY. IT'S HOW I SKATED THROUGH.
WHAT'S THE PLAN?
WE'LL FIGURE IT OUT ON THE WAY UP.
JORDAN!

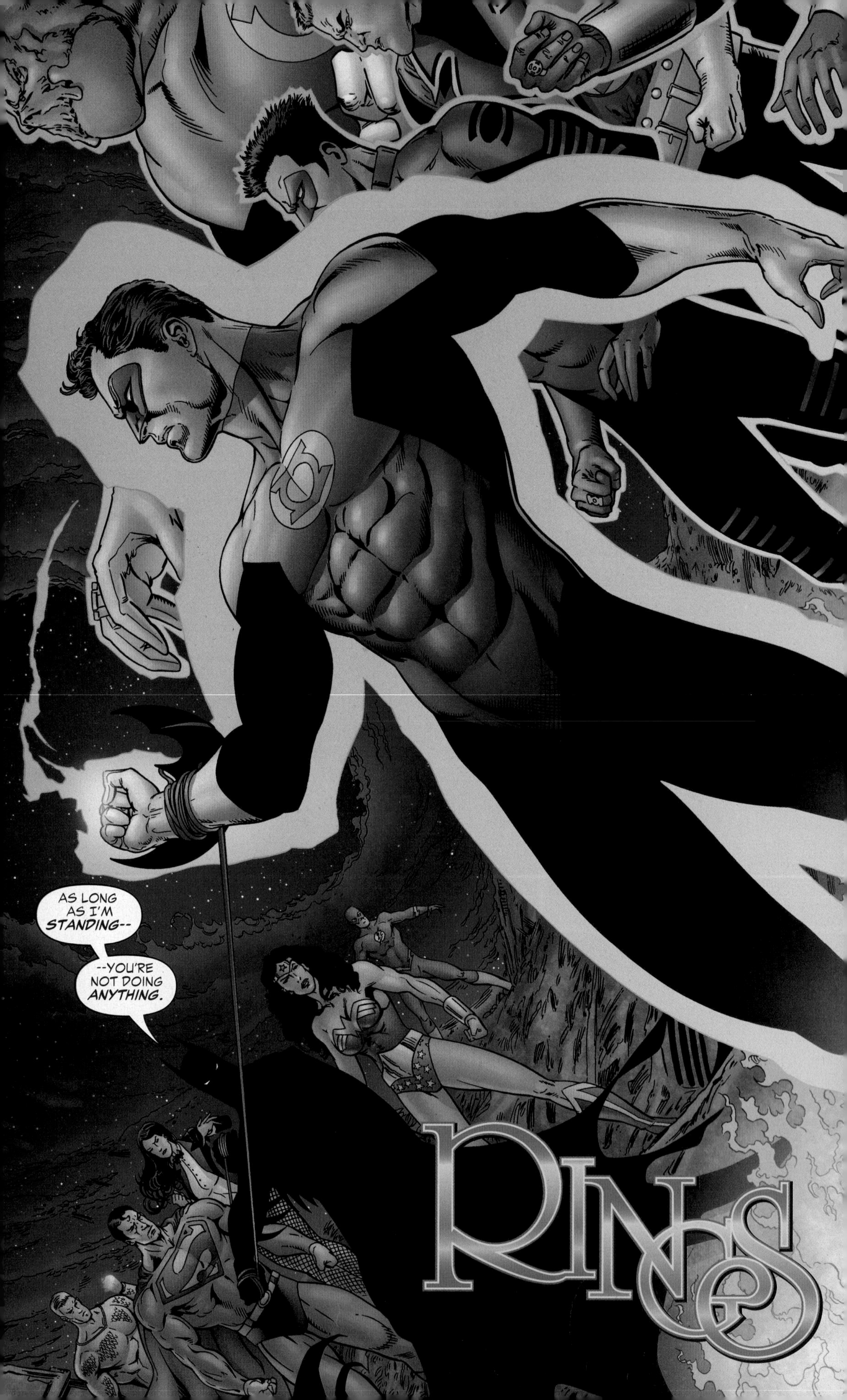
AS LONG AS I'M STANDING--
--YOU'RE NOT DOING ANYTHING.
RINGS

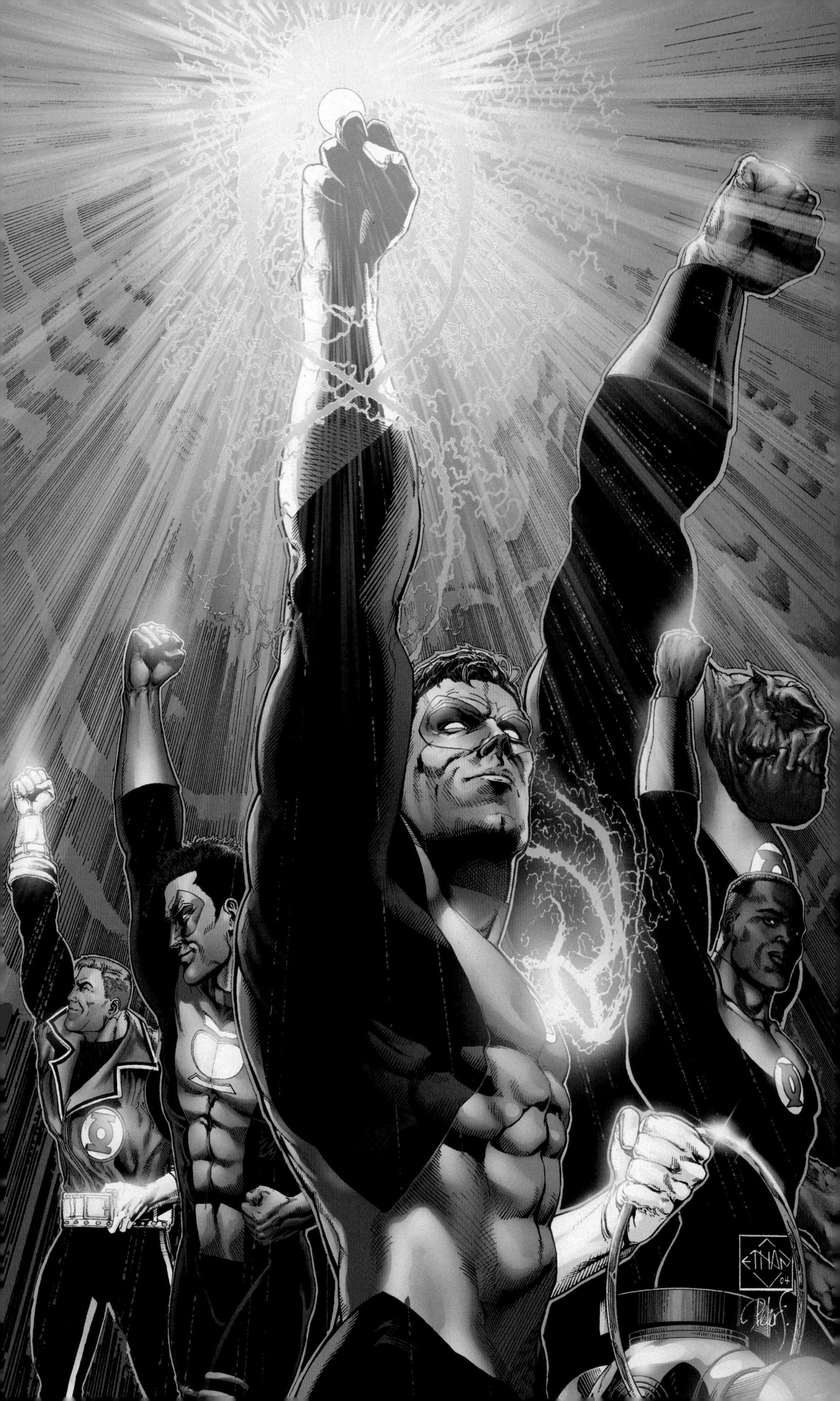

COAST CITY.

BATMAN BELIEVES IN EVERYTHING I *DON'T*.

I WANT AN *EXPLANATION*, JORDAN.

DARKNESS AND *FEAR*.

I LIVE OFF *OTHER* THINGS.

FIGURE IT *OUT*.

FSS

FSSS

FSSS

LIGHT AND *COURAGE*.

WHAT'S THE HELL'S IT DOING?

IT'S *INFECTING* EVERYONE BUT US.

THOOOM

RIOTS ARE BREAKING OUT IN LOS ANGELES. PANICKED COPS ARE *TRIGGER-HAPPY* IN STAR CITY.

IMAGES ARE [FL]ICKERING IN FRONT OF MY EYES LIKE A SUBLIMINAL *SLIDE SHOW*.

JORDAN.

WE'RE *NOT* DONE--

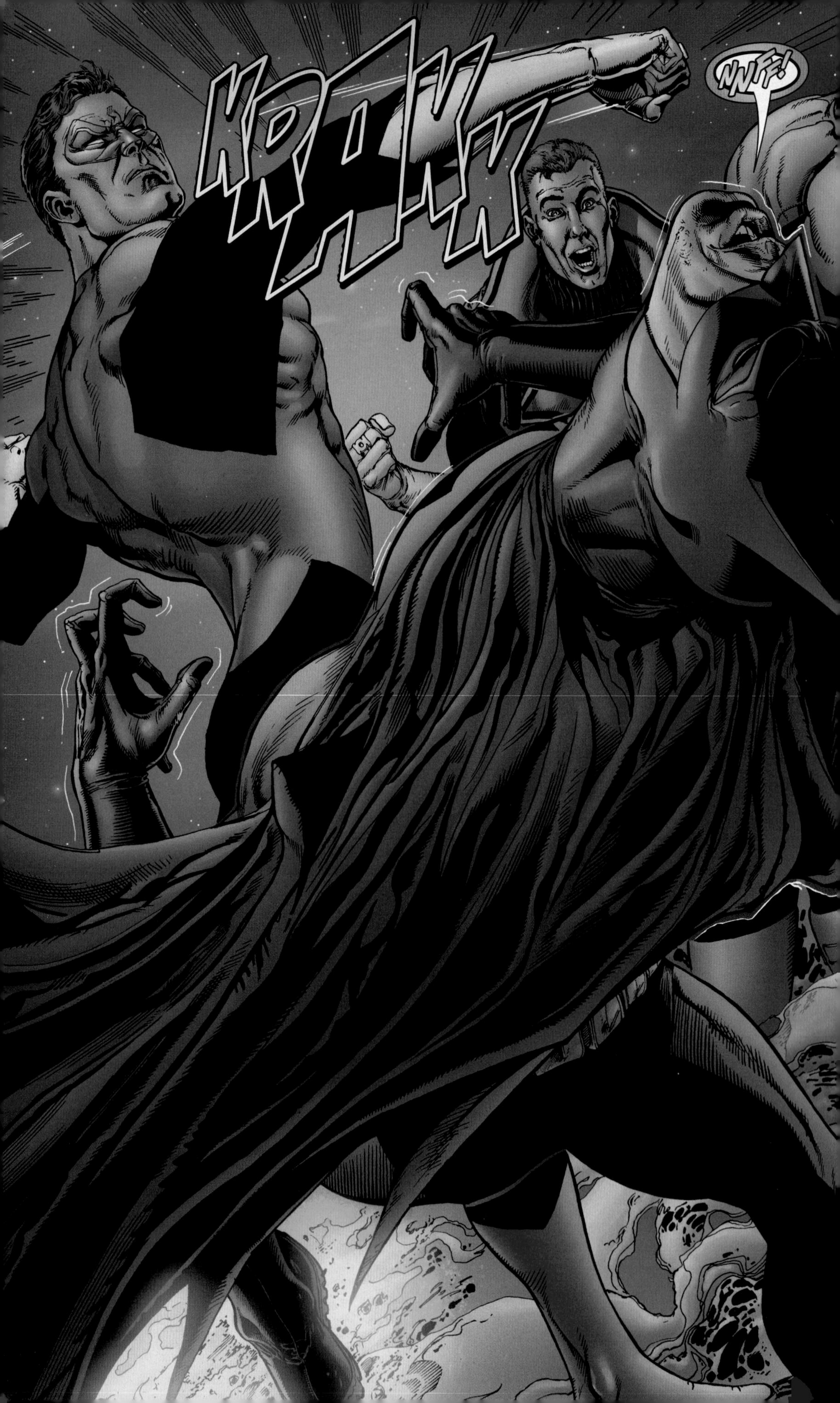
KRANK
NNFF!

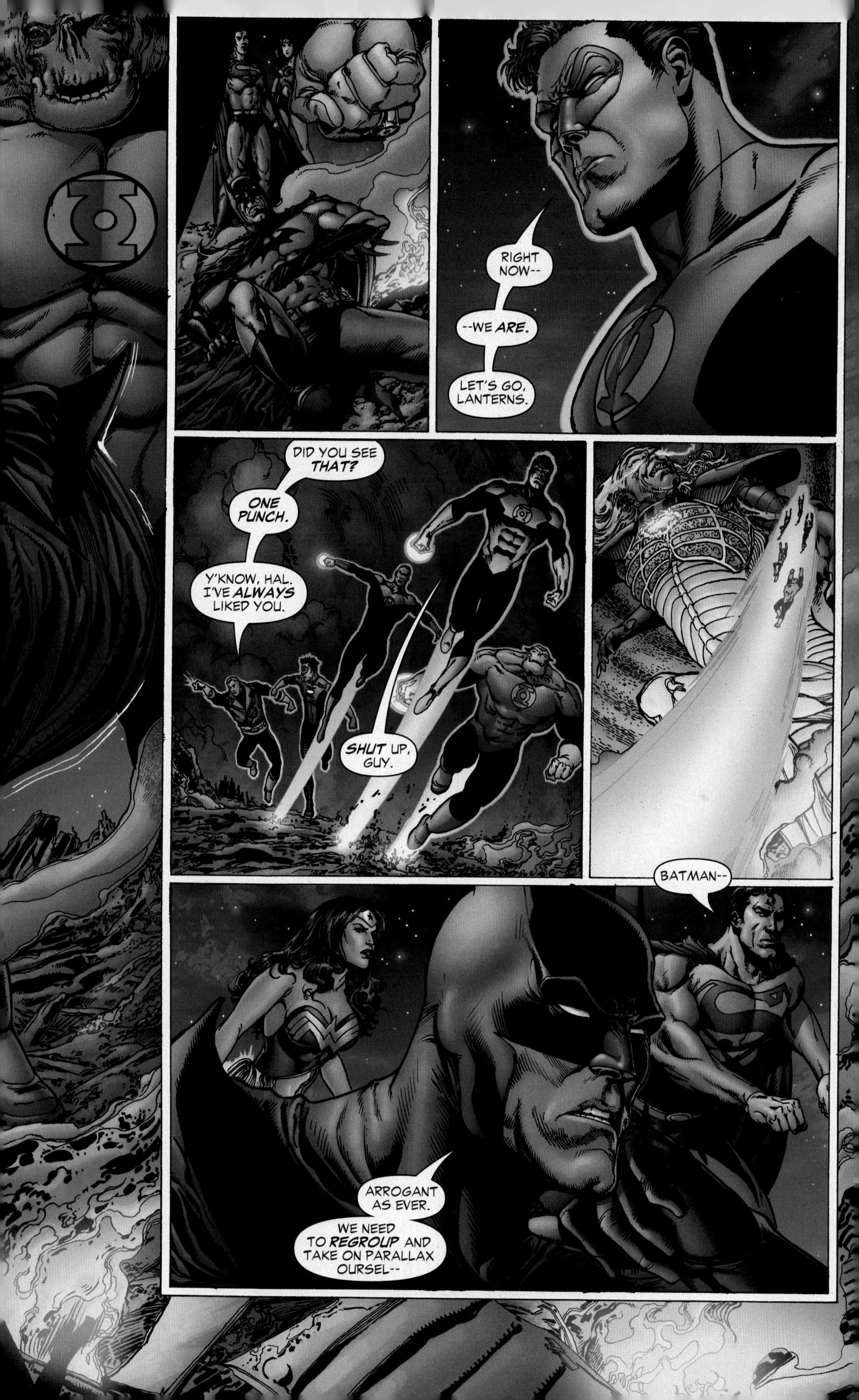
RIGHT NOW--
--WE ARE.
LET'S GO, LANTERNS.
DID YOU SEE THAT?
ONE PUNCH.
Y'KNOW, HAL. I'VE ALWAYS LIKED YOU.
SHUT UP, GUY.
BATMAN--
ARROGANT AS EVER.
WE NEED TO REGROUP AND TAKE ON PARALLAX OURSEL--

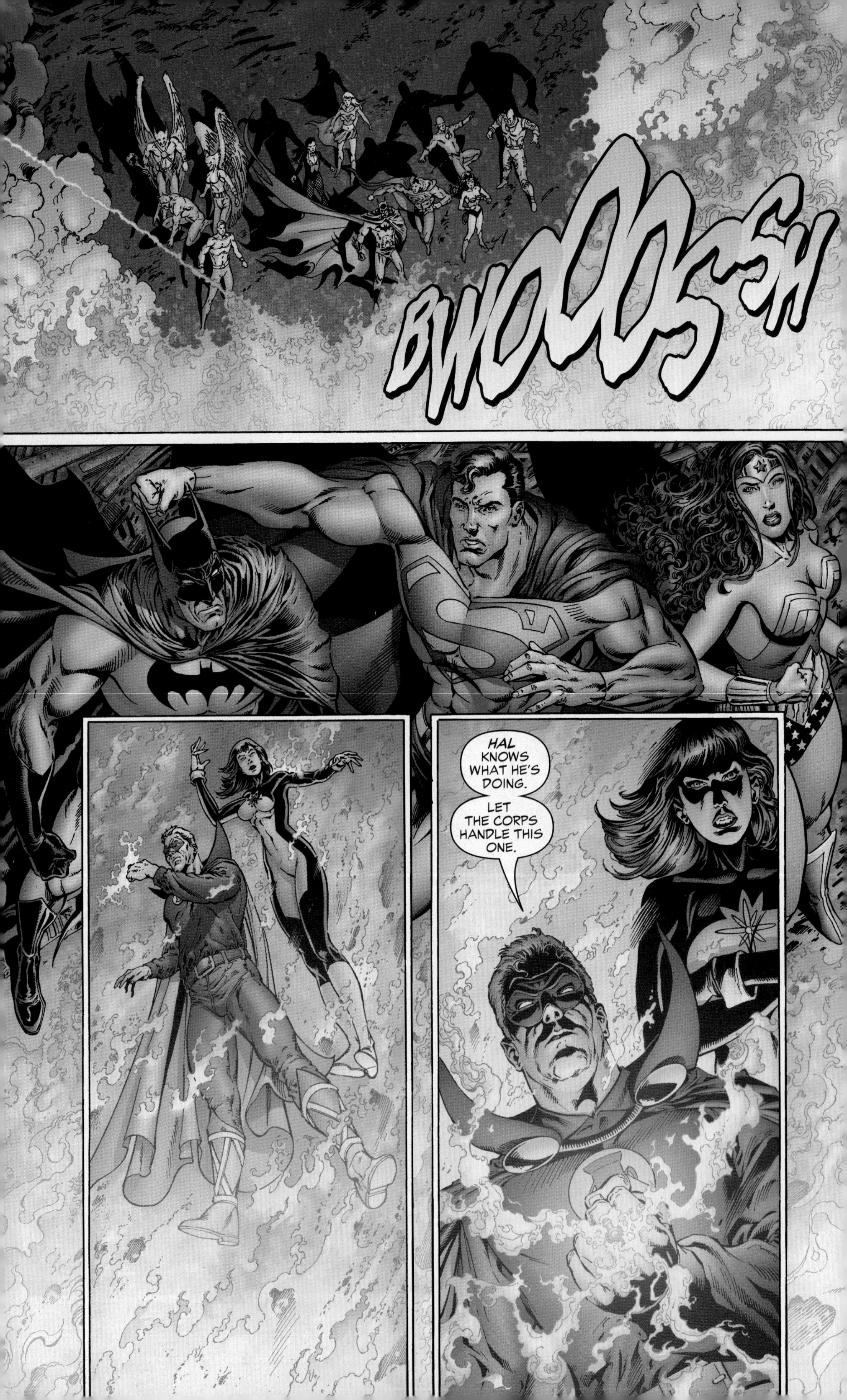
BWOOOSH
HAL KNOWS WHAT HE'S DOING.
LET THE CORPS HANDLE THIS ONE.

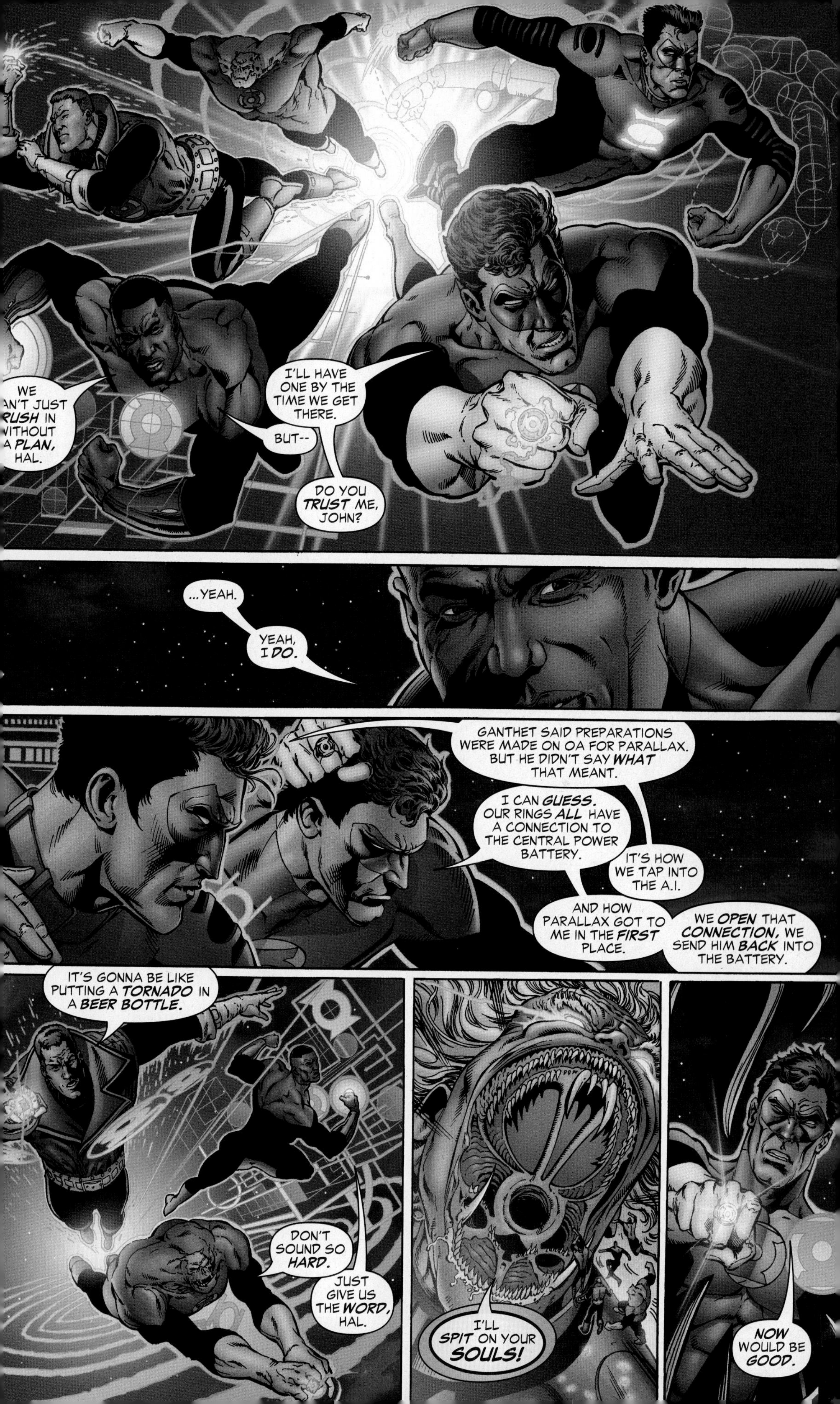

WE ...AN'T JUST RUSH IN WITHOUT A PLAN, HAL.
BUT--
I'LL HAVE ONE BY THE TIME WE GET THERE.
DO YOU TRUST ME, JOHN?
...YEAH.
YEAH, I DO.
GANTHET SAID PREPARATIONS WERE MADE ON OA FOR PARALLAX. BUT HE DIDN'T SAY WHAT THAT MEANT.
I CAN GUESS. OUR RINGS ALL HAVE A CONNECTION TO THE CENTRAL POWER BATTERY.
IT'S HOW WE TAP INTO THE A.I.
AND HOW PARALLAX GOT TO ME IN THE FIRST PLACE.
WE OPEN THAT CONNECTION, WE SEND HIM BACK INTO THE BATTERY.
IT'S GONNA BE LIKE PUTTING A TORNADO IN A BEER BOTTLE.
DON'T SOUND SO HARD.
JUST GIVE US THE WORD, HAL.
I'LL SPIT ON YOUR SOULS!
NOW WOULD BE GOOD.

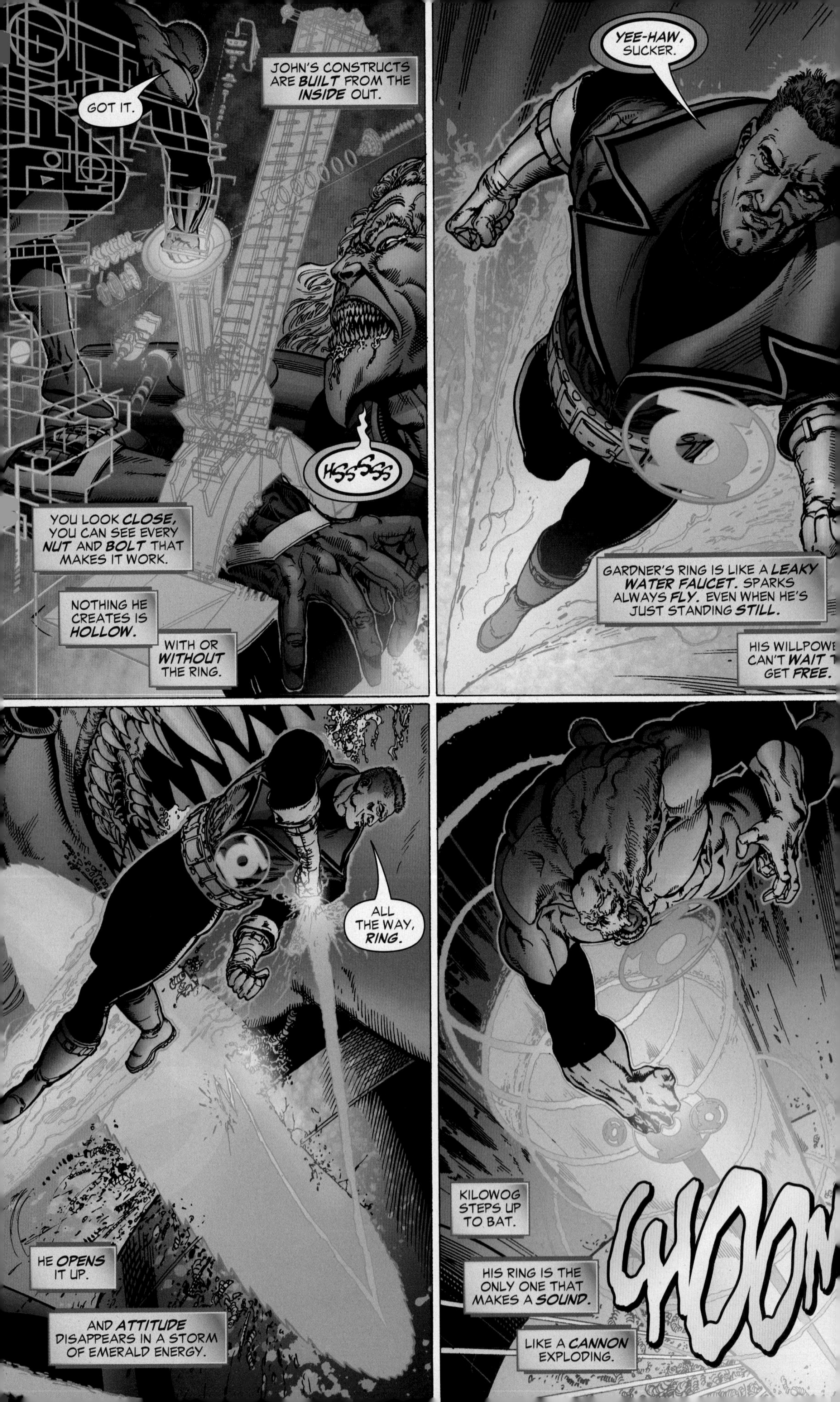

JOHN'S CONSTRUCTS ARE BUILT FROM THE INSIDE OUT.
GOT IT.
HSSSSS
YOU LOOK CLOSE, YOU CAN SEE EVERY NUT AND BOLT THAT MAKES IT WORK.
NOTHING HE CREATES IS HOLLOW.
WITH OR WITHOUT THE RING.
YEE-HAW, SUCKER.
GARDNER'S RING IS LIKE A LEAKY WATER FAUCET. SPARKS ALWAYS FLY. EVEN WHEN HE'S JUST STANDING STILL.
HIS WILLPOWE
CAN'T WAIT
GET FREE.
ALL THE WAY, RING.
HE OPENS IT UP.
AND ATTITUDE DISAPPEARS IN A STORM OF EMERALD ENERGY.
KILOWOG STEPS UP TO BAT.
HIS RING IS THE ONLY ONE THAT MAKES A SOUND.
LIKE A CANNON EXPLODING.

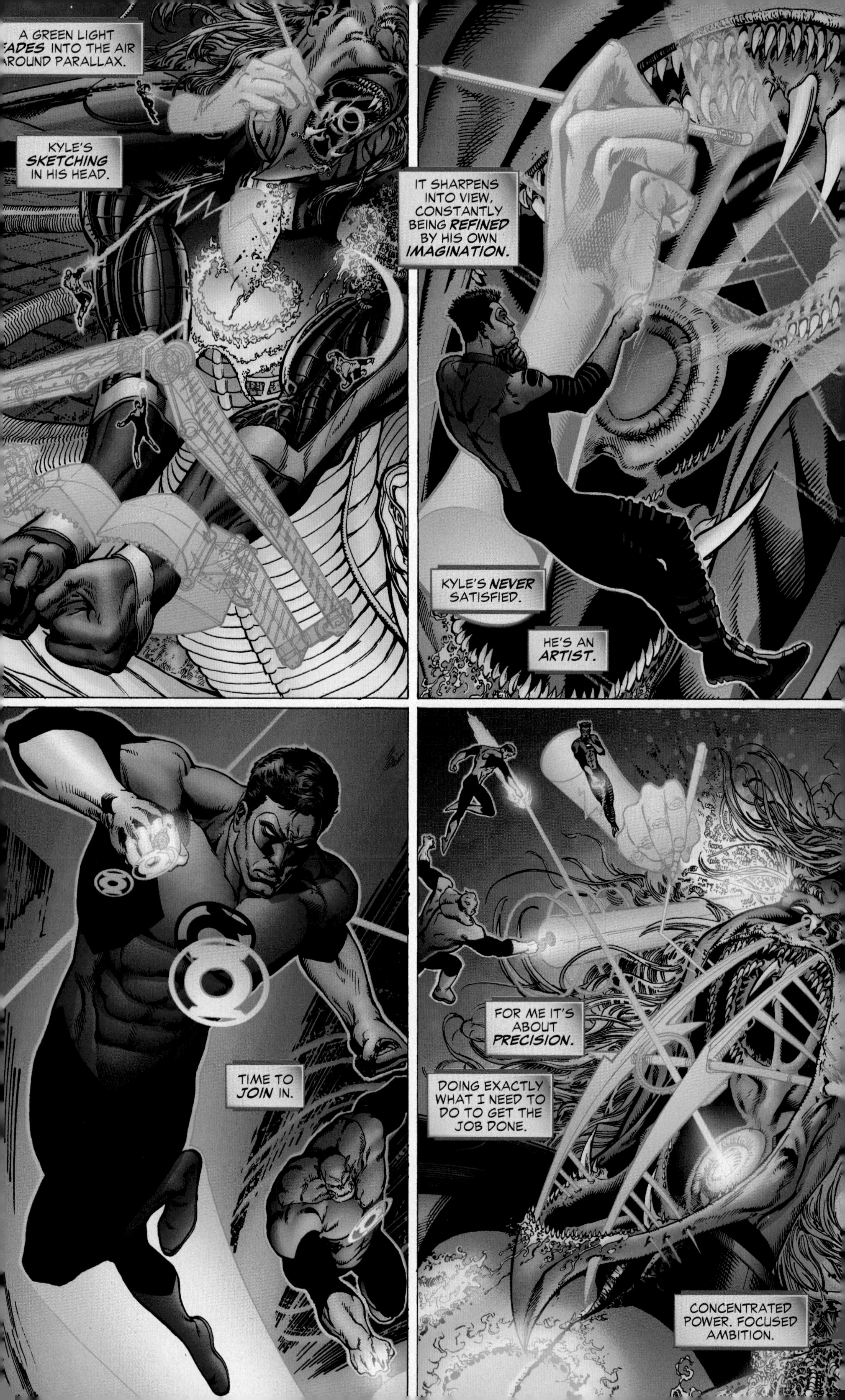
A GREEN LIGHT FADES INTO THE AIR AROUND PARALLAX.
KYLE'S SKETCHING IN HIS HEAD.
IT SHARPENS INTO VIEW, CONSTANTLY BEING REFINED BY HIS OWN IMAGINATION.
KYLE'S NEVER SATISFIED.
HE'S AN ARTIST.
TIME TO JOIN IN.
FOR ME IT'S ABOUT PRECISION.
DOING EXACTLY WHAT I NEED TO DO TO GET THE JOB DONE.
CONCENTRATED POWER. FOCUSED AMBITION.

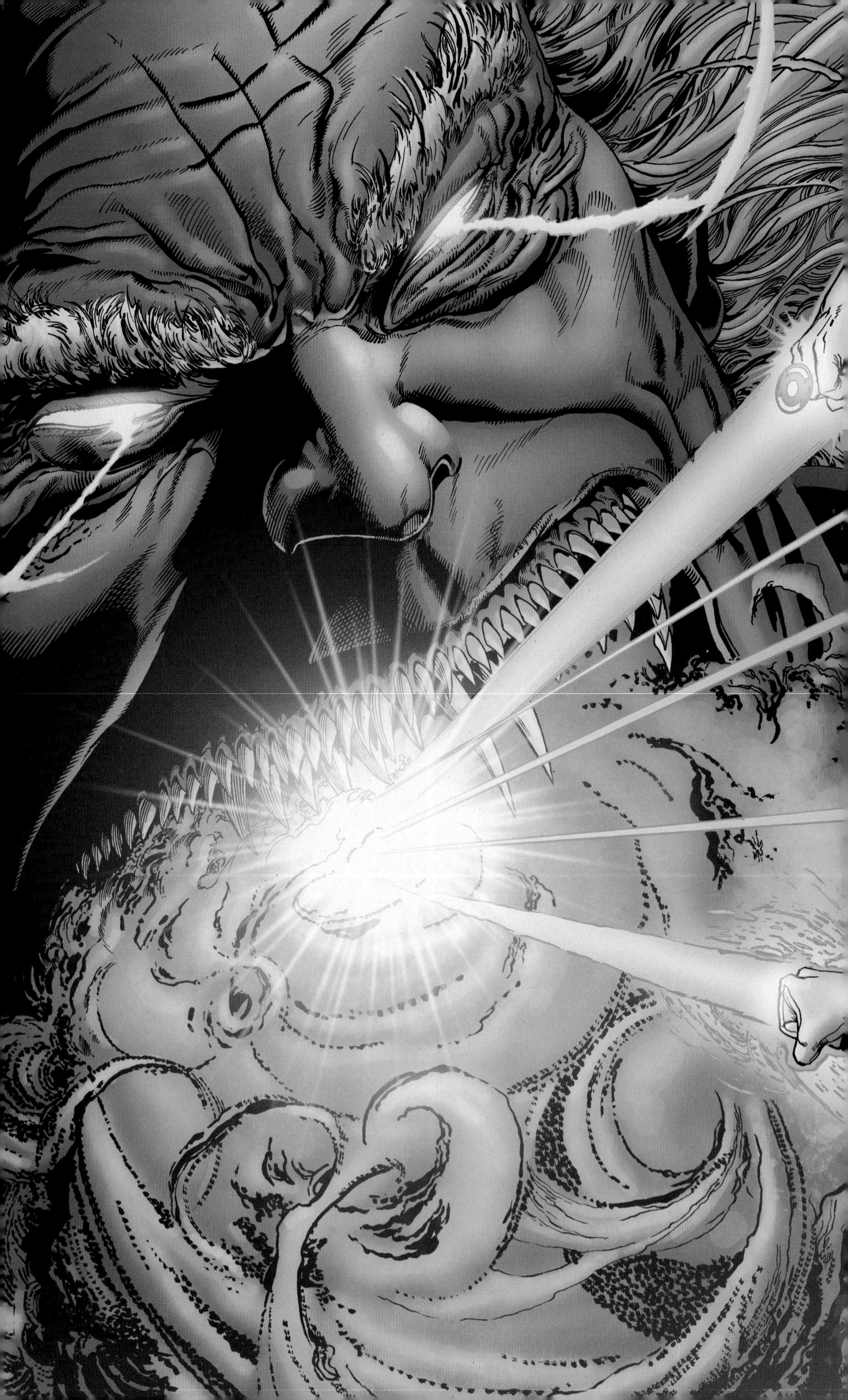

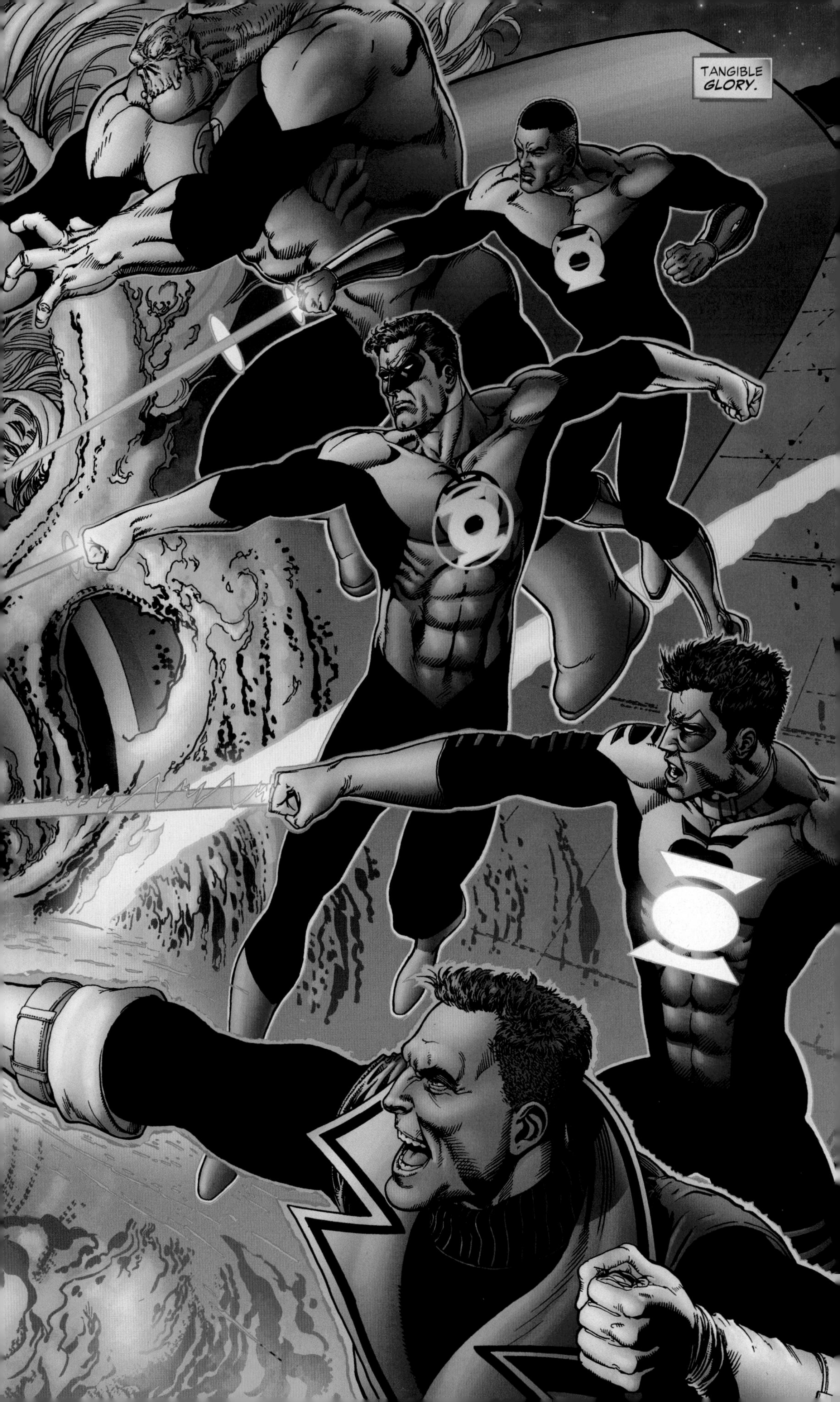
TANGIBLE GLORY.

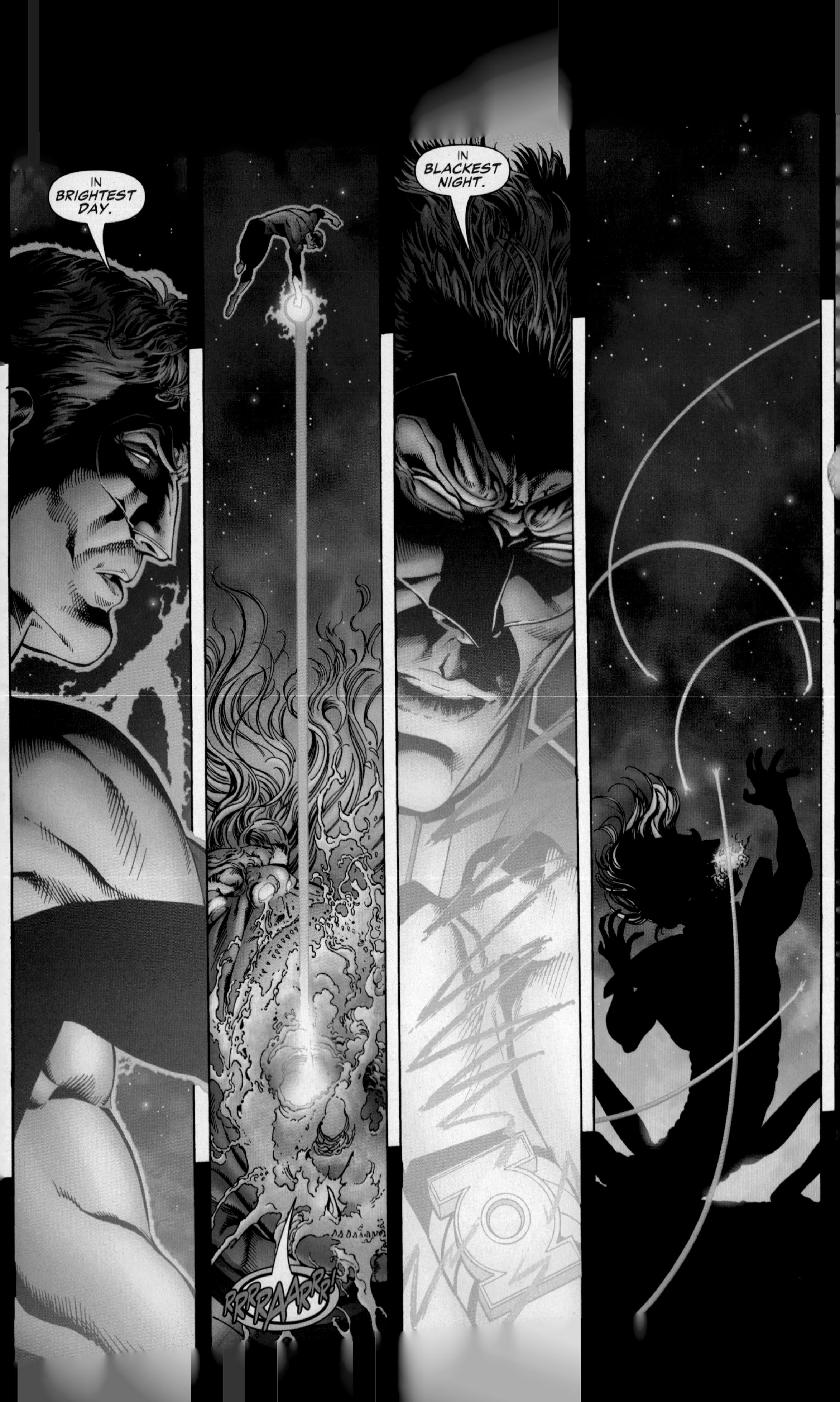
IN BRIGHTEST DAY.
IN BLACKEST NIGHT.
RRRRAARRR!

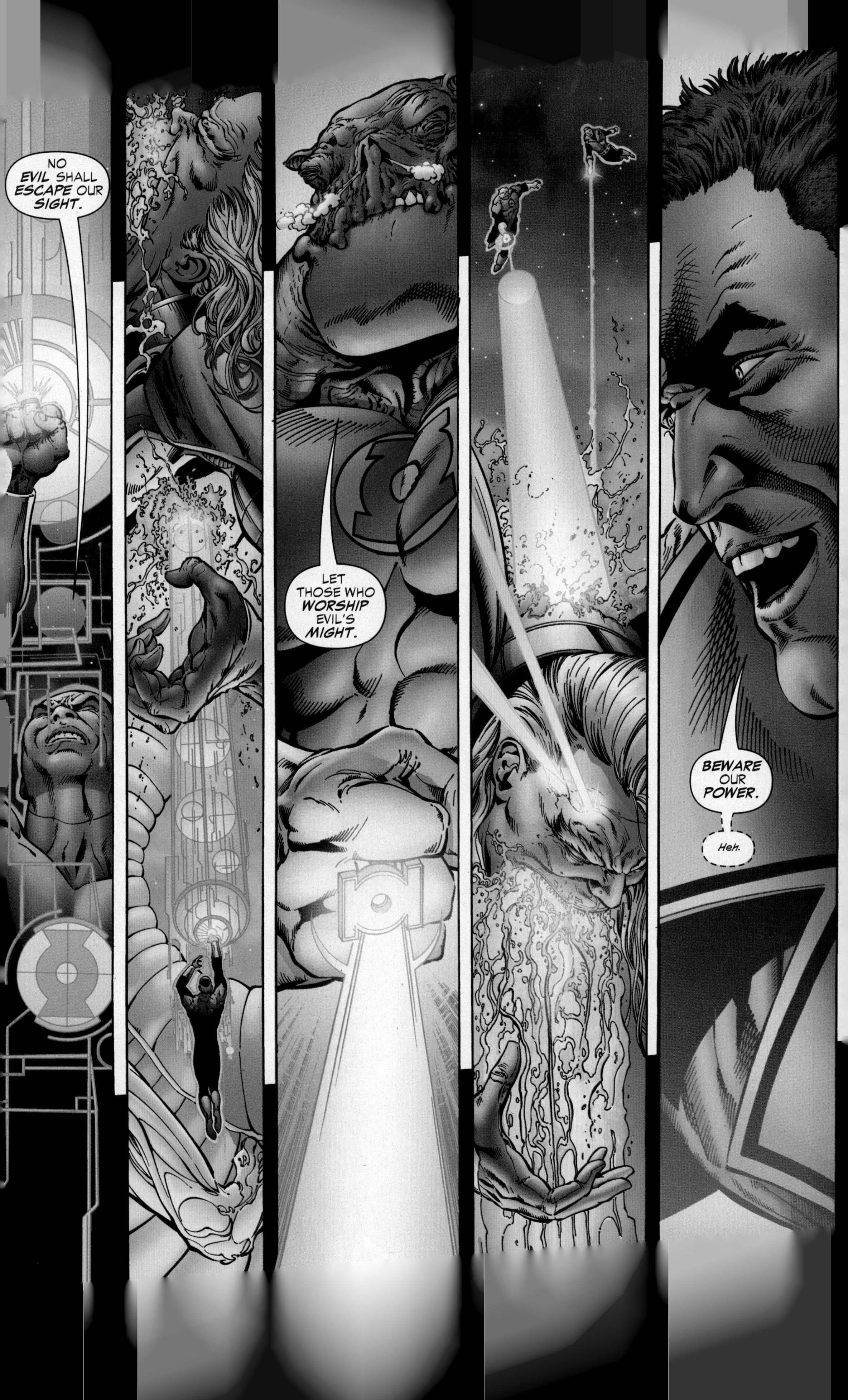
NO EVIL SHALL ESCAPE OUR SIGHT.
LET THOSE WHO WORSHIP EVIL'S MIGHT.
BEWARE OUR POWER.
Heh.

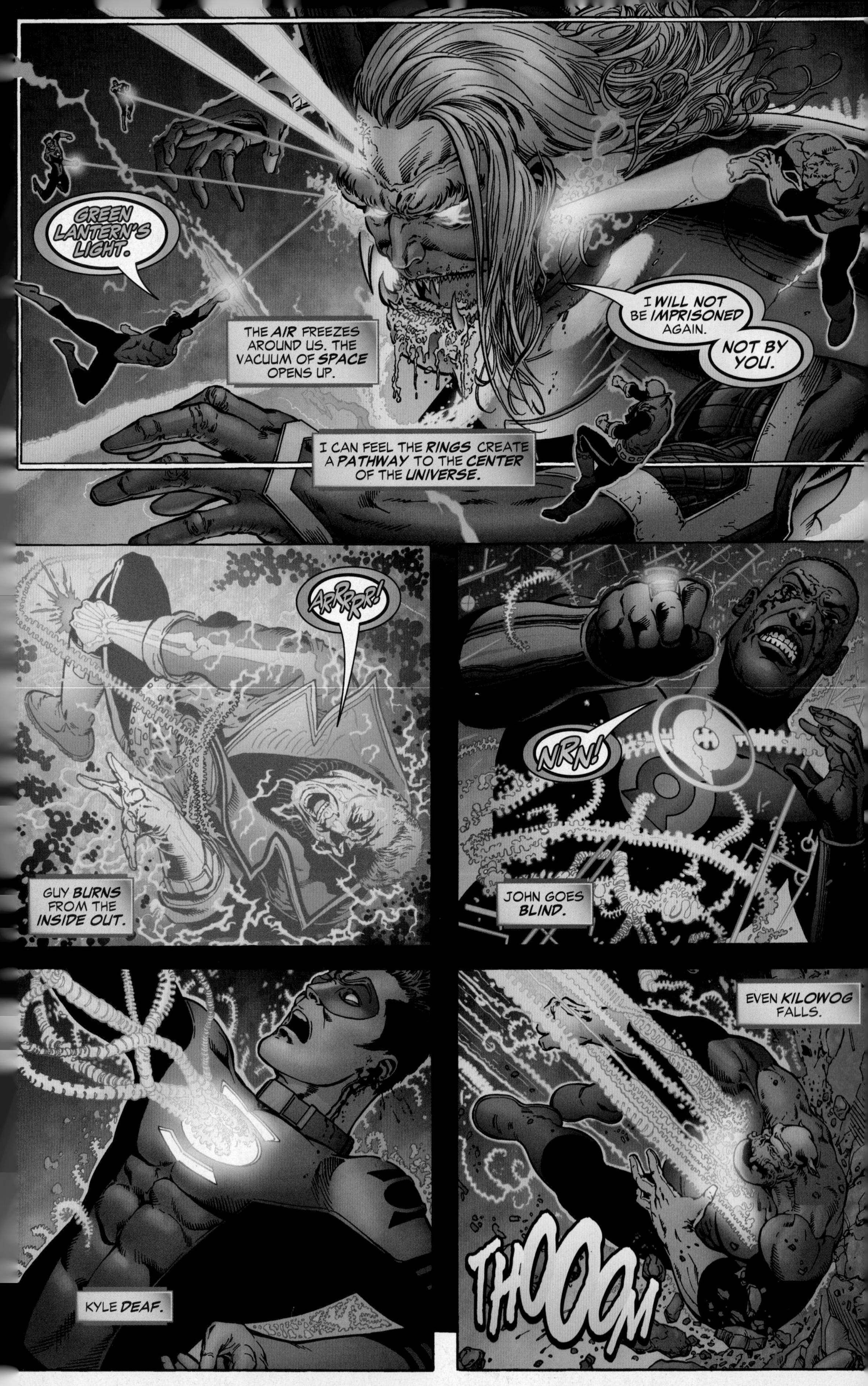
GREEN LANTERN'S LIGHT.
THE AIR FREEZES AROUND US. THE VACUUM OF SPACE OPENS UP.
I WILL NOT BE IMPRISONED AGAIN.
NOT BY YOU.
I CAN FEEL THE RINGS CREATE A PATHWAY TO THE CENTER OF THE UNIVERSE.
ARRRRR!
GUY BURNS FROM THE INSIDE OUT.
NRN!
JOHN GOES BLIND.
KYLE DEAF.
EVEN KILOWOG FALLS.
THOOOM

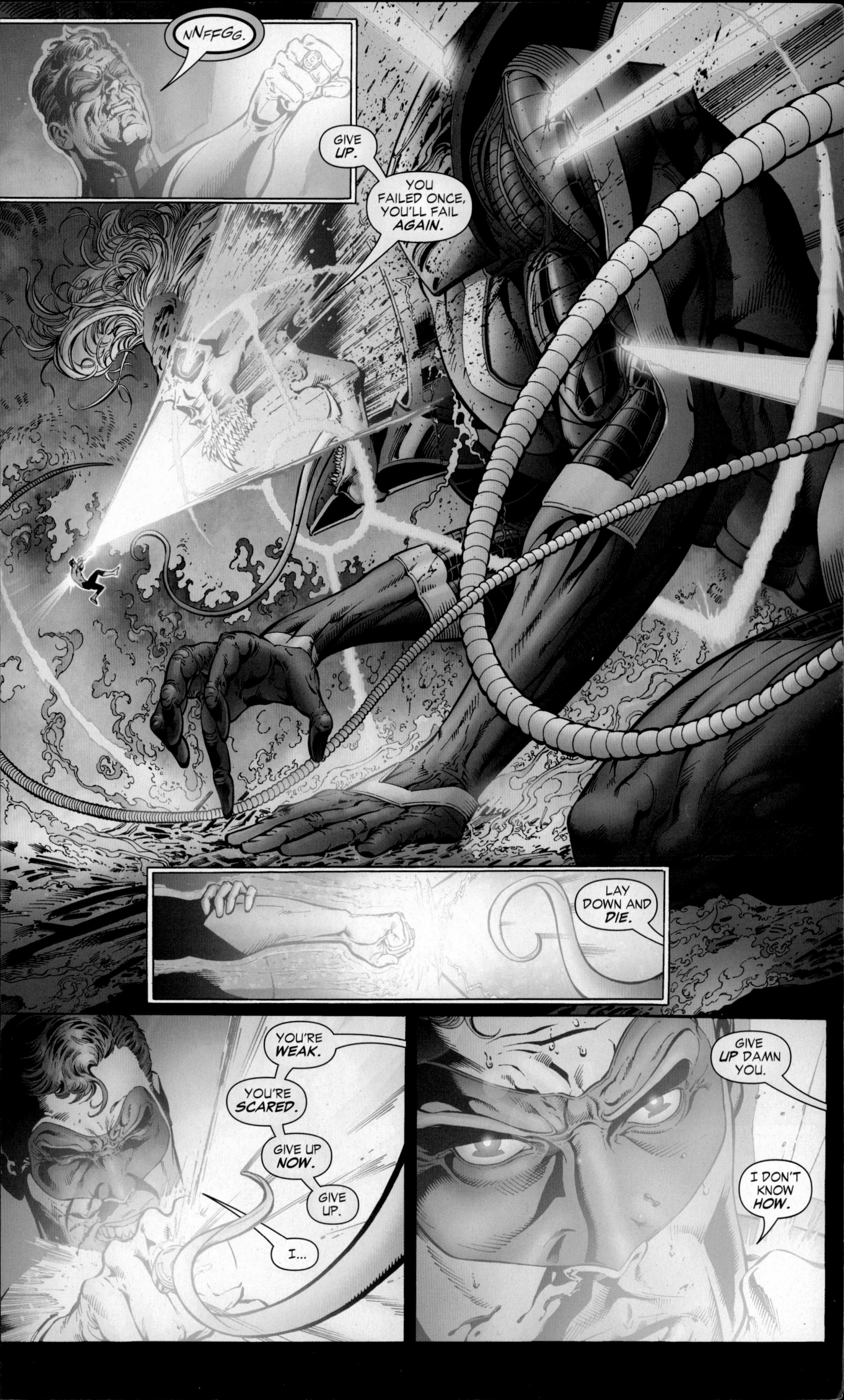
NNFFGG.
GIVE UP.
YOU FAILED ONCE, YOU'LL FAIL AGAIN.
LAY DOWN AND DIE.
YOU'RE WEAK.
YOU'RE SCARED.
GIVE UP NOW.
GIVE UP.
I...
GIVE UP DAMN YOU.
I DON'T KNOW HOW.

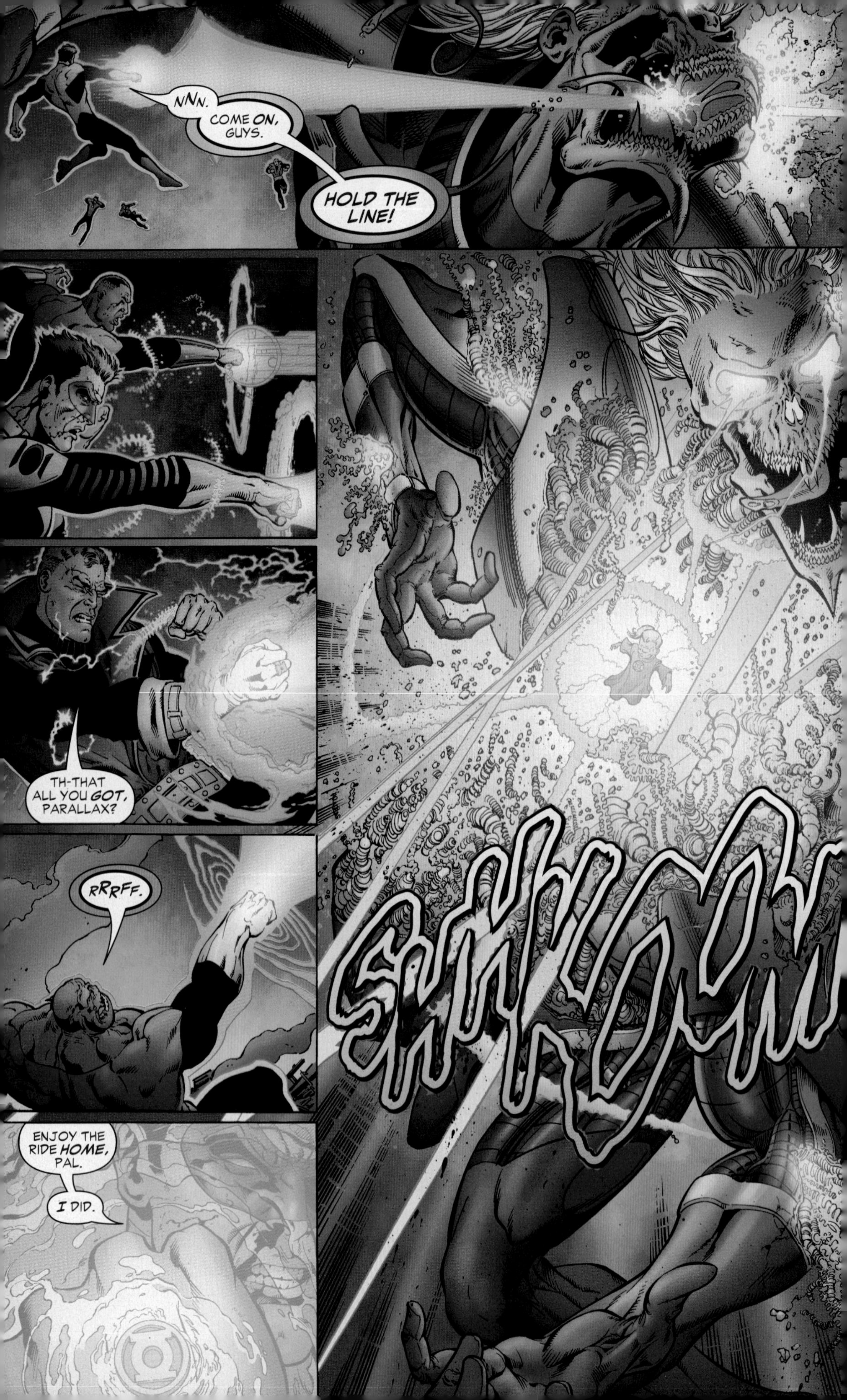
NNN.
COME ON, GUYS.
HOLD THE LINE!
TH-THAT ALL YOU GOT, PARALLAX?
RRRFF.
ENJOY THE RIDE HOME, PAL.
I DID.

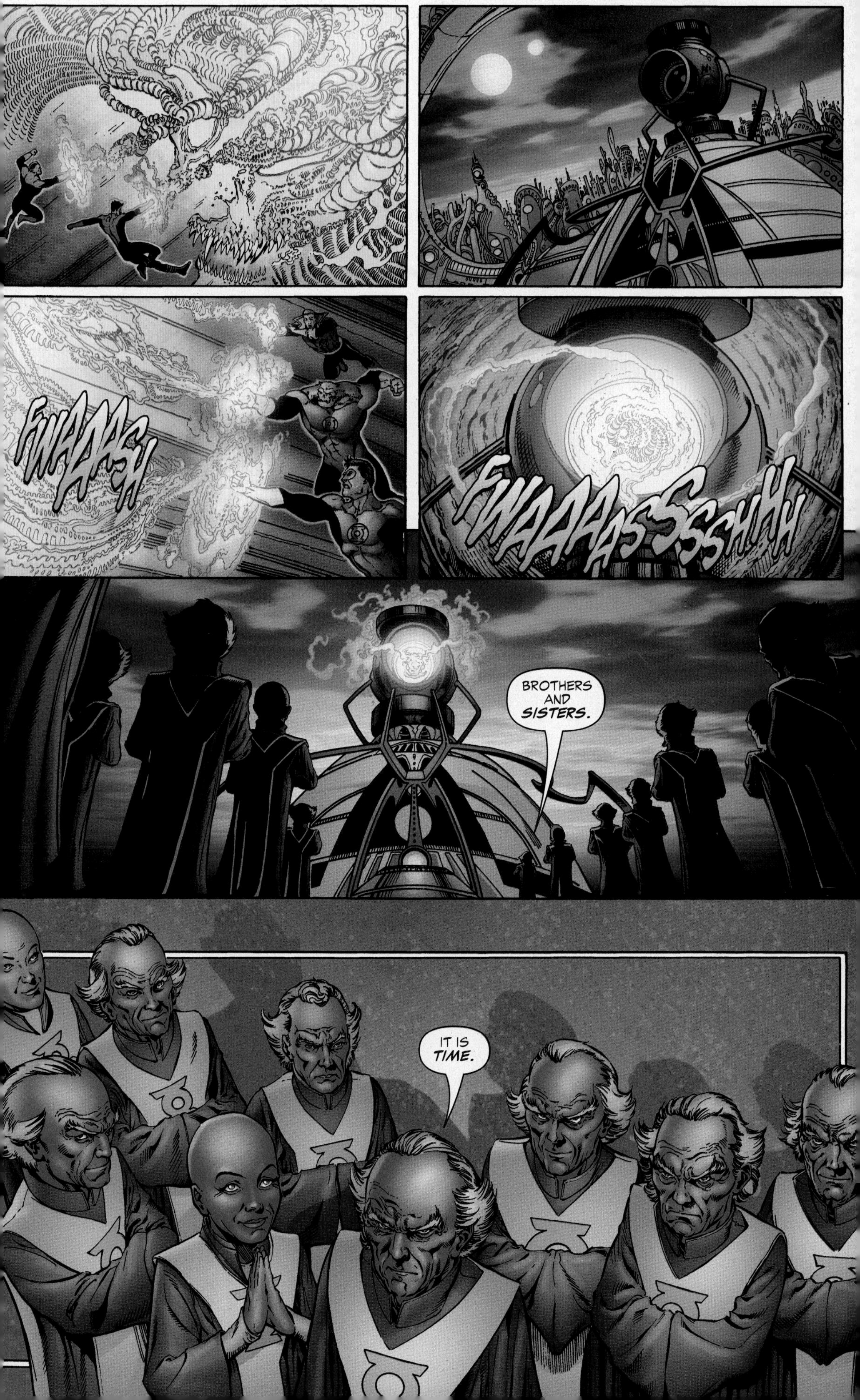
FWAAASH
FWAAAAASSSSHHH
BROTHERS AND SISTERS.
IT IS TIME.

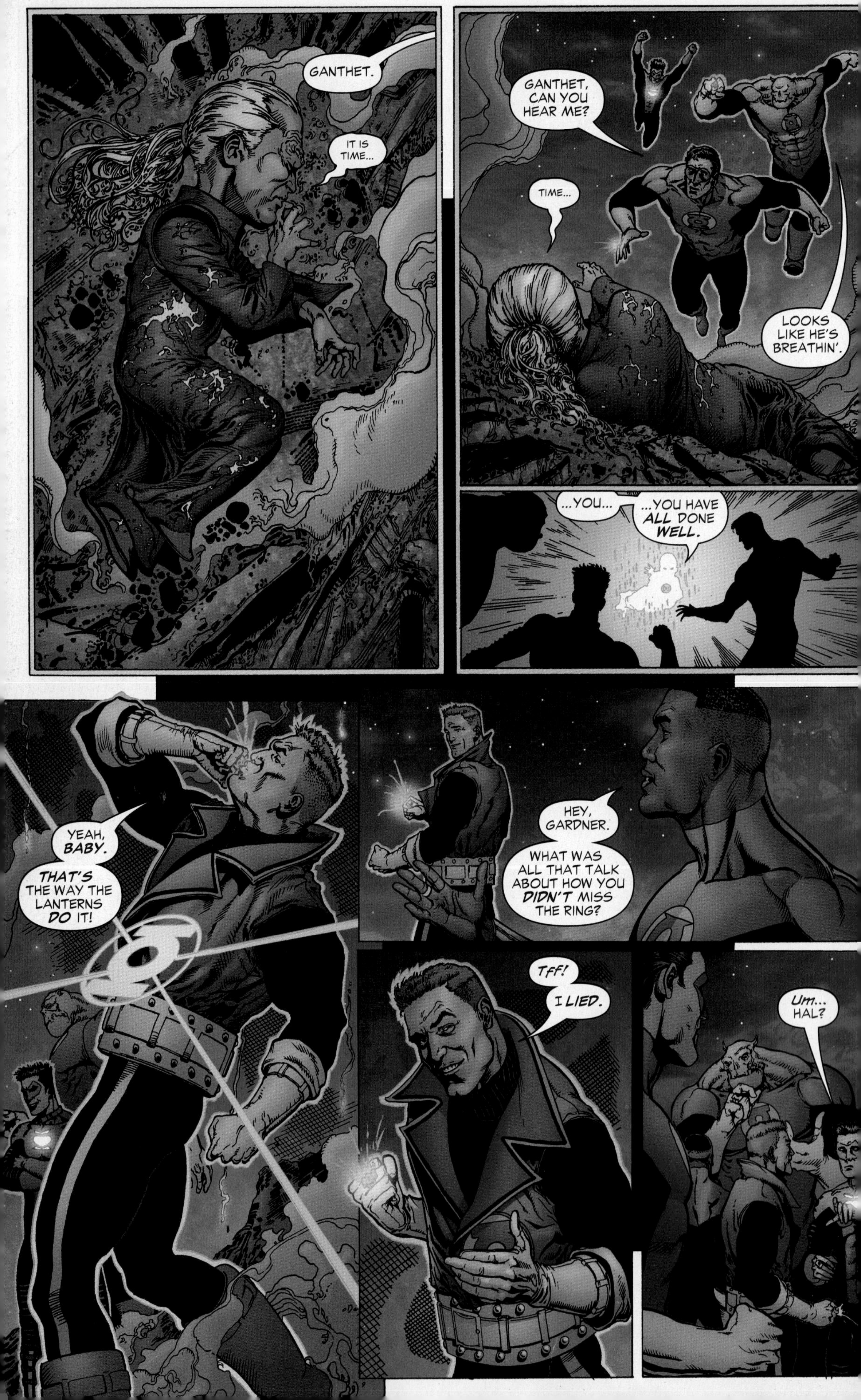
GANTHET.
IT IS TIME...
GANTHET, CAN YOU HEAR ME?
TIME...
LOOKS LIKE HE'S BREATHIN'.
...YOU...
...YOU HAVE ALL DONE WELL.
YEAH, BABY.
THAT'S THE WAY THE LANTERNS DO IT!
HEY, GARDNER.
WHAT WAS ALL THAT TALK ABOUT HOW YOU DIDN'T MISS THE RING?
Tff!
I LIED.
Um... HAL?

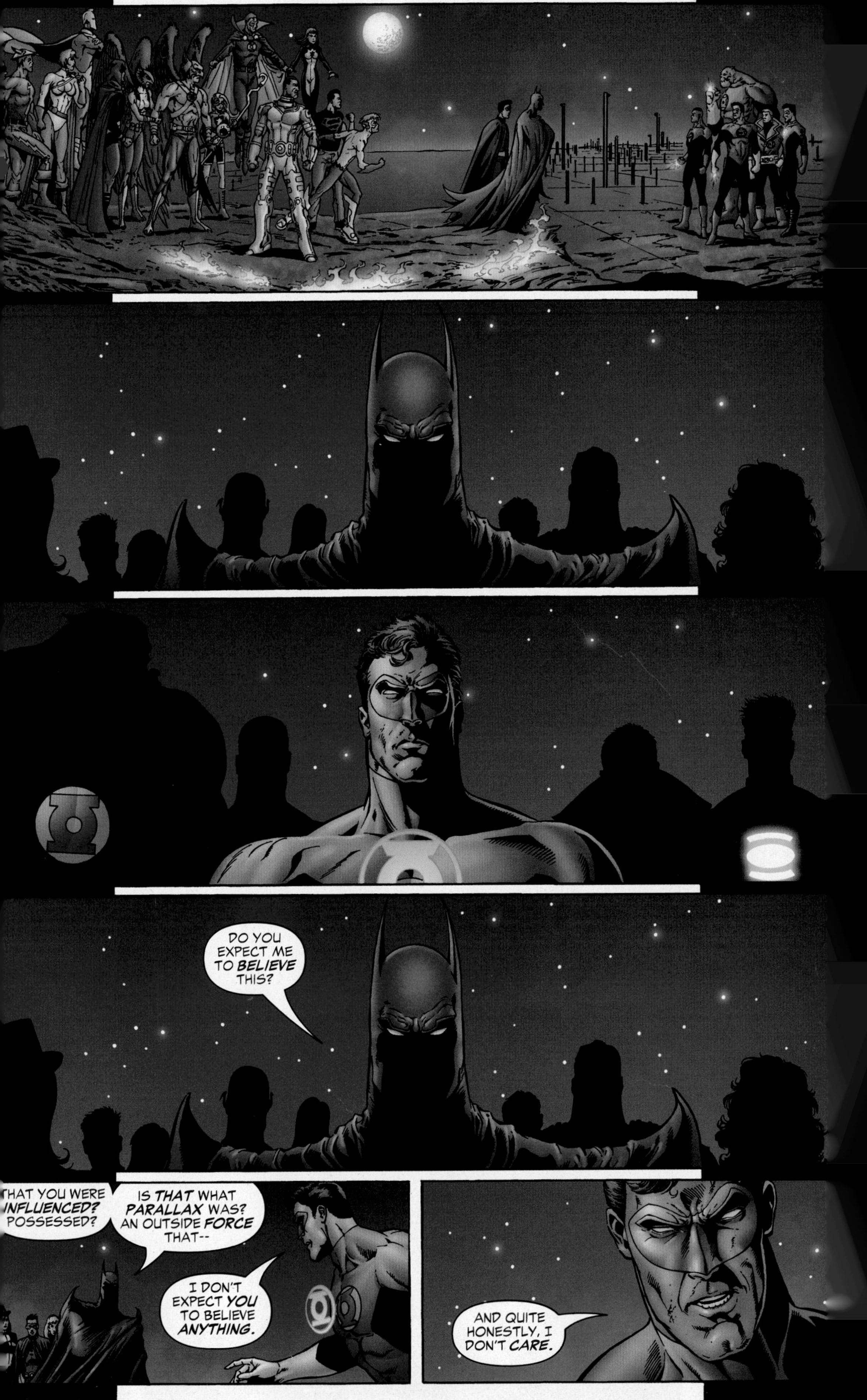
DO YOU EXPECT ME TO BELIEVE THIS?
THAT YOU WERE INFLUENCED? POSSESSED?
IS THAT WHAT PARALLAX WAS? AN OUTSIDE FORCE THAT--
I DON'T EXPECT YOU TO BELIEVE ANYTHING.
AND QUITE HONESTLY, I DON'T CARE.

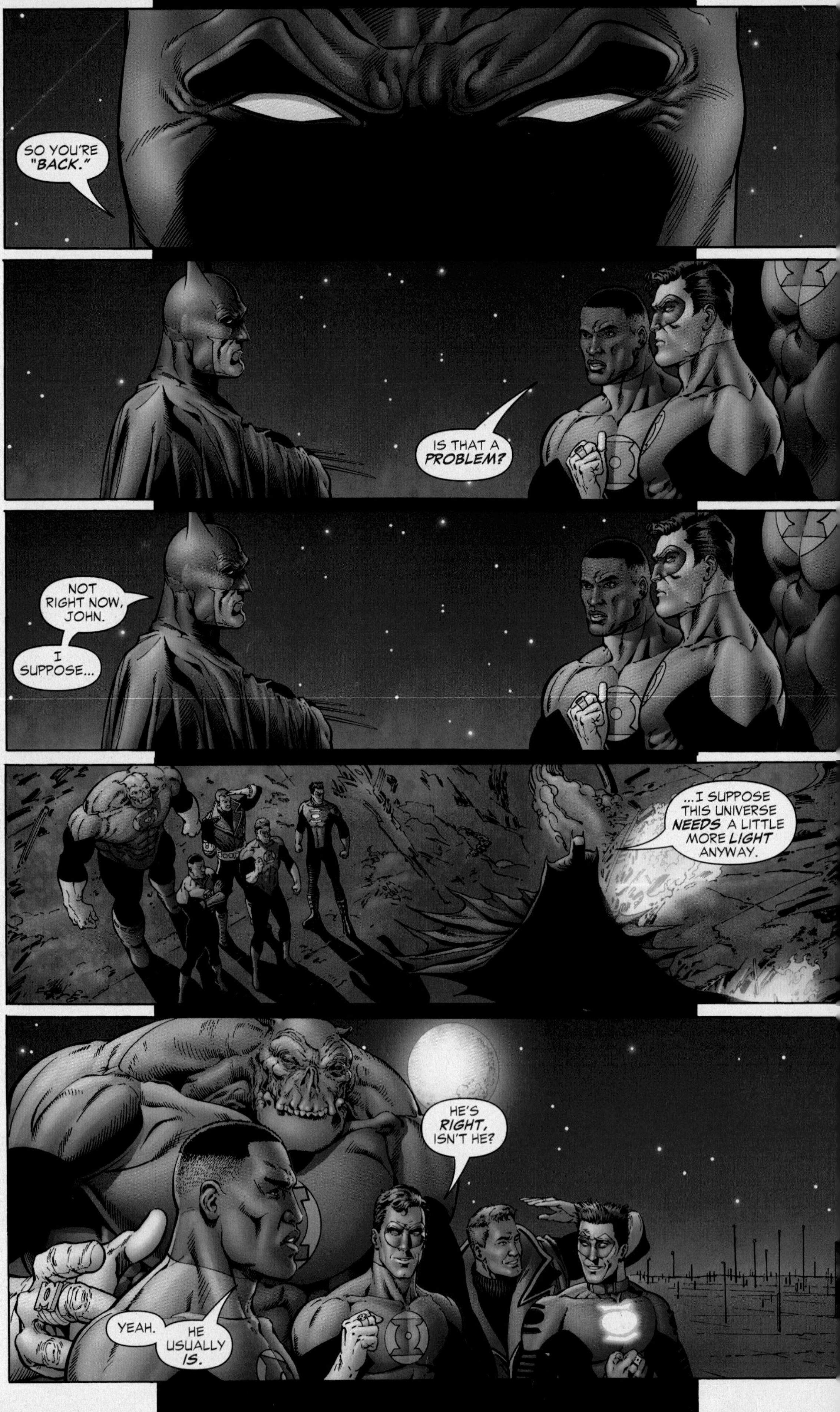
SO YOU'RE "BACK."
IS THAT A PROBLEM?
NOT RIGHT NOW, JOHN.
I SUPPOSE...
...I SUPPOSE THIS UNIVERSE NEEDS A LITTLE MORE LIGHT ANYWAY.
HE'S RIGHT, ISN'T HE?
YEAH.
HE USUALLY IS.

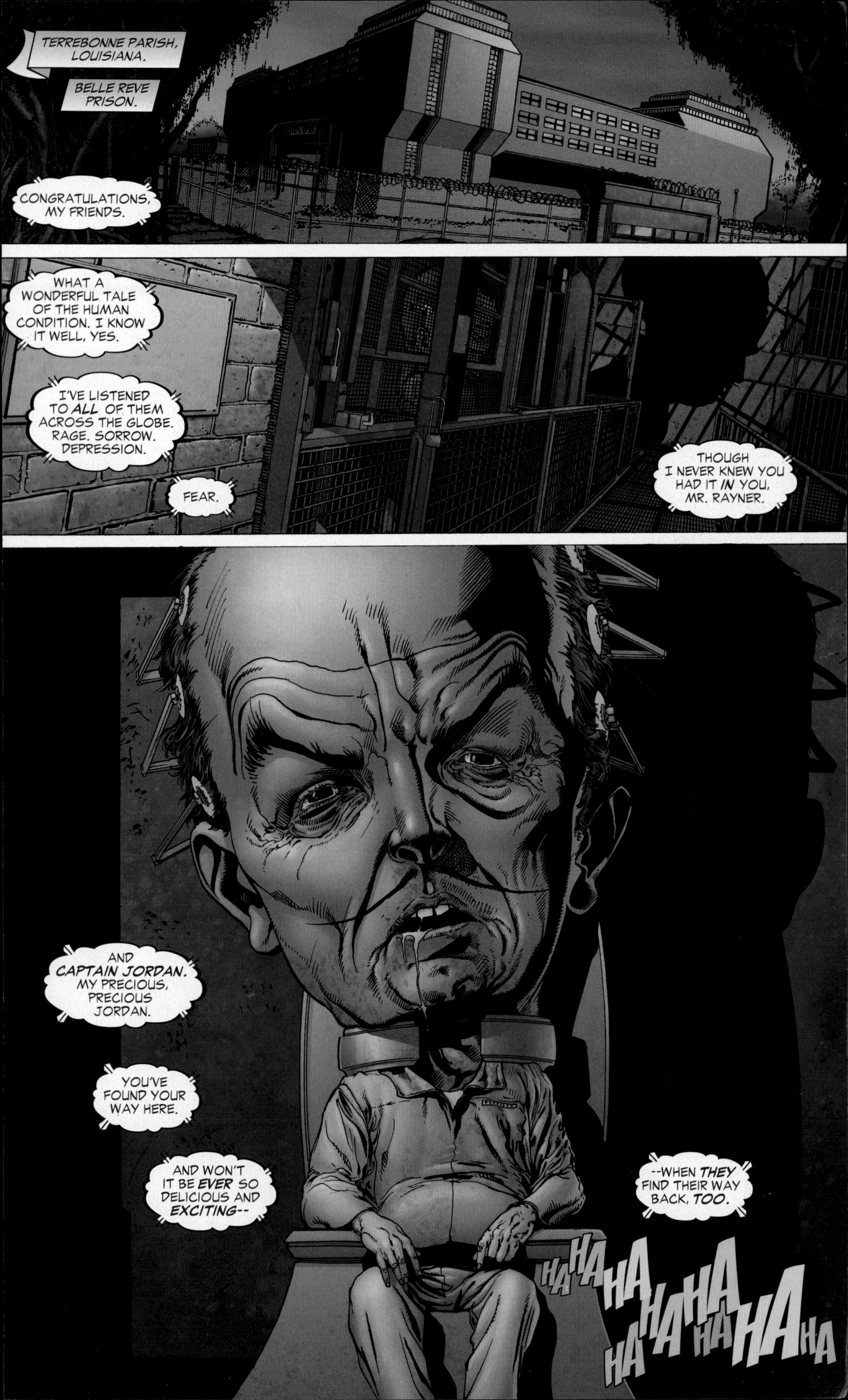
TERREBONNE PARISH, LOUISIANA.
BELLE REVE PRISON.
CONGRATULATIONS, MY FRIENDS.
WHAT A WONDERFUL TALE OF THE HUMAN CONDITION. I KNOW IT WELL, YES.
I'VE LISTENED TO ALL OF THEM ACROSS THE GLOBE. RAGE. SORROW. DEPRESSION.
FEAR.
THOUGH I NEVER KNEW YOU HAD IT IN YOU, MR. RAYNER.
AND CAPTAIN JORDAN. MY PRECIOUS, PRECIOUS JORDAN.
YOU'VE FOUND YOUR WAY HERE.
AND WON'T IT BE EVER SO DELICIOUS AND EXCITING--
--WHEN THEY FIND THEIR WAY BACK, TOO.
HAHAHAHAHAHAHAHAHAHAHAHA

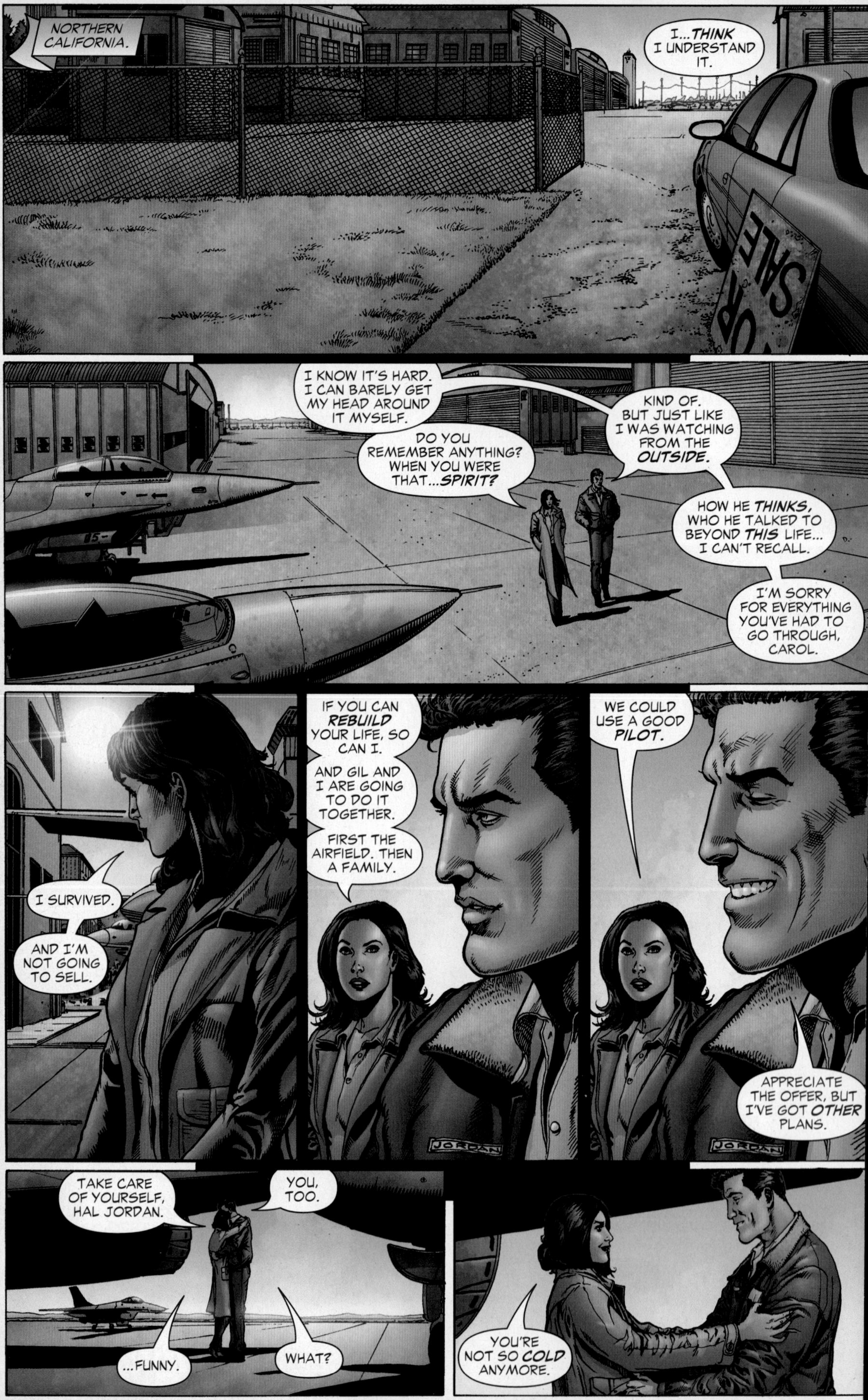
NORTHERN CALIFORNIA.
I...THINK I UNDERSTAND IT.
FOR SALE
I KNOW IT'S HARD. I CAN BARELY GET MY HEAD AROUND IT MYSELF.
KIND OF. BUT JUST LIKE I WAS WATCHING FROM THE OUTSIDE.
DO YOU REMEMBER ANYTHING? WHEN YOU WERE THAT...SPIRIT?
HOW HE THINKS, WHO HE TALKED TO BEYOND THIS LIFE... I CAN'T RECALL.
I'M SORRY FOR EVERYTHING YOU'VE HAD TO GO THROUGH, CAROL.
I SURVIVED.
AND I'M NOT GOING TO SELL.
IF YOU CAN REBUILD YOUR LIFE, SO CAN I.
AND GIL AND I ARE GOING TO DO IT TOGETHER.
FIRST THE AIRFIELD. THEN A FAMILY.
JORDAN
WE COULD USE A GOOD PILOT.
APPRECIATE THE OFFER, BUT I'VE GOT OTHER PLANS.
JORDAN
TAKE CARE OF YOURSELF, HAL JORDAN.
YOU, TOO.
...FUNNY.
WHAT?
YOU'RE NOT SO COLD ANYMORE.

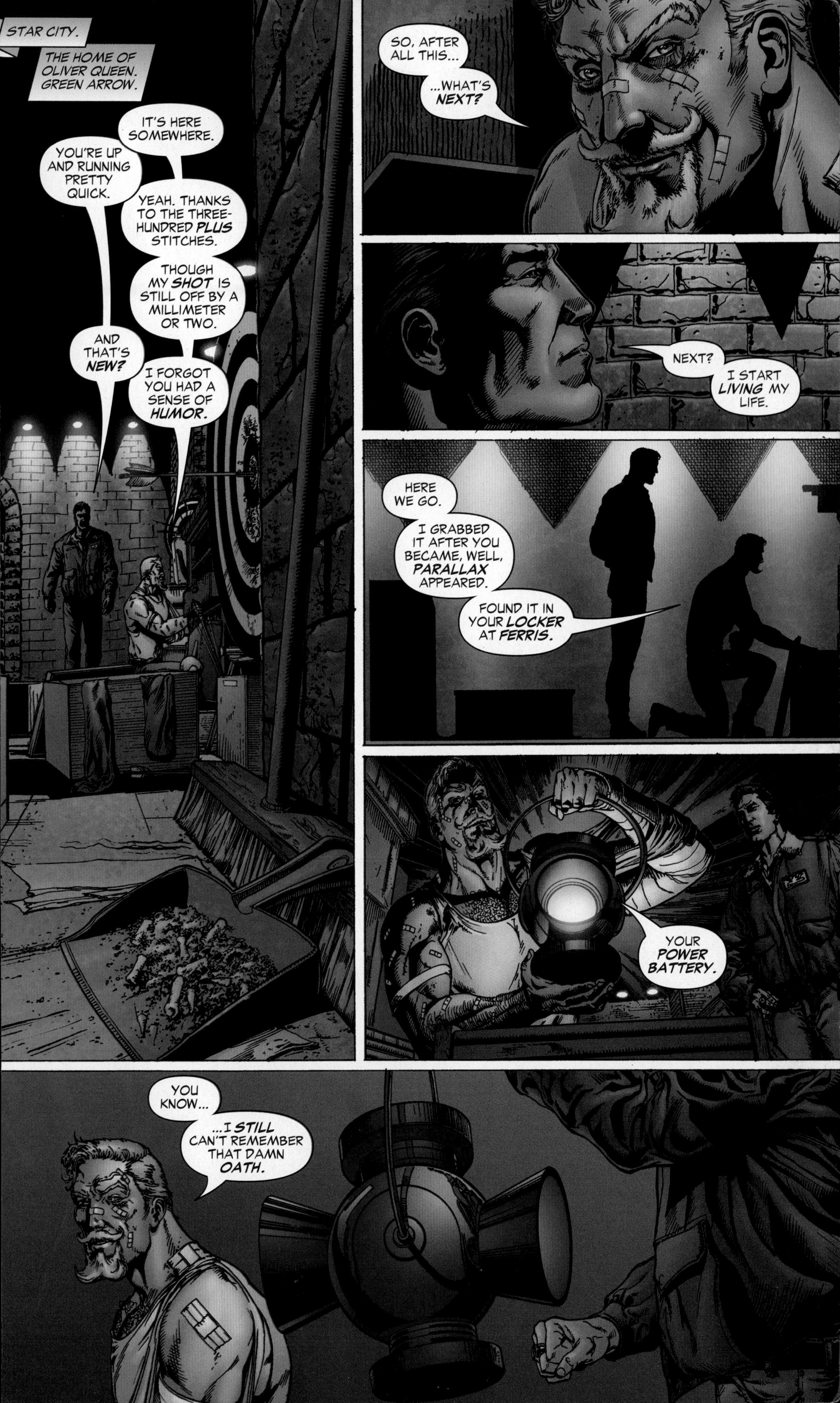
STAR CITY.
THE HOME OF OLIVER QUEEN. GREEN ARROW.
IT'S HERE SOMEWHERE.
YOU'RE UP AND RUNNING PRETTY QUICK.
YEAH. THANKS TO THE THREE-HUNDRED PLUS STITCHES.
THOUGH MY SHOT IS STILL OFF BY A MILLIMETER OR TWO.
AND THAT'S NEW?
I FORGOT YOU HAD A SENSE OF HUMOR.
SO, AFTER ALL THIS...
...WHAT'S NEXT?
NEXT?
I START LIVING MY LIFE.
HERE WE GO.
I GRABBED IT AFTER YOU BECAME, WELL, PARALLAX APPEARED.
FOUND IT IN YOUR LOCKER AT FERRIS.
YOUR POWER BATTERY.
YOU KNOW...
...I STILL CAN'T REMEMBER THAT DAMN OATH.

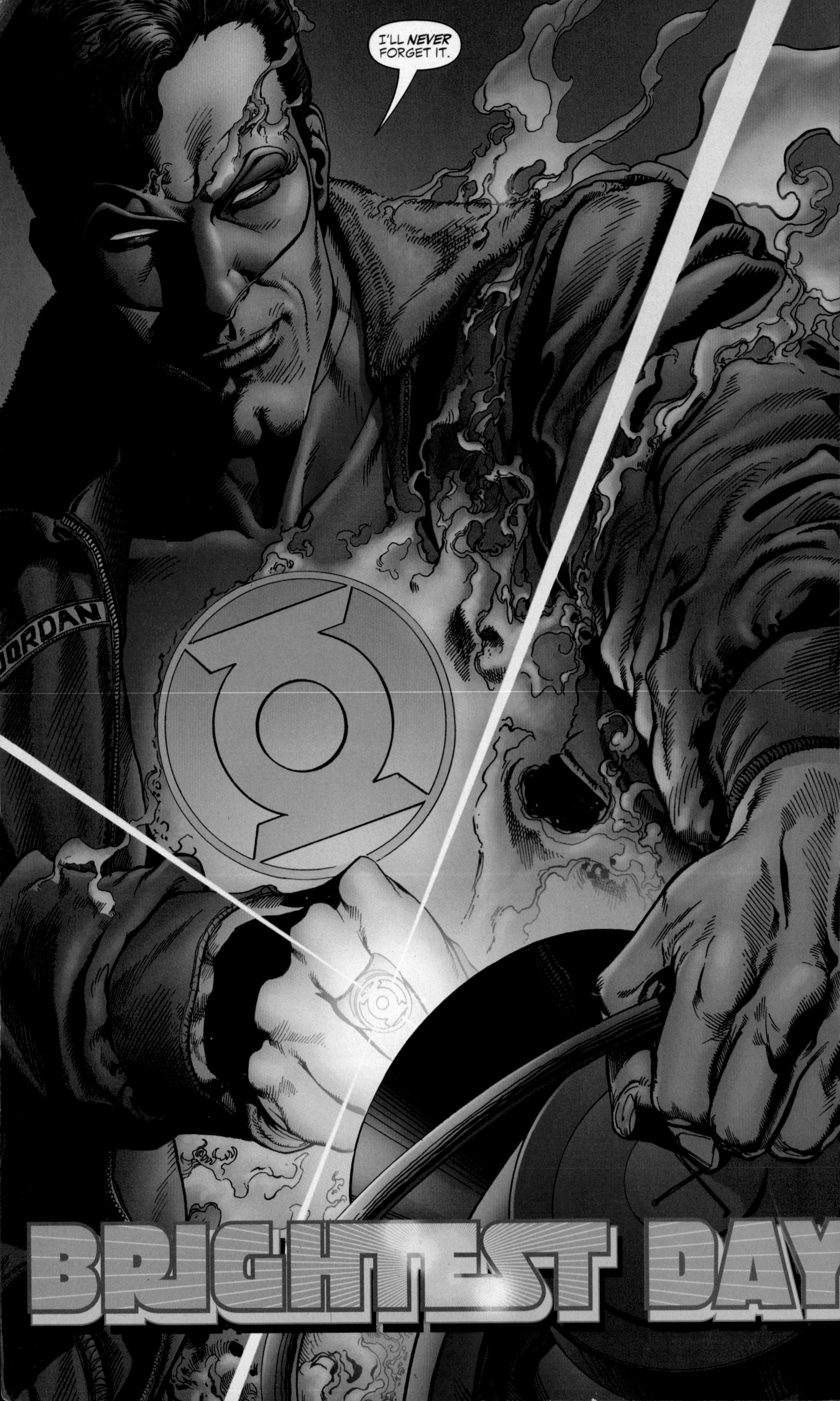

I'LL *NEVER* FORGET IT.
JORDAN
BRIGHTEST DAY

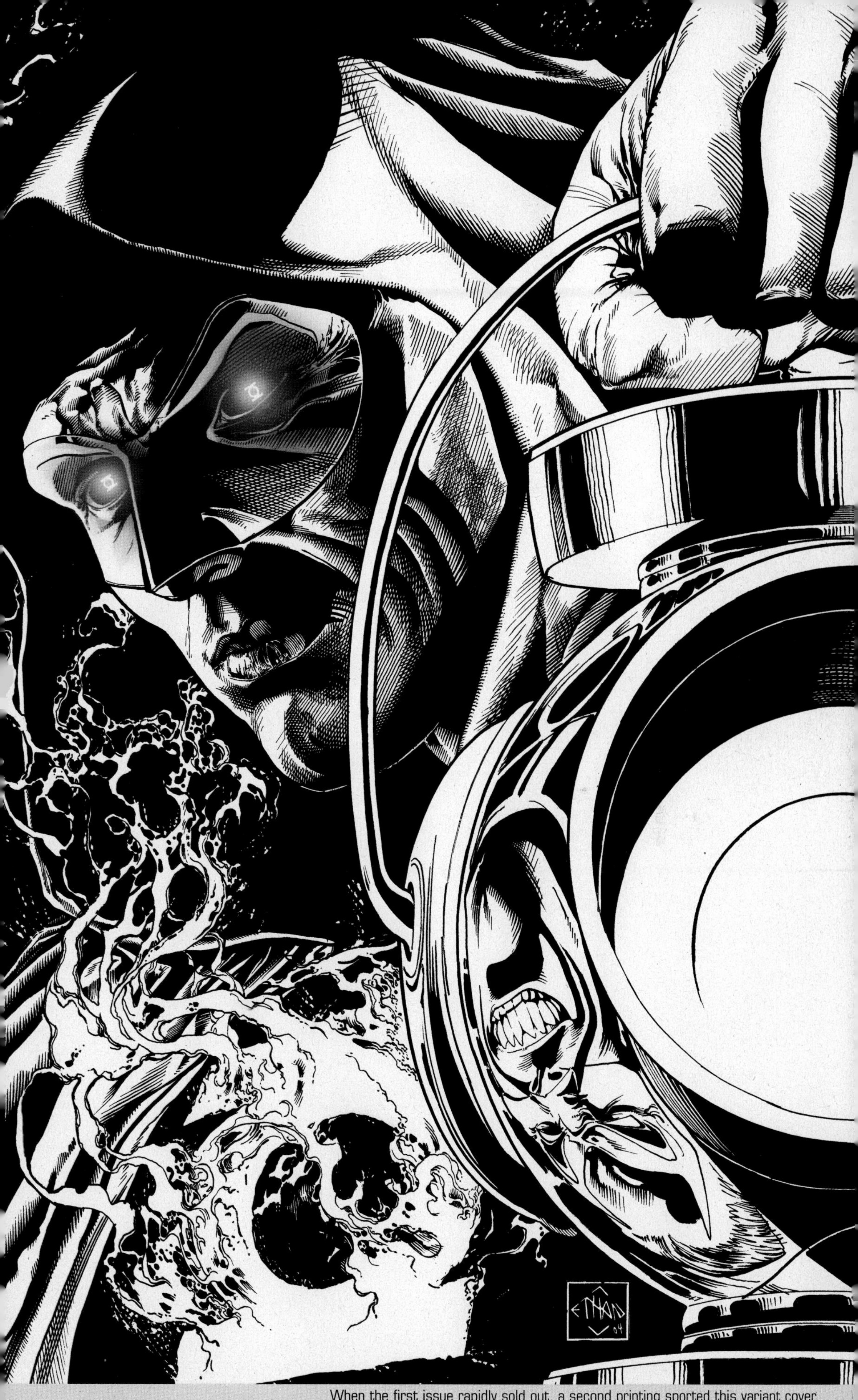

When the first issue rapidly sold out, a second printing sported this variant cover.

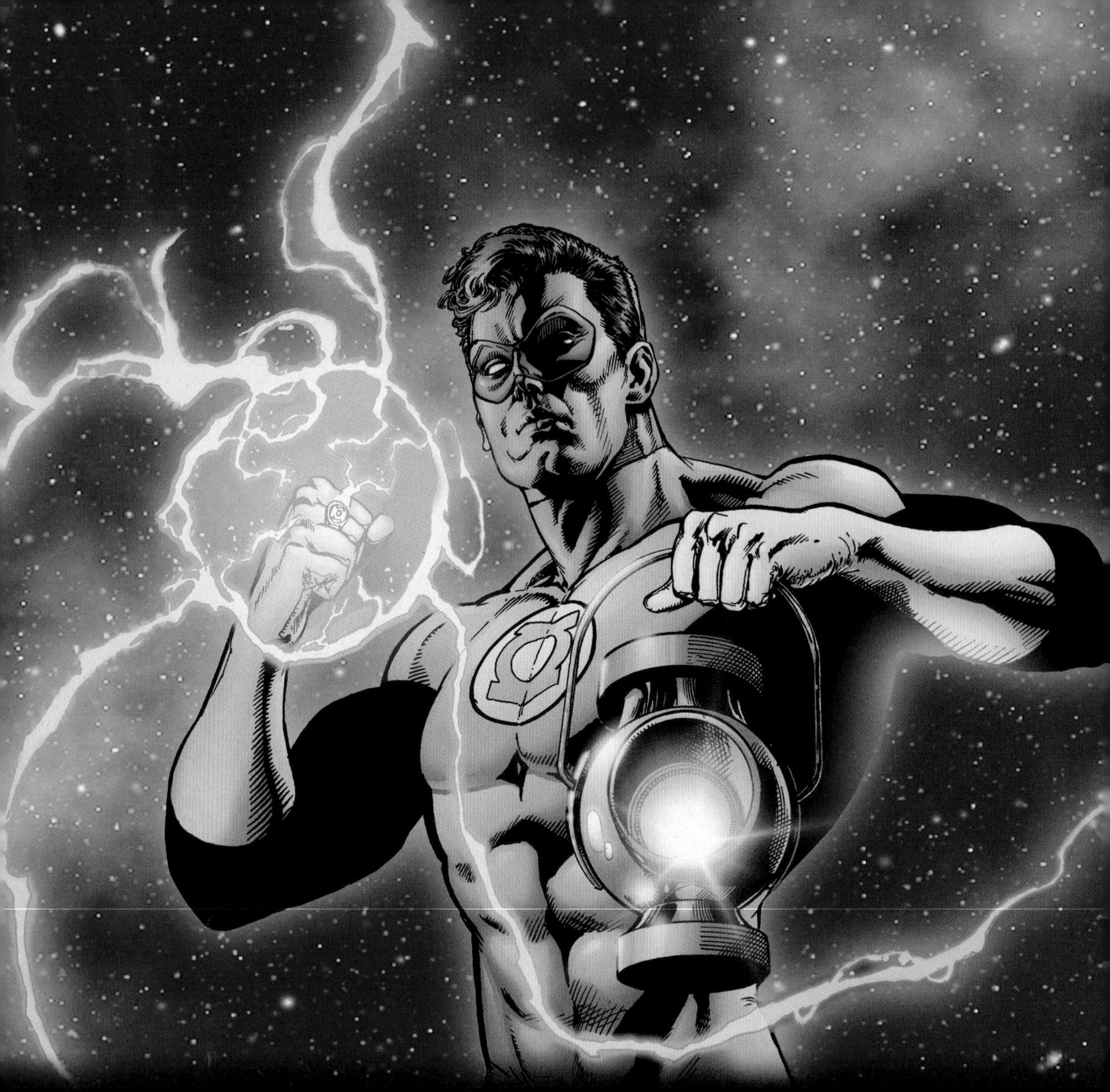

When the second printing sold out, a third printing used this variant cover.

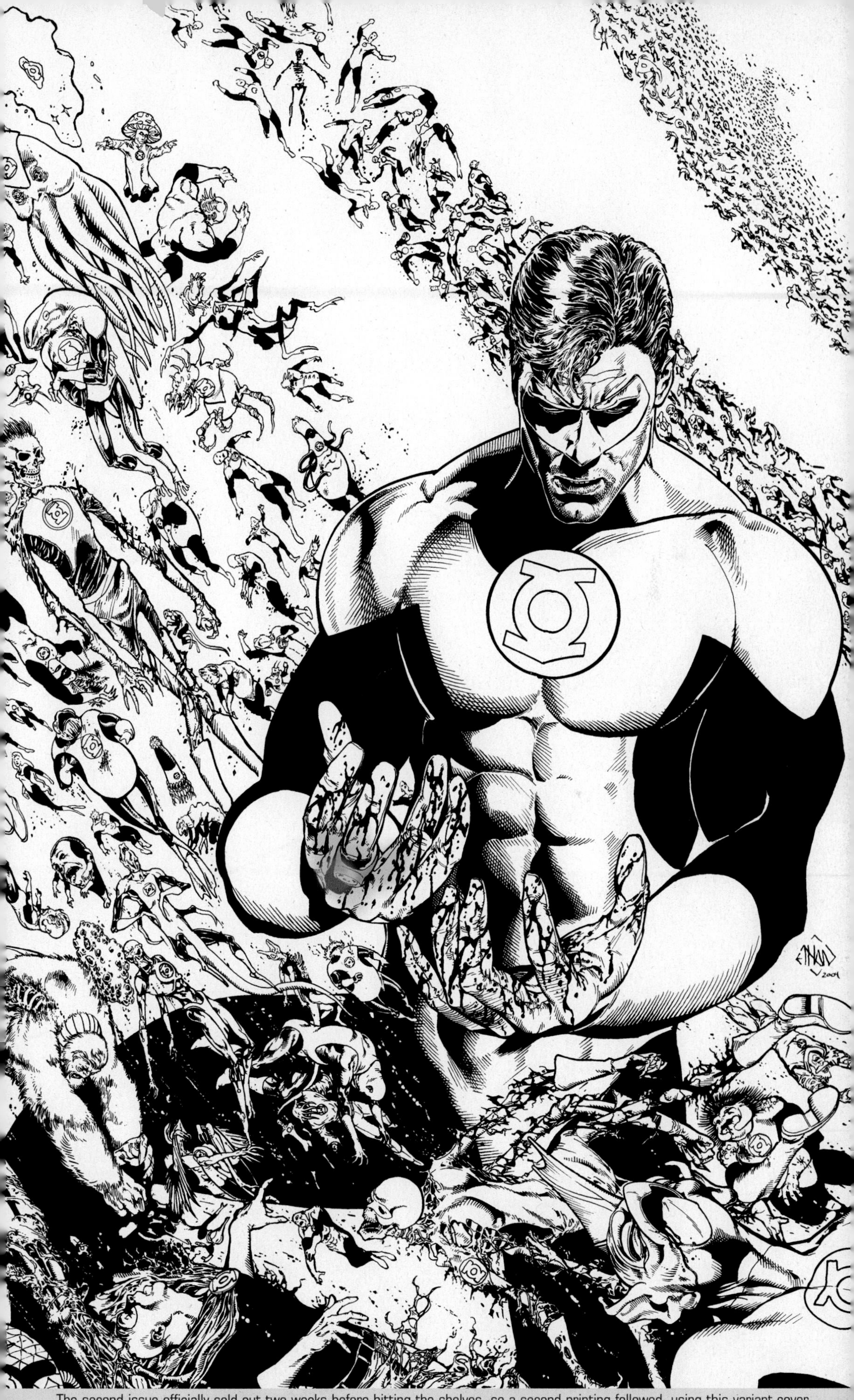

The second issue officially sold out two weeks before hitting the shelves, so a second printing followed, using this variant cover.

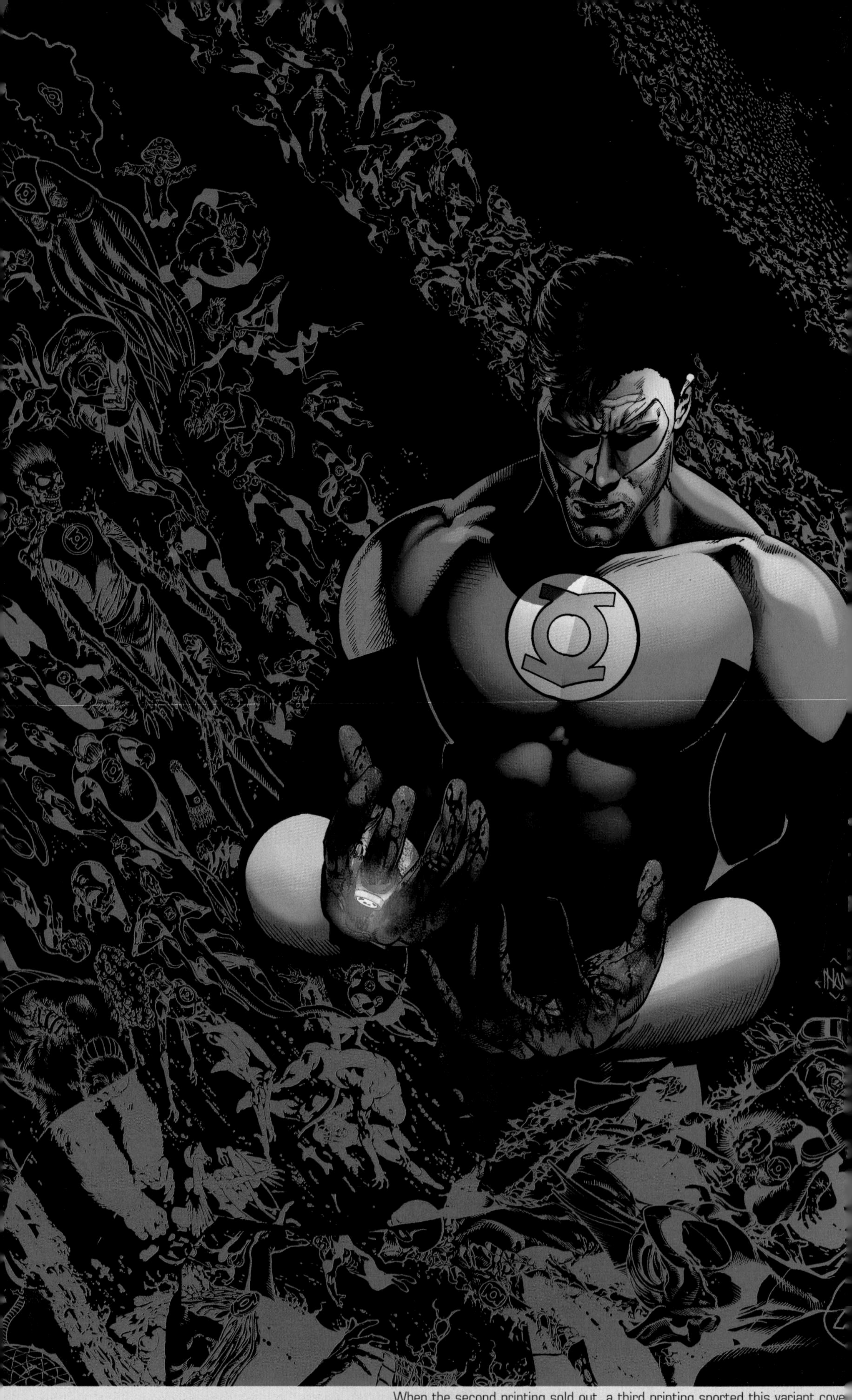

When the second printing sold out, a third printing sported this variant cove

REBIRTH **A 5-ISSUE MINISERIES**
GEOFF JOHNS REVISED 1/21/04

I'm going to outline the basics behind what happened to Hal Jordan before getting into the miniseries outline. It's all tied into Green Lantern mythology, which is what we're looking to restore. Everything needs to be tied back into Hal Jordan, who he was, is and where he's going.

What is Parallax?

Parallax is not Hal Jordan, and never was. Parallax is the yellow impurity in the Central Power Battery. When Sinestro was imprisoned inside the Battery, he made contact with it — able to since his ring was based on the same yellow energy. On the concentrated power of fear. Sinestro gave back the yellow impurity its sentience. (The Guardians removed it when they placed it inside the Battery millions of years ago.) Sinestro manipulated Parallax, and used Parallax to corrupt Jordan and lure him to the Battery.

Hal Jordan was a target of the weapon after Coast City was destroyed — his psyche was in a vulnerable state. For the first time, he was afraid. Afraid he might not be able to stop the next catastrophe.

It was at this moment Hal was influenced by Parallax through the ring. Parallax led Hal Jordan back to Oa, and when Jordan ultimately destroyed the Corps and the Central Battery — he freed both Sinestro and Parallax. Parallax grafted completely onto its new host — Hal Jordan.

Parallax destroyed the Green Lantern Corps.

Kyle Rayner knows this, and Sinestro wants to stop him from telling the truth.

Isn't Sinestro dead?

Parallax seemingly killed Sinestro in GL #50 — but in reality, though Hal broke Sinestro's neck and left him for dead, Sinestro survived thanks to his ring. And Sinestro knew that Hal killing him would be the ultimate event in Hal's life to lead him to become wholly corrupted by Parallax. Sinestro set up his own death alongside Parallax.

Sinestro is going to be built up into a major DCU villain. Sinestro is an intergalactic anarchist, bent on toppling any kind of authority. In his eyes, no one has the right to tell others how to live — save him. And the Green Lantern Corps represent that oppression.

Sinestro doesn't want more power, he hasn't come back to destroy the world; the Spectre/Parallax is about to do that for him. He simply wants to watch his archnemesis continue to spiral down into the depths of madness.

Where is Hal Jordan's body?

When Parallax/Hal Jordan relit the sun, Hal Jordan's infected soul was separated from his body — which still lies in the center of the sun. The power of the Battery has preserved Jordan's body.

Kyle Rayner is the only person who has discovered the truth behind Parallax — in deep space he came across one of the oldest surviving races of sentient beings in the galaxy. Their original home planet had been destroyed by what they called the source of fear. An entity called Parallax that was created by fear. That feeds off fear, and continues to grow. Parallax is a legend in the far corner of the universe.

Kyle retrieved Hal's body from the sun and headed to Earth.

Kyle will be a major key in clearing Hal's name — and when Hal returns as Green Lantern in issue #5, it is with Kyle that he'll team up.

Why did the Spectre choose Hal Jordan as a host?

The Spectre force specifically grafted itself onto the soul of Hal Jordan, and laid the seeds in the minds of the others to find Hal's soul — because the Spectre hoped to "burn out" this monster of fear. The Spectre believed that his power combined with Hal's willpower could destroy Parallax.

(This is where our story opens. Not only has the Spectre failed to annihilate Parallax, but the Parallax force is beginning to corrupt the Spectre's power.)

Who is Hal Jordan?

Hal Jordan is not afraid to fail. Hal believes he can handle anything that's thrown at him. He'll venture into any threatening situation without hesitation.

The Parallax weapon has planted doubts in Hal's mind. Doubts he must shred to overcome it.

Hal's greatest asset has always been his willpower, his belief that he can accomplish anything, and he's going to get that back.

How will Hal Jordan return to the land of the living?

The Spectre can no longer contain Hal's poisoned soul. The Parallax force is overwhelming him and causing chaos across the Earth. In a way, the Spectre must perform a massive cosmic self-"abortion" of sorts that will be witnessed by crowds of our heroes.

As Hal/Parallax is literally torn from within Spectre's body, ripped by Spectre's own claws and covered in a greenish blood, Hal and Parallax separate — then Parallax leaps back inside Spectre. Hal's soul fades from sight as it is called to the afterlife.

Fading away, Hal watches helplessly as Parallax burrows like a parasite back into Spectre. Hal's soul disappears, spinning towards the "light at the end of the tunnel."

But Spectre sends a blast towards Hal's soul, redirecting it — sending it back into his body. The white light in the tunnel turns green.

Hal Jordan will awake in his body, which was brought back to Earth by Kyle.

How will Hal Jordan be absolved in the eyes of our heroes?

If Hal Jordan killed one person, there *may* be a chance at redemption. As Parallax he killed dozens more. We need to absolve him of this. He can have the potential inside him, which was exploited, but he cannot be responsible for these actions.

When the Parallax force is torn from the Spectre, it infects another hero — Batman. Since Hal went "bad," Batman has been the loudest voice denouncing him. We want to bring this to a close for several reasons, the main one being – it's time to move on.

If Batman stays suspicious of Hal Jordan, we'll have to remind the readers about the Spectre, Parallax, etc. We want to start as clean as possible. To us, this was just one story in Hal's life. We're moving on to the next.

Ultimately, it will be Kyle Rayner who is the voice that convinces everyone Hal is back.

NOTE: Parallax only corrupts power, it has none of its own. So inside Batman, it simply corrupts Batman and his inherent abilities.

We want to keep all of this as simple and connected as possible, we want to reach a strong status quo of Hal Jordan as a Green Lantern after this series. His journey will not be one of redemption or guilt, but one of rebuilding.

Rebuilding Hal's life, rebuilding Coast City, rebuilding the Corps, rebuilding a hero. Our theme for the monthly book.

THE ISSUE BREAKDOWNS — I'll be going into much more detail on issue #1. Obviously, scenes will evolve and change slightly during scripting.

ISSUE ONE (30 PAGES)
Pages 1 through 5
We open in space. Space Sector 2814. High above Earth. Suddenly, a space-craft, brittle and burning, flies past us. As if it were bursting out of the sun...

Heading towards Earth.

The craft smashes through the atmosphere, breaking apart. It crashes in the Southwestern desert, skidding across the ground. A pair of hikers see it and approach the craft.

They walk into the hull through a hole and find the pilot.

The pilot is Kyle Rayner. Like Abin Sur years earlier when he has crashed on Earth.

Kyle's costume is phasing in and out. He quickly awakens, claws at his costume, wants it off. Kyle passes out.

A large metal chest-like object is next to him.

Pages 6 through 9
Cut to John Stewart and Hal Jordan. They are approaching Yankee Stadium, surrounded by people. John urges Hal to enjoy himself, finally glad he's agreed to appear in public. To try and become human again. Hal looks on, can hear the people's sins and remorse all around him. It's hard to tune it out, the Spectre's job is never done. He's not supposed to rest. Technically...he's dead.

John convinces Hal to stay and watch the game. Hal actually begins to enjoy himself. Then Hal can't help but ask how Carol is doing.

She's with her new husband. She's fine.

Suddenly, all around them, people are confessing their sins. A husband tells his wife he cheated on her. A man on his cell-phone calls his boss and admits embezzling money. Even John admits that he helped his ex-girlfriend get a job with the D.E.O. because in a way it was easier to break up. John is slightly dizzy. Hal realizes the Spectre will not let him rest...no time for himself. The Spirit of Vengeance calls out.

Hal changes into the Spectre and disappears, leaving a very confused crowd. John is concerned.

Page 10
Cut to Carol Ferris at Ferris Aircraft, brought in to rebuild the company. She's on the phone with her husband, Gil. He's in Chicago on business. Carol feels something is watching her — turns, but the shadow is gone. A passenger plane takes off for the Coast.

Pages 11 through 15
Star City. Green Arrow is investigating a strange occurrence in the city with Arsenal and Connor Hawke. Before they can even begin to wonder where the three men are — they get a call from Speedy. Someone's broken into *their* house.

They race to Oliver's home where Mia is fighting with Black Hand — a Green Lantern villain who was always after his ring. He's tracked the extra power ring given to Green Arrow by Hal Jordan.

Suddenly, Spectre shows up — helps Green Arrow take down Black Hand.

Hal reverts to normal — he wants to have a talk with Green Arrow. "No once could challenge me like you could, Ollie." Hal is very cold toward Arsenal and Connor — telling them to leave. They argue, but Hal waves his hand — sending them away.

Hal feels he's losing himself to the Spirit of Vengeance. He feels he's very close — but when Black Hand attacks Green Arrow, Oliver sees a very different Hal Jordan. He transforms into the Spectre and destroys Black Hand in a hideous way. Spectre disappears.

Green Arrow picks up the power ring Black Hand was after, concerned.

Pages 16 through 18

Cut to Warrior's Bar in New York. It's 3 a.m. Guy Gardner is cleaning the bar, kicks the last drunk out, reminiscing about his life as a Green Lantern with John Stewart. Guy looks over the display — we get a sense of history here. And a sense of how much Hal meant to Guy in reality. "He was never afraid. Could even pick out the most beautiful girl in a bar and walk right up to her."

Guy suddenly begins to feel sick. The yellow power ring on his finger (established in SUPER FRIENDS) crackles with energy.

There's a huge explosion as he takes out the entire bottom section of the building. Warriors' Bar is gone. John rises from the ashes with a badly hurt Guy Gardner. The yellow ring crackled.

Pages 19 through 20

Cut to the Ferris Passenger Aircraft. The pilot flies over what was once Coast City, we get some history here. What happened to the City, how it was destroyed. Suddenly, a flash of green light goes off. And then they see something odd.

Down below, all the roadways, signs, etc. are in place. Only one building stands. A large sign reads: Welcome to Coast City.

The people can't believe this.

Page 21

Cut to Belle Reve, where Hector Hammond, criminal psychic, is acting strangely. Normally, he is unable to move. But he's muttering.

"I know the truth now. I know the truth"

"There are three voices, not two."

Pages 22 through 28

At the JLA Watchtower — Batman, the Atom, John Stewart and others — all examining Guy Gardner's damaged body. Trying to analyze him and find out what is wrong. The yellow ring won't come off.

INTERCUT WITH

Batman is in communication with another group of heroes — Aquaman and others — who are investigating the mysterious building in Coast City. No one can explain what is going on. There is only one building standing. (Aquaman also mentions how the sea life in the waters along Coast City has all but disappeared.)

Batman becomes very concerned after he gets the "address" of the one building in Coast City — it's Hal Jordan's old apartment building, where he lived after being kicked out of the Air Force. And Guy Gardner is wounded. Batman asks, "Where's Hal Jordan?"

A talk between Batman and John — John defending Hal. Arguments of the heroes back and forth about Hal Jordan.

Another group of heroes, including Superman and Alan Scott, in New York, clearing out what was once Warrior's Bar. Mysteries deepen as they find one object has survived the blast.

Standing all alone — a statue of HAL JORDAN, GREEN LANTERN. Untouched and protected.

Alan Scott feels slightly ill as he gets close to the statue. Has to retreat.

Back on the Watchtower, Green Arrow beams aboard. Tells them about his encounter with Hal Jordan. The third strike for Batman. He gets on the JLA communicator, warns everyone.

"Everyone go to red alert. The *real* Hal Jordan is back."

Pages 29 and 30

Cut to Ferris Aircraft. Southern California.

Carol steps out of her office — on the runway, among the planes is

HAL JORDAN.

It begins to rain.

ISSUE TWO
THE BASICS: Hal Jordan has seemingly gone to the dark side again, and the heroes of the world reluctantly unite against him. Meanwhile, Green Lanterns (including John, Guy and Alan) are corrupted and begin turning against their fellow heroes as Kyle Rayner is hunted by a former friend, Kilowog.

We open on something flying through space — glowing green. Heading towards Earth. We don't know who yet. (This is Kilowog, influenced by Parallax using the Spectre's power, hunting down Kyle Rayner.)

Cut to Kyle Rayner. At a camp site. Being taken care of by the hikers. They're looking at the metal chest. Trying to get it to open. They have no idea who the hell this guy is, the spaceship, any of it. A pickup truck is nearby, the chest/coffin loaded in back. On the chest they find a strange pseudo-futuristic tablet. A PARALLAX symbol on it.

Cut to Carol and Hal at Ferris Aircraft — Hal looking to Carol for help. Hal admits his guilt and erratic thoughts and actions of late – especially his self-doubt and fear. Recounts what he used to be like before Coast City, and how he can't understand where his feelings went. Or where the fear came from.

Carol's cell phone rings — Batman. He tells Carol to keep calm, keep Hal there.

The JLA and some reserves appear before Hal. All signs point to Hal going mad with power again. A massive battle between the Spectre and the heroes. John Stewart is corrupted with Alan Scott as they side with the Spectre against the heroes. Hal is barely able to control himself. *Fear* taking him over.

INTERCUT WITH: Inside the JLA HQ, Guy Gardner returns as a Green Lantern (a ring created by John's is put on his finger to destroy the yellow ring), resulting in a fight in the Watchtower. Guy heads towards Earth, joining up with the rest of the "evil" Green Lantern Corps — John and Alan.

Cut to the Southwest. Kyle Rayner awakens with the hikers. He struggles to use his ring, keeping the power level low — he could be detected or, if he uses too much, taken over. He's acting mad. Suddenly, the hikers are incinerated by a green beam from above. Kilowog, influenced by the Parallax force (though we don't know this yet), flies in for the kill, calling Kyle a traitor.

A fight begins, Kyle barely holding his own — struggling not to use the ring. He can feel it infect him. During the fight, the chest/coffin is blown open. And inside —

The body of Hal Jordan, Parallax.

ISSUE THREE
THE BASICS: Kyle goes to his father's home for help while Hal is confronted by the Spectre force, believing the Spectre is corrupting him. Meanwhile, the true nature of Parallax is revealed as Sinestro makes his presence known. Essentially — the "everyone learns the TRUE origin of Parallax" issue.

We open in the home of Kyle Rayner's father. Kyle reaches his father, bloody and beaten, looking for help. He needs to get to the nearest JLA teleportation tube. He's barely escaped Kilowog.

Heroes across the world are suiting up to battle it out with the Spectre and the Green Lantern Corps. The corrupted Corps members have each begun to act out their own fearful fantasies as Hal Jordan did. Guy takes on his former League members, focusing on Batman, John destroying every structure he ever designed (his being an architect will play a large role in GL later on, in the rebuilding of Coast City), etc. Reactions of everyone as they believe another "Zero Hour" or "Crisis" is coming. Some are disappointed (Arsenal), others not surprised (Nightwing).

Hector Hammond continues to freak out, causing Batman to investigate with Martian Manhunter, attempting to learn what Hammond knows about the truth.

As the Green Lanterns make their attacks on the heroes, Hal searches for the true culprit behind these acts — and upon reaching Coast City, discovers that it is himself.

Meanwhile, Kyle and his father briefly bond as Kyle reveals everything to his dad. Who he is, what he does, etc. (Per the GL comic, Kyle's dad already knows he is Green Lantern, though Kyle is unaware of this.) Kyle and his father will head to one of many "secret" teleportation spots the JLA has scattered across the country.

Kyle and his father head to the Watchtower, nothing there. It's all messed up. They find one hero still somewhat conscious, Green Arrow. Green Arrow asks what the hell is going on. Green Arrow still has the power ring, which saved his life. Kyle tells him not to use it — it'll take him over. "What will?" Kyle recounts the story of Parallax — utilizing flashbacks. We'll see Kyle's journey in deep space — the world he found — the legend of Parallax — etc. The Parallax force is fear.

Intercut with: In Coast City, where Hal is being hunted by everyone, confronts the Spectre force, learns of Parallax. "How did I become afraid?" asks Hal. **"Evil escaped your sight. It hid within you."** The Spectre force tells him Parallax is too powerful.

Back to the Watchtower. Green Arrow asks who freed this Parallax thing. Who's behind it? Suddenly, a yellow bow and arrow appears — shooting Green Arrow in the chest. Walking out of the darkness, a smile on his face. The master of the yellow ring — Sinestro.

ISSUE FOUR.
The Basics: Kyle battles Sinestro while Spectre struggles to free himself of Hal Jordan's soul.

A massive battle between Kyle and Sinestro erupts. (Think of it like the first time Darth Vader, Sinestro, battled Luke Skywalker, Kyle. Darth Vader barely moves, using one hand on his light saber while Luke sweats, struggling to hold on to his.) Kyle's father saves Green Arrow's life. Kyle not only has to protect his father and Green Arrow, he also must ward off the influence of the ring.

As Kyle fights Sinestro, he tells Green Arrow to take his father and find the JLA. Tell them the truth about Hal.

The Spectre has lost control, struggling to keep the Parallax force in check. More scenes of Spectre/Hal/Parallax acting out — threatening lives (from Hal Jordan's friends and family to his villains).

Intercut with Green Arrow. He makes contact with Batman, joins up with him at Belle Reve. Entire truth is told, though Batman is still reluctant to believe it — and even if it is true, Hal should've overpowered it. Zatanna helps locate the Spectre and the JLA. Kyle's father is worried about his son.

On the Watchtower, the fight continues. Kyle is beaten to Hell by Sinestro. Sinestro leaves the Watchtower — sensing the moment of Hal's ultimate failure is at hand.

Intercut with the Spectre "aborting" Hal Jordan and Parallax from his body. Hal's soul watching helplessly as Parallax stays, gripping Spectre. When we see the Parallax force we see that it is yellow. (Setting this up for when Parallax is thrust back into the Power Battery.)

Sinestro arrives just in time to witness this and see Hal.

Hal fades away — heading towards a bright white light. Spectre hits Hal with some kind of energy…but Hal disappears. Heading towards the bright light.

ISSUE FIVE. (30 PAGES)
The Basics: Hal reawakens in his own body, joins forces with Kyle and heads to retake the Parallax force himself, believing he knows how to destroy it.

We open with Hal traveling through the white light, suddenly the white light turns a deep green.

HAL IS REBORN

Hal wakes up in his body, still in the coffin on the Watchtower. He coughs, pukes…his hair is brown from here on out. Hal looks down at his body, pulls his armor off piece by piece. He can't stand wearing the Parallax uniform. (We learn the Spectre directed his soul to the body, knowing Hal could help him.)

Hal finds Kyle, wounded badly but still ready to fight. They need to get back to Earth.

Hal sees a statue of himself — wearing his old costume. Time for a quick change.

Meanwhile, on Earth, Hal and Kyle free the Green Lantern Corps members from Parallax's control.

Kyle and the Green Lanterns versus Spectre/Parallax versus Sinestro, DCU heroes help. Sinestro is beaten, but flees back home to Qward. Hal gets Parallax free from Spectre with the help of the rest of the Corps members.

The Spectre is cleansed but Parallax survives, infects Batman.

The Spectre force does not stay to help, like the ending of *Raiders of the Lost Ark*, the Spectre force spirals into the sky.

Many other heroes hurt, are unable to follow Parallax/Batman. Hal tells all the powerful ones to leave this to the "mortals," including him. If Parallax gets in Captain Marvel or Wonder Woman, this fight will go to an entirely different level.

Batman is hunted down by Jordan, Green Arrow, Nightwing, Robin, Black Canary, etc. Batman attacks Jim Gordon, ex-Commissioner. He takes his gun. But shooting a criminal isn't what shows Batman how impossible it is to resist Parallax.

Robin is there, trying to stop Batman. He gets in Batman's way — tells him to put the gun down. This isn't him.

Batman shoots Robin.

Right in the shoulder, Robin falls to the ground. Bleeding.

Hal — normal human form — stops Batman from firing again. A massive fight. Hal gets his ring back from Green Arrow. Parallax leaves Batman, heads back into Hal Jordan.

Everyone waits with bated breath — Hal's about to become Parallax again. But something happens this time — Parallax has no fear to take hold of. Hal's not afraid anymore — and Hal forces Parallax back out.

Together — with all of the GL's — they pronounce the Oath and break apart Parallax, each one sending him back into the rings, imprisoning Parallax back into the Central Battery.

Epilogues:
There'll be many epilogues — between Hal and the Lanterns, Hal and Green Arrow, Hal and Batman & the JLA, etc. (A major moment where Batman apologizes to Hal Jordan — he understands what he went through now. Robin is healing.)

Kyle will head into space with Kilowog and his father. He and his father have made a connection, and Kyle's father has always wanted to fly among the stars.

Hal standing in Coast City, looking up at the building. Deciding it is time to rebuild.

The last three pages will be on Oa. The Guardians on Oa gather together, age and nod in agreement. It is time to rebuild here as well.

"It is time."

THE BEGINNING.

BIOGRAPHIES

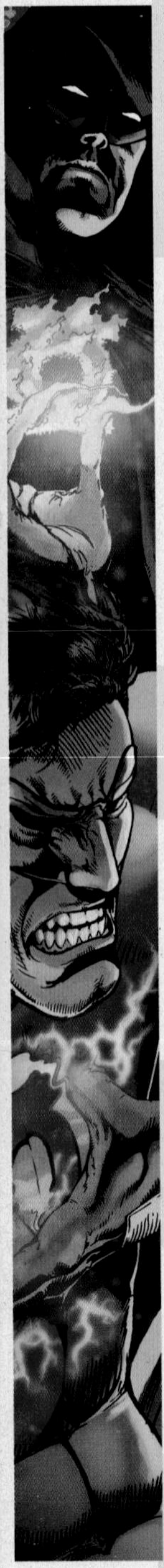

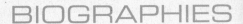

GEOFF JOHNS
Geoff Johns was born on January 25, 1973 in Detroit. It was damn cold.

He attended Michigan State University and studied media arts, screenwriting, film production and theory. After graduating, Geoff moved to Los Angeles where he made a lucky phone call and got a job as an intern for Richard Donner. He then went on to become Donner's assistant for almost four years on Conspiracy Theory and *Lethal Weapon 4*. During that time, he bean writing comics beginning with his favorite title, STARS AND S.T.R.I.P.E., which he created for DC. Eventually, writing turned into a full-time career.

Geoff has written INFINITE CRISIS, THE FLASH, TEEN TITANS, JSA, HAWKMAN, JLA/JSA: VIRTUE & VICE and various other titles for DC Comics and *The Avengers* for Marvel. He lives with his wife, Anissa, in Southern California, still writing for comics and television.

ETHAN VAN SCIVER
Ethan Van Sciver, born on September 3, 1974, has been drawing comics and comic book characters since he was 4 years old. Back then, DC wouldn't return his phone calls. Now look at him. He's working with the best writer, inker, colorist and editorial team in the business. Persistence is key.

At home, Ethan likes to watch terrible old movies, listen to surf music and play Hot Wheels with his son, Hunter. He blames his expanding waistline on the fabulous gourmet cooking of his wife Shari, but it's also probably due to a lot of long workdays putting more lines on Sinestro's face and eating cookies.

His artistic influences are Brian Bolland, Bernie Wrightson, Jack Cole, John Byrne and Todd McFarlane, and his goal in comics is to produce an amazing Plastic Man book one day. We'll see!

PRENTIS ROLLINS
Prentis Rollins has been inking comics since 1993. His credits include *Touch*, *New X-Men*, POWER COMPANY, JLA: INCARNATIONS, IMPULSE, DC ONE MILLION, BATMAN: THE ULTIMATE EVIL and HARDWARE. He is cofounder of Monkeysuit Press. Prentis lives in New York City with his wife and daughter.

MARLO ALQUIZA
Marlo was born in 1970, raised on comics, *Star Wars*, and toys. After graduating with a degree in art from U.C. Berkeley in 1993, he entered the comics industry first working for Image Comics (*Prophet*, *Darkchylde*, etc). He subsequently went freelance and worked with Top Cow (*Darkness*, *Rising Stars*, *Tomb Raider*), and Marvel (*X-Men*). After joining DC, Marlo's work has been found in CATWOMAN, ACTION COMICS and most recently TEEN TITANS. Married, he has a five-year-old daughter and four-year-old son.

MICK GRAY
Mick Gray has been inking comics for nearly 16 years. He has inked many DC titles including HAWKMAN, CHASE, DETECTIVE, ZATANNA, LEGION OF SUPER-HEROES, JLA ADVENTURES, AQUAMAN, SON OF SUPERMAN and PROMETHEA, for which he won an Eisner Award in 2001. He lives in San Jose, California with his wife, Holly, and daughter, Genevieve.

ROB LEIGH
Rob Leigh is a graduate of the Joe Kubert School. His lettering first received critical notice in 1972, when he was sent home with a note for writing a four-letter word on the blackboard of Miss Tuschmann's second-grade class. In addition to lettering, Rob has inked many titles for DC. He lives in northern New Jersey with his wife, Vaughan, and homicidal cat, Barley.

MOOSE BAUMAN
Having puttered around the industry for several years, Moose finally gained credibility and respect by joining DC Comics' stable of creators. He's worked on the monthly GREEN LANTERN series, ACTION COMICS, BLOODHOUND, and HUMAN DEFENSE CORPS, to name just a few. He currently lives with his family in a concrete bunker in Northern California.